FAB Press presents a Spectacular Optical Book
SATANIC PANIC: POP-CULTURAL PARANOIA IN THE 1980s

This second pressing of the FAB Press edition published February 2018

Revised FAB Press edition originally published June 2016
First edition published July 2015 by Spectacular Optical

FAB Press Ltd., 2 Farleigh, Ramsden Road, Godalming, Surrey, GU7 1QE, England, UK

www.fabpress.com

Edited by Kier-La Janisse and Paul Corupe
Page layout by Kier-La Janisse
Layout assistance by Daniela Konishi, Josh Saco and Harvey Fenton
Front cover and chapter illustrations by Mike McDonnell
Frontispiece: Iconic artwork for the original *Advanced Dungeons & Dragons Player's Handbook* by David A. Trampier

TABLE OF CONTENTS

FOREWORD:
MEETING SATAN AND HIS FAMILY
BY ADAM PARFREY 7

INTRODUCTION
BY KIER-LA JANISSE 13

"THE ONLY WORD IN THE WORLD IS MINE":
REMEMBERING 'MICHELLE REMEMBERS'
BY ALEXANDRA HELLER-NICHOLAS 19

THE UNHOLY PASSION: SEX AND GENDER
ANXIETY IN RUSS MARTIN'S EROTIC HORROR
PAPERBACKS
BY ALISON NASTASI 33

DICING WITH THE DEVIL: THE CRUSADE
AGAINST GAMING
BY GAVIN BADDELEY 45

20-SIDED SINS: HOW JACK T. CHICK WAS
DRAWN INTO THE RPG WAR
BY PAUL CORUPE 69

MASTERS OF THE IMAGINATION:
FUNDAMENTALIST READINGS OF THE OCCULT
IN CARTOONS OF THE 1980S
BY JOSHUA BENJAMIN GRAHAM 83

DEVIL ON THE LINE: TECHNOLOGY AND THE
SATANIC FILM
BY KEVIN L. FERGUSON 97

ALL HAIL THE ACID KING: THE RICKY KASSO
CASE IN POPULAR CULTURE
BY LESLIE HATTON 127

"WHAT ABOUT THESE 10,000 SOULS,
BUSTER?" GERALDO'S DEVIL WORSHIP
SPECIAL
BY ALISON LANG 147

THE FILTHY 15: WHEN VENOM AND KING
DIAMOND MET THE WASHINGTON WIVES
BY LISA LADOUCEUR 159

SCAPEGOAT OF A NATION: THE DEMONIZATION OF MTV AND THE MUSIC VIDEO

BY STACY RUSNAK — 173

TRICK OR TREAT: HEAVY METAL AND DEVIL WORSHIP IN '80S CULT CINEMA

BY SAMM DEIGHAN — 201

STEALING THE DEVIL'S MUSIC: THE RISE OF CHRISTIAN METAL AND PUNK

BY DAVID BERTRAND — 217

THE TRACKING OF EVIL: HOME VIDEO AND THE PROLIFERATION OF SATANIC PANIC

BY WM. CONLEY — 231

BEDEVILING BOB: PRANKING "TALK BACK WITH BOB LARSON"

BY FORREST JACKSON — 247

CONFESSIONS OF A CREATURE FEATURE PREACHER: OR, HOW I LEARNED TO STOP WORRYING ABOUT SATANISM AND LOVE MIKE WARNKE

BY DAVID CANFIELD — 263

BOUC ÉMISSAIRE: MANIFESTATIONS OF SATANIC ANXIETY IN QUEBEC

BY RALPH ELAWANI AND GIL NAULT — 275

THE DEVIL DOWN UNDER: SATANIC PANIC IN AUSTRALIA, FROM ROSALEEN NORTON TO 'ALISON'S BIRTHDAY'

BY ALEXANDRA HELLER-NICHOLAS — 291

GUILTLESS: BRITAIN'S MORAL PANICS, SATANIC HYSTERIA AND THE STRANGE CASE OF GENESIS P-ORRIDGE

BY DAVID FLINT — 309

FALSE HISTORY SYNDROME: HBO'S 'INDICTMENT: THE MCMARTIN TRIAL'

BY ADRIAN MACK — 323

END OF THE '80S: PARANOIA AS COMIC CATHARSIS IN JOE DANTE'S 'THE 'BURBS'

BY KURT HALFYARD — 341

AFTERWORD

BY JOHN SCHOOLEY — 355

CONTRIBUTOR CREDITS — 360

FOREWORD:
MEETING SATAN AND HIS FAMILY

BY ADAM PARFREY

Back when he was living in San Francisco and patrolling businesses in a rent-a-cop uniform, Boyd Rice sent me a postcard from the Wax Museum at Fisherman's Wharf. It pictured Church of Satan's Anton LaVey, surrounded by a bunch of skulls. On the back of the card, Boyd Sharpied the comment, "We laughed all night. I know you'd love to meet him."

That was my introduction to Lord Satan himself.

Eventually, I published several books of LaVey's and interviewed him for Nick Bougas' *Speak of the Devil* documentary. But initially I wondered about the man. In the mid-1980s Satanism was no longer given the same pass as it was in the late '60s when *The Satanic Bible* was first released and sold as one of those new unorthodox beliefs that emerged from the hippie era. Satanism had now become the fall guy for all societal evils.

Left: Adam Parfrey in a promotional photo for his book, *Love Sex Fear Death: The Inside Story of the Process Church of the Final Judgment*. Photo by Steven Dewall.

Beyond television exposés like the Geraldo Rivera special, _Devil Worship: Exposing Satan's Underground_ (1988), a small industry of wacky true crime books emerged to reveal the "horrors" of Satanism. One of them, Carl Raschke's _Painted Black: From Drug Killings to Heavy Metal: The Alarming True Story of How Satanism Is Terrorizing Our Communities_, was published by the large New York publisher Harper Collins, and my own collection, _Apocalypse Culture_, became its centerpiece. I found a bit of what I wrote about _Painted Black_ a couple decades ago for some online magazine:

> **"** _Raschke uses a lengthy consideration of Apocalypse Culture to bolster his arguments against "Satanic cultural terrorists." He names one of his chapters "The Aesthetics of Terrorism" (after my essay "Aesthetic Terrorism"), and takes quite a bit of original research from my "Latter-Day Lycanthropy" article for his chapter "The Metaphysics of Violence" within the section he titled "Apocalypse Now." Raschke, a supposed Methodist, dubbed "America's leading authority on contemporary occultism" in his book's flap copy, borrows the work of other researchers while assassinating their character for originally presenting the material. Dr. Joel Norris, another satanic panic journalist, claimed he sued Raschke for stealing his material._

So even if LaVey's shtick was total showbiz, I knew from personal experience that the Satanic rep was a lot to take on, one that invited a huge ration of shit.

Before I first met the man, I read about LaVey more than his actual writings. I knew of his Ming the Merciless look from the '30s _Flash Gordon_ serials, complete with narrow squinty eyes. I wondered whether this Satan motif was all showbiz or some form of sociopathology?

I began to learn that LaVey was not merely reacting to Christianity, but embracing a noir psychodrama situated in a foggy old-time cityscape. It was more or less nostalgia for the good old days. "Dr. LaVey" hardly ever wakened before it got dark, and had a strange collection of objects largely gifted him by fans and followers. He reminded me of the character Durtal from Joris-Karl Huysmans' book _Against Nature_.

So that he could familiarize himself with my sensibility, I mailed LaVey a couple issues of _Exit_, a graphic magazine that I contributed to, and the original Amok Press edition of _Apocalypse Culture_. Apparently he enjoyed them, and soon I was invited to visit the black house, and so I did.

Blanche, his buxom Girl Friday, wore old-style stockings that made her look like a slatternly archetype from the 1940s. I was led to the living room that had a huge electrotherapy machine and great old books filling the bookcases. I noticed volumes of Ben Hecht, weird anthropological texts, the carnival writings of William Lindsay Gresham, and on the walls, both here and in his kitchen, his odd paintings and a poster for the film

Nightmare Alley. LaVey made his appearance by suddenly emerging into the room through the fireplace. What an entrance! We started talking about Hollywood and theremins, and films and writers we both respected. I definitely connected with this man.

If this wasn't enough, Anton's pulchritudinous daughter Zeena soon appeared at the door of my tiny Echo Park apartment bearing a bottle of Stolichnaya vodka. Apparently Zeena was having a bit of trouble starting an acting career for herself, but made rent money through carny routines like a mind-reading act, and Satan knows what else. A couple weeks later I met Zeena's ten-year-old son Stanton (like Zeena, the name of a character from *Nightmare Alley*) who she bore at the age of 14.

This was time for the start of my book publishing company, Feral House, and I was looking for publications that weren't particularly costly to print that would already have an audience. A book Anton wrote called *The Compleat Witch* (its title spelled out in early '70s faux Victorianism) was out of print at the time but apparently available for a new edition. Filled with carny lore, in addition to one of the best bibliographies I had ever read for obscure but fascinating titles, *The Compleat Witch* had its silly ideas, too, like how a favorite salad dressing would reveal your sexual preferences. Anton agreed to change *The Compleat Witch*'s title to *The Satanic Witch*. This would be the first Feral House title.

Soon after Feral House published *The Satanic Witch*, Geraldo Rivera's people filmed his exploitationtastic Satanic special, complete with interviews with Zeena and even stranger "Satanists" like the beetle-browed Michael Aquino of the "Temple of Set," a Psychological Warfare Specialist for the U.S. Army who was accused of child molestation at the Presidio Day Care Center in San Francisco.

As mentioned elsewhere in this book, Rivera's television special was largely responsible for building up the Satanic Panic furor, which also caused the LaVey titles to be banned from independent bookstores and, specifically, from the Barnes and Noble chain. Some months later, many of these bookstores and the Barnes and Noble chain silently reordered the Satanic books when demand overcame the puritanical fad.

The Geraldo Rivera staff also filmed the "8/8/88" event put on at San Francisco's Market Street Strand movie theater that I was involved in. This event was intended to raise money for the purpose of getting Charles Manson retried for the medieval crime of controlling people's minds. The 8/8/88 show was filled with speeches, film clips, and odd musical ideas. Like LaVey, I also played oboe, and for this show I poorly performed the theme from *Valley of the Dolls*. At this time I wish to apologize to Sharon Tate and her family for participating in this juvenile stunt.

Years later, when both Zeena and her boyfriend were not granted leadership of the Church of Satan, paternal resentments rose up and Zeena parted ways with her father. So sad. The newer edition of *The Satanic Witch* replaced Zeena's Introduction with one written by Peggy Nadramia (current High Priestess of the Church of Satan).

Feral House also published two editions of Blanche Barton's LaVey biography, *The Secret Life of a Satanist*, and a couple of LaVey's never before published books, *The Devil's Notebook* and *Satan Speaks*.

But these were not the only incidents of Satanic Panic that Feral House dealt with. We later published two books about the notorious Process Church, the apocalyptic cult/commune from the 1960s and '70s that published and sold provocative but intelligent magazines. In 2009, I edited and published *Love Sex Fear Death: The Inside Story of the Process Church of the Final Judgment* that in part investigated sensational claims about The Process Church in books like Ed Sanders' *The Family* and Maury Terry's *The Ultimate Evil*.

An excerpt from *The Ultimate Evil* reads: "Before the Process divided, it spread seeds of destruction throughout the United States. Those spores were carried on winds of evil across the 1970s and into the present. The terror still reigns with far-flung subsidiary groups united by the sins of their father." These sentences seem to be written by the tabloid press or Jehovah Himself for the Old Testament. But did this cult do anything of this nature? *Love Sex Fear Death* features dozens of interviews with former members of The Process Church and includes more authentic revelations of its time and actions.

Anton LaVey's life has passed. His books sell slower than ever, but the Satanic theme still gets a good deal of press and attention. In these tea party days, Satanic Panic refuses to disappear, rearing its head every month or so in sensationalistic headlines.

~ *Adam Parfrey*

Right: Zeena Schreck, Adam Parfrey and Boyd Rice at the 8/8/88 event in San Francisco.

INTRODUCTION:
COULD IT BE...SATAN?

BY KIER-LA JANISSE

I was eight years old when the hysteria-inducing "memoir" *Michelle Remembers* was published in 1980, but the Satanic Panic first touched my life by way of an uncle who moonlit as a supplements writer for Dungeons & Dragons—which we were warned to never speak about in mixed company— and my mother's refusal to buy the gel toothpaste that beckoned me from a torrent of rotating commercials promising "a new Crest flavor children will love!" Our household brand, Colgate, had not yet caught onto the gel market, but mom was steadfast in her decision. Without a hint of irony, she explained that we could not buy Crest because it was a Procter & Gamble product, and "they worship the Devil." As proof of this, she cited the company's logo, which supposedly boasted a barely-veiled 666.

It would be years before I understood that the Procter & Gamble logo scandal was a real thing and not just an excuse my mother made up to avoid driving over the U.S. border to Detroit to buy me my stupid toothpaste. But I experienced firsthand the furor surrounding heavy metal as the '80s wore on, and the fear that covert Satanic machinations were at work everywhere around us—in our cartoons, commercials, music, movies and, most tragically of all, our daycares. It was a time of Ricky Kasso, Richard "The Night Stalker" Ramirez

Left: Serial killer Richard Ramirez, dubbed "The Night Stalker" by the media, in his most famous courtroom photo in 1985. © AP
Above: The controversial Procter & Gamble logo.

and, later, *Saturday Night Live*'s The Church Lady. The media exploded with headlines and news specials about the supposed Satanic threat, and ambitious journalists tripped over themselves to attach a Satanic mandate to every societal transgression. My mother took these admonitions to heart, but she was also an *ABC Movie of the Week* addict, and lurid accounts like *The Satan Seller* (1973) and *Michelle Remembers* sat on her shelf alongside books like *A Stranger is Watching* (1977) and Flowers in the Attic (1979). She loved the stuff. She had her own baggage, eating up any sordid story about fantastical forms of victimization—and that place where pulp horror met religion was the most salacious of all.

But she wasn't alone; this intersection of dogma and dread had been a pop-cultural preoccupation for some time before the particular anxieties of the 1980s manifested. The Satanic Panic did not exist in a vacuum—its seeds were sown as far back as the late 1960s and percolated through the next decade before reaching a fever pitch in the Reagan era.

In the early 1970s, with the Vietnam War in full swing amidst a rising tide of dissent and the bloodbaths at Altamont and Cielo Drive officially bringing a disillusioned end to the Age of Aquarius, the Baby Boomers looked to unconventional corners of religious experience for answers. Alternative religions flourished, from the Jesus People movement and more radical end-times counterparts to neo-paganism, suburban witchcraft and, of course, Satanism.

In the wake of Ira Levin's book Rosemary's Baby, the Rolling Stones' *Their Satanic Majesties Request* (both 1967) and the scores of celebrities visibly aligning themselves with Anton LaVey's Church of Satan (which had been founded a year earlier), there was a marked societal curiosity and acceptance of occultism, even among the most square pop-cultural day-trippers. Between 1969 and 1972, *Time* magazine ran a pair of cover stories on "The Occult Revival," accompanied by similar

articles in *Harper's Bazaar*, *McCall's*, *Esquire*, *Look*, *LIFE* and Ebony magazines, followed by a proliferation of niche occult-based periodicals and paperbacks. Suburban witches were a sexy fad, as attested to by the release of LPs by Louise "The Official Witch of L.A" Huebner (*Seduction Through Witchcraft*, 1969) and Barbara the Grey Witch (Self-titled, 1970), as well as a range of documentaries, from *Satanis: The Devil's Mass* (1970) and the BBC's

Above: Church of Satan founder Anton LaVey graces the cover of *Look* Magazine, August 1971.

MAN, MYTH & MAGIC ORIGINAL

MODERN WITCHCRAFT
FRANK SMYTH

HW 7038 MAYFLOWER BOOKS $1.25

A Gresham Publication. Vol. 2 No. 4. Monthly 40p.

WITCHCRAFT

The Only Monthly Chronicle
of the Supernatural Satanism and the Occult
THE PROTECTORS (Episode 3 in a gripping Occult serial)
PARAPSYCHOLOGY - a study of the supernormal
THE MUMMIES OF GUANAJUATO
· CHAMBER OF HORRORS
PLUS - THE UNDERTAKER - a trip into the Macabre

The Power of the Witch (1971) to mondo films like *Witchcraft '70* (1970) and *Australia After Dark* (1975). In the October 15, 1971 issue of the *Sarasota Herald-Tribune*, Professor Marcello Truzzi—while sympathetic to the endeavors of many alternative religions, including Satanism—summed up the mainstream appeal of the occult rather succinctly: "You get asked to parties."

Likewise, occult horror cinema found its most rich and prolific period in the 1970s, with acknowledged classics like *The Exorcist* (1973) and *The Omen* (1976) emerging along with a slew of inspired B-pictures such as *Simon, King of the Witches* (1971), *All the Colors of the Dark* (1972), *The Devil's Rain* and *Race with the Devil* (both 1975). Most notably there emerged a strand of horror focused on pedophobia—from the overtly supernatural (*I Don't Want to Be Born* (1975), *Shock* (1977)) to the sociopathic (*A Little Game* (1971), *Devil Times Five* (1974))—that reflected a backlash, conscious or otherwise, against the strides of second wave feminism. The relationship between working women and their children would become a major focal point of the Satanic Panic in the next decade.

All this is to say that, by the time the 1980s rolled around, people had already been groomed to believe that there could be occultists living next door. And after a decade that saw the rise of "latchkey kids" who were left to their own devices while often-absent parents sought to work out their own issues through a variety of spiritual and experimental therapeutic methods, concern turned again to the children. While the publication of *Michelle Remembers* in 1980 spawned renewed international dialogue about horrific child abuse behind closed doors, the double-whammy of the highly-publicized disappearance of Adam Walsh in 1981 (serial killer Ottis Toole later confessed to his murder) and the initial allegations of the famed McMartin pre-school trial in 1983 effectively put an end to the carefree days of Gen-X kids. No more walking home from school alone. No more playing outside until the streetlights came on. No more Jarts.

The result of this reinvigorated watchdogging was a generation of children who increasingly felt the need to operate in secret. 1970s kids who had been taught to problem-solve independently and to speak openly to their parents through a decade of countercultural children's programming (from *Sesame Street* and *Zoom* to *Willie Survive* and *Kids Are People Too*) suddenly faced renewed strictness and anxiety at home. While intergenerational disconnection was certainly nothing new, a chasm opened up between '80s parents and their kids—and it wasn't helped by efforts to target youth culture as inherently vulnerable to a globally-organized Satanic threat.

Many of the essays in this book recount tales of apathetic or lost teens turning to heavy music, extreme movies and role-playing games as a means of escaping a confusing and overwhelming world. For my own part, this included playing with guns, flirting with Nazi iconography and an obsession with serial killers, none of which were considered acceptable pastimes by the various social groups I tried in vain to latch onto. This combination of aimlessness and morbidity that characterized many teens of the era was alarming to parents because they felt it opened up their kids to dark compulsions and temptations. But for parents unable to think of solutions or to accept accountability, a scapegoat as tangible as the Devil proved too tempting in itself.

Even though the media freely bandied around the name of Anton LaVey as the personification of the dark force that had ensnared children and teenagers worldwide, these exaggerated fears had virtually nothing to do with the actual Church of Satan and its adherents as much as a fictional brand of Satanism cooked up by fraudulent "experts." Ironically, if there had been a Satanic conspiracy, every parent and well-meaning preacher in North America would have been playing right into it. They created a ridiculous fervor, provoking an inevitable backlash that denounced the entire Panic as the decade came to a close. And both this hysteria and the response had their respective casualties.

Keeping this in mind, we approached this book from a fairly neutral standpoint, allowing our authors to express their own opinions but being mindful of the lives that were harmed the first time around and being cautious not to encourage history to repeat itself. It would be a mistake to assume that any one exposed fraud invalidates all claims of abuse that came to light during the Satanic Panic. If I learned anything from co-editing this book it's that there *are* cover-ups, cock-ups and conspiracies—but often they're not where you're looking for them.

~ *Kier-La Janisse*

Right: A page from *Ebony* Magazine's occult special, July 1976.

WOULD YOU <u>BELIEVE</u> IT
...SUPERSTITION LIVES!

Interest in the occult, with its symbols and insignia, increasingly is apparent among black Americans who are turning to astrology, European witchcraft and other activities in ever-greater numbers. Other superstitions, such as voodoo, have retained their appeal.

"THE ONLY WORD IN THE WORLD IS MINE":
REMEMBERING 'MICHELLE REMEMBERS'

BY ALEXANDRA HELLER-NICHOLAS

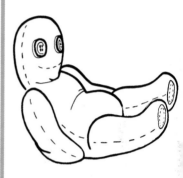

Originally published in 1980, Michelle Smith's notorious "memoir" *Michelle Remembers* is considered the epicenter of the Satanic Ritual Abuse moral panic of the 1980s, as well as one of the most influential media hoaxes of the late 20th century. Co-written by therapist Dr. Lawrence Pazder, the book outlines how Smith became a victim of Satanic Ritual Abuse as a young child, but it's a peculiar text—a mediocre exercise in generic pulp full of hysterical and absurd claims that were once accepted as clinical fact. Today, *Michelle Remembers* is still terrifying, but not for the reasons originally intended. It now reveals disturbing assumptions entrenched in the broader cultural politics of the late 1970s, including widely held attitudes towards gender, race and public morality.

The events covered in the book allegedly took place in the 1950s. The marriage of Smith's parents, her mother Jessica and alcoholic father Jack, was fraught with violence and abuse. During one of Jack's regular disappearances, Jessica aligns herself with the mysterious Malachai and his

Left: Inside flap of the second U.S. edition of *Michelle Remembers*.

fellow Satanists, and surrenders her young daughter to the cult, exposing the child to horrors the book documents in gory detail. The girl witnesses murder and cannibalism. She is the victim of physical and psychological abuse and sexual torture. She is attacked by spiders, raped by snakes, and her body is rubbed with dead human fetuses. Smith is starved, forced to defecate on the Bible, and has horns and a tail surgically attached to her body. She sees babies crucified and kittens murdered, all along with the knowledge that her own mother exposed her to such depravity. She is returned to safety—inexplicably, back home with her mother—due primarily to the direct intervention of Jesus and Mary themselves.   *CATHOLIC*

Jessica died when Smith was 14, triggering her father's final desertion. After spending her late teens at a Catholic boarding school, she became a patient of psychotherapist Pazder in sessions predominantly held at the Fort Royal Medical Center in Victoria, British Colombia. The book picks up her story four years later when Smith's mental and physical health takes a bad turn after a miscarriage. With Pazder's assistance, Smith comes to the realization that she was involved in a Black Mass known as the Feast of the Beast, a ritual that ran for 81 days from September 7 to November 27 of 1955. This rite, which occurs every 27 years, initiates new Satanic priests to continue Satan's work. The timing of Smith's abuse at the hands of the Satanists is crucial to the overall sense of urgency *Michelle Remembers* seeks to create. As the book explains:

> 66 Michelle, in 1977, was remembering the Feast of the Beast that took place in 1955. The next Feast of the Beast, with its new Master Plan, is due—according to experts on Satanism— five years after Satan's return to earth in 1977, the event thought to have triggered Michelle's remembering. That is to say, in 1982, which would be 28 years from the beginning of the year-long ceremonies in 1954, and 27 years from Satan's actual appearance in 1955.

Communist 5-YR PLAN

Michelle Remembers warns of the advent of a new Holocaust in 1982 (just two years after the book was first published), in which Satan would return to again enact horrors during the "Feast of the Beast". This is a conscious association, and a problematic one: the first mention of the Holocaust is extremely tasteless in tone, particularly since the book has been long revealed as a hoax. When telling Pazder that she did not want to be involved in the cult activities, Smith said "I'd rather be in a concentration camp for 50 years." The suggestion here is that what Smith claimed she endured was worse than what was experienced in Nazi concentration camps. Despite having researched trauma and concentration camp survivors, Pazder easily accepts the statement, confirming his belief about the nature of Smith's ordeal. This whiff of anti-Semitism is echoed in later Satanic Ritual Abuse discourse, with Barbara Fister observing that there "were strong parallels between the ritual abuse motif of breeders providing infants for sacrifice and anti-Semitic blood libel, dressing concern about abortion in a familiar guise of evil."

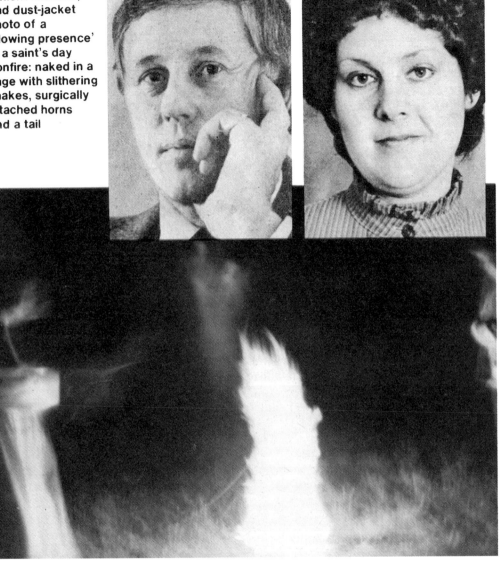

Psychiatrist Pazder; patient Michelle; and dust-jacket photo of a 'glowing presence' in a saint's day bonfire: naked in a cage with slithering snakes, surgically attached horns and a tail

Michelle Remembers attained phenomenal success, and made Pazder and Smith celebrities, key players in the Satanic Ritual Abuse phenomenon as it played out during the next decade. *People* magazine and *The National Enquirer* presented its claims as fact, bringing this memoir to nationwide attention in the United States, and Smith and Pazder went on a cross-country promotional tour. Between advances, rights, and royalties, they made, by some accounts, up to $342,000. Smith and Pazder left their respective partners in the wake of the book's publication and were married, consolidating the blurring of the professional and the personal that permeates the book itself. The two were closely involved in the Satanic Panic right up to its explosive collapse at the end of the McMartin pre-school trial in 1990.

Above: Page excerpt from a *Maclean's* magazine article, October 27, 1980.

The debunking of *Michelle Remembers* is a tale that's just as fascinating—although admittedly less fantastic—as the story in the original book. In retrospect, it's almost incredible not only that people accepted these claims as scientific fact, but that the Satanic Ritual Abuse phenomenon became so influential across the globe. Although now broadly remembered as charlatans, Pazder in particular made Satanic Ritual Abuse an international buzzword, and benefited greatly from peddling the phenomenon on a purely professional level. He positioned himself as the globally recognizable face of "good" in the ongoing battle against Satanic Ritual Abuse, all based on his "findings" as outlined in *Michelle Remembers*. Although he does not use the words "ritual abuse" in the book, Pazder is very much the father of the term, and his use of it in a 1981 American Psychological Association meeting is broadly accepted as its first known recorded appearance of it in this context.

While less immediately remembered today, the book also brought Smith significant media attention, including a 1989 Oprah Winfrey special that focused uncritically on Smith and fellow fraudulent Satanic Ritual Abuse memoirist Laurel Stratford, author of *Satan's Underground: The Extraordinary Story of One Woman's Escape* (1988). Recalling again the links between Satanic Ritual Abuse and anti-Semitism, when *Satan's Underground* was withdrawn, Stratford (real name Laurel Willson) adopted the false identity of a Jewish Holocaust survivor, Laura Grabowski.

CAPTURING THE DEVIL

Throughout *Michelle Remembers*, authenticity is consistently indicated by reference to tape recordings of Pazder and Smith's therapy sessions. These tapes were transcribed and, in later sessions, the reel-to-reel audio tapes were backed up by other types of recordings: including video tape, 16mm film, 8mm film, 35mm film, and a more modern tape recorder. For readers today, *Michelle Remembers'* reliance on the tapes and transcripts as a sign of authenticity may appear bewildering, particularly in an era where audio manipulation on any  home computer is easy. But in a book released only six years after the Watergate audio recordings famously brought down ex-U.S. President Richard Nixon, there was a kind of mass, unspoken awe at the power of tape recordings to capture otherwise inconceivable truths.

Above: Michelle Smith during one of her recorded sessions with Dr. Pazder.

Though *Michelle Remembers* seems at times self-conscious about its potential adaptability to a horror film, it never made the transition from page to screen. But it reads like a random collage of horror vignettes hastily pasted together: a bit of *Frankenstein* here, a touch of Lovecraft there, and some *Rosemary's Baby*, *The Exorcist*, and *The Omen* thrown in for good measure. Cinematic references riddle the book—Smith's ordeal in a hospital recalls *The Exorcist* in places, as indeed does her sudden (and awkwardly superficial) interest with exorcism rites and symptoms of possession. There's even a scene of dental torture that evokes connections with *Marathon Man* (1976), a reference that may have resulted from Smith and Pazder's hopes for Dustin Hoffman to play the role of therapist.

The real reason that *Michelle Remembers* never became a film was due to threats of legal action. Anton LaVey threatened Pazder and Smith with a civil suit as the first edition of the book explicitly stated that Smith was a victim of the Church of Satan (later editions of the book, including the one used for this chapter, scuttled almost all references to the Church of Satan). Smith's father Jack Proby also said he planned to sue if a film adaptation moved ahead, making the optioning of a movie legally impossible. That a film adaptation was even in the cards, however, raises daunting issues about the potential influence of the book: if it made this great an impact based on the book alone, how more far reaching would it have been with a motion picture propelling its terrifyingly conservative ideologies, based on fear, hate and paranoia?

FACT AND FICTION

In the 1981 British publication of the book, publisher Thomas B. Congdon Jr. takes the unusual step of opening the book with "A Note From the American Publisher." Congdon was a renowned and respected figure in American publishing history and, at his passing in 2008, he was considered the last of a dying breed, an old school editor whose dedication resulted in some of the biggest literary blockbusters of the 1970s and '80s, including Peter Benchley's 1974 novel *Jaws* for Doubleday. Congdon's introductory note recalls the Russian doll style literary horror structure of Henry James' novella *The Turn of the Screw* (1898), where a story-within-a-story-within-a-story configuration implies its internal narrative is authentic because the story surrounding it is so believable.

Congdon's preface also establishes a trick the book relies on to present its events as true. Time and time again, Smith's story is presented as authentic simply because men in positions of authority believe her. Says Congdon:

> 66 *She seems as clear as a glass of well water. She appears to be one of those rare people, like Joan of Arc and Bernadette, whose authority and authenticity are such that they can tell you things that would otherwise be laughable—yet you do not laugh, you do not dismiss or forget.*

Later in the book, Smith is said to emit "a cry so violent that it drove her down into the couch." This is verified anecdotally by Pazder's colleague, Dr. Richard Arnot, whose office was next door. Though the room Smith was having her session in was sound proofed, Arnot later told Pazder, "It was a piercing cry of genuine terror."

This implication that male authority is enough to prove Smith's story is most apparent in Pazder himself. Rather than presenting evidence and asking the reader to assess its authenticity, Pazder mediates this knowledge—his verification alone is proof, his belief in Smith positioned as the ultimate evidence. Words like "apparently" and "appears" begin to disappear as early as Chapter 9 and, by Chapter 15, it is implied that Smith is telling the truth simply because Pazder believes she is. At this stage, he is even comfortable telling a local priest that "We've gotten to be very concerned… it seems possible to us that these people were involved in something very definitely anti-Christian. It sounds a lot like Satanism to us."

BAD GIRLS

While men give Smith's story validation, the book makes clear time and time again that women are ultimately to blame for this abuse. Failed mothers are directly responsible for the horrors that happen to this child, and the book ultimately argues that the only solution is a conscious return to the paternal—a shift the book demands in a number of overlapping, unsubtle ways. From this perspective, *Michelle Remembers* should be considered a key document in what Susan Faludi articulated in 1991 as a broader media-driven backlash against feminism during the 1980s.

In light of this, feminism was perhaps a surprising ally of the conservative forces pushing the Satanic Ritual Abuse agenda. On one hand, that the Satanic Ritual Abuse movement sought to allow a voice for the abused to speak up and seek justice for inflicted horrors aligns neatly with the broader feminist mission of addressing imbalances between gender and power. But even without the ensuing fallout that led to the McMartin pre-school hysteria, there was enough evidence in *Michelle Remembers* to prove to any self-identifying feminist that Pazder and Smith's agenda was clearly not driven by a desire for progressive social and political change. As Barbara Fister noted, aside from anything else, Satanic Ritual Abuse anomalously saw women as the predominant abusers, going against the fact that the bulk of sex crimes committed against children were by men.

Michelle Remembers is not subtle in its misogyny. From the very first pages of the book, the maternal failure of Smith's mother Jessica is explicitly stated to be the single central factor responsible for the child's trauma. Although Malachi makes an appearance earlier in the book, Smith's first lengthy, detailed memory of abuse makes clear that women are responsible. Initially, Smith sees this group of women as potential rescuers precisely because they are women; "Mommies" that would look after her and rescue her. Seeing a woman in a long hooded black cape, Smith initially mistook her as another feminine stereotype—a princess—but when the woman tongue kisses her in the first of the book's detailed sexual assaults, Smith notes, "She's not a mommy."

These women, the book implies, are aligned with Satan by rejecting traditional roles as mothers. Smith at times interchanges references to "all those mommies" with "witches" (a term Pazder agrees with), consolidating the book's dedication to its central depiction of the monstrous feminine. On the back of feminism's broader achievements during the 1970s, what Fister notes were "concerns about working women and liberalized abortion laws contributed to the social definition of ritual abuse as a threat." She continues, "the most common site for accusations was the day care center, clearly a locus of social anxieties about working mothers trusting their children to institutional care."

Michelle Remembers' most brutal accusations are directed at Jessica herself as a failed, betraying mother.

Even next to the horrors of abuse, the book languishes in documenting what it considers the greatest crime of all, describing Smith at one point as "a small child trying to deny the unthinkable: total, brutal rejection by her own mother." Smith's greatest achievement, according to the book, isn't recovering from the torture at the hands of the cult, but in going to Pazder who rescues her from the failed monstrous maternal, "to accept his help in facing the horror of what her mother had done." Blaming mothers is a drumbeat throughout the book, and becomes more overt as the book proceeds.

This keep-women-in-their-place conservatism manifests more fantastically with the introduction of two characters for which the book's absurd climax depends—Mary and Jesus themselves. In the depths of her trauma, Smith's cries for "Mommy" are finally met in the figure of Ma Mére. Unlike Jessica, Mary suffered at her child's suffering ("She had sad eyes. They hurt her baby"). And while it is Mary who comforts the tortured Smith, the book makes it clear on a number of occasions that her presence is solely the result of male intervention: Smith believes that Jesus sent his mother because she "needed a mother to stay there with me." The soothing nature of her maternal presence is of value only because it is one that acknowledges the dominance of patriarchy: "Our Father is looking after us," she tells the confused child. "We're all children. We all need looking after. We all need to be cared for. Our Father knows about all his lost children."

Above: Michelle Smith in 1954, a year before her alleged ordeal. Photo from *Michelle Remembers.*

Implicit in *Michelle Remembers* are issues surrounding duty of care, but what today may appear to be unusual, unorthodox or even unprofessional behavior by Pazder must be contextualized in popular notions of what psychiatry was capable of achieving at the time. During the decades preceding *Michelle Remembers*' release, therapy was a common experience, a place to unpack negative experiences from childhood as a way of improving adult lives.

Recovered-Memory Therapy is a loosely defined cluster of clinical methodologies where a therapist would help adult survivors recall repressed, traumatic memories of childhood abuse, allowing a path to personality reintegration (the repressed memories typically manifest in multiple personalities, a disorder increasingly diagnosed in the 1980s and 1990s following the Satanic Ritual Abuse moral panic Pazder and Smith helped trigger). Recovered-Memory Therapy is absent from the *Diagnostic and Statistical Manual of Mental Disorders, 4th Edition* (*DSM-IV*), and its historical notoriety renders it today broadly considered both unscrupulous and unprofessional by the mainstream medical profession.

From this clinical perspective, *Michelle Remembers* also recalls Arthur Janov's "primal therapy," popular in the 1970s with high-profile supporters including John Lennon. Janov maintained that adult neurosis was also the product of repressed traumatic childhood memories, but his practice demanded a kind of practical revisiting of initial trauma to bring it to the fore of the consciousness. A rejection of so-called "talking cures," primal therapy was intended to be a practical way of re-opening the wound, airing it so it can heal. Primal therapy did not attain the same fall from grace in the public eye as Recovered-Memory Therapy, but Janov's failure to convince the broader profession of the virtues of this approach has seen it delegated to history as little more than a passing fad.

From a professional perspective, Pazder's treatment of Smith raises issues for concern, regardless of whether her story was true. Pazder seems incapable at times of separating Smith's story from his own. As early as Chapter 2 he described Smith's first session as "a debilitating emotional experience for both doctor and patient." Not even a hundred pages in, Pazder felt that "he was suffering with her... and he felt instinctively... that he must cry, must give vent to his own feelings. He was a professional, yet he was also a person, and he was being touched by what he was hearing, profoundly touched."

THE PRAYING DOCTOR

The book's victory is the result of science and the church coming together, embodied in the figure of Pazder himself, the praying psychologist. The book's attempt to revamp the *The Exorcist*'s priest and psychiatrist figure Damien Karras (played in William Friedkin's movie adaptation by Jason Miller) lacks the complexity and tensions of the

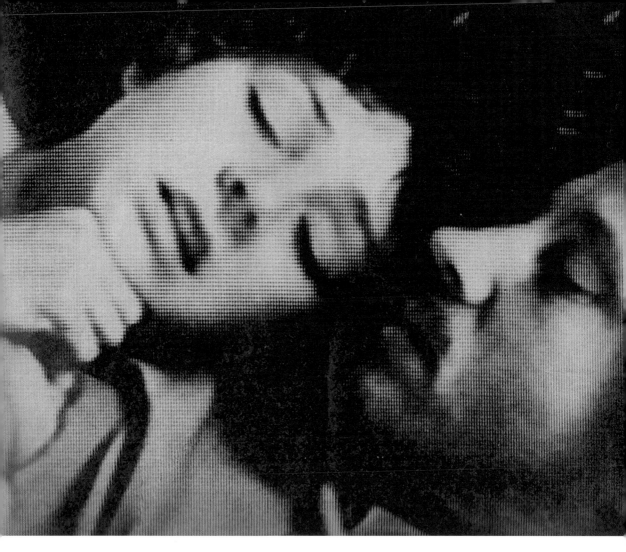

portrayal of the character in Blatty's book, however, and instead opts for a trouble-free merger of the two to trump unruly women.

The church is represented in *Michelle Remembers* as strikingly modern. Priests are hip, understanding allies, some of whom work with gangs and have degrees in sociology: they are profoundly in touch with the complexities and demands of everyday life. The context of this representation of Catholicism is important: in late 1972, Pope Paul VI delivered a speech called "Confronting the Devil's Power" in which he warned of the reality of Satan. At a time when the Church was attempting to show itself as an institution in tune with contemporary world, this speech was controversial, feared to confirm secular suspicions that the Church was entrenched in archaic folklore. By directly referring to this speech in the text of *Michelle Remembers*, the book reveals nothing less than a propagandist inclination intent on converting the Pope's notorious speech into something urgent and valid from both a moral and scientific position.

Above: Smith and Pazder in an unorthodox position during one of their recorded sessions. Image from *People* magazine, September 1, 1980.

To the initially non-religious Smith, Catholicism offers nothing but positivity, and she has little problem accepting its central tenets in her conversion. Science and religion are depicted as the forces required to counteract evil, out-of-control women. Religion is shown to be something also relatively modern, in contrast to the evil that Smith faces, and the activities and language of the Satanists is described throughout the book as both "primitive" and "old." *So what happens when science + Religion conflict?*

In *Michelle Remembers*, this view of religion manifests as outright racism: Westerners are aligned with good (Pazder, we are told from the outset, is "tall, blue-eyed and tanned"), while the evil that torments Smith has its origins in West Africa. Having researched extensively in that continent, the expertize Pazder brought to Smith's case was framed consistently by what he learned of cult behavior there. Pazder's racism is most explicitly revealed in his reference to the "dreaded Ekpe Society of West Africa," who keep kidnapped children in cages, file their teeth into points and train them to be assassins: the "dreaded" is very much Pazder's own archaic reading, and contemporary treatments of the Ekpe do not discuss them in such negative, colonial terms. (1) For Pazder, death and evil smell like Africa, and he constantly links the cult practices of the Satanists Smith encounters with the tribal activities he witnessed in West Africa.

FALLOUT

As early as 1980—the same year *Michelle Remembers* was published—skeptics were investigating the more outrageous claims made in the book. In October that same year, Paul Grescoe wrote an article in *Maclean's* that included interviews with Smith's father and her childhood friends who disputed its central claims. Amongst other things, the Grescoe article emphasized that Jessica was said to be a loving mother and that Smith had two sisters, Charyl and Tertia, contradicting Smith's statement to Mary in the book that "I don't have any [brothers or sisters]." According to the article, Smith's siblings have no recollection of any of the events outlined in the book.

Starting in 1990, *Michelle Remembers'* claims began to unravel in earnest. Investigators could not find anyone to corroborate Smith's memories of events that happened in her house or the cemetery. Smith's husband—mentioned throughout the book as increasingly uncomfortable in discussing the details of her therapy—also could not recall the events outlined in the book. A 1990 article in *The Mail on Sunday* debunking *Michelle Remembers* noted that members of the local Catholic church mentioned in the book made distinct efforts to separate themselves from claims, with Bishop Remi De Roo in particular wanting "to distance himself from these people. More than ten years ago he asked the couple to provide him with details, but they never supplied all the information he required."

Of all the bombshells in *The Mail on Sunday* article, however, this oft-quoted response by Pazder shows he had little interest in pesky distinctions between fact and fiction:

> **"** *It is a real experience. If you talk to Michelle today, she will say, "That's what I remember." We still leave the question open. For her*

it was very real. Every case I hear I have skepticism. You have to complete a long course of therapy before you can come to conclusions. <u>We are all eager to prove or disprove what happened, but in the end it doesn't matter.</u> <u>POST MODERNISM ?</u>

As many commentators on the Satanic Ritual Abuse phenomenon have noted, despite Pazder's feeling that distinctions between fact and fiction had no real significance, that difference matters a great deal for those whose lives were so irreparably destroyed by the false memories extracted during the Satanic Ritual Abuse panic.

REMEMBERING MICHELLE

The legal fallout of false Recovered-Memory Therapy has seen practitioners brought to court by those accused of crimes against their patients (see: *Ramona v. Isabelle*, 1994). More recently, patients themselves have sought legal compensation against the very doctors they initially sought help from in the first place. In 2007, for instance, a Scottish woman won £20,000 in damages against a local hospital for implanting false memories in her about a rape committed by her father (a Scottish National Party politician). In this situation, the court viewed the woman to be as much of a victim of overzealous medical practitioners as her father was a victim of the false claim itself.

This recent legal recognition of false memory recipients as victims of Satanic Ritual Abuse offers another way of thinking about Smith and her now universally mocked memoir. <u>To begin with, while Smith's name is in the book's title, it's always heavily mediated by Pazder's voice. This, in many ways, defies the book's constant demand to listen to the voices of those who have been abused and suffered: by allowing Smith to only speak through a man, issues about her own autonomy are raised.</u> While it's undeniable that the Satanic Ritual Abuse the book outlines is far-fetched and implausible, the evidence that Smith was the victim of a more earthly, everyday kind of abuse is not so clear-cut. Yes, neighbours and Smith's own father said Jessica was a caring mother, but this would hardly be the first occasion where a seemingly normal family hid a dark secret about child abuse. And while many things Smith and Pazder included in their book have been debunked, some smaller details have, to my knowledge at least, remained unquestioned—for instance, maybe Pazder's colleague did hear Smith screaming through the sound-proofed office walls.

British Columbia

Things that go bump in Victoria

It could be the stuff of Halloween nightmares or the fevered imagination of a fiction writer determined to make *Rosemary's Baby* and *The Exorcist* sound as exciting as a Nancy Drew mystery. Yet the book is billed as the true account of a five-year-old girl who, in the demure mid-1950s amid the placid charm of Victoria, B.C., became the victim of unspeakable practices perpetrated by a band of serious Satanists—among them, her mother. In *Michelle Remembers* (Nelson Canada Ltd.), 31-year-old Michelle Smith says the devil worshippers tried to kill her in a car accident rigged to cover up a murder, then fed her the ashes of the murder victim. They held her naked in a cage slithering with snakes, burned and butchered stillborn babies and fetuses in front of her, surgically attached horns to her head and a tail to her spine—and that was just for openers. At the end of 310 pages, plucky little

Bishop Remi De Roo: message from a child

Above: Image of Bishop Remi De Roo, as pictured in *Maclean's* magazine, October 27, 1980.

Satanists did not torture Smith, but this does not mean necessarily that something terrible—albeit less supernatural—did not happen to her. The debunking of *Michelle Remembers* is admirable for its ferocity, but in an ironic way it misses the very lesson that the debunking should teach us: that the world is never as simple as black and white. That *Michelle Remembers* could only be total fact or total fraud does not allow room for something in between, and it is in this space in between where Smith's story—her story, not Pazder's—may lie.

Michelle Remembers is a reminder to rally against binaries. It is not a world of heroes and villains, devils and gods, good and evil. Ironically, both Smith and Pazder as well as those who sought to debunk their story are guilty of the same kinds of either/or visions of morality: they divide the world into good guys and bad guys, allowing little room for what lies in between. For all her desperate pleas that her story be heard, the one that Smith ends up telling in *Michelle Remembers* might be more complex than its authors ever intended.

NOTES:

1. As the *Wikipedia* entry for the Ekpe makes clear, "Formerly the society earned a bad reputation due to what the British viewed as the barbarous customs that were intermingled with its rites." See: http://en.wikipedia.org/wiki/Ekpe.

REFERENCES + BIBLIOGRAPHY:

Allen, Denna and Janet Midwinter. "Michelle Remembers: The Debunking of a Myth". *The Mail on Sunday*, September 30, 1990.

Donavan, Barna William. *Conspiracy Films: A Tour of Dark Places in the American Conscious*. Jefferson: McFarland, 2008.

Faludi, Susan. *Backlash: The Undeclared War Against Women*. London: Vintage, 1992.

Grescoe, Paul. "Things That Go Bump in Victoria". *Maclean's*, October 27, 1980.

Hayes, S. and Carpenter, B. "Out of Time: The Moral Temporality of Sex, Crime and Taboo." *Critical Criminology* 20.2 (2012).

Fister, Barbara. "The Devil in the Details: Media Representation of "Ritual Abuse" and Evaluation of Sources." *Studies in Media and Information Literacy Education* 3.2 (May 2003).

Madeley, Gavin. "£20,000 payout for woman who falsely accused her father of rape after 'recovered memory' therapy", *Daily Mail*, October 19, 2007.

Smith, Michelle and Lawrence Pazder. *Michelle Remembers*. London: Michael Joseph, 1981. (Originally published in 1980).

Above: Michelle Smith in her backyard, as depicted in *People* magazine, September 1, 1980. Photograph by Dale Wittner.

THE UNHOLY PASSION:
SEX AND GENDER ANXIETY IN RUSS MARTIN'S SATANIC EROTIC HORROR PAPERBACKS

BY ALISON NASTASI

While the hysteria surrounding the Satanic Panic swept record shops, daycare centers and TV sets, there was an equally important fictional exploitation of these real-life moral crises that seized North American drugstore and supermarket paperback racks. Paperback presses like Playboy, Putnam, and Tor followed in the footsteps of Ira Levin's wildly popular 1967 book *Rosemary's Baby* with a series of Satanic Panic-inspired novels that cashed in on the lurid confessions of housewives and heavy metal-obsessed teens featured on salacious talk shows. Many of the novels walked the line of satire, horror, and trash, and their fiendish narratives simultaneously responded to and capitalized on real-life scandals like the famed McMartin pre-school trial, and "non-fiction" accounts of sexual abuse (Michelle Smith's *Michelle Remembers*, 1980) and breeding cults (Lauren Stratford's *Satan's Underground*, 1988).

A series of erotic horror novels by Russ Martin captured the real-life Satanic Panic parallels stemming from societal anxiety, fear, and fascination—and took titillation to the extreme. These novels, published between 1978 and 1988—

Left: Cover detail from Russ Martin's *The Desecration of Susan Browning* (1981).

starting with the "unholy covenant of terror and desire" in *Rhea*—were more than just profit-driven attempts to capitalize on Satanic anxieties. They also reflected the increasingly complex view of gender relations at the time, equating fears of feminism with the moral panic that spread throughout the decade. In the novels, a series of female protagonists are stripped of their self-respect and become sex slaves for a nefarious club of devil worshippers known as "The Organization." The covers of Martin's "extraordinary sensual [novels] of vast and organized evil" beckoned readers closer with witchy women and suburban sexpots who were subject to "blind obedience, erotic ecstasy, and Satanic horror."

After the free-loving 1960s and '70s, many Americans buttoned up and brought God back to the center of the family—but the gender and child-rearing climate was out of balance with the word of the Good Book. By 1980, almost half of all families in America belonged to dual income households as feminist ideologies took hold and brought women out of the kitchens and into the work force. The Feminist Sex Wars divided the movement into women who rallied for sex positivity and those who crusaded against pornography, prostitution, and other "deviant" sexual behaviors. The friction between these two opposing groups and the religious tenor of the times is exploited in the Martin paperbacks.

Publication of the Martin series was initiated by Playboy, which was undergoing a brand evolution at the time—inspired by the feminist outcry in the 1970s and strong-armed by the Reagan administration during the '80s (the so-called harmful effects of pornography detailed in the 1986 Meese Report ordered by President Reagan). The Playboy publishing empire was built on glamorizing a swinging, hedonistic lifestyle for the single and affluent man (or at least the wannabe gentleman), who desired the joyously naughty girl next door. The intricacies and contradictions of Playboy's stance on feminism are echoed in Martin's gender-fixated melodramas, explored through various power exchange relationships.

"Scary as hell!" promises *Friday the 13th* screenwriter Victor Miller on the cover of Martin's second novel, 1981's *The Desecration of Susan Browning*. (When contacted for comment, Miller didn't recall the book.) In the paperback, Martin's fright tactics center on the psychological domination, and eventual physical enslavement, of the titular young actress. The book sets the stage for the power dynamics at play in Martin's interconnected stories about the mysterious Satanic "Organization" and its wicked lords and ladies. The word "Satan" doesn't appear until halfway through the book, emphasizing Martin's overarching battle of the sexes. The story even opens with an altercation involving a man, Susan's actor husband Marty, and a woman, whom Marty defends and is revealed to be the book's villainess, Wanda Carmichael.

One key, unique trait of the novels is that Martin writes primarily from the female perspective. While feminine-focused narratives and female-created works of horror have existed since the dawn of the genre (from author Mary Shelley to filmmaking pioneer Alice Guy-Blaché), horror is still labeled a male genre, in which female characters are often portrayed as mere ciphers or victims. Martin is not the first male

Rhea (1978) paperback cover, from the collection of Will Erickson.

horror author to write from a feminine perspective, but his novels are exceptional because they offer readers a chance to understand the emotional and sexual turmoil of his characters. This female point of view supports the voyeuristic quality of Playboy's output: men wanting insight into a woman's likes, dislikes, and sexual fantasies—or in Martin's case, how those desires can be twisted and used against women to control them.

Martin's female protagonists are also symptomatic of Playboy's branching out to prospective female readers. In his 1977 *Chicago Tribune* article, "Playboy Press Courting Women," reporter Mark Metzger cites the publisher's appeal to female readers—the top book buyers overall, according to Mike Cohn, former Playboy Press director—as a key reason for Playboy's survival as a brand in 1976. This move prompted a fast financial turnaround after a disastrous 1975 deficit almost bankrupted the company. "In 1976, we went at it with a vengeance, doing practically nothing for men," Cohn explained. He notes the popularity of Playboy's "fast-paced fiction," offering one "novel of kinky murder in the setting of a woman's consciousness-raising group," Rosemarie Santini's *Abracadabra* (1978), as an example. He also mentions Playboy's "gaudy" romance line and titles containing female-oriented buzzwords like "passion." He adds that, "our paperback line is now primarily original fiction for a mostly female audience." Cohn states that the press wanted to continue to draw female readers through the formerly male-dominated Playboy Book Club, expressing that "two out of three new members are not Playboy Men." He explains: "I obviously don't want to lose the male audience. But I suppose I'm a little greedy. I'd like to see whether we can get women in because we have so many books that are suitable for women." Martin's novels are precisely the kind of "suitable" entertainment that appealed to both male and female readers, without fear of alienation.

For example, in *The Desecration of Susan Browning*, readers are treated to Susan's inner monologue as she watches Marty beat and subdue a rapist in a parked car. "Susan wanted to look away, but the tableau fascinated her, and not only the horror: A thought scrambled across her brain: If he'd do this for a stranger, what would he do for me?" Martin writes. "The idea filled her with a hot excitement that she would later remember with a tinge of shame." Marty's heroic display of masculinity prompts Susan to initiate sex later that night and view her "gentle soul" of a husband in a new light—one which finds her totally helpless against his "skill and strength."

Susan's conflicting feelings about sexual servitude and openness continue throughout the Martin books, present within every female character. This is pushed to the extreme when Martin introduces radical mind control methods that transform women against their will, trapping them under the headship of the "Organization" where they are a commodity to be traded amongst members and their underlings. This mass commodification of women was reflected in the real-world hysterical fears surrounding the Satanic breeders' brainwashing and use of women as cattle. Books like Lauren Stratford's *Satan's Underground* (1988) and Rebecca Brown's *He Came To Set The Captives Free* (1992), as well as Geraldo Rivera's 1988 "Devil Worship" special, popularized stories of women producing children for Satanic sacrifice and black market trade. But a 1990 study from the *Journal of Prenatal and Perinatal Psychology and Health* suggests that Satanic sects engaging in "sadistic sexual orgies, human sacrifice, and cannibalism can be documented as early as the first four centuries A.D."

As far as Middle America was concerned, the devil was threatening the sanctity of suburban households, luring women and children to the dark side in droves. Martin's books brought those fears to light, exploiting subconscious fantasies about control (or lack thereof) and fear of the changing social tide, encouraging a queasy relationship between the reader and female subjects—one where they're both turned on and punished at the same time. "She wondered if there was some part of her that had turned him down precisely because he might be telling the truth, and because some tiny, quintessentially feminine portion of her personality was attracted to the idea of being dominated and enslaved, and relieved of the necessity to make decisions, just as the major part of her was repulsed by the prospect," Martin writes of one character's struggle against her own desires. "The next day she would have it brought home to her that such fantasies are very different from the realities they mimic."

The uneasiness and conflict surrounding sex and gender in *The Desecration of Susan Browning*, emblematic of Martin's books overall, is personified in the diabolical character of Wanda Carmichael. We discover she used to be a heterosexual man, Victor Carmichael, who bartered her soul to Satan for sex reassignment surgery, eventually giving birth to the "Master's" child (her functioning womb a fantastical gift from the Master), who makes an appearance during the climactic, bloody baptismal ceremony. Wanda is wealthy, powerful, and described as strangely attractive, bearing compelling masculine and feminine qualities. Her sex scene with Marty is detailed as a dream, although Martin makes it clear the sex is real. It fills Marty with "a submissive, almost feminine craving." Marty won't admit to loving Wanda (female slaves in later books describe feelings for their masters in terms of "love" and "hate"), but only being completely "fascinated" by her. Susan's denial and anxiety also surfaces at several points, such as when she describes feeling insecure in her womanhood due to Wanda's seduction of Marty, during discussions about several male characters' impotency issues, and during a castration scene.

Once Wanda casts her dark spell over Marty, to make him her obedient pet, he thrusts Susan aside, leaving her in the arms of Maxwell Webster, Wanda's Satanic ally. Wanda's spell—a blood sacrifice that ends with Wanda and Webster bathing their genitals in the gore of a female victim (it doesn't get more straightforward than that)—costs Susan not only her marriage, but also her career and dignity as she inexplicably surrenders to Webster, which devastates the actress. This is part of Martin's simultaneous punishment and celebration of gender roles, where women possess successful, atypical traits, only to be knocked down a peg and made to accept their "femininity" in degrading ways.

The effect of Wanda's evildoing extends to Martin's third novel, 1982's *The Devil and Lisa Black*. Introduced as a young model who informs Susan of Wanda's storied past, the book follows Lisa as she becomes a plaything for the sadistic Satanist. Lisa is caught in a spell that forces her to see a horribly disfigured face in place of her attractive visage—a telling maneuver from Wanda that preys on the most feminine trait of all: beauty. Through the time-spanning novel, we learn that Lisa was once a slave to the Organization. We are privy to her sense of hopelessness, self-loathing, and confusion. Martin spends the majority of the book building psychosexual tension and reinforcing the almighty power of the Satanic order. A priest, who rescues and raises the Antichrist child, is seduced by the Organization's growing harem of disposable female slaves. If a man of God can't control his darkest desires, Martin suggests that no one can. The author also drops hints about human trafficking via countries like the Philippines, alluding to an international Satanic presence.

Martin revisits this global hold the Organization has over the population in 1983's *The Obsession of Sally Wing*, the most provocative of the series, which involves child abduction, human trafficking (with Hong Kong), forced prostitution, and torture. Martin's 1984 book *The Education of Jennifer Parrish*, the last in his Satanic series, is set at a coed boarding school controlled by the Organization. The nefarious institution enslaves the student body using mind control and body swapping.

It's possible that *The Education of Jennifer Parrish* was influenced by the ubiquitous media coverage of the McMartin pre-school trial's preliminary investigation, which brought to light claims of sexual abuse from 360 children. Martin's book saw its first print run during this time, concurrent with widely reported estimates that more than 50,000 child victims were being sacrificed annually by devil worshipers. In a 1991 essay printed in the journal *Society*, professor David G. Bromley contested the outrageous numbers of child victims, stating they were "a [figure] rivaling the 517,347 [combat] deaths from the Second World War, the Korean and Vietnam wars combined." (Bromley's figure does not include the estimated six million Jews murdered in the Holocaust, as cited by the United States Holocaust Memorial Museum, or other civilian casualties.) However,

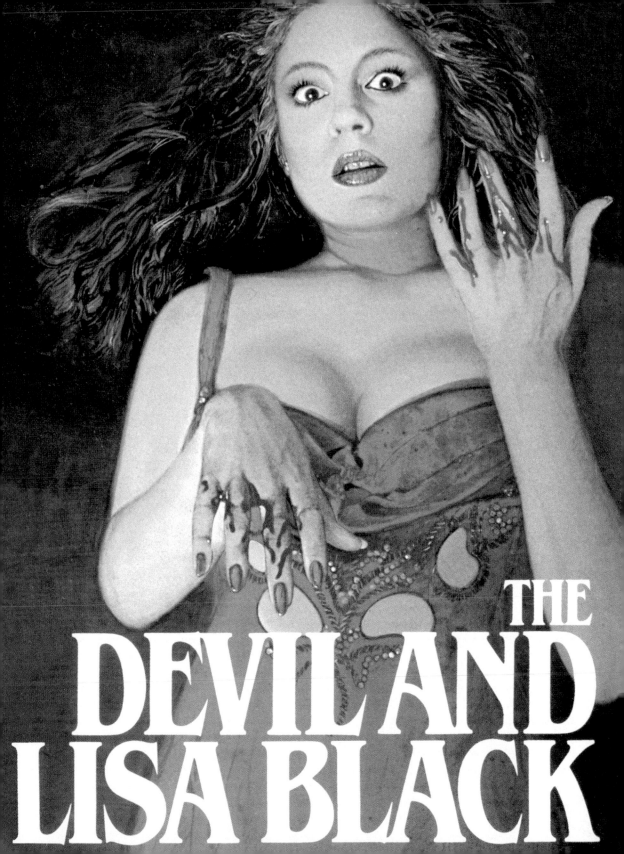

THE DEVIL AND LISA BLACK

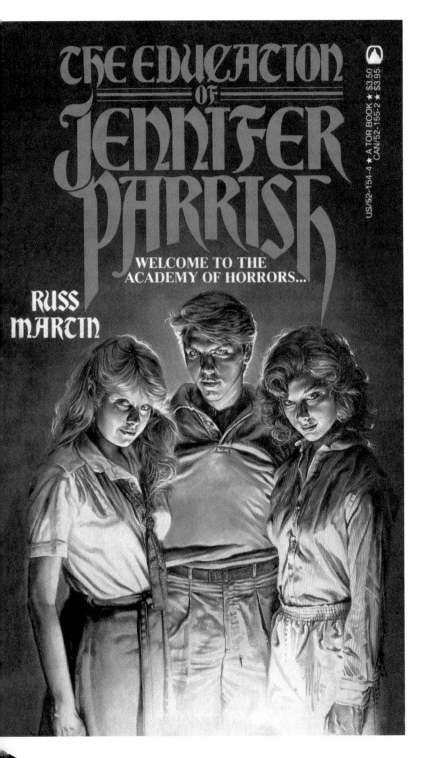

THE EDUCATION OF JENNIFER PARRISH

WELCOME TO THE ACADEMY OF HORRORS...

RUSS MARTIN

US/52-154-4 ★ A TOR BOOK ★ $3.50
CAN/52-155-2 ★ $3.95

he quotes a Sheriff's Deputy in Qallam County, Washington who explained that "the feast period of one or two years (depending on the group) marking this requires a more active level of rituals, sexual behavior and recruitment of children, with abuse being part of the indoctrination. Consider that many day-care abuse cases happened at the end of a 'cycle' in 1982 and 1983, and came to light in 1984 and 1985."

Christie Hefner was named President of Playboy Enterprises in 1982, taking over from her father, Playboy's famed founder, Hugh Hefner. She sold Playboy Books in the first few months of her tenure. The Martin titles were soon picked up by fellow paperback purveyor Tor Books. *The Possession of Jessica Young* was the first book published under the Tor imprint, in August 1982, but is perhaps the most Playboy-influenced Martin book of all. In 2008's *Journal of the History of Sexuality*, Carrie Pitzulo writes about Playboy's progressive stance on women's rights:

> **"** *Hefner also put his money where his mouth was when it came to supporting feminist causes. His help was accomplished through the Playboy Foundation, which was founded in 1965 as the philanthropic arm of the magazine. The foundation's contributions focused on three areas: "the protection and extension of civil rights," "the modernization of laws pertaining to sex, drugs, contraception, abortion and censorship," and "support of research in the fields of human sexuality and population control." The foundation was created to help bring about the social and political philosophy that Hefner had laid out in his rambling editorial series of the previous three years. The series, known as The Playboy Philosophy, ran from December 1962 to May 1965... The foundation contributed money to feminist causes such as the legalization of abortion, access to contraception, and the establishment of daycare centers.*

Still, Hefner's gender politics were undoubtedly complex and often contradictory during this time. *Playboy* magazine openly championed access to contraception and abortion, publicizing international services and feminist viewpoints in ongoing editorials and the "Playboy Forum" letters section throughout the 1960s and '70s. The Foundation supported organizations like the League of Women Voters and the National Conference of Woman and the Law, as well as research regarding the morning-after pill and advances in the birth control pill. *Playboy* even saw a Forum letter of gratitude and request for further contributions from Ruth Bader Ginsburg, the ACLU's Women's Rights Project representative and future Associate Justice of the U.S. Supreme Court. As Pitzulo points out, feminist female Forum readers applauded the company's progressive stance in letters to Hefner, while admonishing the magazine's paradoxical portrayal of women. "These letters show that contemporary observers saw the potential in *Playboy* to offer a useable version of sexuality to both men and women," Pitzulo writes.

It seems likely that this strange and uncomfortable binary of empowerment and objectification fueled an aura of panic amongst Playboy's male and female readership, espousing reproductive, and therefore sexual, freedoms, while upholding the archetype of the desirable woman—one still affixed to the male gaze and not nearly as radical as the feminist Playboy philosophy suggests. In this light, the daycare center, a key site of the Satanic Panic, becomes a fascinating symbol of Hefner's conflicted progressivism—the womb of anxiety. The autonomous woman Playboy promoted—one free from her domestic duties, with only enough time to deposit her children into the care of another (presumably vulnerable to corruption)—is a focal point for this form of embattled feminism. Playboy's feminist history highlights the dual perception of empowerment during a time when America's traditional family values were simultaneously weakening and becoming more entrenched—and there was Martin's panic-stoking fiction to see it through.

The plight of Martin's women is deeply felt in 1982's *The Possession of Jessica Young*, which reads like it could be a manifesto addressing Playboy's social causes. One of Martin's sleaziest characters, a henchman employed by the Organization named Ron, attempts to procure the virginity of Heather, the sister of the psychic, titular protagonist who has similar unrealized powers. He seduces Heather's high school friend Rosa in an attempt to win her through jealousy. "In some ways this was the best part of the whole process, when they were dazzled and bewildered, and just feeling the barest intimations of their helplessness," he muses when we first meet him. Rosa winds up pregnant and asks for financial help to obtain an underground abortion so she can hide it from her family. Ron responds in the most callous way imaginable. Later, we discover she has been brainwashed and enslaved by the Organization. Women are also severely beaten, raped, forcibly drugged, routinely humiliated (for leaving their children, for craving the mistreatment they are forced to endure, for having a "housewife mentality"), and literally lobotomized—in a conceptually frightening surgery scene, where Jessica is shaved bald (hair being a typically feminine point of pride), rendered catatonic, and molested on the operating table by the Organization's thugs.

"We don't know the full potential of your powers, and we can't take a chance," takes on an eerie resonance as Jessica Young—a woman who possesses a unique and powerful gift, yet is rendered totally powerless against the men in her life—reveals the true nature of Martin's series. At once an admission of male anxiety over female agency and a cautionary tale about the liberated woman, Martin forces readers into the uncomfortable space between identification and revulsion.

This notion is emblematic of the Satanic Panic movement and its unsubstantiated first-hand accounts of cultist-related abductions, brainwashing, and breeding. Supposedly fact-based books like *Michelle Remembers* and *Satan's Underground*—pulp fiction disguised as fact—were later debunked, essentially functioning in the same way as Martin's titillating novels. These narratives ask audiences to insert themselves into horror stories that exploit their fears (and desires) of powerlessness and victimization. Feminist advocacy may have been gaining traction in the real world, but Satanic Panic fiction opposed that rising trend. Similar to flesh-and-blood feminists, imaginary Satanist cults represented a force that many people were conceptually aware of without practical or critical engagement. Martin's books suggest that we yearn to feel like we have no choice but to submit to forces that cannot be understood or reasoned with. It's a false dilemma and tale of extremes—one whose mass appeal speaks to its enduring power as exploitive entertainment.

REFERENCES + BIBLIOGRAPHY:

Bromley, David G. "The Satanic Cult Scare." *Society*, 1991.

Brown, Rebecca. *He Came to Set the Captives Free*. New Kensington: Whitaker House, 1992.

Devil Worship: Exposing Satan's Underground. NBC/Universal Television Distribution, October 22, 1988.

Gunelius, Susan. *Building Brand Value the Playboy Way*. Basingstoke: Palgrave Macmilian, 2009.

"Introduction to the Holocaust." *United States Holocaust Memorial Museum*. June 20, 2014.

Leavitt, Judith. *American Women Managers and Administrators: A Selective Biographical Dictionary of Twentieth-Century Leaders in Business, Education, and Government*. Greenwood Publishing Group, 1985.

Martin, Russell. *The Desecration of Susan Browning*. New York: Playboy Paperbacks, 1981.

Martin, Russell. *The Devil and Lisa Black*. New York: Playboy Paperbacks, 1982.

Martin, Russell. *The Education of Jennifer Parrish*. New York: Tor Books, 1984.

Martin, Russell. *The Obsession of Sally Wing*. New York: Tor Books, 1983.

Martin, Russell. *The Possession of Jessica Young*. New York: Tor Books, 1982.

Metzger, Mark. "Playboy Press Courting Women." *Chicago Tribune*. September 25, 1977.

Pitzulo, Carrie. "The Battle in Every Man's Bed: Playboy and the Fiery Feminists." *Journal of the History of Sexuality* 17, no. 2 (2008).

Sachs, Roberta. "The Role of Sex and Pregnancy in Satanic Cults." *Journal of Prenatal and Perinatal Psychology and Health* 5, no. 2 (1990).

Stratford, Lauren. *Satan's Underground: The Extraordinary Story of One Woman's Escape*. Gretna: Pelican Publishing, 1991.

"Two Incomes The Norm...and the Necessity." *Fascinating Families* 25 (2010).

Zirpolo, Kyle, and Debbie Nathan. "I'm Sorry." *Los Angeles Times*, October 30, 2005.

DICING WITH THE DEVIL:
THE CRUSADE AGAINST GAMING

BY GAVIN BADDELEY

"Like the sheep to which Scripture so often compares us, our freest play is within the fold. Outside, there is only the bondage of fear that allows for no real leisure."
–Peter Leithart and George Grant,
A Christian Response to Dungeons & Dragons

The history of role-playing games (RPGs) mirrors the evolution of the Satanic Panic in many respects. Like the Christian campaign that fantasised a Satanic conspiracy threatening society, the RPG hobby—typified by Dungeons & Dragons (D&D)—is an American-born phenomenon that took root in the 1970s, reached its popular peak in the following decade, and gradually receded in the '90s. Although attacks by religious lobbies evolved into a coordinated crusade against the hobby in the 1980s, to suggest that D&D is anything but a game is a fantasy, founded wholly on religious ideology. And as a literal devil's advocate, I'm uniquely qualified to make this statement.

Before I proceed I should probably offer some personal disclosure. In my younger years I played several of the games covered in the following pages, including D&D. Furthermore, I've studied the history of occultism and sorcery extensively in my role as an author, journalist and consultant (I've advised in this capacity for a number of major TV history documentaries and spoken on the subject at several universities). While writing and researching my first book, a 1999 study of Satanism entitled *Lucifer Rising*, I was offered an honorary priesthood in the Church of Satan by its founder Anton LaVey, in recognition of my efforts in uncovering the roots of history's most unholy creed. I liked LaVey and, flattered, accepted.

I'm pretty confident I'd qualify as an "enemy of God," at least as referred to in books by Satanic Panic proponents like Dr. Gary North, but you'll have to take my assurance that I'm not part of a murderous conspiracy on trust. You'll also have to believe me that there is no overlap—chronologically or otherwise—between my interest in D&D and any involvement in Satanism. But this is still likely the first study of the struggle between RPGs and Christian Fundamentalists ever written by an ordained Satanic reverend.

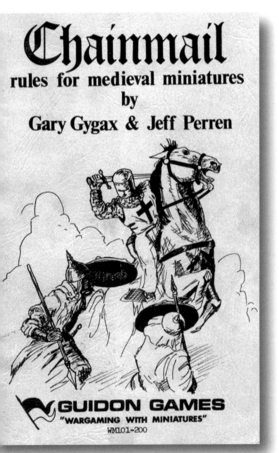

Chainmail
rules for medieval miniatures
by
Gary Gygax & Jeff Perren

GUIDON GAMES
"WARGAMING WITH MINIATURES"
WM101-200

CHAINMAIL ON CAMPUS

If we assume that RPGs weren't the product of secretive Satanic schemes to seduce the unwary into sorcery, their development becomes a little more pedestrian. D&D, uncontested as the pioneering leader in its field, evolved from a 1971 medieval wargame named Chainmail, whose rulebook was penned by Wisconsin wargamers Gary Gygax and Jeff Perren. Tabletop wargaming is a hobby at least a couple of centuries old, whereby players take on the role of generals, commanding imaginary armies—usually represented by model soldiers—recreating historical battles, with conflicts resolved by dice employing pre-agreed rules. (Later versions evolved into boardgames, with cardboard counters replacing model soldiers.) By the 1970s, wargaming was enjoying something of a renaissance, particularly on U.S. college campuses, where it cross-pollinated with several other bookish hobbies and interests, leading to D&D, and ultimately the gaming subculture.

Foremost among these interests was a burgeoning student cult following for the fantasies of the English author and eminent historian J.R.R. Tolkien. Tolkien's heroic fictional sagas set in the mythic world of Middle Earth—peopled with the elves and dwarves of early Medieval European lore—provided the backdrop for D&D. Ironically, bearing in mind future controversies, Tolkien's work has often been identified as a manifestation of the author's own deep Christian convictions, evident in the binary, monochrome morality behind his *Lord of the Rings* trilogy. Tolkien himself downplayed this Christian interpretation, concerned that clumsy evangelism might dilute the broader moral message in his work, but it unquestionably underlies the mythology of Middle Earth, with its simplistic struggle between good and evil.

Few of D&D's Christian critics troubled to delve far enough into the form's origins to encounter this paradox. But in their influential 1987 tract, *A Christian Response to Dungeons & Dragons*, Peter Leithart and George Grant suggest that parents should find more wholesome entertainment for their children to combat the pernicious influence of RPGs, such as reading Christian fiction, including stories by Tolkien. "In defending [RPGs] many people have pointed out the obvious fact that most fairy tales (The Brothers Grimm, J.R.R. Tolkien, or C.S. Lewis for example) are full of witches, goblins, and sorcerers," concede the authors. "But the heroes of these stories aren't the witches and sorcerers." Except, of course, that one of Tolkien's main heroes is Gandalf, a wizard.

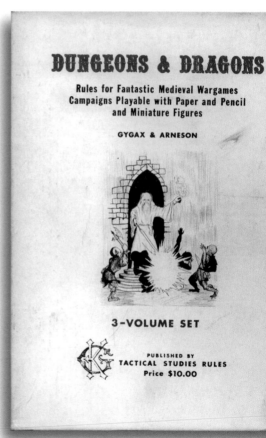

The other factor in the evolution of wargaming into RPGs was a building interest in improvisational theatre and historical re-enactment in the United States. The Society for Creative Anachronism (SCA) was founded at Berkeley University in 1966, the next evolution in the Renaissance Fair movement, outdoor historical weekend events on a loose historical theme that had become popular in the U.S. in the 1950s. The SCA took matters a stage further, not by increasing the (routinely dubious) historical accuracy of their events, but by encouraging all attendees to take part and inhabit the fantasy roles of the colourful characters they portrayed, adding an element of amateur dramatics to proceedings. The Society's brand of interactive American medievalism proved a hit and, by 1970, three "kingdoms" had emerged, all keen to immerse themselves in a fairytale world of knights, damsels and jesters.

D&D synthesized wargaming, Tolkien fandom and medievalist role-playing to create something authentically original. D&D's co-creators, Gary Gygax and Dave Arneson, took their idea to established wargames publishers, but they weren't interested in something so unorthodox. So, in 1973, they founded Tactical Studies Rules (TSR) as a basement operation to publish the game, and printed 1,000 copies of the rules. They swiftly sold out and, through word-of-mouth,

The Adventure Is Yours

With
DUNGEONS & DRAGONS®
Fantasy Adventure Games

D&D® Basic Set opens your world to adventure . . .
D&D® Expert Set gets you involved!
Our D&D® game is the world's most
talked about role-playing adventure. And
for good reason. It's a complete game SYSTEM.
In fact, our Basic game sets the pace for
the additional excitement and character
development you'll find in our Expert Set.

So if you think our Basic Set is great,
GET INVOLVED . . . capture even more
adventure in our Expert version.

For a free catalog write:
In the US: In the UK:
TSR Hobbies, Inc.   TSR Hobbies, (UK) Ltd.
POB 756 Dept.138 DC3 The Mill Rathmore Rd.
Lake Geneva, WI   Cambridge, ENGLAND
53147   CB1 4AD

TSR
The Game Wizards

sales grew exponentially as D&D mushroomed from a niche hobby to a commercial phenomenon, inspiring a number of imitators. By 1980, Gygax's company was effectively a multinational, with the establishment of TSR UK. The following year, the U.S. business monthly *Inc.* rated it the sixth fastest-growing privately held company in the country with revenues of $12.9 million and a payroll of 130, projected to rise to $27 million by 1982.

NONE DARE CALL IT BULLSHIT

Yet D&D wasn't the only cultural phenomena riding the zeitgeist in the U.S. at this point. The Christian Right had also marshalled their forces, successfully organizing to coordinate a campaign that combined political conservatism with Evangelical beliefs, culminating in the foundation of the Moral Majority by televangelist Jerry Falwell in 1979. The following year, Republican candidate Ronald Reagan won a landslide victory in the presidential election on a platform dominated by the Christian Right agenda. America's Christian soldiers were on the march, eager to do battle with anyone or anything that didn't fit with their aggressively puritanical vision of the future, and the RPG hobby was drawn into the building culture war.

Anti-D&D advocates are often notably circumspect in declaring their own positions on the spiritual map, frequently concealing some highly suspect ideological baggage, and prone to quote partisan ideologues as unbiased experts. For example, many tracts and books attacking RPGs reproduce the following quote from author Dr. Gary North:

> **"** *Without any doubt in my mind, after years of study in the history of occultism, after having researched a book on the topic [None Dare Call it Witchcraft (first published in 1976, revised as Unholy Spirits in 1986)], and after having consulted with scholars in the field of historical research, I can say with confidence: these games are the most effective, most magnificently packaged, most profitably marketed, most thoroughly researched introduction to the occult in man's recorded history, period. This is NO game.*

Dr. North's academic credentials are impeccable—at least superficially. He's an Associated Scholar of the Mises Institute, with a PhD in history from California University, who's served as the director of seminars for the Foundation for Economic Education, and worked as a research assistant for a Republican Congressman. North's book *None Dare Call it Witchcraft* is a fairly unorthodox history of the occult by most standards, not least because North not only equates occultism with humanism and liberalism, but also believes magic literally exists, and identifies it as an urgent threat to the modern world.

North's a prolific writer, with over 50 books to his name in a wide variety of fields. What unifies them is a radical right-wing evangelical agenda, which includes advocating Old Testament punishment for "crimes" like homosexuality and abortion. North has a

49

particular interest in education. "We must use the doctrine of religious liberty to gain independence for Christian schools until we train up a generation of people who know that there is no religious neutrality, no neutral law, no neutral education, and no neutral civil government," he explained in a piece for the 1982 Christianity & Civilization symposium. "Then they will get busy in constructing a Bible-based social, political and religious order which finally denies the religious liberty of the enemies of God."

Others have claimed that occultism figured in the very nativity of D&D. In his article "Straight Talk on Dungeons & Dragons," Christian personality William Schnoebelen claims to have been the game's occult advisor during his disreputable past as a "witch high priest":

> **"** *Our "covendom" was in Milwaukee, Wisconsin; just a short drive away from the world headquarters of TSR, the company which makes Dungeons & Dragons in Lake Geneva, WI. In the late 1970s, a couple of the game writers actually came to my wife and I as prominent "sorcerers" in the community. They wanted to make certain the rituals were authentic. For the most part, they are.*

Schnoebelen's part of a very colourful cast who made up the ranks of the anti-RPG crusade. His claims to have been a senior member of a secret Satanic sect, before being rescued for Christ by being "born again," are a familiar feature in the supposed CVs of many of the more flamboyant evangelical preachers. Schnoebelen is unusual both in explicitly stating that he was effectively the occult advisor behind D&D, as well as claiming to have belonged to a large number of unholy organizations, which (according to his official biography) include "Freemasonry, cultural spiritualism (Voodoo, etc.), Thelema (the Aleister Crowley cult), Rosicrucianism, the Catholic priesthood, Mormonism, and various Eastern philosophies." It's when our hero graduates beyond the highest grades of these—in his view implicitly anti-Christian disciplines—that things get really interesting.

Schnoebelen claims to have joined the Church of Satan, an organization that exists (I'm a member), before moving onto "hardcore" Satanism, which is more suspect because of his autobiographical accounts of close encounters with literal demons. From there he claims that the next step was to choose between becoming a vampire or a werewolf (he choose the former in 1979 as he'd heard lycanthropy could be unpleasant). While Schnoebelen stops short of claiming he literally became a member of the undead, he doesn't stop *far* short, and says he craved and drank human blood, slept in a coffin, and dreaded sunlight and garlic. Schnoebelen was "born again" in 1984, ready to dedicate his life to combating his former occult allies, including the fiendish forces behind D&D.

Schnoebelen may be among the more obviously eccentric characters who led the anti-RPG crusade in the 1980s, but he is in several significant respects not atypical. He has a tendency to slip into magical thinking, whereby the supernatural is assumed to be real, which lies behind many of the claims from foes of D&D. He also displays a conspiratorial viewpoint, depicting everything as a covert struggle between otherwordly divine and infernal forces. I'll leave the reader to make their own conclusions on Schnoebelen's plausibility and reliability as an expert, although, in fairness, much of Schnoebelen's writing on the occult begins by at least nailing a few actual facts before plunging deep into more bizarre and contentious territory, suggesting he has at least done some homework, which is more than most of his peers can claim.

But before Dr. North and Schnoebelen's own inquisition into RPGs, the movement seems to have largely gained traction following the 1979 disappearance of University of Michigan student James Dallas Egbert. Clearly a troubled teenager, Egbert's interest in D&D appears to have been casual, but circumstances conspired to make the 17-year-old the first poster-boy of the anti-RPG crusade. An academic prodigy but socially inept, Egbert was under heavy family pressure to achieve at college, struggled with his sexual identity, and had begun taking drugs as a coping strategy. In August, 1979, he disappeared and, after campus authorities failed to locate him, Egbert's uncle employed private investigator William Dear to find the boy. Dear worked out that Egbert had taken refuge in the steam tunnels under the university, and publicly speculated that Egbert was acting out D&D fantasies. In reality, the tormented and possibly suicidal teen was just looking for somewhere secluded to self-harm.

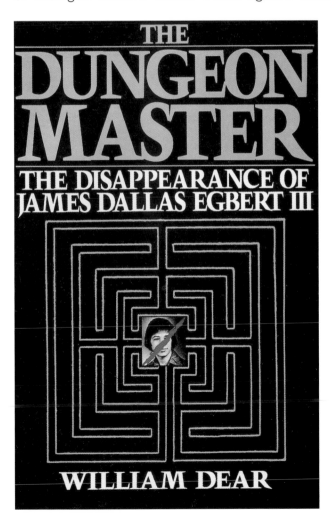

However, the detective's theory—referencing a hobby still regarded as suspiciously weird by the mainstream—captured the prurient imagination of the media. For the first time, RPGs entered the national consciousness, but for all the wrong reasons. Dear located Egbert within a month, but the tormented teenager took his own life a year later. When the detective revisited the case in print in 1985, he confessed that the D&D angle had been a mistake, but he left the myth to take root because he felt that it was less damaging to Egbert's surviving relatives, particularly his younger brother Doug. Dear explained that he was respecting James Egbert's wishes, who did not want Doug to endure "cruel asides from his classmates and friends about his 'faggot brother, the dope addict.'"

Daily Trojan   Thursday, October 8, 1981   3

Dungeons and Dragons causes moral conflict, protest
Evangelists see game as front for demon worship

By Mark Ordesky

Dungeons and Dragons--the very name of this popular fantasy game conjures images of the macabre and the mysterious. To the uninitiated, the game seems incomprehensible; to its players, D&D offers a wild romp through the imagination.

To yet others, however, D&D is not a harmless pastime of its predominantly young players. Evangelists argue the game is a front for demon worship and witchcraft while proponents see it as a wholesome, constructive release. Regardless of which view one believes, if either, the battles which rage over the moral implications of Dungeons and Dragons are as heated as the violent conflicts which take place in the game itself.

Dungeons and Dragons is the prototype of fantasy role-playing games. In such games, players suppress their own personalities and play the roles of fantasy characters like those out of Tolkien or Arthurian legend. Players can become warriors, thieves, wizards, priests, or any of a number of characters from medieval times. These characters travel through an imaginary world of adventure created and controlled by someone known as the Dungeon Master (DM) in search of treasure, fame, and power.

The controversy which now surrounds D&D stems from the "monsters" contained in these manuals are evil enemies. Players gain experience and power in the game by battling such creatures and defeating them.

"There is a built-in reward system in D&D," said one local player. "Being good, stamping out evil where you find it, is rewarded by fame and notoriety. The goal of the game is to live up to the artificial morality of your character."

However, it seems there is more then morality at stake. In another article which appeared in the *Herald Examiner*, a quote from a pamphlet issued by Concerned Christians attacked D&D claiming the game promoted "homosexuality, sodomy, rape, and other perverse acts of sexuality."

Players vehemently deny such accusations. A local high school player commented, "That's a bold-faced lie. It reflects the mentality of these people and their slanderous opinions."

Scott Kilburn, vice president of the university's Fantasy Wargames Club, has similar feelings for such evangelical groups. "They want to come in and dictate what other people should do," Kilburn said. "They are extremely close-minded."

Meanwhile, more fundamentalist Christian groups in California and Utah have been successful in getting D&D banned from public schools, where it had been used in programs for "gifted" students. In Kansas, another evangelist threatened to buy up all the games and burn them if the stores did not stop stocking them.

All the aforementioned actions have taken place this year. Yet D&D has been available to the general public since 1974, and people have been playing games of this type since 1970.

So why the sudden zeal in attacking the game now? Just like anything else, it took a nationally publicized incident to turn the public eye towards D&D: the disappearance of James Dallas Egbert III.

Egbert was a 16-year-old Michigan State student, "a whiz kid," who played D&D in the large complex of steam tunnels underneath the school. When he disappeared, there
(Continued on page 16)

HELPLINE
IS OPEN

8:30 p.m.- 12:30 a.m.
Monday thru Friday

Media panics come and go, and the Egbert story might have evaporated like so many other sensationalist stories had it not caught the attention of New York author Rona Jaffe. Jaffe identified the case as good material for a punchy, topical novel and, concerned that another writer might come to the same conclusion, worked quickly. Her book was published in September of 1981 as *Mazes and Monsters* (presumably to avoid obvious legal issues). Unsurprisingly considering its hasty conception, Jaffe's novel was hardly a sound reflection on the Egbert case or RPGs in general, though, as a work of fiction, why should it be? But it certainly fed the climate of hostility building around D&D.

Yet, once again, Jaffe's book would have enjoyed little cultural resonance had it not caught the attention of executives at CBS. *Mazes and Monsters* was adapted as a made-for-TV movie, debuting on the network in late 1982, that offered an early lead role for a young Tom Hanks. The Egbert tragedy had now broken almost totally free from any factual mooring and entered popular mythology. User reviews on sites like IMDb today largely recommend *Mazes and Monsters* for being laughably bad, with its crass, inaccurate portrayal of a harmless hobby that lends the film a certain camp, comical charm. Though other user reviews also recall it as a malign influence, shown to them as kids by well-meaning but naïve adults to warn of the dangers of D&D.

While *Mazes and Monsters* is often remembered as the flagship of the anti-RPG crusade, religion is conspicuously absent from both the book and film. The titular, fictionalized RPG is portrayed as having a special appeal to oddballs and misfits, but the threat it poses is to their mental stability, not their immortal souls. When the most fragile character—played by Hanks and clearly loosely modelled on Egbert—loses his mind, the game may be the trigger, but grief over his dead brother is the underlying cause. In *Mazes and Monsters*, the danger of RPGs is simply the psychological dangers of becoming too involved in a fantasy world. This is often the first line of attack by anti-RPG crusaders, aware that their more overtly religious, irrational criticisms of the hobby can alienate those who don't share their Christian agenda.

RONA JAFFE'S
MAZES AND MONSTERS

Four players in a dangerous game . . .

Risking their hearts, their minds and their lives.

Sponsored by products of the PROCTER & GAMBLE Company.
WORLD TELEVISION PREMIERE!
A CBS Special Movie Presentation **9 PM CBS ⊚ 4, 10, 35**
TV GUIDE A-63

THE ABOMINABLE THING

On his exemplary RPG advocacy website, *The Escapist*, William J. Walton identifies 1980 as when the first shots were fired in the religious crusade launched against the hobby—the year following Egbert's disappearance in the steam tunnels (though some Evangelicals had referenced the game as early as 1978). His site links to a lecture from Reverend James R. Cotter, a tract by Fundamentalist Christian preacher Albert James Dager and a report from *The New York Times* all from that year. "Due to a long tradition among preachers of prolific cutting and pasting, much of the rhetoric seen in religious anti-gaming materials can be traced backwards to the work of these two men," notes Walton. They're certainly indicative of the charges made against RPGs in the ensuing crusade, and represent a blueprint for the battles to come. Cotter's lecture, dated September 16, 1980, is a catalogue of inaccuracies about D&D. He insists that a character's "only means of defence is the magical powers which you bought and rolled the dice for at the beginning of the game, and the magical powers and strengths of those who are travelling with you," which misrepresents the leading role taken by swashbuckling swordplay in most RPGs. Emphasising the significance of magic in D&D was endemic among Christian critics, symptomatic of their inability to distinguish between the imaginary/fictional sorcery found in books, films and games, and the "real" magic of contemporary occultist practice and history. The same inability to distinguish between fictional invention and any kind of authentic historic belief or contemporary practice has characterized more recent crusades, such as Christian campaigns to have *Harry Potter* books banned from school libraries.

Cotter spends most of the rest of his lecture subjecting D&D to biblical scrutiny. As, for obvious chronological reasons, the Bible has nothing to say on the matter (playing RPGs nearly 2,000 years before they were invented is not one of Christ's recorded miracles), Cotter resorts to comparing sentences from D&D manuals—taken out of context—with reams of biblical quotations. Shakespeare's quote, "The Devil can cite scripture for his purpose," leaps to mind, as any half-capable commentator could find biblical quotes to oppose or support pretty much anything. Cotter concludes with a "warning from Peter telling us to be on the alert for a 'roaring lion,' but at times Satan disguises himself and becomes a cute cuddly kitten. That's what he had done in the game Dungeons & Dragons."

Dager's *Media Spotlight Special Report* on D&D is only marginally more convincing to a sceptic's eye. In fairness, Dager says his report was triggered by the dean of a prominent Christian university, concerned at the building popularity of RPGs on campus. The report was doubtless aimed at an audience inclined to take biblical quotation as incontrovertible evidence, and the Reverend, again, peppers his report with them. Founded in 1977, Media Spotlight describe themselves on their website as "the first ministry on a national scale to specifically address the ungodly nature of the secular media, particularly in motion pictures, television, toys, games, and a myriad of other problems that contribute to Christians living no differently than the rest of the world."

Unsurprisingly, Dager comes out against D&D in his conclusion: "If you are caught up in anything akin to fantasy role-playing games, I beg you to burn the abominable thing." His arguments are somewhat vague and rambling. Dager suggests that success in the game could lead to the sin of pride. The familiar suspicion of anything even mentioning other gods, or sorcery, even in a patently fictional setting is evident, as is Dager's dubious grasp of authentic occultism: "Among the items available for casting spells are 'Wolvesbane'—'Holy Water'—'Garlic,' etc., all part of the esoteric or hidden mystery religious system that characterized the ancient druids and the clerics of the middle ages." Warming to his topic, he even suggests that "it is not without knowledge that Dungeons & Dragons was devised. But it is the knowledge of an evil that mingled the Babylonian mystery religions with a luke-warm 'Christianity.'" Whatever that means.

Cotter and Dager were very much preaching to the choir with little hope of an audience for their message outside of Fundamentalist circles. However, the May 3, 1980 *New York Times* report linked on *The Escapist*; "Utah Parents Exorcise 'Devilish' Game," is perhaps the first example of the RPG panic manifest in mainstream American media. It also shows that the anti-RPG movement wasn't confined to Evangelical Protestants like Cotter and Dager, as the story took place in a predominantly Mormon community (Mormons would play an interesting if minor role in the struggle over the soul of the RPG community). Finally, the article provides a blueprint for the way that the gaming hobby's religious opponents could prevail, even when in a minority and campaigning from a position of evident ignorance.

According to the article, in the small Utah town of Heber City, D&D was introduced as one of the after-school programs —

Utah Parents Exorcize 'Devilish' Game

By MOLLY IVINS
Special to The New York Times

"dragon master," sees the dungeon plan. Players take an imaginary journey

do with lust, and the terminology of magic including a magic circle.

alongside science, sports and Spanish activities — for gifted students at a high school. Even though only those students who had parental permission could attend, other parents expressed opposition. Objections were raised by locals unconnected to the program and a meeting was held, attended by parents of children playing the game and representatives of the PTA, which ruled strongly in favour of the activity. But a second meeting in late March 1980, attended by 300 people—most, presumably, unconnected to the program—reached a different conclusion. "Teachers and school administrators are left feeling variously distressed, stunned or amused at the reaction to the program that they had hoped would stimulate imagination, creativity and teamwork among talented children," *The New York Times* reported. "For the teachers' pains, they have been accused of working with the Antichrist and of fomenting Communist subversion."

So, who were these people who emerged from the woodwork to oppose this after-school program for gifted children? One was Norman Spring, described by *The New York Times* as a non-denominational Christian minister: "Oh it is very antireligious," he said. "I have studied witchcraft and demonology for some years and I've taught against witchcraft. The books themselves have been taken from mythology and from witchcraft and they are filled with demonology, filled with pictures and symbols that you could find in any basic witchcraft book and use the same terminology." Spring was particularly concerned with "incubuses and succubuses"—male and female sex demons from Christian mythology—which he claimed featured prominently in the game.

"These books are filled with things that are not fantasy but are actual in the real demon world," Spring said, "and can be very dangerous for anyone involved in the game because it leaves them so open to Satanic spirits." Aside from Spring's incorrect terminology (the plural for incubus and succubus are incubi and succubi, as anyone who has studied demonology knows), neither mythic entity play a major role in D&D. The notion that any of the game's manuals are filled with images from witchcraft books (whatever those might be) is also patent nonsense. It didn't matter how plausible Spring's claims were—the crucial factor was their impact on local community opinion, which they helped stoke up against the game in true Salem witch-hunting style. (The suggestions that D&D might somehow be "Communistic" is an intriguing thread of paranoid hysteria that never caught on.)

In the end, Douglas Merkley, Superintendent of the Wasatch District Schools, took a pragmatic approach and simply cancelled the program. He had presided over a conflict where the prejudices of an ill-informed minority were able to dictate the agenda for an entire school. His decision set an unhealthy precedent, which would be echoed in countless schools, church halls and family homes in the years to come.

BADD KARMA

Meanwhile, in the summer of 1982, D&D was dragged back into the headlines when Virginian teenager Irving "Bink" Pulling took his mother's gun and shot himself. The circumstances leading to his suicide have since become the source of some controversy. According to the boy's mother, Patricia Pulling, Bink killed himself after being cursed during a high school game of D&D, though none of his peers could recall any such incident.

The boy's state of mind preceding his death became particularly contentious. In the months that followed Bink's suicide, Patricia Pulling tried to sue the school principal on the basis that her son was obviously unstable, and shouldn't have been allowed to take part in an activity that might place him under undue psychological stress. When the case failed, Mrs. Pulling changed her tune, insisting that Bink had been "a happy, well-adjusted kid" until he fell under the malign influence of D&D. A 1983 *Washington Post* article painted a rather different picture of Bink: "He got up one night and killed 17 rabbits and a neighborhood cat for no apparent reason. He was socially isolated, once failing to get even a proforma 'campaign manager' to sign on for him when he wanted to run for school office."

Yet Patricia Pulling maintained her conviction that RPGs were to blame for her son's suicide and, in 1983, founded a pressure group named Bothered About Dungeons & Dragons (BADD), dedicated to the pernicious threat of RPGs. BADD began issuing literature and became a small, but vociferous force in the larger crusade against the mythical Satanic conspiracy that radical Christians claimed threatened America's youth, as Pulling became convinced that the game wasn't just dangerous, but demonic. In particular, BADD targeted parents, educators, the media and law enforcement officials with their literature, which describes D&D as "a fantasy role-playing game which uses demonology, witchcraft, voodoo, murder, rape, blasphemy, suicide, assassination, insanity, sex perversion, homosexuality, prostitution, satanic type rituals, gambling, barbarism, cannibalism, sadism, desecration, demon summoning, necromantics, divination and other teachings." By 1985, BADD's crusade had kicked into high gear, and they petitioned Federal Trade Commission (FTC) demanding labels be put on RPGs to warn that they could cause suicide. The FTC declined, passing the case onto the Consumer Products Safety Commission, who also ultimately rejected the plea.

BADD bounced back, as Mrs. Pulling appeared on respected CBS magazine *60 Minutes* on a segment dedicated to RPGs in September 1985. Presenter Ed Bradley begins with a litany of suicides and murders before stating that "police are blaming D&D." Gary Gygax is interviewed, alongside a TSR representative, but they are very much in the dock, challenged to defend their products. Gygax describes the proceedings as "a witch-hunt," while Mrs. Pulling and her remaining family feature in the role of witnesses for the prosecution. When her daughter starts to cry, Patricia Pulling explains that they "found out later that [Bink] had threatened to kill her if she told us that he was playing the game. She knew it and she was actually scared for her life."

SATURDAY OKLAHOMAN & TIMES   March 23, 1985

Groups Say Fantasy Game Responsible for Teen Suicide

LAKE GENEVA, Wis. (AP) — Millions of high school and college students play the fantasy game "Dungeons and Dragons," fighting hobgoblins and green slime.

Two national groups, however, claim the popular game is far from harmless, blaming it for the deaths of as many as a dozen young people.

The National Coalition on Television Violence and Bothered About Dungeons and Dragons (BADD) have urged their members to write their congressional representatives asking the government to declare the game hazardous.

Lou Brott, spokesman for the Consumer Product Safety Commission of the FTC, said the commission has no jurisdiction in the matter.

Dieter Sturm, a spokesman for TSR Hobbies of Lake Geneva, Wis., which makes the game, said "Dungeons and Dragons" is

only a board game and no more violent than other classic board games such as "Monopoly."

Sturm, director of corporate relations for TSR, derided the groups' proposal to put a warning label on the game.

"You're going to have to label everything from soup to nuts," he said. "What are you going to do, put a label on your dog, saying this animal might bite if you're not careful?"

"Dungeons and Dragons" players are assigned a character with specific traits. Guided by a "dungeon master" who has a book with more information than the players do, the players strive to win a treasure while avoiding various monsters.

About 3 million to 4 million people, mostly young males in their late teens and early 20s, play the game, according to TSR.

Pat Pulling of Rich-

— AP Laserphoto

Patricia Pulling holds a photo of her son along with several books and games from "Dungeons and Dragons," which she blames for the suicide of her son, Irving.

mond, Va., started after a curse was placed BADD after her 16-year-old son, Irving, shot himself to death in 1982. Mrs. Pulling said her son killed himself hours on him during a game of D&D at his high school. She sued TSR, its chairman and the two teachers who led the game,

but the $10 million suit was dismissed by the Circuit Court of Hanover County, Va.

"We know D&D was involved with his death because of the notes (on his game sheets) he left behind," Mrs. Pulling said in a telephone interview.

Mrs. Pulling said her son was "perfectly normal" before he played the game, which was sponsored by the school's program for talented and gifted children.

But some of his classmates later said that Pulling had personal problems not associated with the game.

"Many millions of kids are sold Dungeons and Dragons," Thomas Radecki, head of the coalition and a psychiatrist at the University of Illinois at Urbana-Champaign, said in a telephone interview. "The very least they deserve is the other side of the story — that kids are getting murdered

because of this game."

Radecki's group lists at least a dozen deaths, including five suicides, that it says were connected with the game. Radecki said the game can wrap impressionable teen-agers in a dangerous web of fantasy.

"Aggression research shows that the more violent fantasies someone has, the more likely he is to act it out in real life," he said. "In this game, you're ready at any moment to be assaulted by deadly force."

The game, he admitted, may not spur everyone to violence.

"It doesn't mean every player is going to go out and kill himself or somebody else," he said. " ... There has to be some tendency there (for violence) too."

Sturm emphasized that, in at least one of the incidents cited by Radecki — a murder-suicide involving two teen-age boys in Colorado — police later said the game had nothing to

do with the deaths.

"If you take (the game) outside the context, you're not playing Dungeons and Dragons, you're playing something else," Sturm said. "This is nothing more than a game. It's played around a table, it's not played in real life."

The average D&D player is 12-24 years old and is male, TSR said. In the mid-1970s when the game originated, it attracted primarily college-aged students.

Dr. Thomas Radecki is the segment's professional expert, billed as a psychiatrist who teaches at the University of Illinois Medical School and Chairman of National Coalition on Television Violence (NCTV). But it's not mentioned that NCTV were allies of BADD. Radecki claims to have studied RPGs and discovered 28 fatalities caused by D&D in the preceding five years. "In some of those [cases] it was clearly the decisive element, in other ones it was just a major element, in the thinking of the people at the time they committed suicide or murder," explains Radecki, sounding plausibly professional. But then things get a little odd: "It's not coincidence, not when you have careful documentation, you have careful notes, you have eye-witnesses. For instance, one case the parents actually saw their child summon a Dungeons & Dragons demon to his room before he killed himself."

It's typical of the magical thinking found among Satanic conspiracy theorists, but Radecki's assertion that people literally witnessed a demon conjured courtesy of a game went unchallenged. One of American TV's most reputable current affairs programmes had effectively endorsed the theories of medieval demonology via D&D. Gygax would later reflect on the show as a low-point in the relationship between RPGs and the media, describing it as "wretched yellow journalism." He told Allen Rausch of *Gamespy* in 2004 that:

> **❝** *I've never watched that show after Ed Bradley's interview with me because they rearranged my answers [...] When I sent some copies of letters from mothers of those two children who had committed suicide who said the game had nothing to do with it, they refused to do a retraction or even mention it on air. What bothered me is that I was getting death threats, telephone calls, and letters. I was a little nervous. I had a bodyguard for a while.*

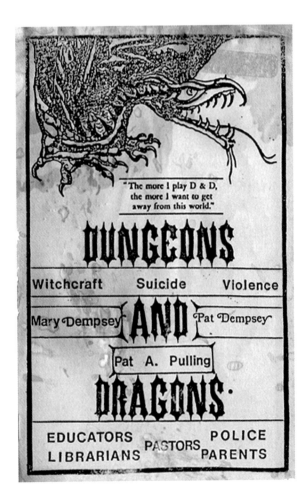

Meanwhile, Pulling was exploring other avenues to push the BADD message in collaboration with Radecki. The pair became involved in a 1985 Missouri case where 19-year-old Darren Lee Molitor cited his D&D hobby as a mitigating factor that helped trigger his strangulation of a teenage girl; it was the first example of a "D&D defence." Pulling later recalled being called by Molitor's attorney, and that her role during the trial was "jury education, explaining to the jury members the game of Dungeons & Dragons and how it is played" But Molitor remembers matters differently, telling RPG advocate Michael A. Stackpole that: "Ms. Pulling contacted either my parents or my lawyer after her husband saw a St. Louis newspaper with my case in it. She and Dr. Radecki did testify at my trial, but it was 'off the record.' In other words it went into the transcript but the jurors were not allowed to hear it because it was ruled irrelevant."

Pulling was reportedly involved in at least two more cases where

Above: An anti-D&D tract disseminated by Pat Pulling and BADD.

defendants attempted a D&D defence though both, like Molitor's, failed. The Committee for the Advancement of Role-Playing Games (CAR-PGa)—a group of role-players founded to counter the anti-RPG crusade—record eight attempted uses of the D&D defence in American courts, starting with the Molitor trial, and finishing with a kidnapping case in 1991. Although all of these defences failed, it only takes one successful court case to set a precedent.

ONSLAUGHT OF THE OCCULT

Despite such failures, BADD was enjoying success on a broader level, as the idea of RPGs as potentially dangerous gained traction in cult crime sectors. In his 1989 book *The Edge of Evil*, leading Kansas youth preacher Jerry Johnston investigates "the rise of Satanism in North America." It's classic Satanic Panic literature, with Johnston endeavouring to convince his readership that a hidden demonic conspiracy is menacing the country. Johnston opens one chapter, "The Onslaught of the Occult," by attempting to attend an advanced seminar on occult crime partially sponsored by BADD: "I find most of the conference-goers worried about security from satanic cult threats, and consequently—as a nonlaw-enforcement [sic] entity—treated pretty much as a persona non grata. So my anticipated goldmine of experts to interview is virtually a bust." Instead, Johnston reads approvingly through some BADD literature that repeats the familiar ludicrous litany of D&D accusations. It's tempting to suggest that had Johnston been welcome, it would equally have been "a bust."

BADD's impact wasn't just confined to America, either. As RPGs became an international phenomenon, so did the crusade against them, as detailed in "The great 1980s Dungeons & Dragons panic," an April 2014 article for the BBC's online magazine by Peter Ray Allison. The article quotes U.K. fantasy author KT Davies, who recalls "showing a vicar a gaming figure—he likened D&D to demon worship because there were 'gods' in the game."

British journalist and Christian Andrew Boyd was instrumental in importing the Satanic Panic across the Atlantic via print and television. After penning his 1991 book *Blasphemous Rumours*, which promoted the (subsequently discredited) Satanic ritual abuse theory, Boyd issued *Dangerous Obsessions* (1996), which regurgitated American conspiracy theories about a demonic cultural attack upon unsuspecting teens. Boyd says:

> **❝** *As long ago as 1987, the* Daily Express *predicted "Cult fantasy games on sale in Britain could drive players to murder and suicide" […] A comparison of the phenomenon in the US and Britain was made in* Police Review, *which found disturbances less marked in the UK because of the difference between the "emotions and reactions" of the two cultures.*

Yet, even if the British police were refreshingly skeptical, the anti-RPG crusade still made its presence felt in the U.K. In his BBC article, Allison interviews veteran roleplayer Andy Smith, who found himself in the uncomfortable position of being both a roleplayer and a Christian, noting that: "While working for a Christian organization I was told to remove my roleplaying books from the shared accommodation as they were offensive to some of the other workers and contained references to demon-worship."

The media was a key target in the strategies of groups like BADD. The same dynamic that helped disseminate the Satanic Panic also facilitated the spread of the anti-D&D agenda. Lurid stories that air sensationalist claims sell more papers—and generate better ratings—than articles debunking hysteria and falsehoods. In an article for *The Skeptical Enquirer* in 1994, the CAR-PGa's Paul Cardwell crunched the numbers on 111 U.S. news articles written on RPGs between 1979-1992, rating them as pro, neutral or negative on a paragraph-by-paragraph basis. Of these articles, 80 were classified as negative overall, nine were neutral, and just three were positive. The statistics tell a clear story, and it's one that favours the mythmakers. A vicious circle develops whereby those making outrageous claims, such as about D&D, only have to convince one credulous, unethical or cynical outlet to print or broadcast them. The result can then be re-employed to offer as "proof" for the next media opportunity, generating a self-fulfilling cycle of baseless assertion.

So, what did TSR do to counter these wild and unwarranted attacks on their products? The short answer is not much. In the wake of Gary Gygax's unhappy 1985 experience on *60 Minutes*, TSR appears to have largely adopted a policy of appeasement. Indeed, CAR-PGa was founded by fans in 1988 explicitly because the "inaction of the game publishers' organization at that time" meant that the fight against crusaders like BADD was largely left to private individuals. The CAR-PGa's Paul Cardwell has an interesting theory on why this might be—in his *Gamespy* interview, Gygax jokes that the controversy "really pushed the sales up," and D&D's sales figures were soaring at the height of the anti-RPG crusade. "TSR seemed to think that this proved that bad publicity was good publicity, and it rarely defends its game," opines Cardwell.

However, as Cardwell notes, there were other factors at play behind the scenes at TSR as D&D made the turbulent transformation from a hobby into an industry. Once D&D had saturated the campus market, they began targeting a younger demographic with an increasingly diverse series of products, including a line of *Endless Quest* "gamebooks" in 1982, followed a year later by *Choose Your Own Adventure*-styled *Pick a Path to Adventure* books for even younger readers. A *Dungeons & Dragons* children's cartoon wasw launched in 1983, produced in Japan and screened on CBS (the network behind *Mazes and Monsters* and the infamous *60 Minutes* episode); it was accompanied by its own line of action figures, plastic playsets and related books. Despite healthy core D&D sales, TSR overstretched itself with this ambitious diversification and, in 1985, the company announced a huge loss and sacked 75% of its staff. Among them was Gary Gygax, ousted from the company he'd founded, as boardroom politics took their toll.

Right: Rear of a Shredded Wheat cereal box circa 1987 showcasing the *Dungeons and Dragons* children's cartoon.

DUNGEONS & DRAGONS™

Hologram

Free inside every special pack you'll find a
Dungeons & Dragons™ hologram. Lurking inside each
hologram is a monster. Who knows which one's inside this pack?
Maybe it's an Orc, or a Wizard, or even a Skeleton!

IMPORTANT – SEE SIDE OF PACK
FOR VIEWING INSTRUCTIONS.

6 TO COLLECT

ACTUAL SIZE OF ITEM
76mm x 50mm

TSR's quest for a younger demographic carried implicit risks. People might be suspicious of college students embracing something odd like D&D. But if their pre-teen kids were becoming involved, it was easy for anti-RPG crusaders to stoke concern among credulous parents into panic. The cartoon brought D&D to the attention of evangelicals like the Texan preacher Phil Phillips, who focussed on finding demonic overtones in children's toys and TV shows. His 1986 book *Turmoil in the Toybox* is a camp classic of Satanic paranoia, condemning the likes of the Smurfs and the Care Bears as covert devilish propaganda. "The fact is that this toy and cartoon series is bringing the occult to younger and younger children in a very real way," observes Phillips in reference to D&D in the 1984 Christian VHS release *Deception of a Generation*.

Phillips claims to have received numerous letters from worried Christian parents who had taken "the pieces of the game, they would throw them in the incinerator, or the fireplace, and screams would come out, because there seemed to be some kind of spiritual forces inhabiting those pieces, and children would drop out of life, they didn't want to study anymore." This curious story echoes accounts from the Middle Ages of occult grimoires that reportedly screamed when burnt, as well as contemporary supernatural manifestations triggered by D&D related by latter-day witch-hunters like Dr. Radecki on *60 Minutes*. Yet, even under such naked provocation, TSR avoided confrontation.

THE BLIND LEADING THE BLIND

One of the most frequent accusations levelled at RPG games by their Christian opponents is that the magic found in fictional RPGs resembles or is modelled on authentic occult practices. My knowledge of the history of the occult, role in the Church of Satan and familiarity with D&D makes me unusually well placed to examine these kinds of claims.

At the risk of crass over-simplification of a complex historical field, there were basically two kinds of magic in the European tradition of the Middle Ages and Renaissance. The first was a scholarly pursuit, often known as "ritual magic" because of the lengthy, complex and exacting ceremonies involved. People haven't changed much, and most such ritual magic operations were usually undertaken in the hope of finding or making money. The second form of magic fits broadly under the umbrella of witchcraft. It largely involved petty acts of vengeful mischief, such as souring milk or causing sexual impotence, though more serious and lethal curses can certainly be found in legal archives. Modern self-styled witches argue that such a view of magic was based upon malicious bigotry and religious fanaticism, and that their historic namesakes were more akin to benevolent herbalists or midwives, ministering to the local community rather than plaguing them. The truth, in my opinion, was likely somewhere in the middle.

Suffice to say that neither variety even vaguely resembles the magic found in RPGs. Generally, spell-casting characters in games like D&D effectively provide heavy weapons support for their sword-wielding allies by conjuring fireballs and lightning bolts to obliterate the opposition. It's the sort of sorcery found in modern fantasy fiction, not in accounts of the activities of our historical ancestors. Indeed we know that the

chief inspiration for the magic system in D&D was derived directly from the dystopian "Dying Earth" fantasies of author Jack Vance, wherein sorcery is rediscovered in the far future as the sun threatens to expire and extinguish humanity. Dramatic, imaginative material perhaps, but hardly connected to history, authentic magical tradition, or indeed modern occult theory or practice.

There have been a few attempts to introduce some authenticity into the magic featured in some RPGs. In *The Seduction of Our Children*, evangelical authors Neil T. Anderson and Steve Russo illustrate the seductiveness of D&D by observing that "Isaac Bonewits, a practising witch, considered it such a good tool for instructing people in paganism that he wrote a special manual showing players how to move from the game into real sorcery." Bonewits' *Authentic Thaumaturgy* was first published in 1978 with the express intention of making the magic in RPGs more "realistic," emphasizing its current inauthenticity. Bonewits was recognized as an occult authority in some circles, though he anachronistically dubbed himself an "Archdruid." *Authentic Thaumaturgy* is pretty obscure, generally considered an interesting oddity—pretty much unplayable—and like Bonewits' take on druidry, essentially an eccentric modern concoction.

One of the most prominent RPG proponents fighting back against these kinds of misperceptions is Michael A. Stackpole, an American science fiction author and game designer who decided to look into BADD and set the record straight in his dissertation, "The Pulling Report." In addition to exposing misleading 'evidence' such as Dr. Radecki quoting from the *Mazes and Monsters* novel as if it were a factual text in a 1985 press release, Stackpole debunks many of the case studies used by BADD to show how RPGs led to teen suicide.

Stackpole also looks at the occult crime seminars conducted by Pulling and her allies across the U.S., attracting sizeable audiences of education, health and law professionals at $100-300 per head. He notes that, "these seminars go beyond 'the blind leading the blind' because the anti-Satanists profit greatly from giving the seminars. Moreover, taxpayers shell out for these dubious educational experiences, then have the disinformation and misinformation used against them when earnest cops try to utilize what they have learned and accepted in good faith." Stackpole concludes that "Pat Pulling is a 'cult crime expert' only in her own eyes and those of her cronies, allies and disciples."

Robert D. Hicks, a former police officer and criminal-justice analyst, made a sceptical study of "cult-cops" (the term coined for Christian police officers who subscribed to Satanic conspiracy theories) for his justly-acclaimed 1990 book *In Pursuit of Satan*. He shares a similarly dim view of the BADD founder's cult-busting credentials: "The most disturbing fact about Pulling is her assumption of professional roles for which she is unqualified [...] Pulling would represent merely a sideshow of America's current preoccupation with things Satanic if she didn't pop up regularly to teach police officers."

Hicks goes on to comprehensively demolish Pulling's extensive CV of purported academic and law enforcement credentials as exaggeration, irrelevant or effective fabrication, and gives a troubling assessment of BADD's impact on the cultural landscape of the 1980s:

" *Perhaps the most remarkable phenomenon is Pulling's extraordinary influence on the police, with whom she has an almost symbiotic relationship. Pulling provides the cult cops with misinformation and then makes claims at seminars based on her access to confidential information provided by cult cops conducting criminal investigations. By citing her information as confidential, she can dangle before her audiences investigative bits and pieces that imply causal connections between game-playing and violence, and make assertions her audience is not likely to question.*

GETTING A LITTLE EDGIER

It wasn't until the end of the 1980s that TSR finally reacted publicly. In the February 1990 edition of *The Dragon*, the official D&D monthly magazine, TSR's James M. Ward explained the company's ongoing policy in a column entitled "Angry Mothers From Heck (and what we do about them)." This column explains that "Avoiding the Angry Mother Syndrome has become a good, basic guideline for all of the designers and editors at TSR, Inc." Ward elaborates that each of the company's products "has to have certain elements that any gamer's mother in this or any other universe would smile at. These qualities must be present in each gamer's role-playing to foster the 'right stuff.'" As an example, he relates how, for the 1989 edition of Advanced Dungeons & Dragons he had "the designers and editors delete all mention of demons and devils."

Ward wasn't the only member of staff eager to try and confound D&D's Christian critics with a moral agenda. Tracy Hickman was hired by TSR in 1982, and subsequently became one of the most influential figures in the RPG world, most notably for the *Dragonlance Chronicles* games and books. Marrying D&D settings with a bestselling range of novels and affiliated products, Hickman's hugely popular *Dragonlance* franchise helped move TSR's accounts back into the black in the late-1980s. He was also a devout Christian (albeit a Mormon, often not recognized by D&D's evangelical critics) who regarded his work as an author and games designer as wholly compatible with his faith, declaring on his website that the "games I designed were always carefully crafted morality tales that reflected my own Christian beliefs."

Most sources agree that, by the time Ward flagged TSR's moral agenda, the great D&D panic was over anyway. It's tempting to hope that perhaps common sense finally prevailed over hysteria. Or perhaps Christians like Tracy Hicks within the RPG community finally overwhelmed the influence of their critics outside of it. In truth, the panic always had a sell-by-date, as those who'd played the games in high school and at college reached positions of influence and authority, making it increasingly difficult to make lies about RPGs stick. "The view of roleplaying games has changed over time," Christian gamer Andy Smith told the BBC's Peter Ray Allison, "mostly because the predicted 'streets awash with the blood of innocents as a horde of demonically-possessed roleplayers laid waste to the country' simply never materialised."

Another factor was the hobby's waning popularity. Just as D&D eclipsed traditional wargaming, a new game emerged that supplanted RPGs in the affections of many gamers—a competitive, collectible card game named Magic the Gathering (MtG). Published with little fanfare in 1993 by Wizards of the Coast (WotC), the game enjoyed a runaway success comparable, if not more meteoric than the heady early years of D&D. Its dominance was underlined in 1997, when WotC bought the D&D brand, dissolving the struggling TSR corporation shortly afterwards. MtG was based in the same kind of medieval fantasy milieu as D&D and, similar to that game, originally featured demons among its menagerie of monsters. And, like TSR, WotC later chose to remove all the demons—even the word "demonic"—from all game materials.

This exorcism happened in 1995, but demons returned to MtG in 2002. For a long time, WotC maintained that the removal was "not because we're worried about offending someone or facing claims that the game is Satanic. It's because we're trying to create rich fantasy worlds, and references to real-world religions and belief systems disrupt those worlds." But in a 2004 article, "Where Have All The Demons Gone?", leading MtG designer Mark Rosewater came clean, explaining that:

> 66 The best indicator of Magic's growth as a genre setting game was Dungeons & Dragons. As such, the Magic Brand Team spent a great deal of time studying D&D's early days. One of the great pitfalls that D&D had when it reached the higher levels of public awareness was a huge backlash against certain parts of its fantasy elements... it seemed like a safe choice in a very unsafe time. Magic was on the cusp of becoming a highly public game. Wizards knew what had happened to D&D when it went through that phase.

Come 2002, on the back of huge commercial success, WotC felt confident enough to start flexing its creative muscles. "It was clear that Magic had the license to start getting a little edgier," observed Rosewater. They clearly felt the same about D&D, steering the product away from the family-friendly puritanism of 1990, into more sophisticated, adult territory. This manifested most overtly in the 2002 publication of The Book of Vile Darkness, an adults-only D&D supplement containing all the sorts of things—drug abuse, sex, torture, human sacrifice—that the likes of BADD already believed were featured in the game, but weren't. In reality, the book's hardly shocking to the internet generation, and the same assumption that had always applied to D&D—that the players would be virtuous heroes opposing any of the iniquities described—still apply in *The Book of Vile Darkness*. Inevitably, not everybody was impressed, and Tracy Hickman fired off an incandescent rant, comparing the book's publication to the 9/11 terrorist attacks. "Invariably, 'mature' subject matter targets immature impulses," he fulminated. "Think about it: EVERY act that is labelled as 'for mature audiences' deals with an immature act or animal-level instinct." Hickman evidently felt deeply betrayed by WotC's decision to finally respond to D&D's Christian critics by confronting, rather than pandering to them: "Now, after OVER TWENTY YEARS of building public relations good will... it is all being thrown out the window. They are gleefully opening the Pandora's box... and there will be NO CLOSING IT again. It literally makes me sick."

By 2002, *The Book of Vile Darkness* represented a controversy that only really interested those within the RPG hobby. In the 21st century, an age shaken by too many real horrors, few could share Hickman's outrage over a game any longer. Patricia Pulling died of lung cancer in 1997, and BADD effectively died with her. In 1992, Dr. Thomas Radecki, her closest ally, had his medical license revoked for "engaging in immoral conduct of an unprofessional nature with a patient." In 2013, he was arrested and, according to the *Pittsburgh Post-Gazette*, accused of "setting up a 'commune' for drugs and sex with patients."

BEARDED FEMALE DWARVES

While the battle with D&D's evangelical foes may be won, the war over the soul of RPGs isn't over. The release of the 2002 medieval-era game FATAL ("Fantasy Adventure To Adult Lechery") sparked controversy in gaming circles by wallowing in sexism, depravity and racism, including potential strength bonuses if a character is "retarded," and chances where foes can be accidentally raped during combat. FATAL swiftly established legendary status within the gaming community as the worst game ever published, with *Something Awful* blogger Zack Parsons later noting that "all the self-righteous preachers and suicide moms in the 1980s made up all sorts of evil lies about Dungeons & Dragons to get it banned. Then along comes FATAL and all those lies are true about it."

Meanwhile, mainstream attention in the RPG world focused on a new version of Dungeons and Dragons, released by WotC in 2014, which no longer required characters to be confined to binary notions of sex and gender. The game notes that players could play "a female character who presents herself as a man, a man who feels trapped in a female body, or a bearded female dwarf who hates being mistaken for a male. Likewise, your character's sexual orientation is yours to decide." From depicting fantasies of violent race war between orcs and elves to addressing issues of gender politics and social justice, it's worth wondering whether targeting the game from a mendacious right-wing perspective inadvertently triggered a backlash, encouraging the birth of a new, politically correct D&D a generation later.

THE
Crusaders®

VOL. 10

By J.T.C.

SPELLBOUND?

69¢

20-SIDED SINS:
HOW JACK T. CHICK WAS DRAWN INTO THE RPG WAR

BY PAUL CORUPE

In his 1972 gospel tract *A Demon's Nightmare*, Christian comic artist Jack Chick depicts a pair of cartoon devils who impishly attempt to distract a busy Christian from church with movies, invitations to drunken parties and female company. But, less than a decade later, Chick's bumbling demons evolved into persistent predators humming in every TV tube, speaking backwards on rock records and lurking in toy aisles of major department stores. As ex-Satanic priests came forward with mindboggling stories of youth corruption, even established and trusted Christian commenters like Chick weren't immune to the simmering culture war. With the Satanic Panic in full swing, Chick created an unprecedented series of inflammatory pop culture-focused gospel tracts in the 1980s, including 1984's infamous *Dark Dungeons*. This cheaply printed comic, which alleged a Satanic conspiracy behind North America's most popular fantasy role playing game (RPG), is probably the Panic's most infamous and widely read piece of religious propaganda.

The face of the Satanic Panic largely played out on daytime talk shows and talk radio, where reformed devil worshippers (and bestselling authors) Mike Warnke and Lauren Stratford mingled with other rising personalities like Gary Greenwald, Bob Larson and Phil Phillips. But these theories and stories were

Left: The original 1978 cover of Jack Chick's *Crusaders* comic, "Spellbound?"

given additional credence with mainstream evangelical audiences by established Christian figureheads like Chick, who has been called the "the most widely read theologian in human history," with more than 750 million copies of his comic booklets distributed worldwide. Chick was no stranger to controversial views and conspiracy-tinged theories, but it wasn't until he met John Todd and Dr. Rebecca Brown, mysterious figures who showed up at Chick's door with exceptional claims about Satan's media empire, that the Panic began to have a noticeable effect on his work.

Chick has always had an interesting relationship to pop culture. As a cartoonist and self-publisher, he spread his message through a decidedly lowbrow, highly disposable medium—newsprint comic books. Once a budding strip cartoonist, Chick found Christ in the 1950s after marrying into a religious family in the wake of World War II. It was then that Chick hit on the idea of combining his love of cartooning with his religious awakening by producing a series of easy-to-understand booklets that could be given away to strangers. It was an indirect way of witnessing that appealed to the shy Chick, who still encourages followers to leave his pocket-sized tracts in public places like park benches and bus stops to be discovered by non-believers.

Chick's earliest religious tracts date to the early 1960s and precede Chick Publications' official establishment in 1970. These early works tended to be optimistic. Feel-good tracts like *Somebody Loves Me* and *Operation Somebody Cares*, meant to comfort distressed readers, were occasionally mixed up with illustrated bible passages, such as in *Creator or Liar?* or *The Beast*. In all cases, the stories end with a suggested prayer that the reader can use to accept Jesus Christ. When Chick first introduced scare tactics into his comics—like in *Somebody Goofed*, *This Was Your Life* or even *A Demon's*

Nightmare—they still carried a message of hope that readers could make choices to avoid the fire and brimstone punishments that Chick doled out to unrepentant sinners. Things started to change in the 1970s, as Chick's positive message of overcoming Satan's influence gave way to a condemnation of those that peddled it. With the help of Fred Carter, a new artist hired in 1972, Chick increased his output and turned out tracts critical of abortions, evolution, feminism, homosexuality and Communism. He was also critical of almost all other major religions (but saved most of his bile for Catholicism). Chick also drew on popular culture—and especially well-known films—to spark reader curiosity. Over the years he released publications called *The Exorcists*, *The First Jaws* (a retelling of the story of Jonah), *Superman?*, *Scar Face*, *Terminator?*, *Home Alone?* and *Scream!* Secular culture also started to leak into the content of his comics—in *Bewitched?* (1972), the devil engineers reruns of a "vampire show" (presumably 1960s soap opera *Dark Shadows*) as a gateway to spiritualism, drugs, Ouija boards and outright witchcraft, themes that would later pop up in *Dark Dungeons* and other related tracts.

In 1974, Chick also started producing full-colour magazine-size comics, under the title *The Crusaders*. In this ongoing series, former street gang leader Jim Carter and ex-Green Beret Tim Clark team up to fight against spiritual corruption and save the innocent. Though *The Crusaders* look like they are intended to sit on drug store racks alongside *Spider-Man* and *Classics Illustrated*, these comics weren't found on newsstands, and sometimes weren't even welcome in traditional Christian book stores. By the 1980s, the Christian Booksellers Association refused to do business with Chick and his publications were outright banned in Canada and South Africa due to his criticism of the Vatican. Increasingly, Chick tended to do business and distribution via direct mail.

The shift towards more aggressive messages in Chick's tracts was the result of more than just the general tenor of the times, it also reflected the influence of a handful of individuals who were able to sway Chick and capitalize on his existing audience of tract distributors and unsuspecting readers. Chick's introduction to John Todd in 1973 set the tone for many of the publisher's more incendiary pop culture-based tracts throughout the following decade.

Todd, a former drug addict and occult bookshop owner, told Chick he was raised a witch and was installed as a Grand Druid on the Illuminati-backed Council of 13, but gave it all up when he read a Chick tract and watched the film *The Cross and the Switchblade* (1970). Todd not only claimed to possess knowledge of an Illuminati conspiracy to start World War III in a battle for Israel's oil, he also further convinced Chick that Satan's insidious influence had spread to pop culture. He said the Council controlled the record companies and indoctrinated youth though rock music, singling out Debby Boone's "You Light Up My Life" as particularly Satanic. Todd further claimed that the cast of *Star Wars* and many popular soap operas were all witches.

Chick based three full-length *The Crusaders* comic books directly on Todd's claims—*Broken Cross, Angel of Light* and, perhaps Chick's first true attack on youth culture, 1978's *Spellbound?*, which focuses on a rock star named Bobby Dallas and ex-druid named Lance Collins, an obvious Todd stand-in, who claims he once had 65,000 witches under his command. Early in the story, Collins recounts rock's secret occult history:

> **❝** *The Beatles opened up a Pandora's Box when they hit the United States with their druid/rock beat in the 1960s. They became so popular that they were able to turn young people on to the Eastern religions. The flood gates to witchcraft were opened. The U.S. will never recover... it was well-planned.*

Collins further reveals the way the Council controlled the rock music industry. Using melodies culled from druid manuscripts, witches would pen lyrics that included "coded spells and incantations." Once recorded, a group of powerful witches would then gather around an album's master tape and call forth Regé, Satan's "top demon," to curse it. When asked about Christian rock, Collins states that, "the words may appear to be God's but the beat belongs to Satan." Collins later incites a record burning, and explains that "Christians will never be effective" as long as they possess playing cards, occult jewelry, rock or country albums, romance books or Dungeons & Dragons games—apparently the first such mention of RPGs in Chick's published work.

Todd was reportedly a charismatic speaker who won over Christians with his message during live tours and television appearances. This allowed Todd to operate a lucrative mail-order cassette tape ministry until past indiscretions caught up with him. Despite his apparent religious conversion, Todd was accused of still practicing some form of witchcraft throughout the mid-1970s and was arrested in 1976 for forcible sex with a minor. Todd largely dropped out of sight in 1979 following the publication of an exposé book, *The Todd Phenomenon*.

Above and Over: Panels from the *Crusaders* comic, "Spellbound?" featuring the John Todd stand-in "Lance Collins." © 1978 Jack T. Chick.

"THIS MASTER WOULD BE SET ASIDE FOR ABOUT SIX MONTHS. IT WASN'T READY FOR PRODUCTION UNTIL IT HAD BEEN *BLESSED."

*BLESSED BY AN EVIL FORCE
(TO A CHRISTIAN THIS IS A CURSE)

"ON A FULL MOON SOME OF THE MOST POWERFUL WITCHES IN THE COUNTRY WOULD ARRIVE TO PUT THE FINISHING TOUCHES ON THE SONG."

HOW HAVE YOU BEEN, SABRINA?

BUSY!

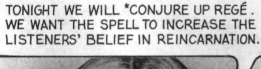

TONIGHT WE WILL *CONJURE UP REGÉ. WE WANT THE SPELL TO INCREASE THE LISTENERS' BELIEF IN REINCARNATION.

"INSIDE 'Z' PRODUCTIONS, THE VERY LARGE ROOM USED FOR THIS CEREMONY WAS BEHIND LARGE, LOCKED DOORS MADE OF OAK.

BLESSED BE!

BLESSED BE!

Todd's departure from Chick's inner circle was quickly filled by Dr. Alberto Rivera, an ex-Jesuit priest who met Chick in 1978. Though Todd believed the Illuminati was pulling the strings behind the scenes, Rivera insisted the Vatican actually controlled the Illuminati and that the popes were anti-Christ figures, among other claims. Chick, who had already shown willingness to accept more outlandish viewpoints, published another round of tracts and *The Crusaders* comics based on his talks with Rivera, which contain whiffs of James Bond-style espionage like assassins, global conspiracies and vanishing ink. When *Christianity Today* and *Cornerstone* magazines published lengthy articles accusing the good doctor of being a fraud in 1981, Chick—true believer to the end—accused them of attempting the same "systematic destruction" used to dismantle Todd's ministry a few years earlier.

THE MAN WHO BROKE AWAY IS DR. ALBERTO RIVERA . . . AN EX-JESUIT PRIEST WHOSE JOB IT WAS TO INFILTRATE AND DESTROY PROTESTANT CHURCHES.

HE READ MANY TOP SECRET REPORTS IN THE VATICAN THAT INVOLVED YOU AND YOUR FAMILY. HE KNOWS CHRISTIANS <u>MUST</u> BE ALERTED TO WHAT'S GOING ON BEHIND THE SCENES.

In the midst of the Satanic Panic, Chick provided a platform for another controversial figure, Dr. Rebecca Brown. In 1986, Chick published Brown's book *He Came to Set the Captives Free*, in which she explains how she managed to bring Christ into the life of one of her hospital patients, a longtime Satanist and witch who was a member of a secret organization known as The Brotherhood. She expands on claims she confronted a werewolf and Satan himself in the Chick-released cassette tapes *Closet Witches 1* and *Closet Witches 2* and a second book, *Prepare for War* (1987).

Brown admits she lost her medical licence in 1984 for misdiagnosing patients (she reportedly began blaming sickness on demonic manifestations), but claims she was kicked out after the hospital was overtaken by witches who perceived her Christianity as a threat. However, the medical board apparently concluded that Brown suffered from paranoid schizophrenia, including demonic delusions, and her stories were later debunked by Personal Freedom Outreach, a religious group specializing in investigating religious cults. Chick apparently believed Brown's story gave further credence to Todd's previous claims of a secret cabal of witches who had infiltrated society and taken their battle for souls into popular culture.

Although Brown wasn't immortalized in any of *The Crusaders* comics, several tracts draw on her stories. Brown claims to have co-written *Satan's Master* (1986)—no longer in print and not currently even mentioned on Chick's website—which shows how Wiccans or "white witches" are still ultimately controlled by Satan. By the end of the tract, a witch who looks remarkably like Brown comes to Christ. Her tale also seems to have inspired *Poor Little Witch* (1987), in which a young girl keeps flubbing a volleyball

Above: Dr. Alberto Rivera, as illustrated in *My Name? In the Vatican?*
© 1980 Jack T. Chick.

until she's told by her gym teacher that she can make the other girls drop the ball if she lights a candle and says a spell. Eventually, she's forced to take part in a Satanic baby sacrifice led by the town's chief of police, until a Christian helps save her.

Brown also says she helped inspire *The Trick* (1986), the first of many anti-Halloween tracts published by Chick Publications. In this one, a coven fills Halloween candy with drugs and crushed glass. Following some child deaths, an "ex-witch" named Becky explains to concerned parents the druid origins of the holiday trick or treating and how deaths caused by poisoned candy are Satanic sacrifices. These themes crop up in later anti-Halloween tracts like *Boo!* And *The Little Ghost*.

Of the approximately 50 gospel tracts Chick created during the 1980s, several seem to borrow from Todd and Brown's accounts to tackle familiar Satanic Panic subjects— everything from the corrupting influence of rock music and narcotics to "new age" beliefs as well as, most famously, Dungeons &

Dragons. *Angels?* (1986) is Chick's pocket-size anti-rock tract that draws largely on the lessons of *Spellbound?*, while in *The Hunter* (1987), the popular high school football star is really a drug pusher for Satan who gives unsuspecting students joints filled with "happy powder" and "PCP cocktails" that ultimately send them to a mental institution.

Related material also appeared in *Battle Cry*, a broadsheet newspaper Chick began publishing in 1983 that offers readers a mix of personal success stories and self-promotion alongside conspiracy theories and straight-up moral panic. Various issues of *Battle Cry* complained about Saturday morning cartoons that depicted super heroes as more powerful than Jesus and accused Van Halen of intentionally inciting student violence ("Runnin' with the Devil") and teen suicide ("Jump").

However, Chick's most famous contribution to the Panic was his *Dark Dungeons* tract, which draws directly from the stories of Todd and Brown as it alleges that fantasy role-playing games were intended to acclimatize players to occult concepts so they could be drafted into a Satanic conspiracy. Released in 1984, *Dark Dungeons* has been called "*Reefer Madness* for the dice-and-pencils set" by *Wired* magazine, and its undeniable camp appeal has made it one of Chick's most infamous publications, even surpassing the more ludicrous storytelling and kitsch of similar works like *Angels?* and *The Gay Blade*, an anti-homosexual tract often cited as Chick's most offensive publication.

Above: Dr. Rebecca Brown immortalized in *Satan's Master*.
© 1986 Jack T. Chick.

The history of Dungeons & Dragons—and especially how it has been depicted in pop culture—is fraught with controversy. In 1974, the same year that Chick met John Todd, Gary Gygax and Brian Blume founded their company, TSR, and began releasing Dungeons & Dragons products. But it wasn't until 1979 that the game was brought to national attention, when Michigan State University student and avid RPG player James Dallas Egbert vanished in a tunnel network under the school as part of a suicide attempt.

The story appealed not only to Christians who wanted the fantasy-themed games condemned, but also to the popular imagination. Author Rona Jaffe fictionalized the story for her 1981 book *Mazes and Monsters*, which was adapted for a TV movie the following year, while elements of a Satan-controlled RPG were woven into a low-budget Canadian film, *Skullduggery* (1983). A fictional RPG also appears in *Cloak & Dagger* (1984)—though it avoids the medieval theme and is based instead on an espionage scenario, the game is shown as a hindrance to the main character that, only when ultimately renounced, indicates that he is finally able to separate fantasy from reality.

As opposition ramped up from Patricia Pulling's Bothered Against Dungeons & Dragons (BADD) and other more explicitly Christian-focused personalities and organizations, Chick staked out his own position by writing and publishing *Dark Dungeons*, featuring illustrations from Fred Carter. The tract begins with friends Marcie and Debbie, who are in the midst of the titular fictional RPG game when Marcie's character, Black Leaf, accidentally springs a poison trap and is killed. After banishing the distraught Marcie from the game, Dungeon Master Ms. Frost tells Debbie that her character, Elfstar, is doing so well that Debbie's now ready to learn how to "really cast spells." Ms. Frost then takes the young player to a witch's coven where she's given "the real power." Debbie reports back the next day that she cast a "mind bondage" spell on her father to get him to reverse his opinion of the game and purchase $200 worth of figures and manuals for her.

Later, when Debbie stops by Marcie's house, she discovers that her friend has hung herself in her bedroom, surrounded by dragon and wizard figurines. Marcie's suicide note explains that she can no longer face life after Black Leaf's death. Hearing about the tragedy, Ms. Frost advises Debbie to forget about it—"Your spiritual growth through

Above and Right: Panels from Dark Dungeons. © 1984 Jack T. Chick.

the game is more important than some lousy loser's life." But Debbie is ready to give up the game, and is by herself crying about this turn of events when she's approached by Mike, who explains he's been praying and fasting for Debbie since he knows she's engaged in "spiritual warfare." Mike takes her to listen to a preacher who explains that those who think they've achieved power through the occult are really trapped in a "dungeon of bondage." The preacher orders the evil spirits to leave Debbie, who accepts Jesus into her life and burns her occult effects, including her Dark Dungeons material, that evening.

Like *Angels?*, *Dark Dungeons* has important connections to *Spellbound?*, the Todd-inspired *Crusaders* comic that had already advised Christians to get rid of their Dungeons & Dragons games six years earlier. Even though Todd was widely discredited by 1984, a preacher that strongly resembles him also appears at the end of *Dark Dungeons* to deliver a sermon that's remarkably similar to the one by the character Lance Collins in the earlier book. Again, the preacher rails against witchcraft and advises the congregation to get rid of their occult material, including rock music, charms and RPG games. Interestingly, the original version of the tract also advised readers to burn books by fantasy authors such as J.R.R. Tolkein and C.S. Lewis, a reference that Chick has attributed directly to Todd's influence and that has since been deleted.

Although Chick doesn't publish circulation numbers for each tract, it's safe to assume that in the more than 30 years it has been in print, hundreds of thousands—if not millions—of copies of *Dark Dungeons* have been printed as part of the more than 750 million tracts that Chick claims to have distributed. Because it was intended for a secular audience, the tract quickly fell into the hands of RPG circles who were amused by the tract's claims that these type of games are addictive, encourage suicide and are a form of mind control to acclimatize teens to notions of magic and fantasy that would make them susceptible to Satanists.

Despite the tract's widely mocked views, it did help tip the scales to spark some changes. TSR removed explicitly demonic characters from the game in 1989 when it published its second edition of Advanced Dungeons & Dragons, and Christian Dungeons & Dragons equivalents like 1984's DragonRaid began to appear that allowed gamers to play parent-approved versions of their preferred pastime, similar to the "White Metal" phenomenon. But, like Christian rock that couldn't escape its roots because of that secret "druid beat," many organizations turned their noses up at DragonRaid, which was even accused by BADD of using biblical scripture as a form of "magic," even though it was primarily intended as a learning tool about the teachings of Jesus.

While Dungeons & Dragons has diminished in popularity since the 1980s, *Dark Dungeons* continues to live on and was updated as recently as 2013 to modernize its characters' wardrobes. The tract, now available for free on Chick's website, is accompanied by online articles like William Schnoebelen's "Should a Christian Play Dungeons & Dragons?" and "Straight Talk on Dungeons & Dragons." Like Todd, Schnoebelen is a self-described former witch high priest who says he was saved by reading a Chick comic.

But just as notable is *Dark Dungeons'* cultural impact as a piece of appropriated kitsch—an RPG game ostensibly based on *Dark Dungeons* was released in 2010, while another company created *Demonic Deviltry*, a fake tract against RPGs in 2012 as a promotional campaign for its game *Demon: The Fallen*. In 2014, Chick's tract was adapted for a tongue-in-cheek 30-minute film that expands the story and plays up some of the tract's most ridiculous elements. Made with Chick's blessing, the basic plot remains relatively close to the original, but here a raucous frat party turns into a gaming session as students chant "RPG! RPG!" and Marcie has an implied same-sex crush on Debbie.

Without Chick and his original, tragic tale of Black Leaf and Elfstar, it's hard to know whether the movement against fantasy and role playing games would have gained as much traction as it did throughout the 1980s. As the figure behind an established outlet for fundamentalist Christian thought, Chick was able to elevate and disseminate these viewpoints to a mass audience in a way that other Christian authors and personalities only dreamed of. No need to visit your pastor or a religious bookstore—anyone could find a copy of *Dark Dungeons* at a local Laundromat or tucked under their car's windshield wiper. However, this level of visibility also led to the tract's infamy among non-believers, especially as it was passed around, co-opted and satirized by the very gamers it sought to demonize.

Fearing Satan's influence had spread its wings into our shared culture, Jack Chick and other personalities like Todd and Pulling that railed against Dungeons & Dragons may have been opposed to the very idea of role-playing as it preyed on players who had difficulty separating fact from fiction. But having cast themselves as mighty heroes in a dramatic, fiery war with the Lord of Darkness and his immortal forces of evil, it seems these particular crusaders for Christ were even more immersed in dangerous role-playing than anyone who has ever dared to roll a 20-sided die in a wood-panelled basement.

Right: A still from L. Gabriel Gonda's film adaptation of *Dark Dungeons* (2014).

REFERENCES + BIBLIOGRAPHY:

Chick, Jack. *Dark Dungeons*. Ontario, CA: Chick Publications, 1984.

Chick, Jack. *Spellbound?* Ontario, CA: Chick Publications, 1978.

Fowler, Bob. *The World of Jack T. Chick: (The History of the World According to Jack T. Chick)*. 2nd ed. San Francisco, CA: Last Gasp of San Francisco, 2001.

Kuersteiner, Kurt. *The Unofficial Guide to the Art of Jack T. Chick: Chick Tracts, Crusader Comics, and Battle Cry Newspapers*. Atglen, PA: Schiffer Pub., 2004.

Raeburn, Daniel K. The Imp #2, "Holy Book of Jack Chick" Chicago, 1998.

Schnoebelen, William. "Should a Christian Play Dungeons & Dragons?" accessed May 10, 2014, https://www.chick.com/articles/frpg.asp.

Schnoebelen, William. "Straight Talk About Dungeons & Dragons?" accessed May 10, 2014, https://www.chick.com/articles/dnd.asp.

God's Cartoonist: The Comic Crusade of Jack Chick, directed by Kurt Kuersteiner (2008).

Dark Dungeons, directed by L. Gabriel Gonda (2014),

MASTERS OF THE IMAGINATION:
FUNDAMENTALIST READINGS OF THE OCCULT IN CARTOONS OF THE 1980S

BY JOSHUA BENJAMIN GRAHAM

Many North American evangelical and fundamentalist Christians in the 1980s felt that they were losing control of their culture to a malevolent force, a slide that began in the 1960s. The Nixonian backlash against free-love, hippies, race riots, civil unrest, and rising crime rates included much criticism of the media's role in fomenting rebellious youth. By the early 1980s, a scapegoat was needed, and a muscle-bound space barbarian appeared on television who seemed to fit the bill. *He-Man and the Masters of the Universe* confirmed some of the fundamentalists' worst fears. He-Man's malignant, Satanic agenda was hiding in plain sight, right there in the title; he wanted to master the universe. And to do so, he was parading around in his underwear in the living rooms of good Christian homes, telling innocent children, "I have the power." This was blasphemy if they'd ever heard it, and they were incensed that a sinful North America wasn't even blushing.

How did He-Man—explicitly designed by Mattel to be an innocuous do-gooder—become so insidious to the religious right? This is a character who pledges on screen to "uphold what is right and protect the innocent," and who becomes distraught in the episode "The Problem with Power" because he believes that he may have inadvertently killed someone by knocking over a pile of rocks with his super-human strength. Apologists for the existence of a Satanic conspiracy, in their scramble to explain how the innocent children of godly parents were transformed into an unholy scourge of Satanic teenagers, began reading the occult onto toys and cartoons and drawing a direct line of causation from the child collecting He-Man action figurines to the Satanic high priest ritually murdering children in the same suburban basements. Fundamentalism already had an infrastructure and a widely distributed audience, and by spreading the suspicion that the occult was hiding in plain sight, it played a major role in disseminating Satanic Panic. It's true that the mélange of anodyne, pseudo-pagan mythology in He-Man's home planet Eternia didn't exactly correspond with the fundamentalist Christian paradigm but, in almost every way, fundamentalist Christians took He-Man far more seriously than anyone else.

Fundamentalist critiques of youth culture were nothing new, of course. Preachers had been railing about iniquity at the moving pictures since the invention of film, but the main points of contention up until the 1980s—exemplified in Fredric Wertham's sardonic attack on comic books, *Seduction of the Innocent* (1954)—was run-of-the-mill violence and sexuality. Reformers sought to clean up the airwaves with more educational programming, and groups like Action for Children's Television, formed in 1968, pressured the American Federal Communications Commission to ban advertising during children's programming altogether. The industry could see the writing on the wall, and it had a plan in the works that would sidestep the criticism and increase profits at the same time. By the 1980s, children's cartoons were dominated by shows that were essentially half-hour commercials for toys, shows like *G.I. Joe*, *Transformers*, *Care Bears*, *My Little Pony*, *M.A.S.K.*, *She-Ra: Princess of Power*, and *He-Man and the Masters of the Universe*.

Parental concerns about sexuality and violence were somewhat ameliorated by this new imaginative cartoon milieu of quasi-New Age mythology in which inoffensive narratives of good versus evil included plenty of marketable extra equipment and characters who inflicted very little actual bodily harm. *G.I. Joe*, for example, was a bloodless war cartoon without bullets that ended each episode with the characters wandering into a child's life and delivering euphemistic public service announcements. The character Roadblock, for example, is careful not to define the nature of the "trouble" a potential child molester wants to bring. After the child hangs up the phone with a stranger, Roadblock says, "All he wanted to bring you was trouble. Remember, never tell anyone you're home alone, and never give anyone your address."

He-Man also tagged pro-social messages to the end of its episodes. For example, "In today's story, He-Man used something even more powerful than his muscles to beat Skeletor. Do you know what it was? If you said, 'his brain,' you were right. And just like a muscle, your brain is something you can develop to give yourself great power." Other PSAs included bromides such as "the people who succeed are the ones who work for what they want," "animals, like all living things, should be treated with kindness and respect," and "be good to your body, and it will be good to you." How could anyone object to those messages? Mattel certainly thought this would be enough to keep most secular parents happy—and buying action figures.

Fundamentalists saw things differently. They saw the morality tags at the end of cartoons—probably correctly—as a cynical attempt to placate concerned parents. Self-proclaimed media critics began to proliferate on the church lecture circuit, and they were taking aim at cartoons. Jeffrey S. Victor, in *Satanic Panic: The Creation of a Contemporary Legend*, discovered in his research that by the end of the 1980s a host of Satanic experts was at the disposal of fundamentalists:

> **❝** *I found that fundamentalist churches were an important part of a communication network for the dissemination of the Satanic cult rumour stories. The ministers of several of these churches gave sermons condemning occult practice and Satanism. Some churches held meetings about the Satanic cult rumours and some held special prayer sessions. A few churches invited out-of-town religious 'experts' on Satanism to speak to their congregations. Members of a few of these churches even organized adult study groups which used videotapes of 'Geraldo' talk shows as documentation for their studies. The rumors were discussed in church newsletters and, thereby, circulated more widely.*

Victor points out that he didn't find evidence that the pastors had started the Satanic rumours themselves, but they certainly didn't hesitate to sweep in and capitalize on them. Two of the self-appointed fundamentalist experts who rushed to cash in on the anxiety over the occult in television cartoons were Phil Phillips and Joan Hake Robie. Phillips' *Turmoil in the Toybox* book was something of an instant hit in 1986 for its

Left: Peggy Charren, founder of Action for Children's Television.
Photograph by Barbara Alper.

small publisher. As of its 11th printing in 1990, the publisher claimed that over 135,000 copies were in print. It was followed up by Robie's sequel, *Turmoil in the Toybox II*, and other titles followed, including Phillips' *Saturday Morning Mind Control* and Robie's *Teenage Mutant Ninja Turtles Exposed*, *The Truth about Dungeons and Dragons*, and *Halloween and Satanism*. The pair also teamed up to ferret out even more hidden signs of the occult in *Horror and Violence: The Deadly Duo in the Media*.

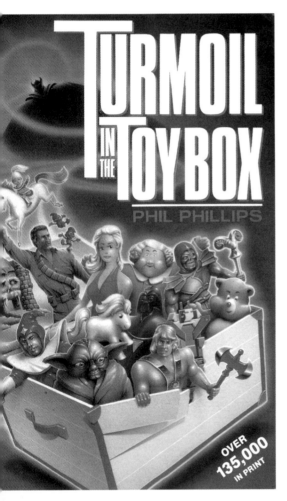

These books, for the most part, follow a formula of relating anecdotes about cartoons, toys, and games that they consider un-Christian and jumping from unproven assertions to outrage and back. The tone is aggrieved and beleaguered, at times bizarrely counterfactual, as when Phillips asserts, without any irony, that the vast majority of the world is Christian. In *Turmoil in the Toybox*, he writes that, "Christians generally are not depicted on television as intelligent. In fact, by excluding an accurate representation of Christians, television is not very representative of the vast majority of the world." What's telling about these books is the way in which they echo secular critiques of violence on television that approach the problem from a public health perspective. They try to lead into their warnings about the spiritual health of children using language that is prescriptive and authoritative, the language of dispassionate sociological concern. But the books are all imbued with a sense of dread about the future of youth.

The rise of visual media in the second half of the 20th century was accompanied by inevitable anxiety about the loss of textual authority in a post-textual culture. The Gospel of John begins "In the beginning was the Word, and the Word was with God, and the Word was God" (John 1:1) and the entire Protestant project was founded on the belief that the text of the Bible could be interpreted in the vernacular by the average Christian in his own home. Thus, for the Protestant, the presence of a Bible in each household became a source of authority. The "word" was in nearly every Protestant home. As John puts it, "the Word was made flesh, and dwelt among us" (John 1:14). When television arrived, it, too, went forth to every home, subject to the interpretation of every individual. Here was the image made flesh, dwelling among us.

Christians weren't alone in the 1980s in feeling that television had deeply unsettled the authority of print culture, and they found an unlikely ally in media critic Neil Postman. His analysis of television as a medium, *Amusing Ourselves to Death*, argued that:

> **"** *We are now a culture whose information, ideas and epistemology are given form by television, not by the printed word. To be sure, there are still readers and there are many books published, but the uses of print and reading are not the same as they once were; not even in schools, the last institutions where print was thought to be invincible. They delude themselves who believe that television and print coexist, for coexistence implies parity. There is no parity here.*

This was a struggle to the end between competing epistemologies, and Postman claimed that the authority of public educators had already been undermined. Children were spending their weekdays at the school and the bulk of their free time in front of the television. With only a few hours left over a week at church, what hope did Christian parents have of capturing the attention of their youth?

Television was creating a new mythology and shared cultural experience through the sheer force of its ubiquity, and even among the secular there was a growing call to more strictly regulate television programming. By the late 1960s, academics and behavioural researchers were beginning to look at the issue seriously and consider what influence television might have on developing young minds. Part of this cultural anxiety was a very real concern about the spiking crime rate, and while a whole host of cultural influences were taking the blame, many were asking whether it was in any way related to viewing violent scenes and scenarios on television.

Lyndon Johnson's National Commission on the Causes and Prevention of Violence of 1968 included a report on *The Mass Media and Violence*, and it reveals a lot of anxiety about already having lost control of the

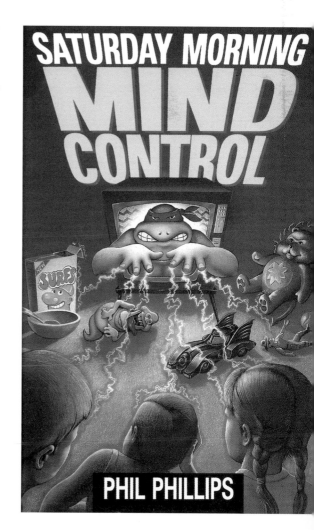

SATURDAY MORNING MIND CONTROL

PHIL PHILLIPS

younger generation. An appendix section titled "What we can expect from television" predicts that in the future things will only get worse: "there will be an increase in conflict content with violence as a means of problem solving." Authors Baker and Ball theorize, tautologically, that men turn to violent television because comedy somehow undermines their fragile masculinity: "TV comedy today emasculates the American male; action, adventure, violence, strengthen him. He actively seeks out the latter." Moreover, while the report takes pains to point out that the evidence for television's pernicious influence is still emerging, it's not above blaming television for a lot of the unseemly youthful behaviour of the 1960s: "It should take a considerable degree of obtuseness to prevent the suspicion that mass media have contributed (along with the way mixed adult and child audiences respond to them) to the behavior of today's youth which so perplexes some of their elders. The 'generation gap' can be considered partly the result of inadvertent social training which has instilled in children values their parents did not mean to instil in them". Of course, the commission delved into all sorts of explanations for a societal trend toward violence in an attempt to be comprehensive, but television was set up to take a lot of the blame for all varieties of evil.

The American Surgeon General's report of 1972, *Television and Growing Up: The Impact of Televised Violence*, picked up where the presidential commission left off, with a growing suspicion that there was a direct line from too much childhood television watching to delinquency and a rising crime rate, but there still wasn't enough evidence to prove it scientifically. The report begins, "It would be difficult to overstate the pervasiveness of television in the United States" and declares that both children and adults were watching up to two hours a day. It concludes that there was a "preliminary and tentative indication of a causal relation between viewing violence on television and aggressive behavior" but that it operated only in "some children" and "in some environmental contexts." The evidence was not particularly damning, and it was accompanied by some very high-minded and optimistic suggestions for the future of television. If only the medium could be harnessed for good, perhaps it could help usher in a future utopian age, one in which "power tactics might become unnecessary if broadscale identification with victims could be encouraged and reinforced, and television might be an important tool in such a movement."

The Surgeon General's report singled out cartoons for their incidents of violence, pointing out that "cartoons were the most violent type of program in these years" but there was already a trend among the networks toward ameliorating the consequences of cartoon violence. The report pointed out that, "as many violent incidents occurred in 1969 as in 1967, but a smaller proportion of characters were involved, and the violence was far less lethal." They also noted that a cartoon's level of violence correlated with its popularity, which incentivized violent content. The Surgeon General's committee was clear about its limitations, explaining that such inquiries are usually the result of political pressure that "urgently desires an answer to some question far too complex for easy solution." Regardless, the tone is unshakeable in its optimism that television, if given proper guidance and incentives, could elevate itself. The greatest Western narratives, after all, from Homer to *Beowulf* to Shakespeare, were steeped in violence, yet upon them was built an entire civilized discourse. "There is a considerable body of literature on the symbolic meanings of primitive (and not-so-primitive) myths and legends, which often are extremely violent. Anthropological literature supports the contention that, whatever else it may do, such folk literature communicates conventional social values and moral standards, and also provides folk interpretations of the pervasive conflicts and problems of life in a given society at a particular point in its history." Here the report is talking about fairy tales, children's stories that contained violence many parents didn't consider shocking merely because it had become so familiar and become so internalized. Many of these folk tales even contained magic and occult themes that fundamentalist Christian parents didn't seem at all bothered by.

But was it a stretch to think of contemporary children's cartoons as an emerging folk literature? The Surgeon General's committee didn't think so: "It would be desirable to look upon television drama and cartoon programs—crude as they may be–as folk literature in this sense. It would be important, in order more fully to understand the role of television in American life, to investigate the latent symbolic 'messages' that even violent television plays and cartoons may convey over and above the content of individual scenes." This was a rational, cool-headed call to begin to theorize and analyze children's cartoons to tease out what their symbolism might mean for western culture, the way academics had analyzed other literatures and other mediums. As Postman suggested in the 1980s, although not very hopefully, "The problem, in any case, does not reside in what people watch. The problem is in that we watch. The solution must be found in how we watch." Maybe there could be new ways of watching television—consciously and with analytical intent—that could tame the medium, make it safe for children and a catalyst for positive social change. On the other hand, fundamentalist pundits were ready to sweep in and tell their

Above: Ted Koppel, Filmation's Lou Scheimer and ACT's Peggy Charren debating the idea of cartoons as veiled advertisements on ABC's *Nightline* in 1983.

audience exactly what the symbols of this new folk discourse meant, and their analysis lacked any of this nuance or subtlety. "What is the difference between a violent television program and a traditional fairy tale filled with gory incidents and terrifying incidents?" Phillips and Robie asked in *Horror and Violence: The Deadly Duo in the Media*. For them, it was in how the experience of print culture was mediated and controlled by parents:

> **"** A fairy tale is generally read to a child while he or she is sitting in the parent's lap. This closeness gives the child a feeling of security. The reading of even the most frightening incidents is in the voice of one of the most important and trusted persons in the child's life. That familiarity adds distance to the incident. Also, the child's questions can be answered, and mysteries can be solved as they occur. The parents can soothe any fears that may arise. On the other hand, most children view television when they are alone, frequently in a darkened room. Parents are often in another part of the home while murderers, monsters, and mayhem parade in front of their vulnerable youngsters.

On the surface, this analysis is remarkably close to Postman's assertion that "how we watch" is crucial to making television viewing less harmful, but here the TV is malevolence personified, sitting with your "vulnerable youngsters" in a "darkened room." Phillips and Robie were trying very hard to imitate more serious discourses about television's role in society, but they had a very difficult time doing so without an underlying tone of hysteria.

In 1982, the National Institute of Mental Health picked up where the Surgeon General had left off and published *Television and Behavior: Ten Years of Scientific Progress and Implications for the Eighties*. This report begins in a similar vein, rehashing the ubiquity of television, pointing out that "more Americans have television than have refrigerators or indoor plumbing." The report considered experimental studies and field research on the effects of television viewing on behaviour. Television was then being blamed for promoting bad health and nutrition, causing emotional disturbances, and provoking violent copycat behaviour. Language about "television literacy" began to appear as "a way to counteract the possible deleterious effects of television and also to enhance its many benefits." There's even a chapter on "television's health-promoting possibilities" which discusses "therapeutic uses of television." Almost all of the findings of the report, however, are couched in hesitant language warning that more study is needed and that almost all of these findings are preliminary.

The report's discussion of violence on television shows that it's something that's actually very difficult to clearly define and subsequently quantify: "Most of the definitions [of violence] involve physical force, including hurting or killing. Some definitions include psychological violence and violence against property; others do not. Some include comic violence, accidents, and acts of nature, such as floods and earthquakes."

During the Satanic Panic that followed, during which attempts to control young minds through inculcation of occult symbols were read onto cartoons, spiritual violence was included in this definition.

Phillips' *Saturday Morning Mind Control* provides a helpful list for parents who are trying to figure out which shows to prevent their children from watching. If a parent finds any of the following in a cartoon, he or she should put that show on the banned list: demons, spirits, familiars, pentagrams, goats' heads, occult practices, seeing into the future, levitation, mind control, divination, communication with the dead, witchcraft, amulets, wands, staffs, magical powers, or books of spells. This is where these advice books deviate sharply from the seemingly reasonable advice about managing viewing hours and discussing content. Phillips makes it clear that these occult powers aren't just harmful in a metaphorical sense; rather, there is actually a demonic realm that your child could summon up by accident: "Our concern also is that children can participate, and are participating, in a spiritual reality without their knowing it. It is our contention that when children imagine and role-play that they have occult power, they actually open themselves up to the acceptance of an occult mind-set." It's not clear exactly what accepting that occult mind-set might lead to, but further on Phillips makes another demonic innuendo. He claims that "our children are being taught by TV today to call on demons for power," and then asks ominously, "What if one answers?"

The question of "what if a demon answers?" is one that others promoting Satanic Panic were quick to answer. Bob Larson, whose syndicated call-in radio show *Talk-Back* provided breathless descriptions of Satanic horrors to audiences each week, warned in *Satanism: The Seduction of America's Youth* that "even a casual brush with such supernaturalism could lure [your child] into further investigation." Larson, incidentally, never gave up on the demon-industrial complex. He returned to the public eye recently in a 2013 Vice News documentary, *Teenage Exorcists*, in which his prepossessing daughter and her friends travel Ukraine casting out Slavic demons with the help of a translator, and during an appearance on *The Daily Show with Jon Stewart* in which Larson demonstrates his new exorcism service that's now available over Skype for a suggested donation of only $295 per hour. Larson took the stories of many of the callers to his radio show, many of them teenagers, and used them in his book as evidence that there was widespread animal sacrifice, child abuse, and ritual human sacrifice taking place in North America. Both the book and the radio show have undeniable entertainment value, and Larson even seems to approach the issue with the cheek of a carnival showman: "Do you believe what I've written above? Do I believe it? Yes, but I can't blame you if your credulity is stretched... In fact, the story of ritualistic abuse of children remains largely untold simply because it is so unbelievable." The circular reasoning is air tight.

Gary Greenwald, a pastor who made himself famous by lecturing on the idea that backmasking had placed subliminal Satanic messages on heavy metal and rock records, produced a video about demonic cartoons featuring Phillips called *Deception of a Generation*, in which Phillips and Greenwald sit in armchairs and discuss clips and commercials from a typical Saturday morning lineup, commenting on their spiritual and occult implications. In one exchange, they point out that children might not have to become full-fledged Satanists to be influenced for evil:

> Phillips: Children don't have to wind up in the backyard sacrificing chickens to a moon god to be affected by the occult within the toys and cartoons.

> Greenwald: You say some have even yelled out in parking lots "He-Man is more powerful than Jesus Christ!"

> Phillips: Right. All that has to happen is for Satan to divert them from a pure and sincere relationship to God, and he's won. He doesn't have to get them totally involved in the occult. Although, that can happen, and this creates a desire and a taste for it.

Greenwald is very clear about what parents should do: "I tell you what. You have a responsibility as a parent to stop the children from having these toys, from watching these cartoons." He then points at the camera and raises his voice like he's performing an exorcism: "In the name of Jesus, I break every stronghold and I command that Satan loses hold upon your household and I praise God for it." This series of videos was often distributed to churches to share with their congregations. Pastor Greenwald couldn't have been more clear; He-Man had blasphemed against Jesus and must be tossed out of your home. Robie was also proscriptive, telling her readers in *Turmoil in the Toybox II*: "Any toy representing violence or associated with occult practices should be prohibited from Christian homes." Because of pronouncements like these, not having He-Man action figures in the home became a form of countercultural expression in many fundamentalist households.

By 1985, the *He-Man* cartoon had reportedly gained nine million viewers and Mattel had raked in $500 million in action figure sales and another $500 million in product licensing fees, so the fundamentalist critiques seem to have had little practical effect. Parents who saw some of the episodes without demon hunting would have seen fairly innocuous stuff. In "The Problem with Power" episode, for instance, He-Man is upset because he may have accidentally killed a man, and he renounces his power by throwing away his magic sword. He's been tricked into thinking this, and retrieving his sword accounts for the third act of the episode. He-Man's action figure lineup seemed to have lots of weaponry for sale, yet despite all this armament, He-Man's producers point out that on-screen mayhem is held to a minimum. When the show was being developed, Filmation's educational consultant, Stanford University Communications Professor Donald Roberts, urged that none of the characters should get killed or "really hurt." In the midst of warfare, He-Man usually deplores violence. Thus, says Roberts, battle scenes are "really antibattle scenes."

This is certainly true. Skeletor can shoot lasers from his fingers, but characters mostly step nimbly out of harm's way.

HAIL THE NO.1 HERO!
THE TOP-RATED CHILDREN'S SHOW IN SYNDICATION
Stronger
THAN YEAR-AGO PROGRAMMING
AVERAGE MARKET RATING
UP +43%
TOTAL KIDS
UP +125%
O. 1 WITH TOTAL CHILDREN
86 MARKET TIME PERIODS
Stronger
THAN NOVEMBER PERFORMANCE
AVERAGE MARKET RATING
UP +25%
TOTAL KIDS
UP +48%
NEWEST CLEARANCES
RAISE STATION TOTAL TO 14
HE-MAN AND THE MASTERS OF THE UNIVERSE™

Yet an article in *The New York Times* lays out the He-Man controversy in 1985 and some potential legislation to limit its airing. The reporter visits a "He-Man Workshop" taking place at a church where concerned parents are discussing, among other things, the merits of Prince Adam's sense of humour, or lack thereof. They ask, "Are the one-dimensional characters a problem?" One parent even offers a bit more sophistication, adding, "Isn't it just a modern version of *The Odyssey*?" Mattel representatives, of course, have answers that anticipate these secular criticisms. They cover the familiar ground brought up in the presidential commission, the Surgeon General's report, and the NIMH report: "We try not to have He-Man hurt any living creature, and the good guys always win," said Lou Scheimer, president of Filmation, the animation studio in Reseda, California that produces *He-Man* and *She-Ra*. He stated that most of the show's critics have never watched the program carefully, or they would notice "that we've given children a lot of positive messages."

And they have, but the messages seem like non-sequiturs. The moral of "The Problem of Power" is the general theme of safety, and wearing your seatbelt is combined with not playing with matches. This isn't even obliquely related to the content of the episode, but it does provide talking points when Mattel representatives had to issue a statement to concerned parents.

He-Man was a marketing machine, built according to guidelines to give the least offence while taking in the most profit. Mattel used the warnings and findings of the Surgeon General and the National Institute of Mental Health to stave off criticism from anxious parents with a ready-made discourse that focused on health promotion and pro-social television. The occult and magic were only used because these allowed for violence without consequences, among the characters or from the FCC. Fundamentalists saw this development as pernicious. They were still against violence, but at least violence had been comprehensible. Now, their children were being trained by what they saw as occult symbolism into horrible, unspeakable violence said to be committed in Satanic cults, out of range of parental surveillance. Maybe if parents could control what their children were watching, if they could keep these occult cartoons out of their homes, they could stop the scourge of Satanism that was sweeping the continent.

REFERENCES + BIBLIOGRAPHY:

14 Life Lessons from He-Man. 2006. Online video.

Baker, Robert K. and Sandra J. Ball. *National Commission on the Causes and Prevention of Violence (U.S.) Mass Media and Violence*. Vol IX. November, 1969.

Ball-Rokeach, S.J. "The Politics of Studying Media Violence: Reflections 30 Years After The Violence Commission." *Mass Communication and Society*. 4.1 (2001).

Bixby, Scott. "My $295 Dollar Skype Exorcism." *The Daily Beast*. February 2, 2014.

Blake, Patricia, and Meg Grant. "A He-Man for All Seasons: Zapping the Forces of Evil on Daytime TV." *Time*, 125.1 (1985).

Collins, Glenn. "Controversy About Toys, TV Violence." *The New York Times*. December 12, 1985.

Deception of a Generation. Phillips, Phil, and Gary Greenwald. 1984.

G.I. Joe "Roadblock – Don't Give Strangers Your Address". Hasbro, 1985. TV show.

He-Man and the Masters of the Universe. "The Problem With Power." Mattel, 1984. TV show.

Larson, Bob. *Satanism: The Seduction of America's Youth*. Nashville: Nelson Books, 1989.

National Institute of Mental Health (U.S.). *Television and Behaviour: Ten Years of Scientific Progress and Implications for the Eighties. Summary Report*. National Institute of Mental Health, 1982.

Postman, Neil. *Amusing Ourselves to Death: Public Discourse in the Age of Show Business*. New York: Penguin Books, 1985.

Phillips, Phil. *Horror and Violence: The Deadly Duo in the Media*. Lancaster, Pa: Starburst Publishers, 1988.

Phillips, Phil. *Saturday Morning Mind Control*. Nashville: Oliver-Nelson Books, 1991.

Phillips, Phil. *Turmoil in the Toy Box*. Lancaster: Lancaster, Pa: Starburst Publishers, 1990.

Robie, Joan Hake. *Turmoil in the Toybox II*. Lancaster, Pa: Starburst Pub, 1990.

Surgeon General's Scientific Advisory Committee on Television and Social Behaviour. *Television and Growing Up: The Impact of Televised Violence: Report to the Surgeon General United States Public Health Service. U.S. Department of Health, Education, and Welfare*. Washington, 1971.

Victor, Jeffrey S. *Satanic Panic: The Creation of a Contemporary Legend*. Chicago: Open Court, 1993.

Wertham, Fredric. *Seduction of the Innocent*. Port Washington, N.Y: Kennikat Press, 1972.

Left: Cover image from ACT's *Television, Children and the Constitutional Biennial*, 1986.

DEVIL ON THE LINE:
TECHNOLOGY AND THE SATANIC FILM

BY KEVIN L. FERGUSON

Satanism conjures images of medieval, pre-technological rituals, ancient in their wickedness and responsive only to age-old tools, traditions, or symbols. But a cycle of 1980s horror films that included Eric Weston's *Evilspeak* (1981) and Robert Englund's *976-EVIL* (1988) contributed to Satanic Panic by integrating technophobia and Satanic ritual. Are these films simply updating Satanism to appeal to a new, technology-mediated, postmodern decade? Or are they not actually demonstrating some basic equivalence between Satanic Panic and '80s technophobia? While the mix of Satanism and technology in this film cycle might appear like an awkward attempt to reach new audiences, fears of Satanism were paradoxically informed less by an ancient dread of secret Satanic ritual than by a newly modern concern over controversial communication technologies that posed threats to traditional family structures. These techno-devil films demonstrate how the Satanic Panic and technophobia manifest the same cultural anxiety: that new communication networks were fracturing family bonds and irrevocably damaging North American youth.

As with other moral panics of the North American 1980s that involved children, such as those around the crack baby, the welfare mother, or child surrogacy, the Satanic Panic was primarily an adult anxiety fantasized onto youth culture.

Left: Clint Howard in Eric Weston's *Evilspeak* (1981).

Historian Michel Foucault, writing about 19th century sexuality, explains the basic process: adult authority figures invent new "privileged objects of knowledge" which then become "targets and anchorage points for the ventures of knowledge." In other words, new types of people are literally invented and named in order to demonstrate, contain, and process otherwise hidden cultural anxieties or desires. Thus, each new object of knowledge serves as a kind of vessel for new medical, cultural, legal, political, and social attitudes. This process is not always negative (for example, consider "the vegan" as a contemporary object of knowledge used to promote an environmentally conscious and healthy way of life). But when new objects of knowledge become overburdened with cultural signification and capture the attention of mass media, they can easily turn into moral panics. The widespread public fear of an underground Satanic conspiracy within North America in the 1980s is a perfect example of this.

While there are earlier examples of films concerned with demonic possession of children (*The Exorcist*, 1973) or of technology run amok (*Demon Seed*, 1977), the 1980s was an especially fertile time for mixing these two themes as new telecommunications technologies raised questions about the relationship of children to the larger world. Both *Evilspeak* and *976-EVIL* feature bullied male characters from broken families who call on Satan to get revenge.

Both films also demonstrate a particular interest in communication technologies. In the 1980s, 976- and 900-numbers were seen as both a hot new industry and a regulatory nightmare. In this context, *976-EVIL*'s foregrounding of telecommunications as a vessel for Satan would have resonated with real-world anxieties over children accessing pornography or running up huge bills through a simple phone call. *Evilspeak* has a similarly ambivalent relationship to technology, captured in the film's poster art, which features the new Apple II computer used by the nebbish lead character both to complete homework and to translate a Latin Satanic ritual. The fear here is twofold: that new technology makes dangerous knowledge more available and that youth culture's naïve interaction with telephones and computers will lead them to become unthinking slaves to the devilish machine. Ultimately, *Evilspeak* and *976-EVIL* simultaneously inform discourse about Satanic Panic while also undermining claims of widespread Satanism by highlighting the true anxieties of the decade.

Evilspeak begins in the Middle Ages with Father Esteban (Richard Moll) being exiled from Spain for practicing Satanism. In the present time, orphan Stanley Coopersmith (Clint Howard) attends West Andover military academy as a "welfare case" where he is often bullied. The academy was built on land Esteban owned after he left Spain, and while Coopersmith is cleaning out the cellar as punishment he discovers a passageway that leads to a Satanic altar. Coopersmith takes a book and uses his computer to translate the Latin of what turns out to be Esteban's diary. Coopersmith installs a computer in the altar room and attempts unsuccessfully to follow the diary's instructions for a Black Mass. After the mysterious death of some academy staff and the killing of his pet puppy, Coopersmith goes into a rage and murders a teacher. With the mass complete, Esteban possesses Coopersmith, levitating through the cellar into the chapel above to murder everyone. A postscript informs viewers that Coopersmith,

Remember the little kid you used to pick on?
Well, he's a big boy now.
Evilspeak

the sole survivor, is in a catatonic state at an asylum. But, a final computer image of a pentagram with the words "I will return" suggests Esteban/Coopersmith's revenge is unfinished.

976-EVIL has much in common with *Evilspeak*, focusing on an unpopular adolescent from a single-parent home dominated by religious zealotry who fulfills a supernatural fantasy of revenge. After an opening scene where a man is murdered by a mysteriously exploding pay phone, we are introduced to Spike (Patrick O'Bryan), a James Dean-like figure who has lost at cards to a gang of bullies. His younger nerdy cousin Hoax (Stephen Geoffreys, known to audiences as vampire "Evil Ed" from *Fright Night* (1985)) adores Spike but lives with his Christian fundamentalist mother. Returning home, Spike notices a card advertising "For Your Horrorscope 666 Dial 976-EVIL" (the last "O" of "Horrorscope" is stylized as a pentagram). He dials the number, which suggests he steal money to pay off his gambling debts. Aunt Lucy catches him, but as they argue, fish suddenly fall from the sky. Aunt Lucy takes this as a sign from God and, the next day, tells her story to Marty Palmer (Jim Metzler), a reporter for *Modern Miracle* magazine.

At high school, Hoax is bullied until Spike intervenes. That night, Spike calls 976-EVIL, but decides against following the advice to steal again. From Dante's diner across the street, Marty has been watching Spike, and saves him from being run over by a mysterious car. Next, Hoax finds the Horrorscope card, and follows its instructions to go on a date with Spike's girlfriend Suzie, until he's humiliated by bullies. Calling the number again, Hoax is given instructions

to perform a Satanic ritual to win back Suzie, but it results in her death by a horde of spiders. At school, Hoax is bullied again, but is able to easily beat off his attackers with newfound physical strength.

Meanwhile, Marty is poking around the school, finds the Horrorscope card and visits the call center, "After Dark Enterprises." The owner, Mark Dark, shows him the dusty Horrorscope recording device, but claims it has been turned off for months. Returning later at night with the high school counselor Angella, Marty sees the 976-EVIL number speaking to Hoax and is attacked by a pay phone. Hoax, fully transformed, has gone to the El Diablo theater to murder the bullies. At home, he murders his mother and her pet parrot. Marty and Angella arrive, but the inside of the house has been transformed into a frozen-over hell. Spike arrives to save Angella from Hoax; after a brief fight Spike throws the possessed Hoax out of a window into the fiery pit of hell. A concluding scene shows Mark Dark in his office looking at Hoax's photograph as a new phone call comes in.

DIAL TONES: NEW CONNECTED NETWORKS IN THE 1980S

Underlying the cultural shifts in the North American 1980s related to children and families were changes in communications technologies. On one hand, the influence of personal computers on the decade cannot be overstated; even for those unable to own one, the public image of the computer as primarily a personally liberating device—argued most famously in Apple's watershed "1984" television ad—shaped the direction of conversations about how humans interact with computers. But on the other hand, in addition to radical changes in computing technology and production, there were also simpler but no less profound changes in the use of already existing telecommunications infrastructure. The telephone, over a century old, was put to brand new social purposes in the 1980s as the development of premium rate lines opened up opportunities for businesses to create new services and cater to new markets.

For a new use of an old technology, national 900 numbers and their regional 976 counterparts had an extraordinarily rapid rise and fall in the 1980s. They were breathlessly described in trade publications at the time as "truly... the hottest business of the late '80s, with growth predicted in the billions of dollars per year." As one of the fastest-growing segments of the telephone industry, they attracted a great deal of attention from businesses, consumers, and soon regulators alike. Local 976 numbers had been used since the early 1970s for specialized uses, and the national 900 number was later developed by AT&T as a way for television networks to poll their audiences in real time. Initially, 900 numbers carried no premium rate charge for customers and thus were "primarily used by corporations as promotion or information tools... and for sports lines underwritten by national advertisers."

In the mid-1980s, however, AT&T restructured the 900 program into a premium line, began splitting profits with content providers, and allowed for higher rates. Business exploded, and since success relied heavily on advertising, 900 numbers quickly became a highly visible commodity, particularly on television. In addition to the relatively straightforward polling 900 numbers, where callers provided information (should Eddie Murphy kill Larry the Lobster?), from the new 900 number structure "a quirky and cluttered industry [has]... blossomed" that let callers receive a variety of information and entertainment, including messages from Santa Claus, the Easter Bunny, or Psychic Friends, sports scores, health information, stock tips, details on government grants and—most notoriously—sex.

Despite representing only a small percentage of 900 number traffic, the so-called "dial-a-porn" numbers would soon result in the collapse of the business. The industry attracted great scrutiny in the late-'80s as federal regulators struggled to come to grips with the explosion in services, particularly those aimed at children and those for adult entertainment. In doing so, they had to balance legitimate business interests with consumer protection practices. For instance, the same dial-a-porn number might either offer a therapeutic outlet for safe sex between consenting adults during a chilling time of AIDS, or motivate unhinged depravity in normally innocent youth. For instance, in describing how new regulations were affecting legitimate businesses, one trade paper noted the lurid case of a boy who allegedly raped a four-year-old after listening to dial-a-porn.

Seen specifically as a threat to children, a Federal Trade Commission official in 1991 even went so far as to describe 900 numbers as being responsible for "the newest and most serious abuses" in children's advertising. Major newspapers picked up the stories, generally foregrounding the problem of 900 numbers as one of a threat to children. In 1988, AT&T and other regional companies, under pressure of government regulations as well as complaints from consumer and parents' groups, stopped paying providers of some adult 900 numbers a share of caller profits. Bell Canada discontinued its 976 numbers in 1989. The industry that had worked so hard to attract and build up a new business model was now backpedalling from a major image problem.

Two legitimate concerns were impossible for either the industry or regulators to ignore—that 900 numbers allowed children to easily access inappropriate material including pornography, and that children could unwittingly run up high phone bills that their parents would be forced to pay. Federal and state regulations specifically addressed the latter by requiring refunds and the ability to block 900 numbers, and the phone industry, recognizing an image problem, worked itself to cut out the former by removing financial incentives. But despite these paired efforts to clean up the industry, what was impossible to address at the time was the new tele-consciousness that the 900 numbers created—namely the simple, stubborn fact that "the telephone network is designed for everyone to reach everyone," as a public relations manager for Southern Bell put it.

Scholar Jeanne Freiburg describes how television advertisements for 900 numbers further helped construct this new mode of '80s tele-consciousness. Speaking of popular cultural tropes such as Wendy's "Where's the Beef?" advertisements, Joe Bob Briggs's low-brow movie reviews, and sardonic cult movie presenter Elvira, Freiburg identifies a new media strategy in the decade that created "a distinct sense of comradeship" between viewers and television characters by having characters actively voice negative opinions or frustrations that viewers at home might share. For example, Elvira

Right: Nancy's phone call from Freddy Krueger gives new meaning to the catchphrase "Reach out and touch someone" in *A Nightmare on Elm Street* (1984).

satirized the respectful role of movie host by mocking acting performances, talking over dialogue, and addressing viewers with complaints about the film being shown. In the resulting "market-sanctioned institutionalization of discontent," these dissatisfied figures became popular precisely because they gave an outlet for home viewers' own discontent.

What makes these media figures unique in the 1980s is that they used classic advertising strategies in order to elicit a response in viewers, and yet they were not doing so to sell a particular product. Rather, the media strategy of discontent "achieved a marketability of its own," and the 900 number industry likewise capitalized on both creating and promising to fulfill this discontent. Building on the "long-established acceptability of seeking emotional response through mass communication technologies," 900 numbers restructure social interaction so that passive consumers can now buy active participation in a larger network in order to satisfy their discontent. In other words, the 900 number represented not just passive absorption of information, but also the promise of active agency within a larger sphere outside of the home. This production and consumption of agency by youth in particular was the true hidden anxiety for '80s parents: more than simply being able to hear dirty words, youth were buying, and buying into, a new tele-consciousness of discontent and agency.

The anxiety over youth telephone use is seen in any number of media texts from the period. The bidirectional nature of phone calls is made a source of disgusting body horror in *A Nightmare on Elm Street* (1984), when monster Freddy Krueger possesses heroine Nancy's phone, licking her through the mouthpiece.

Ferris Bueller's Day Off (1986) represents youth phone use as a source of comedy when Bueller and his friend Cameron fool their high school dean by imitating adults. The music video for Aerosmith's "Sweet Emotion" (1991) mocks the unreality of phone sex and how it enables callers to disguise or transform their true identity on the network. Each of these texts portrays youth bedrooms as fully functioning, self-contained environments, connected to the outside world by television and telephone. Scenes of youth bedrooms show us how fully the telephone has been transformed from a shared household tool to a personal device offering semi-private access to the outer world (this trajectory being continued with the development of multi-line telephone plans and the contemporary cell phone industry). Seeing filmic youth use phones in their bedrooms taught children and adults alike that phones were agency-producing devices, carriers of the new tele-consciousness that brought with it both liberation and danger.

Many of these same concerns are evident in today's rhetoric about a "touch-screen generation" of children accessing inappropriate media online or being overly "wired." Indeed, mid-1990s concerns over children using personal computers to access internet pornography are nearly indistinguishable from the earlier arguments against 900 numbers. Media texts from the decade often portrayed computers and technology as the natural province of youth, although youth users invariably lacked an adult understanding of the consequences of computer use. For example, in Ferris Bueller's Day Off, Ferris uses a Macintosh computer to hack into his high school network to change his attendance records. In Weird Science (1985), two high school students easily hack into a government supercomputer and literally create a superwoman. In The Manhattan Project (1986), a high school student builds a nuclear bomb as his science fair project.

However, WarGames (1983) remains the best example of anxiety over youth's technology-driven interaction with the larger world: a high schooler hacks into a military computer and nearly starts World War III by playing a game, which is really a live missile defense system. WarGames develops the trope of interacting with computers as gaming consoles rather than as computing machines or analytical devices. "Gamifying" computer use strengthened associations of computers to youth culture and presented computers as bewilderingly complex devices that only youth could have intuitive knowledge of. Films like D.A.R.Y.L. (1985) and The Wizard (1989) play on this by showing cyborg youth freely mixing with technology and demonstrating a new kind of technologically mediated relationship to their environment. As if youth needed another source of alienation from their parents, youth computer expertise and the dangers it introduced has come to represent a wedge in family bonds.

While the concept of the North American "family" has dramatically changed since World War II, splintering into any number of formations, conservative commentators of the 1980s were still able to call up the "traditional family" as something under assault and in need of defense. Evangelical organizations like Focus on the Family, the Moral Majority, and the Christian Coalition of America sought political change that would protect traditional "family values," including restrictions on birth control

Right: Ally Sheedy and Matthew Broderick in WarGames (1983).

and abortions, opposition to same-sex marriage, and censorship as a way to protect children. Mobilizing an emerging conservative base and finding a receptive audience in Reagan-era Washington, conservative leaders espoused a reinvestment in "family values" as a cure to the ills of the modern world and a necessary defense against future generations' further weakening.

STATIC ON THE LINE: CONTEXTS FOR THE TECHNO-DEVIL'S RECEPTION

Evilspeak and *976-EVIL* circumscribe two well-worn filmic traditions: movies about possessed children and movies about technology run amok. Demonically possessed children in horror films such as *The Exorcist* and *The Omen* frighten audiences because they undermine cherished assumptions about children's innocence and purity. Out-of-control machines in science fiction films such as *2001: A Space Odyssey* (1968), *Westworld* (1973), and *Demon Seed* suggest that even benign technology contains dystopian possibilities.

What is so notable about *Evilspeak* and *976-EVIL* is that they mix these two traditions, connecting images of possessed youth with scenes of youth using technology. Both films are R-rated, which suggests that the filmmakers were addressing an adult audience rather than the teen one represented by the films' protagonists, and neither film seems particularly interested in making a moral point, preferring instead to emphasize horror elements like gory special effects, atmospheric settings, and narrative rescue. For example, the tagline for one version of the *Evilspeak* poster addresses an older audience by accusingly asking viewers to "Remember the little kid you used to pick on? Well, he's a big boy now." But both films are grounded in contemporary settings, so while not morally didactic, they do offer viewers opportunities to reflect upon contemporary youth culture and its associated problems such as bullying, parents, revenge, and school. Thus, as with many genre pictures, both *Evilspeak* and *976-EVIL* mix a number of elements that film audiences were familiar with: slasher motifs, iconography of contemporary youth style, fetishization of technology, and demonic possession as narrative explanation for supernatural events in an otherwise realistic world.

These films were also primarily received in a historical context where horror films were becoming increasingly associated with gore. Describing how horror films were pushed to the margins as the conservative blockbuster became the new norm in the 1980s, James Kendrick describes the interaction between horror filmmakers and audiences:

> **"** *Despite mainstream Hollywood's attempts to curtail horror film production in the 1980s by not producing such films and by using CARA [The Motion Picture Association of America's Classification and Ratings Administration] to put a brake on the extremity of the content in independently produced horror films, the genre flourished in the 1980s thanks in large part to a core of dedicated fans who not only enjoyed but demanded increasingly graphic and gory content.*

The push and pull of horror film production particularly centered on horror's increasing use of gory and graphic images. While general audiences might watch a film and only see gratuitous gore, discerning horror audiences would be able to read the same film in a more nuanced way. Kendrick attributes this particularly to the success of fan magazines like *Fangoria*, which "made the horror genre more gruesome by focusing on the most graphically violent aspects of its films while simultaneously denying this screen violence any true impact by fetishizing the makeup effects technologies used to create it." As a result, these fan magazines created a culture of specialized knowledge that horror audiences were able to deploy when watching gory films.

This fan culture of technical knowledge was no doubt part of the strategy in getting veteran horror makeup maven Kevin Yagher to work on *976-EVIL*. For example, in a preview of the film in the fan magazine *Cinefantastique*, Yagher's contributions were emphasized in both images and text, although the article also takes pains to give credit for a unique artistic vision to first-time director Robert Englund, most famous for his role as iconic horror villain Freddy Krueger in the *A Nightmare on Elm Street* series (the fifth entry of which was in the theaters around the time that *976-EVIL* was released). The brief report repeatedly quotes Englund as aiming for "atmosphere over gore" in his film. Attempting to distance himself from the expectations established by the gore of the films he acted in, Englund positioned his film as "a classic gothic horror story," while at the same time hiring Yagher to bring some of the expected "drippy stuff" to the film. Englund did, however, voice the Satanic Horrorscope, so one might argue that his star persona as Freddy was too strong a selling point to totally avoid. Englund's (and Krueger's) name was also prominently featured on advertising materials, which almost always portrayed the demonic high school character in a decidedly non-gothic pose.

Kendrick argues that the twin turn to over-the-top gore and the behind-the-scenes fan magazines were preemptive strategies to package horror's potentially controversial public image. As a result, the double "dissociation of horror violence from reality helped to separate the horror genre from real-world anxieties during the 1980s." But while this is true for most '80s horror, films like *Evilspeak* and *976-EVIL* that specifically raise a contemporary social problem are notable exceptions. This tension is apparent in the contradiction between Englund's stated desire to make a "gothic" rather than a "drippy" film and the resulting gruesome images of slashed faces, severed hands, and impaled corpses. Working against the general tendency of the Reaganite ideology of pacifying entertainment, *Evilspeak* and *976-EVIL* transgressed expectations by mixing horror elements and contemporary technology. Their relatively poor critical reception is a function of the unexpected juxtapositions, which made it difficult to receive the movies as either straight gory horror or as social problem films.

While received more favorably by critics than *976-EVIL*, *Evilspeak* faced its own difficulties when the British press branded it a "video nasty" and the Department of Public Prosecutions banned it. A particularly '80s anxiety, the video nasty raised fears that children would be able to easily access obscene material at home. *Evilspeak* was prosecuted in the United Kingdom under the *Obscene Publications Act 1959* before

Parliament passed a new *Video Recordings Act 1984* which required later releases of the film to be censored in order to receive certification. British tabloids heavily publicized the video nasties and often linked them to particularly gruesome tales with headlines like "Youth Tried Rape After Seeing Video" or "Fury Over the Video Rapist." Reports of raids on video stores and collector's homes emphasized to the public how serious the problem was. As a result of the tabloid attention, video nasties became a target point for the supposed problem of the influence of horror on youth, so much so that scholar Kate Egan argues that tabloid and legal attention transformed video nasties into "a recognisable film genre within Britain" today. Thus, in reading *Evilspeak* as a techno-devil film, we can also see how its status as a video nasty informs perceptions of the film's violent goriness.

As with *976-EVIL*'s special effects, for tech-savvy audiences the computer technology in *Evilspeak* was a part of the fan discourse that coded the film's reception. For example, while only giving the film two out of four stars, Rob David's review in the computing industry publication *InfoWorld* trumpets "a new era in cinema... heralded by *Evilspeak*, the first movie with a microcomputer as a star," although he also humorously notes that the starring Apple II "must have been a newly released version because it was operated without software or electricity. A single disk drive was thrown in for special effects." Reviewer Bill Landis also wryly comments that "on a personal level, believing that computers could be frightening or fascinating was extremely difficult, having worked at programming jobs that were either drudgery or frustration personified."

Clearly, some viewers were both interested in and distracted by the unrealistic aspects of computer use. A second review in *Infoworld* by John Barry complements David's assessment that *Evilspeak* is "perhaps the first feature-length film to have as a main character a personal computer." But where David and Landis joke about the realism of *Evilspeak*'s computing, Barry sees the film as metaphoric of "the compulsive computer mentality" since "Coopersmith bears a strong resemblance to the obsessive-compulsive personality *Psychology Today* refers to as the 'hacker.'" "Hacker" would still have been a relatively novel term in 1981; in fact, the Oxford English Dictionary provides two competing definitions that both first date to 1976: the one we are most familiar with today, "a person who uses his skill with computers to try to gain unauthorized access to computer files or networks," and the more neutral "a person with an enthusiasm for programming or using computers as an end in itself." Coopersmith takes part in the "unauthorized" tradition of computing, and as such is an early representation of teen computer use as dangerous, illegal, and in this case, murderous.

Even non-technology-focused reviewers noted the importance of the computer. Alain Garsault paired *Evilspeak* with the Marty Feldman comedy *In God We Tru$t* (1980) to show that "cinema has taught us that God and the Devil live today in computers." If *Evilspeak*'s star computer is metaphor, it is metaphor for the latent deviance of youth and how little restrains that deviance—that we are but a few BASIC commands away from devilry.

CROSSED WIRES: THREE TECHNO-DEVIL CONCEPTS IN EVILSPEAK AND 976-EVIL

Evilspeak and *976-EVIL* not only contributed to discourse around Satanic Panic, but also tellingly reveal the decade's true anxieties over youth technology use. This is seen in three central concepts that link techno-devil films: communication tools as Janus-faced outlets offering both emotional comfort and liberatory promise, games misunderstood as a consequence-free model of the world, and the disruption of traditional religious family values by outside influences. Just below the in-your-face gory elements that drew audience attention, the circulation of these three central themes in *Evilspeak* and *976-EVIL* mark them as techno-devil films with a particularly attuned '80s sensibility.

The difficulty of regulating dial-a-porn services made it clear that the 1980s telephone was a Janus device, offering new access to information from inside the home, but also bringing the dangerous outside world into the family. Thus, the unintended double entendre of AT&T's famous 1979 advertising appeal to "reach out and touch someone" is that someone might reach back. Likewise, even before the development of the public internet, the early 1980s computer was readily portrayed as a sentient device that could intelligently respond to the new '80s tele-consciousness of discontent and agency. By offering a new outlet for personal connection, the '80s telephone and

Above: Coopersmith (Clint Howard) with the brand new Apple II computer in *Evilspeak*.

computer offered both a way to fulfill older emotional needs and a promise of a new liberatory agency. This is true for both *Evilspeak* and *976-EVIL*, where the central nerd relies on the "long-established acceptability of seeking emotional response through mass communication technologies." But when both are frustrated in satisfying their emotional needs, they turn to technology as a possible liberation from their past selves.

As an orphan and "welfare case," *Evilspeak*'s Coopersmith is constantly seeking an outlet at the academy for his emotional needs. The film presents him initially as rather well adjusted: he is studious and responsible with schoolwork, he has an "above-average IQ," he persists in activities that challenge him, and he has one friend that repeatedly sticks up for him. One scene defines Coopersmith's resilient attitude: he begs the cook to let him keep the runt from a litter of puppies, although the cook argues that they should let nature take its course. Coopersmith responds that "it's a tough world out there; you got to be able to kick and scratch if you want to survive. I found that out right after my parents died. From what I can tell, like these other pups, it's the ones that can do the most pushing and shoving that get the biggest piece of the pie." For all the grief heaped on Coopersmith throughout the film, his attitude, while cynical about the world, is remarkably positive about how to survive. Because of this, viewers can sympathize with Coopersmith as a "fish out of water" character, rather than fear him as an intractable social misfit (as his counterpart in *Carrie* was). Furthermore, viewers might consider his later techno-obsession with Satanism as something that could easily happen to youth of any background (even, as we see, to a Senator's son).

Thus, Coopersmith turns to the computer as emotional outlet. While not yet truly a mass communication technology, in *Evilspeak* the computer does offer Coopersmith emotional outlet and response, an open line to Satanic friendship rather than just a source of information. In fact, the immediacy of the back and forth when Coopersmith questions Esteban presents the computer as equal parts internet chat room and spirit medium. We first see Coopersmith using the computer for homework, modeling the physics of a catapult he later builds (and which the bullies destroy). He tells his teacher he wants "to check my configurations so it'll be really accurate," showing how Coopersmith initially considers the computer as a reference resource, but also foreshadowing how crucial "accuracy" is both in designing catapults and performing Satanic rituals. When he is told he must stop using the shared computer since others are scheduled, he steals it and takes it to the cellar. Here, the computer becomes more than a source of information, integrating into a larger info-spiritual network by occupying the centerpiece of a Satanic altar. This is more than fetishizing the machine: when it becomes part of ritual, the computer is elevated from being a simple tool to manifesting a higher power.

Above and Left: Technology and ritual meet in *Evilspeak*.

But before fully embracing the machine, the film offers Coopersmith a choice of emotional alternative in the form of Fred, the puppy he rescues from the cook and keeps in the cellar. When the drunken Sarge threatens the puppy, Coopersmith watches in satisfied horror as the computer flashes a pentagram and Sarge's head—in a nod to *The Exorcist*—is twisted completely around, killing him. But Coopersmith is unable to intervene later when Bubba drunkenly sacrifices the puppy in an attempt to finish the Satanic ritual. Discovering the puppy's body, Coopersmith repeats in shock "we were a team, Fred." Devoid of any human or animal friendship, the film leaves Coopersmith with no alternative than to turn to Esteban to form a new "team." The technology-mediated desire for emotional connection is then made literal as Esteban possesses Coopersmith's body. Finding liberation in Satanic possession, Coopersmith also allows Esteban to fulfill his promised threat "I will return."

But is this really a return or just another exile? Once it is part of a larger info-spiritual ritual, the computer functions as a Janus machine to facilitate the continued, cyclical shift between exile and return, or discontent and agency. After the massacre, when Esteban has fulfilled his promise to return, we learn that rather than continue to terrorize the community or reestablish a Satanic practice, Esteban/Coopersmith is permanently put in an asylum. And yet the final shots of a pentagram and Coopersmith's computerized face are accompanied again by the words "I will return." While no doubt this coda anticipates possible sequels, it also raises the interpretive question of whether or not the Devil can ever truly return, or only temporarily manifest. In other words, in emphasizing cyclical Satanic returns over permanence, *Evilspeak*'s narrative conclusion argues that Satanic communication is Janus-faced: that possession is always imminent but impermanent, that constant vigilance is required, that the line is always open for a return call.

976-EVIL quickly shows nerdy Hoax's need for emotional outlet through communication technology. The film first stages an unsatisfying proto-telephone network in the form of a pneumatic tube that connects Spike and Hoax's bedrooms. We never see Spike use this, but Hoax sends three very banal messages (the first reads simply "Hi Spike, Hoax!"). While Spike's invention has failed to bring him closer to his cousin, the tube does later provide an avenue of escape for Marty and Angella to cross over Hell's gaping fiery pit. Thus, the pneumatic tube's tangible physical size, unlike the mysterious nature of the small, hidden telephone wire, suggests a return to older communication as a form of rescue. In fact, 976-EVIL often valorizes romantic notions of the recent past, particularly in the way that Hoax looks up to Spike, who is modeled on 1950s teen rebels with his motorcycle, leather jackets, jeans, coiffed ponytail, zip gun, and bad boy demeanor. This is contrasted with the gang of bullies, who have a more contemporary exaggerated punk style, with skateboards, dyed hair, ripped T-shirts, chains, and names like "Airhead" and "Rags."

Above: The bullies (including a young Darren Burrows) in 976-EVIL.
Top right: Richard Moll as Esteban in Evilspeak.

In one scene Hoax makes his nostalgic longing clear: Spike is arranging a date with his girlfriend Suzie by his Harley when Hoax arrives on his Vespa. Spike and Suzie are embarrassed as Hoax brags about punching out his muffler in metal shop so that it would sound like Hoax's. He then tells Suzie, to Spike's chagrin, about their plans to take a cross-country bike trip over the summer (if his mom will let him), adding comically that the trip would be better "with a couple of babes riding on the back." The film punctures Hoax's dream as he crashes when he tries to drive off. Hoax's nostalgic masculine fantasy of a cross-country motorcycle trip with his hero cousin is clearly unattainable, and yet for that reason it becomes the one human thing that remains once Hoax is fully possessed by Satan. In the final confrontation, Spike tries to speak to what remains of Hoax by reminding him of the motorcycle trip—"the open road, Grand Canyon, Painted Desert, the Mississippi, New Orleans"—even offering Hoax the use of his Harley. Once again, this dream is skewered when the reverie gives Spike just enough time to throw Hoax out of a window into hell. Thus, 976-EVIL juxtaposes two fantastic but unrealizable possibilities: a nostalgic return to 1950s freedom of movement and a supernatural embrace of 1980s freedom of communication.

Unlike Coopersmith, Hoax's desire for emotional contact is portrayed as deviant. When first introduced, Hoax is secretly looking at naked women in *National Geographic* magazine. In a later scene, Hoax uses a telescope to spy on Spike and Suzie as they have sex, afterwards using the pneumatic tube to send a message "Nice Babe Hoax." Once they leave, he sneaks into Spike's room and steals underwear that Suzie has left. He next follows the Horrorscope's advice and takes Suzie on a date while his cousin is occupied. He even "rescues" her from a harmless daddy longlegs, telling her about the poisonous gray hermit spider he has at home. But this scene, where Hoax is on the cusp of developing his first normal emotional attachment, falls apart when the bullies show up, smash the spider, find Suzie's underwear, and shove Hoax into a garbage can. In the next scene, Hoax resorts to the Horrorscope to receive instructions for a ritual to "capture his prize": "a small circle of salt with star within, adding one insect will punish her sin. The juice of my weed will implant my seed and make you one of my kin."

At home, Hoax prepares his bedroom for the ritual, outlining a pentagram and noticeably putting the phone inside a circle of candles. Initially in his childish pajamas, he takes his shirt off and squeezes devil's-root on his torso as the phone, left off the hook, chants at him. Intercutting with Suzie in her apartment preparing a meal, the

supernatural effect of Hoax's ritual as spiders attack her is revealed. Hoax, who initially thought he was only going to scare Suzie, seems to have second thoughts and quickly kills his spider, but a smash cut suggests that this action kills Suzie too. After argumentative confrontations with his mother and with Spike, Hoax, devoid of any companionship, decides to fully embrace the Satanic connection he made over the telephone. As with *Evilspeak*, though, the offer of permanent liberation is instead one of transient possession, as Hoax gradually transforms into a lizard-like Satanic figure.

The spider ritual in *976-EVIL* shows the desperate lengths Hoax would go to for emotional contact, but it also reveals the second concept of techno-devil films: that games are misunderstood as a consequence-free model of the world. The emphasis on games and contests in both films suggests that for youth, experience is a game: through games youth learn about their world, but they also must understand that games are not the world. That lesson—that the real world has consequences—is absent in both films. Hoax clearly did not know that following the ritual would result in Suzie's death since he rushes to her house after, looking shocked when he sees her body. In the next scene, he is hiding the spider cage in his closet when his mother interrupts and takes his telephone. As soon as she leaves, we see him in closeup, shaking in anger,

Left: Hoax (Stephen Geoffreys) summons the spiders in *976-EVIL*.
Above: Suzie (Lezlie Deane) is punished for not returning Hoax's affections.

repeating to himself "You shouldn't have done that, Mama." This marks a turning point for Hoax, for now he has neither remorse for killing Suzie nor respect towards his mother and Spike. Invoking his mother's religious language, the next day at school he brags to Spike about having killed Suzie, since "she was a dirty Jezebel whore, and I took care of her for you." When Spike pushes him away, Hoax threatens "it's gonna be different from now on."

Transformation, change, and difference are all classic tropes of horror and high school, but here Hoax's conscious embrace of the possibilities of difference turns this from a film about possession to one about embodiment. In the following scenes, Hoax's body monstrously transforms. This is the gateway argument of Satanism: that simple games or play with Satanic ritual will lead to more serious transformations and devilry. Ironically, Hoax is initially more skeptical about the Horrorscope than Spike, rolling his eyes when he first calls the number and laughing "oh brother" at the corny pre-recorded dialogue. Whereas Spike was driven to call the number out of financial desperation, Hoax does so mainly out of curious boredom. In this update on the Faustian theme of a man selling his soul to the Devil, it is the idler of the two cousins who is most susceptible

Robert Englund gets behind the camera to deliver a tale of jealous adolescence and the worst possible phone counseling number.

to games of distraction. Hoax's lack of serious industry (he has wasted time tinkering, building the pneumatic tube, and punching out his Vespa's muffler), has left him particularly susceptible to seeing the world as a game. Thus, Hoax's naïve following of the Horrorscope's advice shows the danger of even pretending to play at the occult— that quitting may be impossible.

The film makes a similar suggestion about Spike's gambling. In his first scene, Spike loses the pink slip on his Harley gambling with the bullies, and the Horrorscope suggests he

Above and Left: Hoax transformed (image on left as captioned in *Fangoria* #73).

steal from his Aunt Lucy to keep the motorcycle. This leads to a second moral dilemma when the Horrorscope next tells him to steal a pair of leather motorcycle gloves. He does, but immediately regrets it and returns them. As supernatural punishment, Spike is almost run over by a mysterious, driverless car. Even when his gambling luck surprisingly turns around and he wins all of the money from the bullies, this is just the Horrorscope's way to keep Spike busy while Hoax dates Suzie. In these examples, the Horrorscope is portrayed as a jesting, gambling force; in other words, an active presence in the youth's lives trying to trick them into playing a game for real. This is matched by the playfulness on display throughout *976-EVIL*, especially in the many visual puns: characters eat at Dante's diner (where a sign advertising shuffleboard has had its H and L removed), see movies at the El Diablo movie theater (where the "B" and "O" are not lit up, leaving "Dial"), and Spike gets his motorcycle repaired by Virgil, the hellish guide from Dante.

The first scene at the After Dark call center particularly uses visual humor to make a point about the discrepancies between entertainment and reality. As the camera tracks through a short hallway, taking the point of view of Marty, it peeks inside a number of rooms to show tableaux of workers operating 976 numbers: a beer-drinking man reads off horse-racing picks (with names like Deadly Nightshade, Devil's Moon, Mother's Curse, Merlin's Hex, Dark Omen, and Belladonna); a wino in a tinsel-covered room pretends to be Santa Claus; and a "petite 17-year-old nymphet with desires most men can't satisfy" turns out to be a frumpy housewife talking to a priest. We end with the Horrorscope, a comically dusty and spider web-draped device locked away in a janitor's closet. Unlike the human operators we had just seen, the Horrorscope is a homebrewed pile of wires, machines, boxes, and switches—an experiment in automation that Dark hoped would allow him to fire staff. But Dark presents his "pet project, his baby" as a failed dream, blaming consumer taste for a declining interest in the supernatural: people are "just into Ewoks and E.T. and football and phone sex." But we also see the techno-devil impulse at work here: by marking the Horrorscope as the only technologically-mediated phone service in the building, the film asks viewers to see technology as the real threat. When it is revealed in the final scene that Mr. Dark is Satan, his admiration for his "baby," which

was a success after all, is obvious: Satan in the modern world will not show up with pointy ears and red cape, but in the form of the latest communications technology.

If *976-EVIL* compares Spike's gambling to Hoax's phone calls, *Evilspeak* explores a wider range of games and play: soccer, computer simulations, beauty contests, even bullying. A shock cut early in the film connects

Above: The automated Horrorscope of *976-EVIL*, "locked away in a janitor's closet."

games with religious ritual: after being excommunicated, Father Esteban beheads a woman in a Satanic ritual, and her flying head is matched with a soccer ball being kicked in the present day. In this framework, it is natural to expect youth to "play" with religious ritual. While Coopersmith is terrible at soccer, he still wants to play and be part of the team. Thus, unlike Hoax, Coopersmith understands the value of gaming; he does not just want to be like one role model, but wants to be part of a larger team. In this, his possession by Esteban marks Satanism as a kind of team sport that offers communion with a larger group. This follows with the film's criticism of religion and the military, two other organizations that demand obedience to group think. In a speech right before Coopersmith/Esteban begin their massacre, the Reverend compares life to a soccer game, with Satan as a losing coach and God as referee and scorekeeper. After warning the players not to cheat in life, the film mocks the Reverend's closing lesson—"you better be on the winning side of this or there will be hell to pay"—when a spike from the chapel crucifix brains him. Instead, the film's conclusion supports Coopersmith's competing life lesson: "it's a tough world out there; you got to be able to kick and scratch if you want to survive."

The central part of the film tests Coopersmith's argument, staging a debate about the possibility of self-reliance, or whether to treat life as a team sport or a singular one. On the one hand, Coopersmith tries to conform to larger teams (military life, the soccer team, social groups), but on the other he increasingly comes under the influence of one figure—Esteban. In a number of mysterious ways, Esteban's spirit insists that Coopersmith finish the ritual: the computer magically turns itself back on, begins actively to communicate with Coopersmith and even murders interlopers like Sarge, the secretary, and a teacher. But Coopersmith misunderstands the computer, and it becomes a game for him to solve the computer's puzzle, for example when the computer rejects the input of dog's blood instead of human blood. The computer's insistence on properly completing the black mass demonstrates the underlying logic in common between computing and Satanic ritual: that both are bound by exacting laws. The fear here is twofold: that new forms of knowledge (such as automatic translation of devilish texts) are easily enabled by technology and that youth culture's naïve interaction with computers will lead them to become unthinking, robot-like followers. Coopersmith must follow the ritual exactly, just as he must use the computer to make sure his catapult class project is accurate. But like Hoax, Coopersmith gets caught up in following the ritual without considering the consequences.

```
BY THE DREADFUL DAY OF JUDGEMENT,
BY THE FACE OF THE UNHOLY MAJESTY AND
BY THE BEASTS BEFORE THE THRONE...
BY THE FIRE WHICH IS ABOUT THE THRONE
I CONJURE AND COMMAND THEE OH PRINCE
OF DARKNESS IN THE NAME OF HE WHO SPAKE
AND IT WAS DONE.
SATAN, LUCIFER APPEAR FORTHWITH AND
SHOW YOURSELF TO ME.
            BLOOD
      CONSECRATED HOST
    *DATA INCOMPLETE*
```

Above: The computer itself directs the Black Mass in *Evilspeak*.
Over: A selection of scenes from *Evilspeak*.

Likewise, 900 numbers with their pre-recorded responses cultivate an environment of unthinking automation. Thus in *976-EVIL*, the Horrorscope line is surprising since it wraps its devilish instruction in blandly generic introductory content. While *976-EVIL* portrays individualized attention as a source of horror, that kind of personal connection is the precise fantasy of anyone calling into a dial-a-service.

The technological theme of automation and slavish obedience to the machine in turn informs the third techno-devil concept seen in both films: the disruption of traditional religious family values by outside influences. Children are the primary target points of anxiety about family values because they are seen as being most susceptible to untoward influence. In both films, parents are absent or dead, and children have especially difficult circumstances to cope with in the absence of a traditional home environment. *Evilspeak* replaces the traditional home with the highly disciplined structure of a military academy and *976-EVIL* with an overbearing maternal figure. Of course, neither of those proves to be acceptable substitutes, and in part Coopersmith and Hoax (and Spike) are simply running away from their home environment as much as they are seeking out Satan.

While Coopersmith's deceased parents are only briefly mentioned, *Evilspeak* does devote some time to Bubba's mother Mrs. Caldwell. The Reverend gives her a private tour of the academy (offering some plot exposition along the way), where we learn that her husband is a senator. Thus, as a senator's son and privileged child of the academy, Bubba's bullying is presented not as sociopathic, but as perfectly normal. Further, Bubba's attempts to complete the Satanic ritual emphasizes that Satanic play could affect any child, whether poor or privileged. The Colonel, trying to secure increased military funding, makes the argument to Mrs. Caldwell that "the military is the backbone of this country, our only hope in preserving this democratic way of life of ours," lamenting that they must admit people like Coopersmith for financial reasons. And indeed when the Colonel later paddles Coopersmith for a minor infraction, we see how sadistic life at the military academy is, and how the film portrays supposed government, military, and religious leaders as corrupt and violent. "Traditional" family values are just as psychotic as Satanic ones.

The environment of *976-EVIL* is, in a sense, the exact opposite: there is too much maternal involvement in Hoax's life, which has stifled him. Overall the film presents a nostalgic, 1950s small-town vibe, with youth life centered around the diner, movie theater, and high school. The intrusion of '80s culture on this idyll—whether the 976 numbers or the punk subculture—makes this a darker place, a wasted vision of '50s nostalgia closer to *The Wild One* (1953) than *Pleasantville* (1998). Hoax's environment is media-saturated; the home is dominated by the sound of televangelists, which is nicely contrasted with another key space in the film, the projection room of the El Diablo movie theater, which plays a "Continuous Horror Marathon." Hoax's mother Lucy is constantly needling Hoax and Spike about following God's laws, although neither of them seems particularly inclined to agree. When it rains fish after Spike first calls the Horrorscope, Aunt Lucy takes this as a sign of blessing from God, although

Hoax assumes Spike had instead hatched an elaborate prank. At the film's end, after Hoax's total transformation, hellish graffiti on the walls of the home conflates a hatred of mother with hatred of religion: "Go to Hell Mommy."

These images, along with Hoax's murder of his mother, shockingly mark not only how evil Hoax is but also how little parents seem to matter. After murdering his mother, he turns to her pet parrot, which is repeating her constant nagging "not on the couch." When Hoax crushes it, he suggests that he saw his mother as little more than a parrot herself. The emptiness of parental concerns is further shown when the film specifically invokes the parental and legislative fears that shut down dial-a-porn. In one scene, Hoax's mother bursts into his room, waving a phone bill and complaining that Hoax has been tying up the phone line and running up a large bill. He was using it to perform Satanic ritual, but she wanted to use it to call in a pledge to a televangelist. Call Satan or call God? What's the difference? In *Evilspeak* and *976-EVIL*, traditional religious family values are no different than Satanic ones.

HANGING UP

Coopersmith and Hoax are central film examples of that new 1980s object of knowledge: the Satanic youth corrupted in the techno-devil film. The cycle of '80s horror films that placed Satanic themes in technological environments do not just update Satanism to appeal to a new, technology-mediated audience, but rather demonstrate a basic equivalence between Satanic Panic and '80s technophobia: that new communication networks would fracture family bonds and irrevocably damage North American youth. Both God and the Devil live in the computer and telephone line, even if at the time new technology was primarily a metaphor for something yet unable to be understood. And while it might be easy to dismiss these movies as just trashy gore or video nasties, Suzanne Moore argues that their power to shock has less to do with their imagery and more with their underlying message: "What remains the most shocking thing about these kind of movies is that although hell is loosely bound to vaguely religious imagery, they make it abundantly clear that it is actually located in the heart of the family and in the minds of its young men." Discussing *976-EVIL*, Kevin Thomas finds great irony in the fact "that the strictly raised Hoax is far more vulnerable to the temptations of the Devil than his older cousin Spike," which further suggests how the threats to traditional family values in these films are really only threats to traditionalists.

The techno-devil trope was not exhausted in the 1980s; anxieties resurface and resonate in more recent techno-horror: *Brainscan* (1994) (video games), *Ringu* (1998) (video tapes), *Pulse* (1993) (the internet), *One Missed Call* (2003) (cell phone voice messages), *The Lords of Salem* (2012) (radio) and *V/H/S* (2012) (Skype). Ultimately, *Evilspeak* and *976-EVIL* inform cultural discourse about Satanic Panic but then redirect the focus to anxiety about the impact of communication technologies on the family. As such, they are key texts to interrogate cultural assumptions about the susceptibility of youth to techno-devilry.

REFERENCES + BIBLIOGRAPHY:

Andrews, Edmund L. "F.C.C. Obtains Concessions On Children's '900' TV Ads," *The New York Times*, May 9, 1991.

Andrews, Edmund L. "F.C.C. Takes Steps to Combat Abuses on '900' Numbers," *The New York Times*, March 15, 1991.

Barry, John. "The Computer Nerd as Metaphor." *InfoWorld*, March 8, 1982.

Counts, Kyle. Review of Evilspeak, *Cinefantastique* 12.2/3 (April 1982).

David, Rob. Review of *Evilspeak*, *InfoWorld*, March 8, 1982.

Davies, David. *The Million Dollar Phone*. Montpelier, VT: Data Communications Group, 1991.

"Phone Companies Take Steps Against Dial-a-Porn Services," *The New York Times*, January 19, 1988.

Egan, Kate. *Trash or Treasure: Censorship and the Changing Meanings of the Video Nasties*. Manchester: Manchester University Press, 2007.

Foucault, Michel. *The History of Sexuality: An Introduction* (1976), trans. Robert Hurley. New York: Vintage, 1978.

Freiburg, Jeanne. "900 Numbers and the Desire for Response," *Studies in Popular Culture* 13.1 (1990).

Garsault, Alain. "Messe Noire," review of *Evilspeak*, *Positif 248* (November 1981).

Kendrick, James. *Hollywood Bloodshed: Violence in 1980s American Cinema*. Carbondale, IL: Southern Illinois University Press, 2009.

Kerekes, David and Slater, David. *See No Evil: Banned Films and Video Controversy*. Manchester: Headpress, 2000.

Kleinfield, N.R. "Business Dials 1-900-PROFITS," *The New York Times*, May 8, 1988,

Landis, Bill. Review of *Evilspeak*, *Soho Weekly News*, March 9, 1982.

Miller, Cyndee. "'Dial-a-Porn' Protests Spur Moves to 'Hold All Calls'". *Marketing News* 22.3 (1988).

Moore, Suzanne. "To Hell and Back," *New Statesman & Society*, December 16, 1988.

Polinien, Gilles. "Messe Noire," review of *Evilspeak*, *L'ecran Fantastique* 20 (1981).

Rosin, Hanna. "The Touch-Screen Generation," *The Atlantic* (April 2013).

Ross, Philippe. "Messe Noire," review of *Evilspeak*, *Revue Du Cinéma* 364 (1981).

Szebin, Frederick C. Review of 976-EVIL, *Cinefantastique* 18.4 (1988).

Thomas, Kevin. Review of 976-EVIL, *Los Angeles Times*, March 27, 1989.

Underwood, N. "Pulling the Plug," *Maclean's*, January 16, 1989.

ALL HAIL THE ACID KING:
THE RICKY KASSO CASE IN POPULAR CULTURE

BY LESLIE HATTON

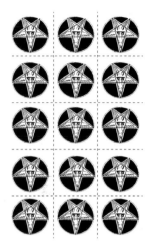

In the summer of 1984, there was something evil in the affluent community of Northport, Long Island.

Seventeen-year-old drug dealer and self-professed Satanist Ricky Kasso savagely murdered fellow teenager Gary Lauwers, stabbing him at least 32 times according to the coroner's report, including gouging out his eyes. Ricky was furious because Lauwers had stolen several hits of mescaline and hadn't paid him back. The two others present during the murder—James "Jimmy" Troiano and Albert Quinones—alleged that Kasso screamed at Lauwers to "say you love Satan," but the poor kid could only confess that he loved his mother before succumbing to his many injuries.

The absence of Lauwers' presence among the drugged-out burnouts in Northport barely caused a stir and his family never filed a missing persons report. It was like no one actually cared that much about Lauwers, despite stories that, over two weeks, Kasso himself had led at least a dozen teens into the woods to boast over the putrid corpse of his victim. On July 4, that most patriotic of days, it became clear that something was rotten in the state of America, or

Left: Image from Tommy Turner and David Wojnarowicz's
Where Evil Dwells (1985).

at least Suffolk County, New York. Nearly three weeks after the last time anyone could remember seeing him alive, an anonymous tip (from a teen who'd heard about Kasso's corpse tours) led police to Lauwers' shallow grave in the Aztakea Woods.

Before they could even confirm the facts of the case, the police issued a press release that included details immediately seized upon by a sensationalist media; words like "drugs," "ritual," "cult" and "Satanism" provided the

intended shock value. Meanwhile, Kasso confessed to the crime soon after his arrest and committed suicide in prison within 48 hours of being charged. Now there were two dead teenagers and a lot of wild speculations, and local residents were appalled.

What kind of terrible influences could lead a middle-class boy to do such a thing? Why, Northport was a suburban paradise! It offered gorgeous houses, manicured lawns and excellent schools: everything a kid could want. Drugs and heavy metal music were soon rounded up as potential suspects in this conspiracy, one where Satan was the criminal mastermind.

With Kasso dead, there were only two other living witnesses to the crime, teenagers Jimmy Troiano and Albert Quinones. Quinones quickly testified against Troiano to ensure his own immunity, while Troiano was charged with second-degree murder and gave no fewer than four different accounts to his defense attorney of what had actually taken place. The only thing that was clear about the whole sordid mess was that someone had to pay and that it was probably going to be the Devil. Or drugs. Or possibly heavy metal. Soon, the death of Gary Lauwers would become fodder for the likes of 20/20 and Geraldo Rivera, who aided and abetted the "Satanic Panic" hysteria that had captivated the imagination of the God-fearing public during the decade.

Top: Main Street, Northport, Long Island.
Above: Gary Lauwers' shallow grave in the Aztakea Woods.

While the question of "why" may never be completely or satisfactorily answered, one thing seems almost certain. Rather than the murder having been the result of the evil influence of popular culture, in the case of the "Acid King" Ricky Kasso, it was the other way around. Whether in music, movies or on TV, the actions of Ricky Kasso have been influencing popular culture for the last 30 years. With all that attention being paid to such a horrific crime, people are still asking why and still not getting any answers.

Despite a 2011 *NY Daily News* article claiming that the Lauwers murder resulted in "dozens of books, plays, movies and songs," the real number is probably far less. This is typical of the media hyperbole the incident has engendered over the years. Still, Ricky Kasso's status as a pop culture icon is not insignificant, and possibly the biggest output of Kasso-inspired pop culture was conjured by the news media itself. There were dozens of newspaper and magazine articles and a couple of high-profile television shows that covered, in whole or in part, the murder, the trial and the aftermath. Of course, a story about a teen killing another teen would cause consternation, if not abject terror, in the American (and global) public, especially in the pre-Columbine world of 1984.

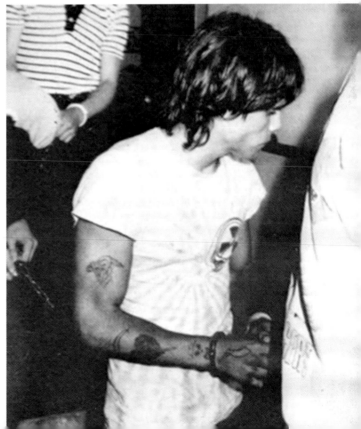

Top: Ricky Kasso.
Right: Jimmy Troiano.

Yet, it was the language in the initial press release from the Suffolk County Police Department that made things worse:

> 66 *Kasso… is a member of a satanical cult and worships and partakes in rituals honoring the devil… Kasso further indicated that on this last stabbing of the victim, he heard a crow cry out. This was an indication to him as a satin [sic] worshipper that the devil had ordered him to kill Lauwers.*

The press pounced on these lurid details the way Kasso pounced on Gary Lauwers in the Aztakea Woods. Even though Suffolk County Police Department media relations assistant William McKeown later produced a heavily edited (and spell-checked) version, it was never shared with the Northport Police and no one there, not even Suffolk County Police Chief Bob Howard, knew about it. Not that facts have ever gotten in the way of a good story.

In the summer of 1984, even those close to the case were blaming Satan. Detective Lieutenant Robert Dunn, head of the Suffolk County homicide division, was quoted in *Newsday*: "This was a sacrificial killing. It was pure Satanism." "We learned that he was very deeply involved in Satan along with a number of boys," said Ricky's father, Richard Kasso, Sr. in an *Associated Press* article from July 10. "He would go to the library and read about witchcraft, devil worship. He wore emblems, T-shirts, upside-down crosses. He wouldn't discuss it with us." More than one article associated Ricky with a local group of so-called Satanists called The Knights of the Black Circle, despite no evidence supporting the connection.

But by December 1984, Satan was out and drugs were in as the reason behind the killing. *The New York Times* asserted, "the prosecutor and defense lawyer preparing for the trial of the sole defendant, which is scheduled to begin January 8, now say the killing had nothing to do with a Satanic cult. Instead, they said, the killing grew out of a pervasive use of drugs and violence induced by hallucinogens." Still, Old Scratch wasn't going away without a fight, at least not in the mind of prosecutor William Keahon.

The New York Times reported Keahon's opening statement at Jimmy Troiano's murder trial on April 4, 1985:

> 66 *Mr. Keahon said the defendant and the friend, Richard Kasso, forced [Lauwers] to pledge his love to Satan. Mr. Troiano also participated in several other satanic rituals that preceded the killing, Mr. Keahon said in his 35-minute opening argument.*

Keahon's statement is included in David St. Clair's 1987 book *Say You Love Satan*, probably the most well-known document of the events leading up to Kasso's murder of Lauwers and the trial itself. In the preface, St. Clair states that he did "weeks of research in Northport and the surrounding towns... trying to understand."

The book hints strongly at parental neglect being a factor in the murder, but never actually comes to any conclusions. Any thought-provoking analysis that can be found within its 411 pages is overshadowed by ridiculous prose about drug use and heavy metal music and the notable absence of any citations, despite featuring quotes that are strikingly similar to those found in a *New York Times* article from April 1985. The book also includes at least one quote that appeared in David Breskin's *Rolling Stone* article "Kids in the Dark," which is more an oral history told by Kasso's peers than an indictment.

St. Clair places so much emphasis on the first time that Kasso supposedly smoked marijuana in 1977, it almost reads like that Season 4 episode of *Taxi* where Reverend Jim's bright Harvard future is destroyed when he ingests a pot brownie and immediately becomes a drug-addled degenerate. St. Clair: "The decision he made at that moment affected the rest of his life and the lives of everyone around him." His tone drips with condescension in the several discussions of the role that heavy metal music played in the lives of these kids. This isn't surprising given that both the *New York Post* and the *Long Islander* ran headlines indicting the genre. On July 7, Lieutenant Robert Dunn, who never met an incendiary sound bite he didn't like, was also quoted in an *Associated Press* article where he attributes the rise in Satanic rituals to their depiction in rock videos, saying, "Society ought to evaluate what goes onto our screens." St. Clair outright mocks these kids, including a sarcastic passage about Judas Priest, of whom Lauwers was a fan: "There's a lot of shit out there but the lyrics of Judas Priest are the truth, man. And when you're sixteen, the truth is where it's at." Both Kasso and Troiano were big fans of Ozzy Osbourne (the latter even had a crude OZZY tattoo on his arm), but St. Clair's liberal quotes from Osbourne's 1983 hit "Bark At The Moon" during the section of the book that describes Lauwers' murder are puzzling. As one online review of *Say You Love Satan* observes, "Sure they may have listened to *Bark at the Moon*, but [St. Clair] wrote as if Ricky swallowed acid and saw Ozzy pop out of the speakers and hand him a knife."

Before his description of the grisly murder, St. Clair notes, "There is great debate about what actually happened at this point." Considering that even Troiano and Quinones couldn't produce consistent, non-conflicting police statements (or in the case of the latter, sworn testimony), this is a significant understatement. St. Clair even delves into Kasso's own thoughts after the murder—a neat trick, since Kasso's statement was deemed inadmissible in court because he gave no interviews and killed himself soon after he was arrested. Even Lauwers is not spared from St. Clair's tawdry speculations when he discusses how Lauwers himself was into Satan worship, casting a new light on the term "victim blaming." St. Clair: "Had the murder not occurred, one wonders how long it would have taken Gary to exchange Satan for Jesus."

It's too bad St. Clair's distaste for drug use and heavy metal meant he didn't pay attention to some of the other discourse about Ricky Kasso that was taking place in film and music during the middle of that decade.

Writer, painter, filmmaker and AIDS activist David Wojnarowicz and filmmaker Tommy Turner are associated with the Cinema of Transgression, an underground film movement of the 1970s and '80s characterized by zero budgets, non-mainstream filmmakers and actors, and a distinctive aesthetic of violating taboos and boundaries. Together Wojnarowicz and Turner depicted the earliest cinematic incarnation of Kasso in *Where Evil Dwells* (1985). It was intended as a full-length film, but was never finished due to a lack of funds and an unfortunate fire that destroyed some of the reels. The only remaining evidence of *Where Evil Dwells* is a 30-minute trailer, but the original shooting script gives, in narrative form, a detailed interpretation of the events before, during and after the murder.

According to Jack Sargeant's book *Deathtripping*, Wojnarowicz and Turner (like St. Clair and Breskin) also traveled to Northport to interview "local teens" and perhaps also read Breskin's *Rolling Stone* article, because one scene of the script recreates a statement made by Lauwers' girlfriend Michelle DeVeau after her mother told her about the teen's death:

> I ran into my grandmother's kitchen, grabbed the biggest knife I could find and booked out into the backyard. And I just started hacking away at a tree, started freaking on a tree. That poor tree. One of these big oak trees. It's gonna die.

Top: David Wojnarowicz, image from the book *In the Shadow of the American Dream: The Diaries of David Wojnarowicz* (1999), edited by Amy Scholder.
Above: Tommy Turner in Richard Kern's *Submit to Me Now* (1987).

From Turner and Wojnarowicz' script:

> *Girl wigs out grabs huge carving knife out of silverware drawer and turns runs out of house over to tree in back yard and starts stabbing it like crazy. Stab stab stab.*

The script is characterized by an attention to detail that comes from a place of empathy or at least a genuine attempt at understanding, and stands in stark contrast to the way St. Clair smugly distances himself from his subjects. As Turner remarked in an interview, "I identified with [Kasso], in a way," though he also conceded that Kasso's "stupidity" lay in the fact that "he didn't try and escape and see that he could just leave that world and go into another world."

The remaining footage of *Where Evil Dwells*, assembled into a half-hour preview for the Downtown New York Film Festival in 1985, successfully generates an atmosphere of escalating horror: long-haired teens hang out in a parking lot smoking and drinking, then play pranks on highway drivers by dangling a dummy over an overpass. Someone digs up a decrepit corpse, a reference to when the real-life Kasso was arrested and charged with grave robbing. The scene where Kasso kills Lauwers is graphic and intercut with clips of a wounded bird in a forest and shaky cam, point-of-view footage of an old wooden rollercoaster, perhaps indicating a life out of control.

The soundtrack incorporates "0_0 (Where Evil Dwells)," a song from Wiseblood, a band comprised of JG Thirlwell (a.k.a. Clint Ruin) and The Swans' Roli Mosimann. Like Turner and Wojnaorwicz's film, the song title comes from a *NY Daily News* headline.

The song's lyrics arose from Thirlwell's "immersion" in tabloid scandals and, as he says, "it fit with the conceptual themes that were going into Wiseblood: sick, macho and violent, and married well with the brutal drum machine track" (the 0_0 came from the pattern on the drum machine they used). The song is loud, unhinged and grotesquely masculine, with Thirlwell mentioning Northport, mutilation and murder, and repeatedly growling the phrase, "Kasso killer, Long Live The New Flesh!" (33) The latter was the tag line for 1982's *Videodrome*, David Cronenberg's surreal trip into TV violence, VHS tapes and BDSM. Thirlwell adds: "I liked that line and had written it in a notebook. It seemed to engender the idea that Ricky Kasso was the figurehead of a movement."

Other artists were tackling the Ricky Kasso story in their own unique ways. According to the book *Confusion Is Next*, the Sonic Youth track "Satan Is Boring" was inspired by Kasso. Although it doesn't go into detail about the murder, the line "Satan flirts, I'm prepared" is a fitting description of someone dabbling in Satanism. Big Audio Dynamite, the band formed by influential DJ Don Letts and Mick Jones of The Clash in the 1980s, had the distinction of being mentioned by name and quoted in a newspaper article in 1987. Their song "Sudden Impact!" condemns the media for sensationalizing the case and the families for ignoring the drug problem: "Newspapers sell disaster and

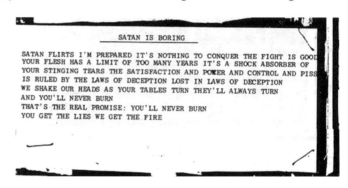

SATAN IS BORING

SATAN FLIRTS I'M PREPARED IT'S NOTHING TO CONQUER THE FIGHT IS GOOD
YOUR FLESH HAS A LIMIT OF TOO MANY YEARS IT'S A SHOCK ABSORBER OF
YOUR STINGING TEARS THE SATISFACTION AND POWER AND CONTROL AND PISS
IS RULED BY THE LAWS OF DECEPTION LOST IN LAWS OF DECEPTION
WE SHAKE OUR HEADS AS YOUR TABLES TURN THEY'LL ALWAYS TURN
AND YOU'LL NEVER BURN
THAT'S THE REAL PROMISE: YOU'LL NEVER BURN
YOU GET THE LIES WE GET THE FIRE

sin, and when the dust storm comes they say the devil rides in."

Not everyone in 1985 was as astute, however. Right after Troiano's acquittal, 20/20 aired a special called "The Devil Worshippers" which not only played up the Satanic angle that wouldn't die, but conflated real life and reel life. A voice-over intones over B-roll of a video rental store, "Each [store] offering seemingly harmless types of entertainment like movies... take a look at the number of movies that involve Satanism. Most were popular films in their day, but even today if one is inclined to believe in Satanism, it's a way to actually see the devil and perhaps be inspired." Kasso is also discussed briefly in Geraldo Rivera's inflammatory 1988 NBC special *Devil Worship: Exposing Satan's Underground*, but is secondary to Rivera's obsession with Satanic Ritual Abuse, a phenomena debunked by a series of FBI reports a few years later. Geraldo does, however, beam in Ozzy Osbourne for an interview about a separate incident and in a truly hilarious moment, quizzes him: "Do you feel a sense of responsibility, Oz?"

Although they may not have had the high-profile notoriety (or the big NBC budget) of Geraldo Rivera, there were those who had something meaningful to say about the Kasso/Lauwers story. One of the better representations came from a movie that was about a totally different murder. *River's Edge*, directed by Tim Hunter in 1986, was based on the 1981 murder of 14-year-old Marcy Conrad in Milpitas, California. Her body "had been dumped in the foothills outside town and remained unreported for two days while [Jacques] Broussard [who was convicted of the murder in 1982] brought his friends to see it, after bragging of the killing." There were other similarities in the movie, too, like the preponderance of heavy metal music and the cloud of drug abuse and disaffection that surrounds all the characters in the film, even the one who ends up reporting the crime to the police.

In his analysis of the film, Glenn F. Bunting, who covered the arrest and trial of Broussard beginning in 1981, touches on some of the issues that were also raised by the Kasso case, characterizing *River's Edge* as "the story of a group of stoned, comatose teenagers who saw their friend's murdered corpse" and describing the "dozens of reporters who swamped the... town to write about the shredded moral fiber of the post-Vietnam generation." Even Bunting's closing remark in his article reflects the same contemptuous tone of much of St. Clair's book, convicting the parents, but still calling rock music and drugs as witnesses for the prosecution:

> 66 *There's much to learn from Marcy Conrad's death—the combination of drugs, TV violence, deafening rock music, arcade games and, most of all, neglectful parents have anesthetized our children. It's too bad* River's Edge *missed the point.*

On the other hand, a 1987 play by *Rolling Stone* writer David Breskin and playwright Rick Cleveland was praised because it didn't try to force audiences to learn anything. Their collaboration, taken from Breskin's article and also titled *Kids in the Dark*, tells the story "almost completely in the words of the teens and young adults [Breskin]

interviewed" without going into "any deep psychological or sociological analyses" of them. Cleveland's empathy may have arisen from a personal connection; he admitted to being a former drug dealer as a teen saying, "when I read [Breskin's article] I tended to put myself in each one of the kids' shoes."

The Dead Milkmen's 1988 sardonic punk song "Bad Party" references Kasso for shock value and to take the piss out of pretentious, boring party guests. "Shut your mouth, get in the car, cause Ricky Kasso wants to drive" and "When we get there, we'll say we love Satan/Ricky always thinks that's funny." A more lyrically in-depth but sonically glam-rock take was found in Faster Pussycat's "Cryin' Shame" in 1989. Like "0_0 (Where Evil Dwells)" it mentions Northport, Lauwers' shallow grave and also name-checks the Aztakea Woods. The narrator is clearly disturbed by the events in question, especially the lack of reaction amongst the local teens: "Wake me when it's over and it's done/why can you see the poor boy bleed/does it make you numb?"

Nearly a decade after the murder had taken place, it was still being digested by popular culture. The Electric Hellfire Club's "Psychedelic Sacrifice" tells the tale of The Acid King who lives in Northport, Long Island, as well as the Knights of the Black Circle. Using a blend of dance music, techno and psychedelia, the song doesn't shy away from vivid descriptions of Lauwers "screaming for his mama/while Ricky tore out his eyes" and condemns the murder through mockery: "Say you love Satan/all the drugs you've taken/were a sacrament in his name."

In 1993, actor and director Jim Van Bebber wrote, directed and starred in the short film *My Sweet Satan* as a way to appeal to investors for his project *Charlie's Family* (eventually released as *The Manson Family* in 2003). *My Sweet Satan* loosely follows the trajectory of the St. Clair book, but opens with Ricky's jailhouse suicide, then cuts back to scenes of Ricky and his friends, and the murder itself, before revisiting Kasso's suicide and Troiano's response (here the character is "Jimmy Thompson"). Although updated contemporaneously, the film maintains a creepy, graphically realistic vibe, much like *Where Evil Dwells*, although Van Bebber had not seen Turner and Wojnarowicz's film at

Above: A still from David Breskin and Rick Cleveland's play *Kids in the Dark* (1987).
Top right: Terek Puckett, Mike Moore and Jim Van Bebber in *My Sweet Satan* (1994).
Bottom right: A behind-the-scenes photo from *My Sweet Satan*, © Asmodeus/Mercury Films.

the time. As "Ricky Kasslin," Van Bebber is shown to be volatile and violent as voice-overs from his peers call to mind the oral history format of Breskin's article. Drug use and metal music are prevalent, as is Kasslin's fascination with Satanism, but the film shares a punk credibility with brethren like *River's Edge* and *Where Evil Dwells*. In an early scene, Ricky is shown walking towards the camera, shirtless, tattooed and defiant, while behind him the screen is filled with a giant mural of an American flag on the side of a building; there can be no denying that this happened in America and could happen again. The murder scene is even more explicit than the one in *Where Evil Dwells* and, like that film, includes a point-of-view shot where the Kasso-inspired character appears to stab at the viewer's face. The film screened at the first New York Underground Film Festival and won best short.

Left: An original hand-made poster for *My Sweet Satan*, by Michael Capone.
Above: Jim Van Bebber as Ricky Kasslin. *My Sweet Satan* images © Asmodeus/Mercury Films.

Unfortunately, as time passed, the depictions of what happened in Northport in 1984 grew less and less believable, with little focus on the root causes and more exaggerated claims about the influence of Satan. 1997's *Black Circle Boys* fast-forwards the story to a post-Marilyn Manson world and is told from the point of view of "Kyle." Although "Shane" (the Kasso character) is into Satan, he's more into being in a band, even though he can't sing or play any instruments. Shane racks up a body count of three during the course of the movie and unlike the real Kasso, hides the bodies.

Peter Filardi (screenwriter of 1996 teenage witch film *The Craft*) directed *Ricky 6* in 2000. Even if one wasn't familiar with Vincent Kartheiser from TV's *Mad Men*, he seems an odd choice to play Kasso, and his character's decline from drug dabbler to full-blown, murderous psychotic takes only 18 months and not six years. Like *Black Circle Boys*, the film is also told from the point of view of Kasso's best friend, here named "Tommy." While neither film provides many insights into the "why" behind Kasso's homicidal activities, both do show the effect they have on his friends and peers and *Ricky 6* even presents a couple of dreamlike sequences that attempt to show what may have been going on in the real-life Kasso's mind.

Better to light a candle and curse your friends...

Following its initial festival run, beginning at the Fantasia Film Festival in Montreal, *Ricky 6* disappeared and remains unreleased to this day. While grotty fan uploads exist online, the only place any of its footage has appeared in any official form is in the documentary *Satan In The Suburbs* that aired on television later that same year, where it was used as "dramatization" footage to accompany new interviews. The documentary featured then-current interviews with not only Troiano, but also Troiano's

Above: Vincent Kartheiser as the title character in Peter Filardi's *Ricky 6* (2000), as captioned in *Fangoria* #197.
Right: Kartheiser during a fantastical LSD sequence in *Ricky 6*.

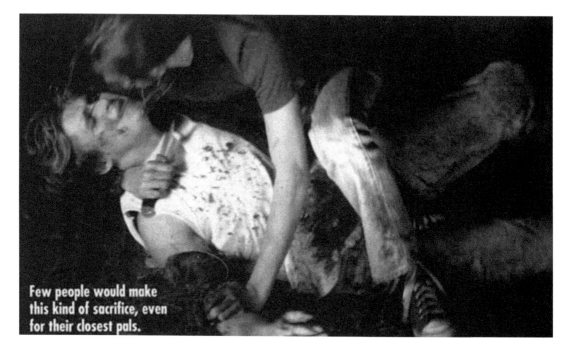

Few people would make this kind of sacrifice, even for their closest pals.

defense attorney Eric Naiburg, Prosecutor William Keahon, Chief Bob Howard and Lauwers's father Herbert, who still maintained that his son was "not involved in any drugs." It's the most even-handed of the non-fictional accounts of the events leading up to and including the murder, as well as its aftermath, covering the Satanic Panic that resulted but indicating—as Chief Howard notes on camera—that "Satan became Ricky's scapegoat" and a "satanic cult never existed." The doc also talks about heavy metal, rock videos and drugs, but never deems them culpable in the murder, although it does again strongly hint at parental neglect being a factor: "If the kids were getting into trouble, many parents weren't around to know about it."

A narrator reads parts of what may be Kasso's official police statement, probably the only document of the crime in any pop culture output that accurately represents Kasso's point of view. In a decidedly chilling moment when discussing Lauwers' murder, Troiano looks at the camera and says, "I knew exactly what was going on and I still, I didn't stop it," which gives one pause considering the defense strategy Naiburg utilized in 1985, that Troiano could never know what truly happened the night Lauwers was killed due to his heavy LSD use.

Although pop culture depictions of the story have been few and far between in the intervening years, there are a couple of more recent examples. The 2006 film *Under Surveillance* uses the events as the basis for a story about a Satanic cult, while Vancouver punk band Nü Sensae revealed in a 2010 interview that their song "Cat's Cradle" was inspired by the murder, as supported by the lyric, "I know a kid to kill." Other songs—Aesop Rock's "Catacomb Kids," Ill Bill's "Ricky Kasso" and "Severed

Above: Vincent Kartheiser (Ricky) and Patrick Renna (Gary - here named "Ollie") in *Ricky 6*, as captioned in *Fangoria* # 197.

Heads of State," Kent 3's "The Ballad of Ricky Kasso"—used Kasso's name but without furnishing much insight into the story.

One of the most perceptive comments about the Lauwers murder came from Reverend Graham Walworth, pastor with the Trinity Episcopal Church in Northport. In 1984 he argued that teenagers' purported belief in Satanism was just another "form of revolution, a rejection against the standards their parents represent," noting shrewdly "we give our young people everything that is essential except a meaning for life." Kids on the margins will often seek out unpopular culture as a way to find meaning in their own lives. It's highly unlikely that one joint, Ozzy Osbourne song or copy of *The Satanic Bible* could have set Kasso and Lauwers on a collision course towards Hell. There are millions of people who smoke pot, listen to Ozzy and/or read about Satanism and who don't become murderers. Unfortunately for Gary Lauwers and his family, Ricky Kasso was one who did.

Perhaps the most horrifying aspect of the murder wasn't the dubious role of Satanism, the drugs or the heavy metal, but the fact that Kasso left Lauwers' body in the woods for two weeks to rot, all the while bragging about it and bringing kids to see it, and that it took so long for anyone to do anything about it. Yet, out of all the pop culture interpretations, the only two that address this facet of the story are *Where Evil Dwells* and Faster Pussycat's "Cryin' Shame": "For weeks under the leaves/He just sat there dead."

It's as if the apathy of Kasso and his peers has been too difficult to deal with; the concept that there isn't anything to blame is too terrifying to accept. In the case of Kasso, the reasons why he rebelled against society and killed Lauwers will never truly be known because of the involuntary or willful ignorance of those who actually knew him. The many unanswered questions surrounding the case have certainly contributed to its lingering impact; ironically while the case itself was colored by apathy, no other case from the Satanic Panic era has inspired as many artistic explorations as that of "Acid King" Ricky Kasso.

In 2014, doom metal misanthropes Electric Wizard released *Time To Die*, an album that features samples from the segment of the *20/20* episode "The Devil Worshippers" that discusses the Kasso murder. When asked in an October 2014 interview if Kasso was the "personification of the Electric Wizard ethos," guitarist Liz Buckingham replied: "Yes. In a lot of ways. Drugs, woods, Satan, killing, metal... When I was a kid, that stuff happened right near where my family was living at the time. I remember reading about it in the newspaper in the back of my dad's car. That picture of Ricky in his AC/DC shirt, the whole Satanic Panic. I was totally obsessed and continued to be for many years."

Likewise, singer/songwriter Brendan Brown of Wheatus, who grew up in Northport, said in a 2011 interview, "the impact [the murder] had on my life and music is complete. I would have been a very different person had Ricky not sacrificed his classmate to the Devil, two blocks away from my house in 1984."

REFERENCES + BIBLIOGRAPHY:

Adams, Gregory, "The kids in Nü Sensae are not all right," *Straight.com*. June 16, 2010.

Aesop Rock, "Catacomb Kids." *None Shall Pass*. Definitive Jux, 2007.

Big Audio Dynamite, "Sudden Impact!" *This Is Big Audio Dynamite*. 1985, CBS Records.

Black Circle Boys. Dir. Michael Carnahan. 1997.

Bovsun, Mara. "Satan runs amok on L.I. as a teen confesses to grisly murder." *NY Daily News*. November 29, 2011.

Breskin, David. "Kids in the Dark," *Rolling Stone*. November 22, 1984.

Bunting, Glenn F. "'River's Edge' Not Quite As He Recalls." *Los Angeles Times*, July 4, 1987.

California Office of Criminal Justice Planning. *Occult Crime: A Law Enforcement Primer*. 1990.

Christiansen, Richard. "'Kids in the Dark' Turns A Chiller About Murder Into A Real Winner." *Chicago Tribune*, April 3, 1987.

Christiansen, Richard. "The Young Aliens: Dramatizing Teen Despair With No Holds Barred." *Chicago Tribune*, April 19, 1987.

"Coast Youth Who Boasted Of Killing Girl Is Sentenced," *The New York Times*. December 5, 1982.

Devil Worship: Exposing Satan's Underground. NBC/Universal Television Distribution, October 22, 1988.

Faster Pussycat, "Cryin' Shame." *Wake Me When It's Over*. Elektra Records, 1989.

"For Ricky Kasso, there was no 'light at the end of the tunnel'." *Lakeland Ledger*, July 15, 1984.

Gr8grendel, "Review of *Say You Love Satan*". *GoodReads.com*. http://www.goodreads.com/review/show/18656925?book_show_action=true&page=1.

Gruson, Lindsey. "L.I. Murder Trial Opens: Confession is Described." *The New York Times*. April 5, 1985.

Ill Bill, "Ricky Kasso." *Howie Made Me Do It 3*. Uncle Howie Records, 2013.

Ill Bill, "Severed Heads of State." *The Grimy Awards*. Fat Beats Records, 2013.

Kent 3, "The Ballad of Ricky Kasso." *Screaming Youth Fantastic*. Bag of Hammers, 1994.

Lanning, Kenneth V. "Satanic, Cult, Ritualistic Crime: A Law Enforcement Perspective". *Police Chief*, Volume 56, Issue 10. October 1989.

Lanning, Kenneth V. U.S. Dept. of Justice, Federal Bureau of Investigation, FBI Academy. *Investigator's Guide To Allegations of "Ritual" Child Abuse*. January 1992.

McFadden, Robert D. "Youth Found Hanged in L.I. Cell After His Arrest in Ritual Killing," *The New York Times*. July 8, 1984.

Moore, Nathaniel G. "Interview: Wheatus," *Verbicide Magazine*. January 27, 2011.

My Sweet Satan. Dir. Jim Van Bebber. Asmodeus, 1993.

Osborn, Sam. "The Robbed Innocence of The West Memphis Three," *Vice*, January 10, 2012.

Quittner, Joshua C. "Grisly Lauwers Murder Still Haunts Suburban Northport." *Schenectady Gazette*. May 1, 1987.

Ricky 6 (a.k.a. *Say You Love Satan*). Dir. Peter Filardi. Spice Factory, 2000.

River's Edge. Dir. Tim Hunter. Island, 1986.

Rosenbaum, Ron. "The Devil In Long Island." *The New York Times*, August 22, 1993.

Sargeant, Jack. *Deathtripping: The Extreme Underground*. Soft Skull Press, third revised edition, 2008.

Satan in the Suburbs. Dir. Scott Hillier. Image Group, 2000.

"Satan Is Boring Lyrics." Sonic Youth Information Database. Accessed May 26, 2015. http://www.sonicyouth.com/mustang/sy/song27.html.

"Satanic Ritual' is Now Ruled Out in June Slaying of Youth in L.I. Woods," *The New York Times*. December 27, 1984.

Sharbutt, Jay. "Cauldron Boils Over Geraldo's 'Devil Worship': 'Satan' Wins Ratings, Loses Advertisers." *Los Angeles Times*, October 27, 1988.

"Slayings Blamed on Devil Worship, Drugs," *The Lewiston Daily Sun*. July 10, 1984.

Sonic Youth, "Satan Is Boring." *Death Valley '69 12"*. Homestead, 1985.

St. Clair, David. *Say You Love Satan*. New York: Dell Publishing Company, Inc., 1987, 310, 312.

The Dead Milkmen, "Bad Party." *Beelzebubba*. Enigma Records, 1988.

"The Devil Worshipers." *20/20*. Disney-ABC Domestic Television. May 16, 1985.

The Electric Hellfire Club, "Psychedelic Sacrifice." *Burn, Baby, Burn!* Cleopatra Records, 1993.

"The Road Not Taken: Part 1" *Taxi*. Disney-ABC Domestic Television. April 29, 1982.

Thirlwell, JG. E-mail to author. July 2, and September 29, 2014.

"Trial Makes Young Visitors Uneasy," *The New York Times*. April 11, 1985.

"Two Held After Ritual Killing In Which Youth's Eyes Cut Out," *Ottawa Citizen*. July 7, 1984.

Under Surveillance. Dir. Dave Campfield. Fourth Horizon Cinema, 2006.

VanBebber, Jim. E-mail to author. September 17, 2014.

Wheatus, "Teenage Dirtbag." *The Lightning EP*. Montauk Mantis, 2000.

Where Evil Dwells. Dir. David Wojnarowicz and Tommy Turner. Deathtrip Films, 1985.

Wiseblood, "0_0 (Where Evil Dwells)." *Dirtdish*. K.22, 1987.

Newsweek

November 14, 1988 : $2.00

Trash TV

From the Lurid To the Loud, Anything Goes

Geraldo Rivera

"WHAT ABOUT THESE 10,000 SOULS, BUSTER?"
GERALDO'S DEVIL WORSHIP SPECIAL

BY ALISON LANG

Ozzy Osbourne looked baffled.

It was October 25, 1988, and the lead singer of Black Sabbath had been patched in via satellite to a television monitor within a seemingly endless wall of screens in an NBC studio. Clad in a black suit jacket with white polka dots, his hair delicately feathered, he'd been called in as one of a group of talking heads to weigh in on a very special prime-time spin-off of *The Geraldo Rivera Show* titled *Devil Worship: Exposing Satan's Underground*.

The program had just aired a segment exploring the case of Thomas Sullivan, a 14-year-old boy from New Jersey who had stabbed his mother to death with his Boy Scout knife and then slit his own throat. Sullivan had been fascinated with Satanism and in a grainy clip of TV footage, an image of his bedroom walls flashed by, plastered with posters of his heavy metal heroes—including what appeared to be a Black Sabbath poster.

Rivera began flitting around his guests for response. He first sidled up to Detective Paul Hart, the New Jersey policeman in charge of Sullivan's case. "You're not a theologian, you're a cop—do you think Tommy was possessed?" he asked.

"Possession is a state of mind," Hart replied, a little obliquely.

Rivera then turned to another guest—Rev. James Lebar of the New York Archdiocese —and asked whether, in the eyes of the Catholic Church, demonic possession was possible. "It certainly is," the Reverend said. "It's not only possible, but it is a reality."

Rivera then turned to Osbourne, a floating head in the monitors. "Every single kid...who committed a violent act in Satan's name was also into heavy metal music," he said. "What's your response to that, Oz?"

Osbourne crossed his legs and uncrossed them. "Well...I don't rightly know," he said. "All I do is make music. I don't sit down to purposely freak everybody out. When I was young and writing music, my world was dark and dingy...I came from a working class family, we had no dough, no prospects. And not all my songs are about Satan—"

Before the singer could continue, Rivera cut him off, leaping to an interview with Sean Sellers, a convicted murderer and self-proclaimed Satanist in Oklahoma whose crimes included murdering his mother and stepfather in their beds.

So began the broadcast that *The New York Times* would the next day dub an "obscene masquerade." The Osbourne exchange was typical of Rivera's leapfrogging between so-called experts, confused interviewees and real-life criminals and victims.

The show opens with a montage of various clips visited throughout the program, scored to Motley Crue's goofy paean to an evil sex kitten, "Looks That Kill"; shots of metalheads headbanging at a concert, a self-proclaimed "breeder" of babies for Satanic sacrifice, a shot from one of Anton LaVey's rituals, amateurish pentagrams and 666's scrawled across gravestones, and footage of actual crime scenes paraded garishly across the screen. The montage then cuts to a clawed monster hand rising within a swirl of dry ice and Charles Manson dancing a jig.

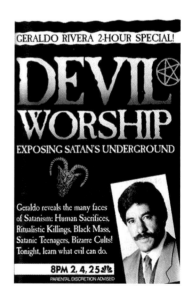

GERALDO RIVERA 2-HOUR SPECIAL!

DEVIL WORSHIP

EXPOSING SATAN'S UNDERGROUND

Geraldo reveals the many faces of Satanism: Human Sacrifices, Ritualistic Killings, Black Mass, Satanic Teenagers, Bizarre Cults! Tonight, learn what evil can do.

8PM 2, 4, 25

PARENTAL DISCRETION ADVISED

Top: Geraldo Rivera with Ozzy Osbourne and Sean Sellers onscreen behind him.
Middle: A rather uncomfortable Ozzy Osbourne.
Bottom: An advertisement for Geraldo's *Devil Worship* Special.

This is only a sampling of the dizzying array of ideas, individuals and events that Rivera gathered under the umbrella of Satanism in order to "prove" his central idea: Satan lives in America, and he's coming to ensnare your kids in his cloven hooves. "The operating thesis (of the special) was that (Charles) Manson was not alone," Rivera wrote in his 1991 autobiography *Exposing Myself*. "From kids who dabble in satanic rituals to heavy metal devotees who self-mutilate, to cults that kill, devil worship is a reality involving tens of thousands of Americans in wildly varying degrees."

Today, the special (which you can watch in full online) comes across as tabloid TV trash at its cheesiest and most exploitative. It's a relic from a bygone era; its hysteria is both deeply hilarious and troubling in its amped-up ignorance. It was also the highest-rated two-hour special NBC had ever aired, reaching nearly 20 million households that evening. The program effectively stoked the embers of the Satanic Panic, leading to copycat features on other talk shows such as *Sally Jessy Raphael* and *The Oprah Winfrey Show*. Ultimately, *Devil Worship: Exposing Satan's Underground* is an example of tabloid TV at its crappiest and most effective: it got its point across by muting and tokenizing certain voices while amplifying others to a shrill fever pitch.

1988 marked the continuation of a major transitional period in Geraldo Rivera's career. Two years earlier, his eight-year tenure as a respected, if controversial reporter for *20/20* had come to an end. Broke and disillusioned, Rivera went against the advice of his agent and took a $50,000 gig with Tribune Broadcasting to host a syndicated, one-time only live broadcast called *The Mystery of Al Capone's Vaults*. The two-hour special featured Rivera plowing through the rubble of the vault, located beneath the Lexington Hotel in Chicago, offering a

blustery play-by-play of what the team might find. Famously, it was empty (save for a few broken bottles that Rivera speculated might have been used for bathtub gin.) In *Exposing Myself*, Rivera recalls his immediate feeling that the special was a "colossal failure." He retreated that evening to a hotel room with a bottle of tequila.

The show ended up a ratings smash, reaching over 30 million American households. Rivera was offered a daytime talk show and a gig as a regular contributor to *Entertainment Tonight*. Along with Morton Downey Jr., Rivera helped to usher in a new kind of daytime talk show known as "confrontainment": loud, bombastic and occasionally exploitative. This tone extended to the ongoing *Geraldo Rivera* specials, which were slowly becoming ratings leaders in their evening timeslots.

Above: Geraldo Rivera in *The Mystery of Al Capone's Vaults* Special, 1986.

As part of Rivera's fifth prime time special, *Murder: Live from Death Row*, he nabbed an exclusive interview with Charles Manson. As described by Rivera, "that weird little man with the unforgettable Satanic gleam in his eye" agreed to the interview because of the popularity of Rivera's show amongst San Quentin inmates; he himself was a regular viewer. The interview with Manson did little to discourage the show's tonal histrionics, and didn't bring any new insights to the table. Still, it was nonetheless compelling enough to commandeer the attention of viewers in over one million households. It opened a gateway to a week's worth of Geraldo programming, and provided a lurid new topic to explore on a two-hour special, scheduled for Halloween night: Satanism.

The segments were selected and the roster of guests was chosen. Lt. Colonel Michael Aquino was then the High Priest of the Temple of Set, an offshoot sect from the Church of Satan, as well as a colonel in the U.S. Army. He vividly recalls being contacted by Rivera's producers to appear on the program, namely because it wasn't an invitation as much as a threat. In 1987, Aquino and his wife Lilith had been accused of sexually abusing the daughter of an army chaplain named Larry Adams-Thompson as part of the Satanic Ritual Abuse frenzy that swept the army. Even though the Aquinos were 3000 miles away in Washington at the time of the alleged abuse, they endured a search warrant and a sweep of their home by police. Gradually, it was determined that the accusations were unsubstantiated, and all charges were dropped. Then the Rivera show producers called.

"They said, 'If you are on this panel, you can talk about this situation yourself—if you are not there, other people are certainly going to talk about you, and you won't be able to refute anything," Aquino says. "There was a definite current of hostility—an ominousness—if I didn't come. It seemed to be a little bit of media blackmail."

Meanwhile, the show had managed to line up a member of the Church of Satan: Anton LaVey's daughter, Zeena Schreck (nee LaVey).

Schreck was named the Church's official spokesperson in 1985 at the age of 21 after her father began his retreat from public life. She found herself defending an already-controversial (and waning) religious movement on live television with very little support from her parents or the Church itself. It was a role she was told would be temporary; it ended up lasting five years. She recalls her first national syndicated TV appearance on

Above: Geraldo Rivera in a publicity shot for Devil Worship: Exposing Satan's Underground (1988).

The Phil Donahue Show in 1986, where she was the sole female on an all-male panel. "I was a kid," she says. "That really made people sit up and take notice. They sat up primarily for how strange it appeared – here's three very aggressive and stern supposed experts on occultism and crime against this one very young girl. It was like bullying. But Donahue was pretty fair. He was balanced in his approach." By 1988, she had logged a number of appearances on local and national television, and reluctantly agreed to appear on "Devil Worship." There was added pressure, too: Geraldo's producers said they had footage of her speaking at a Satanic rally, and Schreck feared it would be used out of context.

"I was a little bit leery about doing it," she admits. "I was feeling the impossibility factor of these interviews—that I was up against a lot of things. It seemed impossible to get through to people on a logical level. At the same time, I thought (if I showed up) that at least I'll have a fighting chance to say something."

Along with Aquino, Reverend James LeBar and former FBI agent turned cult investigator Ted Gunderson, Schreck was seated on a dais facing the audience in a studio. Other guests—including more occult experts, parents, cops and others—were also planted throughout the audience, so Geraldo could beeline to them for a quick response.

All the *Geraldo* specials are characterized by their host's unique style—what author Jane Shattuc calls "intimacy with swagger." Rivera goes from folksy buddy to hard-nosed, grilling newsman to empathetic and paternal, sometimes within single segments. In the *Devil Worship* special, all these personas become amplified to a comical effect.

Above: The *Devil Worship* panelists. From left: Zeena Schreck, Michael A. Aquino, Reverend James LeBar and Ted Gunderson. Image © Zeena Schreck.

Some examples of this:

- The grilling of convicted murderer Charles Gervais, patched in from a Louisiana prison. While Gervais told the court he and Michael Phillips murdered Andre Daigle simply to prove they could, Rivera seems fixated on the idea that Gervais, an occult dabbler, had committed the murder to acquire 10,000 souls. "Did you really think they were going to give you 10,000 souls—this Devil?" he barks, as an anxious-looking Gervais stumbles through his replies. "Get to the point about Satanism, Charlie. Listen, what about these 10,000 souls, buster?"

- Counting down the names of serial killers as if they were football players or pro wrestlers: "Berkowitz! Lucas! Ramirez and Manson!... are the all-stars in the halls of infamy!"

- In a segment on lesser-known Satanic crimes, the camera zooms in on the business card of Kansas serial killer Bob Berdella. "His business card seemed straight from hell!"

- Midway through the segment on Satanic Ritual Abuse and the McMartin pre-school trial: "Now, incest is certainly not new. But more and more of it is taking on the dark overtones of Satan."

Within the silliness, there are crasser moments. The broadcast also marked the opening date of the trial of Joel Steinberg, a criminal lawyer accused of murdering a six-year-old girl named Lisa he adopted with his partner Hedda Nussbaum. The defense, in their opening statement, declared that Nussbaum had an interest in Satanism. Rivera pulled Maury Terry—author of *Untamed Evil*, a book that claimed the Manson, Zodiac and Son of Sam murders could be attributed to a global Satanic network—from the audience. Terry holds up a book that he claims is Nussbaum's diary, saying there was evidence that Nussbaum attempted to call cult deprogrammers. The program then shows a drawing allegedly done by Lisa that, according to Terry, depicts the child wearing a robe for Satanic rituals. This is perhaps the most unsavory moment in a program that thrives on them: the attribution of Satanism to an already sensational case characterized by neglect and child/partner abuse feels exceptionally lurid.

For the panelists, the rapid-fire nature of the program was deeply frustrating. "We expected we'd have more time to say things, give opinions and impressions, and were limited to quick sound bites," Aquino says. "It wasn't a panel as much as a bunch of talking heads, saying a few quick answers here and there."

During Rivera's grilling, Aquino responds calmly, explaining that Satanism was founded by agnostics and atheists, not bloodthirsty sex freaks, and that *The Satanic Bible* was largely considered a polemic—not to be taken literally. He points out that many of the individuals portrayed in the special were lapsed Christians. "By our own standards, the people you've shown in these clips would not be Satanists," he says. "Rather, they would be failures of a conventional religion."

During one commercial break, Rivera sidled up to Aquino.

"He said, 'Try to limit your sentences to words not more than two syllables—we're dealing with an audience with the mental capacity of 13-year-olds here, and they won't be able to understand you if you start getting philosophical,'" he recalls. "I said, "'Well, okay, Geraldo!'"

"He truly had contempt for his audience," Schreck says.

Schreck herself wasn't given Aquino's level of airtime. She realized—too late—that she was a silent player in the circus. "I could hardly say anything," she recalls. "It was mind boggling. There would be these long periods of just obscene descriptions of things that—to me —appeared like mentally ill people being given a platform to describe their fantasies of Satanic abuse. It was like pornography. After these long periods of sitting and waiting, Geraldo would swing over to me and say 'Zeena, what do you have

to say about that?' and I was totally stunned. I thought 'What the hell? This is insane.'"

In the 1997 book *The Talking Cure: TV Talk Shows and Women*, author Jane M. Shattuc discusses the essential tension that exists within "confrontainment" talk shows like those hosted by Rivera. "The topics of the shows play on the bogey of the loss of social order and on the need for authority as much as they titillate through the possibility of transgression," she writes.

Through this lens, individuals like Schreck, Aquino and Ozzy Osbourne were merely dominos within the landscape of the Satanism special—set up to be knocked down. The beautiful young female Satanist, the vampirish Aquino with his forked eyebrows and the teased, tousled heavy metal icon didn't need to speak. They were the evil

Top: Zeena Schreck and Michael A. Aquino.
Above: Zeena Schreck. Images © Zeena Schreck.

placeholders within the puzzle, counterbalanced with the solid, soothing presence of white, square, comforting and largely male authority figures—cops, detectives, authors and priests—along with women who represented mothers and victims.

"I felt at the very beginning that the media was kind of glomming onto the idea of boogeymen Satanists—it was a very easy, catch-all, vague, amorphous thing that they didn't even really believe existed," Schreck says. Within Geraldo's Satanism special, it's possible to see the cartoonish interplay of good and evil forces at work at their most simplistic level, which is, one suspects, exactly what the producers intended. Take the show's Haitian "voodoo" segment as an example. About half an hour into the special, Rivera cuts to a pre-taped segment filmed in Brooklyn, New York. The camera lingers over a dark dingy room lit with candles, where a sober Rivera voice-over mentions that in some religions, exorcism is real. The camera zooms into the back room of what Rivera calls a "curio shop," where a group of black people are dancing, shaking noisemakers and, in one man's case, swigging from a bottle. Rivera explains we're watching a voodoo priest who regularly performs exorcisms. Cut back to the dark room, where Rivera comments on the "throbbing traditional music." The priest holds a live chicken aloft, and women of various ages form a circle, but it's otherwise very difficult to tell what's going on. "The priest's incantations build to a crescendo," the voiceover continues. "Then, in a moment of almost sexual release, the devil was purged from the patient!" We glimpse a pile of white feathers poking from a bucket— herein lies the chicken, presumably slaughtered.

The segment uses the sexualized language and sense of menace so commonly ascribed to African-American music and physicality while depicting a murky, unexplained religious practice and a decontextualized, highly stereotypical depiction of Haitian culture. While it's arguable that other people Rivera consulted for the special were depicted with a similar lack of context, most were allowed to speak for themselves via some sort of representative. This Haitian segment stands alone as the vague "black mysticism" segment of the show, and then we're spirited away to another volley of clips, sequences and accusations, mostly from concerned white folks.

Above: *Bring Me the Head of Geraldo Rivera*, an album by Radio Werewolf, a music/ performance collective featuring Zeena and Nikolas Schreck. Image © Zeena Schreck.

By the end of the broadcast, Schreck was furious. Her attempt at making one final comment—during the closing monologue, a big no-no—led to her mic being shut off.

"Even now, talking about it, I feel my chest tightening up," she says. "He's wrapping it up, and he hasn't let me say anything. Why the hell did they even ask me to come? Why'd they invite me? I'm sitting over here at the end, like I'm the caged animal, there she is, the vicious beast. This is the thing we're supposed to be scared of. This is what Satanists look like, down here on the end. He only wanted me as a visual. As far as he was concerned, I was just a bimbo."

"This was pure entertainment, no analysis, no documentary," Aquino says. "It was very annoying to all of us on the panel, to be used that way. When the Satanic Ritual Abuse stuff exploded in the '80s, the Temple of Set—our serious metaphysical religion—became viewed like Al Quaeda. I spent most of that decade trying to defend (the religion) in two syllables or less. When you're serious about your religion, you can't turn it into a comic book story."

When asked if she'd do the special over again, Schreck pauses. "You know—no, because it wasn't fun," she says. "But I don't regret it. A lot of people look back at the '80s and say wasn't that exciting, wasn't that interesting, how edgy things were, they look back with nostalgia, and I don't have that warm cozy nostalgic feeling looking back at my youth at all. I had emotional breakdowns, I was extremely depressed after leaving the country, and had to quickly pull myself together, not just because of the media. Still, I think if you have strength of character, you can use that as fuel to not only be a survivor but to transcend simply being a survivor, use an internal alchemy to turn something rotten and horrible into gold."

Above: Zeena Schreck's original receipt for the hotel room provided by *The Geraldo Rivera Show*. Image © Zeena Schreck.

Zeena Schreck *is a Berlin-based interdisciplinary artist, writer, animal rights activist and initiated Tibetan Buddhist yogini. In 1990 she resigned from the Church of Satan and renounced all forms of satanism. She teaches traditional tantric Buddhism at the Buddhistische Gesellschaft Berlin and is founder and spiritual leader of the Sethian Liberation Movement, within which she teaches Vajrayana Buddhism, Shaktism and authentic Gnostic Sethian theurgy. www.zeena.eu / www.zeenaschreck.com*

Lt. Colonel Michael Aquino *is the former High Priest of the Temple of Set. He has published a number of books, including* The Temple of Set I, The Temple of Set II, MindWar, *and* Extreme Prejudice: The Presidio Satanic Abuse Scam.

REFERENCES + BIBLIOGRAPHY:

Aquino, Michael A. *Extreme Prejudice: The Presidio 'Satanic Abuse' Scam*. Createspace, 2014.
Aquino, Michael A. Phone interview by author. October 14, 2014.
Devil Worship: Exposing Satan's Underground. NBC/Universal Television Distribution, October 22, 1988.
Marguiles, Lee. "Geraldo Rivera's 'Murder' Special Tops TV Ratings." *Los Angeles Times*, April 15, 1988.
Rivera, Geraldo, and Paisner, Daniel. *Exposing Myself*. New York: Bantam, 1991.
Schreck, Zeena. Skype interview by author. October 15, 2014.
Sharbutt, Jay. "Cauldron Boils Over Geraldo's 'Devil Worship': 'Satan' Wins Ratings, Loses Advertisers." *Los Angeles Times*, October 27, 1988.
Shattuc, Jane M. *The Talking Cure: TV Talk Shows and Women*. New York: Routledge, 1997.
"Topics of the Times; NBC's Obscene Masquerade." *The New York Times*, October 28, 1998.
State v. Gervais, 546 So.2d 215, Court of Appeal of Louisiana, Fourth Circuit, June 8, 1989.

THE FILTHY 15:
WHEN VENOM AND KING DIAMOND MET THE WASHINGTON WIVES

BY LIISA LADOUCEUR

There are a few reasons why the 1985 song "Possessed" by British metal band Venom could be considered objectionable. Seasoned fans of the group, whose raw, lo-fi sound, outrageously blasphemous songs and over-the-top image helped spawn the extreme subgenre known as Black Metal, may have thought the title track of their fourth album to be disappointing—shoddily produced, self-indulgent, lacking menace. Parents of those fans may have taken issue with lyrics such as, "We drink the vomit of the priests/Make love with the dying whore"— if they could make them out through the noisy racket. And those metal enthusiasts who had already abandoned Venom for the newer, heavier sounds of Slayer and the like, might have found the song—like the band—to be little more than a joke that was no longer funny.

Regardless of the song's merits (which in retrospect are many) there was certainly no sane reason for "Possessed" to have ever been made a matter before the U.S. Senate. Except that 1985 was not a sane year in America. It was the year a rich and powerful politician's wife went on a crusade against the evils of rock 'n' roll. It was the year ABC aired the

Left: Publicity shot of King Diamond.

20/20 TV special "The Devil Worshippers," igniting a national hysteria about anything related to the occult. Even still, "Possessed"—which was released on an independent record label in England and with limited profile outside of the metal underground—was placed on a list of "Filthy 15" songs used as evidence in a Senate committee hearing on "porn rock." It remains one of the most bizarre moments in the history of music censorship, one that that serves to highlight how easily a confluence of special interest groups can create moral panic out of nothing, and how heavy metal's flirtation with the devil can sometimes come back to haunt it.

Conservative religious types raging against rock for being the devil's music was not new to the 1980s. They said it about Elvis in the '50s and the Beatles in the '60s. In 1971, former DJ turned evangelist Bob Larson wrote in his book *Rock & The Church* that:

> **❝** *The latest and most disturbing scene in the blasphemy of rock is called "Satan Rock," performed by such groups as The Damnation of Adam Blessing, Coven and Black Sabbath… Many hippie communities now practice occultism to the accompaniment of their own special rock musical liturgy.*

But, barring the odd publicity-generating protests by religious leaders or radio censorship, even widely popular groups (such as Led Zeppelin, The Rolling Stones) who dabbled in overtly occult themes generally came out unscathed.

By the time heavy metal proper had found its way into the Sony Walkmans of millions of American teens, the country was in the grips of what is often dubbed the "culture wars," but was no less than spiritual warfare. Highly organized, politically connected and well-funded evangelical groups were pitted against a secular entertainment industry they claimed was out to destroy the fabric of their nation, their families, their children's very souls. They didn't like sex, they didn't like drugs, they didn't like swearing and they most certainly didn't like alternative religions. Their most pointed attacks accused artists and labels of brainwashing young people, through subliminal messages, into worshipping that biggest of bogeymen, the Devil himself.

A frightened public had already been convinced by sensationalist journalism and tabloid TV that what they saw in *Rosemary's Baby* was really happening, and thus accepted the challenge to "Save! The! Children!" from murderous baby breeders lurking in backwards-masked lyrics, spandex pants and studded wristbands. It seems silly now, but in the era when reporter Connie Chung could go on the nightly news and say AC/DC stands for "Anti-Christ Devil Child" with a straight face, it's no wonder that what Frank Zappa called an "ill-conceived housewife hobby project" to protect kids from metal was taken so seriously.

Mary Elizabeth Gore (née Aitcheson and better known by her nickname Tipper), was a photographer at a newspaper with a masters degree in psychology. In the '80s, she was also married to Al Gore—future Vice President of the United States, but then a Congressman from Tennessee. The Gores lived in Washington, and had four children.

According to Al, it was their oldest daughter who tipped off Tipper to the shocking state of modern music:

> 66 We had been letting them watch MTV and buy and listen to any music they wanted. One day when Karenna was 11, she bought an album that had some explicit lyrics on it, and then she and her girlfriend asked Tipper about several of the words. A short while later, our two younger girls, then six and eight, asked Tipper to watch a video on MTV that featured strippers and women in chains. That's how Tipper discovered that "good old rock 'n' roll"... had ratcheted up the quotient of explicit sex and sexual violence and that it was being marketed directly to kids.

The record was *Purple Rain*, by Prince. The song was "Darling Nikki." The offensive words, presumably, included "sex fiend" and "masturbating."

Not long after, in April 1985, Tipper Gore called a meeting at St. Columba's Church in Washington, D.C. The subject was "porn rock." Her hope, she wrote in her 1987 book *Raising PG Kids in an X-Rated Society*, "was to generate a discussion of the issue, raise public awareness, and begin a dialogue with people in the industry." One of the speakers that night was Jeff Ling, a musician and youth minister, who gave a slide presentation "graphically illustrating the worst excesses in rock music, from lyrics to concerts to rock magazines" that were targeting children. More than 350 people showed up. Amongst them were several of Tipper's friends, who just happened to be a who's who of powerful socialites, including Susan Baker (wife of then-Treasury Secretary James Baker), Sally Nevius (wife of Washington city council member John Nevius) and Ethelann Stuckey (wife of former Georgia congressman Williamson Stuckey). Together, 20 of these "Washington Wives" formed a non-profit organization they called Parents Music Resource Center—the PMRC.

Tipper Gore was not amused by W.A.S.P.'s latest offering.   12/19/85 R/S

An antiratings group called the Musical Majority was formed; among its members were **Cyndi Lauper**, **Don Henley**, **Prince**, **Lionel Richie**, the **Pointer Sisters** and **John Cougar Mellencamp**.

Several recording stars appeared before the Senate committee, providing some of the best Washington television since the Watergate hearings. **Frank Zappa** logically, and wittily, debated the meaning of our First Amendment rights, while **Dee Snider** showed America that metal has some brains, after all.

Unfortunately silent amid the brouhaha were most of the fans, the kids who stand to lose the most if these moves toward de facto censorship succeed.

161

Immediately, the PMRC called on the recording industry to warn parents when an album contained explicit content "contributing to the delinquency of minors." They wanted a rating system similar to the one for movies, with labels and lyrics printed on the outside packaging. Surprisingly, mainstream media took up their case—a *Washington Post* editorial applauded the wives for fighting "filth, violence, sado-masochism and explicit sex." The Recording Industry Association of America (RIAA) disagreed, and while the PMRC and the RIAA bickered about the issue via letters, the Senate Committee on Commerce, Science and Transportation (which counted Al Gore as a member) announced it would hold a hearing on record labeling.

At this point, Satan seemed an afterthought to the issue of so-called "Porn rock." But as the PMRC prepared for the Senate hearings, staff started collecting examples of offensive lyrics—and they found plenty to be offended by in heavy metal. They zeroed in on 15 songs in particular, which they dubbed "The Filthy 15." Each one had a designation: X for explicit sexual references, D/A for drugs and alcohol, V for violence—and O for occult. Nine of the 15 artists were heavy metal.

Readers with even a passing knowledge of '80s music will find the list confounding. Not because Top 40 pop singer Cyndi Lauper is on there ("Shebop" is about female masturbation, after all, which remains a taboo subject even today). What's bizarre is that the PMRC somehow chose AC/DC, Black Sabbath and Mötley Crüe and didn't label them with an O. AC/DC, whose biggest hits at the time included "Highway to Hell" and "Hells Bells" and were front page news that summer because serial killer Richard "Nightstalker" Ramirez

The Filthy Fifteen

ARTIST	SONG	RATING*
JUDAS PRIEST	"Eat Me Alive"	X
MÖTLEY CRÜE	"Bastard"	V
PRINCE	"Darling Nikki"	X
SHEENA EASTON	"Sugar Walls"	X
W.A.S.P.	"(Animal) Fuck Like a Beast"	X
MERCYFUL FATE	"Into the Coven"	O
VANITY	"Strap On Robby Baby"	X
DEF LEPPARD	"High 'n' Dry"	D/A
TWISTED SISTER	"We're Not Gonna Take It"	V
MADONNA	"Dress You Up"	X
CYNDI LAUPER	"She Bop"	X
AC/DC	"Let Me Put My Love into You"	X
BLACK SABBATH	"Trashed"	D/A
MARY JANE GIRLS	"My House"	X
VENOM	"Possessed"	O

*(Proposed) X = Profane or sexually explicit O = Occult D/A = Drugs or alcohol V = Violent

was apparently a fan, were included instead for explicit sex. Black Sabbath, who pretty much created the occult heavy metal template, were picked for drug and alcohol references. And the PMRC found the most offensive thing on Mötley Crüe's album *Shout at the Devil*—which had an inverted pentagram for cover art, liner notes warning "this record may contain backward masking" and a title track that had millions of kids raising their fists in a devil salute, was using the bad word "bastard"?

Compared to those chart-topping, internationally known groups, the lone examples of the horrors of Satanic music on the Filthy 15 were relatively obscure. How the hell did Venom and Mercyful Fate land on the PRMC's hit list? Neither Gore nor any representative has ever explained the process of whittling down the apparent ocean of offensive material to these 15 particular tracks—the list appears to have been completely arbitrary. But one can imagine staff thumbing through articles on these bands in issues of magazines like *Kerrang!* or *Metal Forces* and coming across Satanic references so blatant they'd be hard to ignore.

Venom was formed in 1979 in Newcastle-upon-Tyne, a former coal mining town in the far North East of England famous for its football team and its ale. In the beginning there were three members, each with a stage name torn from Anton LaVey's Satanic Bible: bassist/vocalist Cronos (Conrad Lant), drummer Abaddon (Anthony Bray) and guitarist Mantas (Jeffrey Dunn). As Cronos explains,

> **❝** *I thought it would be lame to be singing about Satan and demons and all the dark forces, and then for me to say, "Hello Jeffrey and Anthony!"… That was always my problem with Ozzy. He'd sing about dark figures then spoilt it all by going, "Oh God, help me!" Wrong! That was stopping one step short of where I wanted to take this band. We were prepared to go beyond the Hammer Horror of Black Sabbath.*

Venom wasted no time in realizing that intent: the first single was called "In League with Satan," which would also appear on their debut full-length, 1981's *Welcome to Hell*. The album cover was black, emblazoned with a goat's face in an inverted pentagram—the Goat of Mendes—a Satanic symbol that would soon become the band's trademark. Inside, things were no less subtle: the word "Hell" appears more than 35 times. The sound was a mix of punk rock and speed thrash, delivered in the most crude way possible (due in part to the fact the tracks were initially recorded as mere demos), with vocals ranging from whisper to scream to full-on Regan MacNeil.

The band's follow-up, 1982's influential *Black Metal*, was equally packed with references to Hell, Satan, Lucifer, Baphomet, and the Devil, as was 1983's concept album *At War With Satan*. In case it wasn't obvious from their bondage leather attire and theatrical postures (or ludicrous tracks like "Aaaaaarrghh"), the approach was all so over-the-top that clearly Venom were taking the piss. Or, as metal biographer Ian Christe put it, practicing "mock devil worship [that] merely expressed the desire to smash societal restraints and carve a space for unfettered fun." The women of the PMRC however (who may have been exposed to Venom through its 1984 concert video, *Seven Dates of Hell*) weren't exactly known for their sense of humour.

Copenhagen-based band Mercyful Fate took Satan much more seriously—or at least its lead singer did. King Diamond (birth name: Kim Bendix Petersen) had long been interested in horror but started seriously investigating the occult after experiencing a glass levitating while in the studio working on the band's first demo. Like the members of Venom, he came across Anton LaVey's *The Satanic Bible*. Unlike many influenced by LaVey's book, he actually subscribed to the philosophies of the Church of Satan, and became a card-carrying member who spent time with LaVey himself, saying "If you look at Black Sabbath, they were interested in the occult but they were never Satanists. They were like standing on a hill looking over, while I was in the middle of it."

The first Mercyful Fate record, a self-titled EP released in 1982, was inspired by horrors fictional, historical and biblical, featuring the songs "A Corpse Without Soul," "Nuns Have No Fun," "Doomed by the Living Dead" and "Devil Eyes." The cover illustration showed a nearly naked nun, crucified and about to be lit on fire by ominous men in robes. As the band gained popularity in Denmark, a local priest took issue with their imagery and tried to get them banned from radio. King Diamond, debating him on the radio, responded simply, "This is a drawing of the religion you stand for. They did this for real to millions of people!"

With its first proper record, 1983's *Melissa* (featuring Filthy 15 song "Into the Coven"), Mercyful Fate crossed over internationally, where King Diamond became the black-and-white-painted face of Satanic metal. Alongside his spectacular falsetto vocals and a mic stand constructed from real human bones, King's Satanism became Mercyful Fate's distinguishing characteristic both inside and outside the metal community.

MRS GORE   MRS BAK

Despite their relative low-profiles in the mainstream music world, both Venom and King Diamond certainly earned their spot on a list of occult music. And on the morning of September 19, 1985, as the Senate committee hearing on record labeling convened, they both became cemented in American political history. The hearing was videotaped, and it's fun now to watch it, especially to see musicians Frank Zappa (in a suit) and Dee Snider of Twisted Sister (the only artist from the Filthy 15 list to appear), shock the packed room by speaking intelligently and compellingly about free speech. Or to watch a Florida Senator display album art from W.A.S.P., or minister Jeff Ling quoting gross scatological lyrics by The Mentors. It's easy to chuckle even, knowing that the eventual outcome of the PMRC's outrage would be the fairly benign "Parental Advisory: Explicit Lyrics" sticker, perhaps the greatest promotional tool for marketing music to under-age buyers the record companies could ever have dreamt of (the creation of the warning sticker was agreed on before the hearings). However, within the detailed transcripts are signs that, for the O-for-occult-branded artists, the attacks were just beginning. Two expert statements were presented that morning :

Left: Tipper Gore and Susan Baker at the PMRC Hearing, 1985.
Above: Senator Paula Hawkins at the PMRC Hearing, 1985. Photos by James Colburn.

> **❝** Most successful heavy metal projects one or more of the following basic themes: extreme rebellion, extreme violence, substance abuse, sexual promiscuity/perversion, including homosexuality, bisexuality, sadomasochism, necrophilia, etc.—and Satanism.
>
> > –Dr. Joe Stuessy, Professor of Music at the University of Texas at San Antonio

> **❝** The heavy metal groups themselves state that this is all in fun and that they are not into Satan worship. Whether this is true or not is not important… Heavy metal portrays the power and glory of evil. Adolescents with emotional and/or drug problems, which I treat every day, become further involved in delinquent behavior, violence, acts of cruelty and Satan worship... Heavy metal is presented to kids as a religion. The adolescents are vulnerable.
>
> > –Dr. Paul King, Medical director of the adolescent program at Charter Lakeside Hospital, a psychiatric and addictive disease facility

Above: Twisted Sister's Dee Snider at the PMRC Hearing, 1985.
Photo by James Colburn.

In the months following the hearing, the PMRC refocused its campaign on the dangers of devil worship, hawking a "Satanism Research Packet" for $15 and giving "Satanism and Youth" seminars across the country. Tipper Gore's book featured a wealth of examples from the heavy metal world to rail against. Ozzy, Dio, Venom, Slayer, Black Sabbath, Mötley Crüe, Celtic Frost, Mercyful Fate, W.A.S.P, Iron Maiden and King Diamond all get name-checked, while Lyrics to Venom's "Sacrifice" and Slayer's "Reign in Blood" are reproduced. In a chapter entitled "Playing with Fire: Heavy Metal Satanism," Tipper wrote:

> **"** This childhood fascination with the occult has led to one of the most sickening marketing gimmicks in history. Just as some in the music industry emphasize sex or violence in their songs, others, specifically heavy metal groups, sell Satan to kids. The demonic, it turns out, is lucrative… Many kids experiment with the deadly satanic game, and some get hooked.

One amusing thing about the PRMC's high-profile campaign against Satanism in metal is that Venom and Mercyful Fate, operating oceans and cultural worlds away from mainstream American media, were generally unaffected by the controversy. (Both bands were about to go through line-up changes and break-ups, but not because of any outside pressures.) In fact, King Diamond later looked back at landing on the PMRC's list and proclaimed, "I guess the worst thing that ever happened to us was kind of good." And in a 2012 interview with filmmaker Sam Dunn for the documentary *Metal Evolution: Extreme Metal*, Venom drummer Abaddon reveals their band didn't even know it was happening.

SD: You had no idea that you were on the Filthy 15.

A: I had never even heard of it. I knew about things like PMRC and that kind of thing, and I didn't take it very seriously. I didn't know what Filthy 15 was. I had no idea.

SD: This was the list of songs

that the PMRC identified as being evidence of the music that was corrupting the youth of America. And you were on there for the song "Possessed" because of occult themes.

A: That just sounds lazy to me. That sounds like nobody's listening to enough Venom to find the worst song. That sounds like they've just set something out with Possessed written on it. There's a lot worse than that.

For many metal bands, censorship was generally seen as a mild annoyance, an opportunity to generate publicity. Iron Maiden played along when their "Number of the Beast" caused a tizzy. And, on a good day, it was a chance to outwit one's opponents through debate. (Glen Benton, leader of Satanic death metal band Deicide, famously used to call into Bob Larson's Christian talk radio show, and the pair of them engaged in outrageous theatre). In his interview with Dunn, Abaddon recalls the time he was pitted against a priest on the BBC, and how he made light of an absurd situation.

66 *It was on a TV program called Newsnight. A couple of kids in America had decided to kill their school teacher. What happened was, they didn't do it, they kind of bailed out. They went back home, they threw on a Venom record, Welcome to Hell, then they went out, looked for him and killed him. And everybody said if they hadn't have played Venom records they wouldn't have gone and done it. And my argument was … whether it was Venom, whoever, it just happened to be whatever was closest at hand. But this thing got as far as Newsnight and they asked me to come in. And what happened was it was a guy, he was a bishop of somewhere or other, and the government or whoever had given him loads of money to buy really expensive equipment so they could play our records backwards. And live in the studio he put on Welcome to Hell and he started spinning it backwards and he said, "Do you agree that that says 'I worship Satan and I love Satan and all this sort of stuff?'" And I went, "No, I don't deny that at all, but do you understand that it's on an album called Welcome to Hell and it's on a song called 'In League With Satan' and it's got a pentagram on the front? I didn't have to hide anything; it's all there in English. You've just got to pick it up and fucking read it, you don't have to buy all this equipment to play it backwards—it's the same forwards as it is backwards."*

It's funny, but while Venom and King Diamond were going about their business recording and touring, it was metal fans that would soon become the target of America's war on devil worship. Across the country, law enforcement was buying into the Satanic Panic, and ramping up efforts to sniff out occult crimes. Increasingly, specially designated "occult cops" (small town cops, many of whom came from the anti-cult Movement, where they learned to deprogram people practicing alternative religions as to avoid another Jonestown) were dispatched to investigate such common (albeit still criminal) bored teen activities as graveyard vandalism and graffiti, ready to declare every spray-painted 666 or candle residue proof of a Satanic gathering and potential site of child abduction and abuse. Tabloid TV talk shows were stocked with guests who claimed to have been victims or participants in gruesome rituals involving the kidnapping, torture and even murder of children and babies. The fear of Satanic Ritual Abuse was real and, by this point, it's clear worries about occult references in metal had snowballed into an old-fashioned witch hunt. As pointed out by author Jeffrey S. Victor, "the moral crusade against Satanism arises out of the social changes which affect children, or at least, out of the change believed to affect the well-being of children."

For those freaking out about the erosion of traditional family values, including increased divorce and women's rights, and the thought of children of working parents left to strangers at daycare or their own mischievous devices, Satan in music was a convenient scapegoat. Rather than examining the actual socio-economic causes of, say, teen suicide, better to create a bogeyman that comes from outside our own bodies, minds, and souls. In the case of bands like Venom, Mercyful Fate, Black Sabbath, AC/DC and the like, they had the added "benefit" of being foreigners, evil outsiders that could easily be accused of invading the homes of American families without Americans having to examine their own culture.

In this environment, something as harmless as listening to music with occult lyrics, or wearing a band T-shirt with a pentagram on it, could be considered sinister and suspicious. This went on for years. With the truth about the existence of Satanic baby-breeding cults in question, the anti-Satan brigade also looked to new, tangible examples of the threat. They found it, and a link to heavy metal, in teenage suicide.

In 1986, the parents of John McCollum filed a lawsuit against Ozzy Osbourne, claiming subliminal messages in his song "Suicide Solution" had contributed to their son's decision to end his life. Then, in 1990, Judas Priest was accused of having the subliminal message "do it" on one of their records by the parents of James Vance and Raymond Belknap, who shot themselves after getting drunk and listening to Priest. This fear of "back-masking" had reached a fever pitch in America after the TV show *Praise the Lord* (flagship show for the largest Christian network in the world) blasted musicians for being members of The Church of Satan and hiding messages in songs. Both cases were ultimately dismissed, but got extensive media coverage, further planting in the public consciousness the connection between heavy metal and dangerous behavior.

In *The Satanism Scare*, author James T. Richardson commented on the Judas Priest case:

> 66 *Although Satanism played a minor role in this case, future heavy metal cases may include more direct references to Satanism, depending on alleged Satanic involvements of those being sued, and on the views of judges and attorneys in the cases. Popular beliefs and accusations that heavy metal and its stars are deliberately exposing youth to Satanic messages are widespread. Such claims fit neatly with the*

religious fundamentalist belief structure, which in turn complements others' more secular concerns that heavy metal music fosters anti-social behavior, including suicide, among youth.

Plenty of organizations benefited from this false crisis being pinned on heavy metal — religious groups, politicians, police and even the recording entertainment industry. For them, there was minimal fall-out from the PMRC's Filthy 15 list, the labeling campaign, the tabloid TV specials and even the court cases. Frank Zappa managed to get a cool song out of it; his "Porn Wars" is a mash-up of titillating quotes from the hearings. But for others, there were real world consequences. Not for Tipper Gore, of course. Sure she was declared "Asshole of the Month" in *Hustler* magazine. But, according to her husband's biography, "the worst part of it all was that, for a while, our daughter Karenna had to defend Tipper to her teenaged friends."

No, the victims were teenagers who hung posters with pentagrams and goats in their bedrooms, who sewed Venom patches onto their jean jackets, who borrowed *The Satanic Bible* from their libraries after reading about it in heavy metal magazines. These teens then found themselves targeted by their parents, their schools, their police, as potential sociopaths. The most devastating example of this remains the case of the West Memphis Three: Damien Echols, Jessie Misskelley Jr. and Jason Baldwin, aged 18, 17, and 17 respectively, who in 1994 were tried and convicted of the murder of three young boys in West Memphis, Arkansas, without any real evidence other than the suspicion that Echols, who had expressed interest in metal music and the occult, was a devil worshipper. The three spent almost 20 years in jail (Echols on death row) until new DNA evidence led to their release in 2011. That is the legacy of Tipper Gore, of tabloid TV specials, of the "occult cops" and the Filthy 15. That is the power of Satan.

REFERENCES + BIBLIOGRAPHY:

Baddeley, Gavin. *Lucifer Rising*. London: Plexus, 1999.
Christe, Ian. *Sound of the Beast: The Complete Headbanging History of Heavy Metal*. New York: HarperCollins, 2003.
Gore, Al, and Tipper Gore. *Joined at the Heart: The Transformation of the American Family*. New York: H. Holt, 2002.
Gore, Tipper. *Raising PG Kids in an X-rated Society*. Nashville: Abingdon Press, 1987.
Larson, Bob. *Rock & the Church*. Creation House, 1971.
Metal Evolution: Extreme Metal. Dir. Sam Dunn. Banger Films, 2014.
Raspberry, William. "Crying Foul Over Filthy Lyrics." *The Washington Post*, June 25, 1985.
Record Labeling: Hearing Before the Committee on Commerce, Science and Transportation, United States Senate, First Session, on Contents of Music and the Lyrics of Records, United States, September 19, 1985.
Richardson, James T. *The Satanism Scare*. New York: A. De Gruyter, 1991.
"Venom Biography - The History of the Ultimate Metal Band." *Official Venom Website*.
Victor, Jeffrey S. *Satanic Panic: The Creation of a Contemporary Legend*. Chicago: Open Court, 1993.

Right: Black Metal pioneers Venom in a publicity shot

This one's for the PMRC.

SCAPEGOAT OF A NATION:
THE DEMONIZATION OF MTV AND THE MUSIC VIDEO

BY STACY RUSNAK

In the 1980s, battles over family values, abortion, pornography, drugs, and prayer in school, flooded newspaper headlines and the nightly news. Acting in the name of "national security," important moral entrepreneurs framed this cultural crisis as a diabolical conspiracy by a powerful underground network of Satanic cultists intent on undermining the moral fabric of American youth. In the midst of this cultural crisis, a new music video-focused cable TV channel launched. MTV (The Music Television Network) provided a space where America's culture wars played out for the younger generation. Many videos offered some critique of the dominant hegemony, often misinterpreted by adults searching for answers to explain teen suicide, drug use, or a display of "deviant" sexuality. Though it eventually became the total expression of youth popular culture, MTV also fueled the moral panic with its images of androgynous rock stars, Satanic symbols and anti-authoritarian messages.

MTV AND HEAVY METAL

There was nothing like MTV on American airwaves when the network officially launched on August 1, 1981—not even a

Left: W.A.S.P.'s Blackie Lawless in an anti-PMRC publicity photo by Ross Halfin.

173

formula for how such a network should be run. Very few people, aside from possibly those that worked there, thought that the channel would ever amount to anything. Though MTV had only 200 videos initially, most of which were from marginal British and Australian bands, the station realized the potential in marketing to a young audience aged 12 to 35 that were being underserved at the time. MTV founder John Lack labeled teenagers as the least-interested demographic in TV, because TV was the medium that was least interested in teenagers; young children had cartoons, and adults had the news and prime time sitcoms and dramas. By serving up a steady stream of music videos, MTV gave the untapped teen audience what it wanted, and eventually the network became the hub around which popular culture rotated. From 1981-1992, MTV's "Golden Age," the network celebrated and influenced America's youth culture through fashion, art, sexuality, advertising, race and politics.

In the early days, MTV catered mostly to white suburban and rural communities, partly because urban centers were not wired for cable, or the cable channels were simply inaccessible. After considering market research, MTV decided to focus on rock music because of its popularity with white, middle-class teenagers. But as competition with radio programs and imitation networks increased, MTV expanded to include other popular genres, including heavy metal. By 1983, MTV was investing more wisely in the mounting popularity of the heavy metal genre, which set it apart from radio and other TV networks. These outlets often steered clear of the controversial genre, as televangelists, congressmen, law enforcement agencies, doctors and journalists were already spreading the notion that "extreme" music styles like heavy metal were dangerous to children.

From the beginning, the music video and heavy metal was a match made in Heaven (or maybe Hell). Heavy metal bands had visual value; they were theatrical, used over-the-top set designs, and wore glamorous, attention-getting costumes and make-up. Although these factors were ideal for the video format, parents often regarded these bands' music lyrics as "offensive" because of references to the occult, violence, sex, and drugs and alcohol. In 1984, Susan Baker and Tipper Gore, along with wives of other high-ranking members of Congress, formed the Parents' Music Resource Center (PMRC) in response to the perceived moral crisis of the "lewd" lyrics. Responding to the PMRC's concerns, the Recording Industry Association of America (RIAA) agreed to voluntarily sticker potentially offensive releases in 1985, and the PMRC soon set its sights on MTV.

The PMRC was only one group responsible for the moral panic spreading through middle-class America. Mass media also lent credence to parental fears regarding a nationwide Satanic network that was preying on the youth culture via heavy metal. Prime time news show 20/20 aired "Devil Worshippers" on May 16, 1985, a special that put parents on high alert. The program featured a checklist of symbols associated with the occult: pentagrams, upside crosses, the evil eye, the number 666, the goat -headed man, death, desecrated churches, fire, chains, and blood drinking; icons and themes easily found in 1980s music videos.

Ozzy Osbourne's music video for "Mr. Crowley" (1980) is rife with this kind of imagery. The video begins with a flash of lighting over a silhouette of a haunted mansion. Inside, a young, innocent-looking girl in white twists and turns in bed, suffering from some sort of nightmare. The camera cuts to Ozzy, made up as a vampire, and a quick series of crosscuts indicate that the vampire Ozzy is haunting the young lady's dreams. The next four minutes of the video is a concert

performance by the band, followed by a last minute return to the young lady. Ozzy stalks and then bites his victim. A close up on the girl's face captures an erotic, rather than a fearful, expression. The camera cuts back to the concert and zooms in on the same girl standing in the crowd. Her white gown replaced by a skimpy red dress, she smiles to reveal vampire-like teeth, clearly corrupted by Ozzy's charm.

Similarly, Motley Crüe's video for "Looks that Kill" (1983) sees the band carrying torches and chasing a group of "untamed" women around a cavernous, dark setting. In what seems like a display of misogynist bravado, the band corrals the scantily-clad women into a cage. The women cower and avoid eye contact with the band members. Like in Ozzy's video, there is a cut to a performance

sequence. The band members, dressed in red and black costumes, whip their long hair around and wear make-up and heels. Tommy Lee's drum set and Vince Neil's headband are adorned with the pentagram popularized by Church of Satan founder Anton LaVey. Parents were also wary of Def Leppard, whose "Rock of Ages" (1983) video begins with an image of hooded men, haloed by a red haze. A burning tree is shown with a link of chains across the top branches. Moments later, a large black leather glove squeezes a goblet of thick red liquid until it bursts. The color red, the fire, and the implied blood drinking are all associated with Satan. Likewise, W.A.S.P.'s video for "I Wanna Be Somebody" (1984) plays into parental fears regarding heavy metal

Top: Ozzy Osbourne in a publicity photo for his album Blizzard of Ozz (1980).
Middle: From Motley Crüe's video for "Looks That Kill" (1983).
Bottom: From Def Leppard's video for "Rock of Ages" (1983).

and its connections to teen suicide and substance abuse. This video begins with a lock being sawed off of a door that is then opened by a skeleton hand, revealing the band playing. Lead singer Blackie Lawless looks into the camera and makes a throat-slitting motion with his finger, while guitarist Chris Holmes chugs a beer, smashes the can and throws it on the ground.

Heavy Metal videos also made use of traditional medieval and horror imagery. Dio's video for "Holy Diver" (1983) opens with the camera tilting up through twisted, knotty branches that give way to a superimposed image of a demon, before cutting to a decrepit-looking church. Singer Ronnie James Dio wields a sword and battles with a man wearing a skinned animal's head over his own, brandishing an axe. The weapons and costuming seem vaguely reminiscent of the Dungeons & Dragons role playing game, which was also criticized for its occult connotations. Iron Maiden's "Number of the Beast" (1982) video begins in a foggy cemetery at night and a medium close-up of a werewolf fills the frame. As the song kicks in, the half-shadowed face of singer Bruce Dickinson appears, with a piercing and hypnotic stare. There is a cut to a man in a goat's head mask and other images

flash before our eyes: the vampire from 1922's *Nosferatu*, the scarred face of the titular creature from *The Amazing Colossal Man* (1957), Godzilla, a skull face, explosions, flames, and a pulsating, spellbinding spiral. A woman in pink whirls onto the stage with her tuxedo-clad partner, changing momentarily into a werewolf. A caricature of the Devil joins the cast, and Eddie, the band's "mascot," enters from the left, looming over the stage in jeans, a leather jacket and shaggy hair. Similar in dress to many heavy metal fans, perhaps it is this last image that was so disturbing for parents, who might have recognized something of their own teenagers in Eddie.

Top: Iron Maiden, from the rear of "The Number of the Beast" album (1982).
Above: From Iron Maiden's video for "The Number of the Beast" (1982).
Opposite: Promotional artwork for Dio's "Holy Diver" (1983).

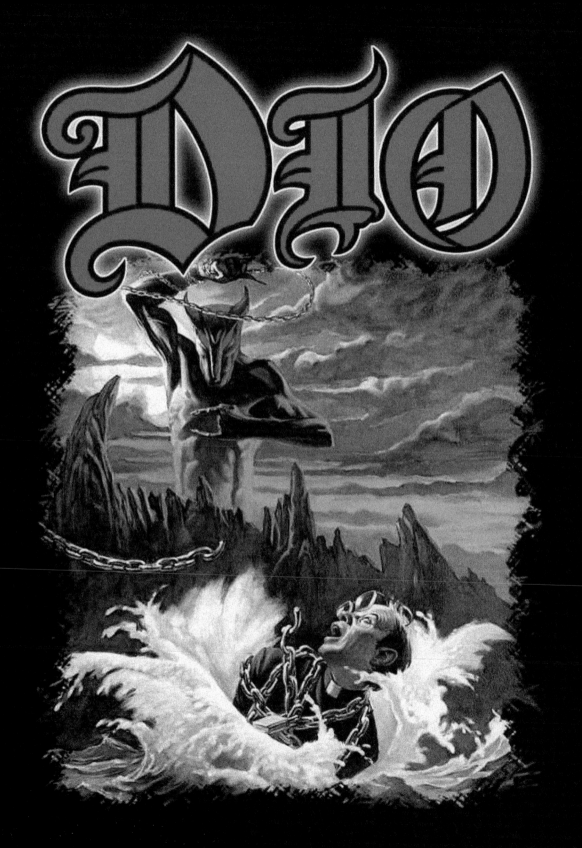

WHO NEEDS TO HANG AROUND?
I'VE GOT DUNGEONS & DRAGONS®
ADVENTURE GAME

DUNGEONS & DRAGONS® BASIC SET
A FANTASY ROLE PLAYING GAME FROM
TSR HOBBIES INC.
THE GAME WIZARDS

Hell on earth

a sobering view of what Satan's up to

BOB LARSON

SATORI™
Presents

Alison's Birthday

A young girl
comes of age. . .

and an evil
destiny
awaits her.

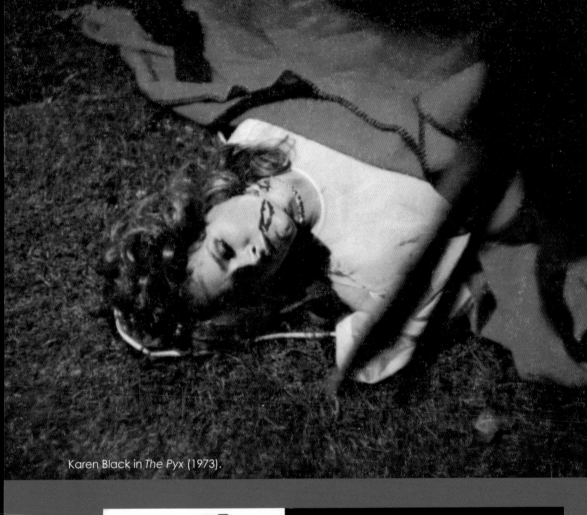

Karen Black in *The Pyx* (1973).

DARK DUNGEONS

J.T.C.

Heaven help us all when
THE DEVIL'S RAIN!

Absolutely the most incredible ending of any motion picture ever!

BRYANSTON Presents A SANDY HOWARD Production • Starring ERNEST BORGNINE • EDDIE ALBERT in "THE DEVIL'S RAIN" • Also Starring WILLIAM SHATNER
KEENAN WYNN • TOM SKERRITT • JOAN PRATHER and IDA LUPINO as Mrs. Preston • with the Special Participation of ANTON LAVEY, High Priest of the Church of Satan
Written by GABE ESSOE, JAMES ASHTON, and GERALD HOPMAN • Produced by JAMES V. CULLEN and MICHAEL S. GLICK
Directed by ROBERT FUEST • Executive Producer SANDY HOWARD • A BRYANSTON RELEASE • COLOR

PG PARENTAL GUIDANCE SUGGESTED

75/106

DEVIL'S RAIN

Images this page: Jim VanBebber's *My Sweet Satan*. © 1994 Asmodeus/Mercury Films.

1986. BEER. PRIEST. VIDEOCAMERA.

Poster by Standard Design.

IT BELONGS ON FUCKIN' MARS MAN

LET'S LEGALIZE DRUGS, THAT IS A FACT

JUDAS PRIEST

DC/10
MADONNA'S A DICK

I'M READY TO ROCK

HELL, YEAH

HEAVY METAL PARKING LOT

PRIEST RULES

SHE'S TRIPPIN' JACK DANIELS

a documentary by JEFF KRULIK and JOHN HEYN

I'M ON ACID, THAT'S WHERE I AM

RICK TREMBLES' MOTION PICTURE PURGATORY

DREAM DECEIVERS (1992)

ONLY THING THAT MIGHT GET YOU OUT OF YER FUNK WATCHING THIS DEVASTATINGLY DEPRESSING DOC ABOUT JUDAS PRIEST FAN JAMES VANCE'S HORRIBLY BOTCHED XMAS '85 SUICIDE ATTEMPT COULD BE THE BLOOD-CURDLING INFURIATION THAT'LL SWELL UP INSIDE YOU LISTENING TO HIS DRONING MOM'S PIGHEADED, SANCTIMONIOUS, SELF-RIGHTEOUS, "TOLD-YOU-SO'S" WHILE JUSTIFYING HER ATTEMPTS TO SUE THE METAL BAND FOR HER SON'S DISFIGUREMENT! "HE DOESN'T EAT IN FRONT OF PEOPLE CUZ HE HAS TO USE ONE FINGER & ONE TOOTH," SHE TELLS THE CAMERA MATTER-OF-FACTLY WITH A SMIRK!

BAND WAS GREETED BY ECSTATIC FANS OUTSIDE THE COURTHOUSE AS THEY *ACTUALLY* WENT TO TRIAL IN NEVADA, LOOKING FOR SUBLIMINAL MESSAGES THEY WERE ACCUSED OF INSERTING INTO THE MUSIC THAT EGGED ON VANCE INTO BLOWING HIS BRAINS OUT AT A PLAYGROUND RIGHT AFTER HIS 18-YR OLD BUDDY, SUCCEEDED INCHES AWAY FROM HIM! AFTER INEFFECTIVELY TRYING TO FIND THE WORDS "DO IT" IN THE SONG "BETTER BY YOU, BETTER THAN ME," THEY FESS UP TO BACKWARDS RECORDINGS THEY DID ONCE RELEASE & THEN PRESENT THE "DANGEROUS" RESULTS!

Actual BACKWARDS MESSAGE FRONTWARDS:

"I ASKED FOR A PEPPERMINT, I ASKED FOR HER TO GET ME ONE"!

Actual Quotes:

"THE MUSIC WAS LIKE A NARCOTIC"!

"WE WENT LOOKING FOR AN EASY WAY OUT; WE OBVIOUSLY THOUGHT THERE WAS SOMETHING BETTER OUT THERE"!

"I WOULD LIKE TO CALL CERTAIN PEOPLE MURDERERS"!

SURVIVED CUZ HE AIMED 12-GAUGE UNDER HIS CHIN, WHEREAS HIS PAL HAD IT IN HIS MOUTH!

Actual Quotes:

"GOD KNEW WHAT HE WAS DOING WHEN HE MADE ME (HIS) MOM"!

"I TOLD HIM, 'IF YOUR MOM HADN'T BEEN PRAYING FOR YOU, YOU WOULD'VE DIED THAT NIGHT' & HE NEVER CHALLENGED ME AGAIN"!

"JUDAS PRIEST'S ANSWER TO LIFE WAS DEATH"!

R.I.P.

ABUSIVE ALCOHOLIC STEPDADS EXPLAIN "WHOOPING" METHODS, LIKE HOW THEY'D TELL KIDS TO GO GET THE BELT SO THEY HAD TIME TO THINK ABOUT WHAT WAS COMING! DEFENSIVE MOM IS GRILLED BY BAND'S LAWYER: "YOU KNEW HE WAS UNHAPPY," SHE ASKS, "I DON'T UNDERSTAND WHY YOU'RE ASKING ME ABOUT HIM BEING UNHAPPY, WHAT DO YOU MEAN BY UNHAPPY," MOM INDIGNANTLY RETORTS, "MY QUESTION'S A SIMPLE ONE; HE WAS UNHAPPY PRIOR TO HIS SUICIDE ATTEMPT, WASN'T HE"? "I DON'T REMEMBER," SEZ MOM!

YOU WANNA ROOT FOR VANCE TO PULL THRU SO MUCH THAT HIS SIDING WITH MOM'S CRACKPOT THEORIES MAKES YOU WONDER IF HE WAS ONLY DOING IT TO GET THE BAND TO MAKE A FLESH & BLOOD APPEARANCE WITHIN HIS PROXIMITY! "HOSPITALIZED 3 YEARS LATER FOR DEPRESSION & DEAD OF AN OVERDOSE," THE FILM GRIMLY ENDS! RARE 16MM SCREENING OF *DREAM DECEIVERS: THE STORY OF JAMES VANCE VS. JUDAS PRIEST* AS PART OF POP MONTREAL'S FILMPOP FEST AT BLUE SUNSHINE (3660 ST-LAURENT), SUNDAY SEPTEMBER 25, 6:45 PM!

THE GRIP OF EVIL

NUMBER 96

BASED ON THE TV SERIES

BEV AND VERA – TRAPPED IN A NIGHTMARE

Paperback tie-in to a Satanic-themed episode of Australian soap opera Number 96. Image from the collection of Andrew Nette at Pulpcurry.com.

Dee Snider of Twisted Sister at the 1985 PMRC Hearing. Photo by James Colburn.

Clint Howard in Evilspeak (1981).

PREGATE DIO DI TROVARE OCCUPATO...

Backward Satanic Messages of Rock and Roll Exposed

Jacob Aranza
Introduction by Louisiana State Senator BILL KEITH

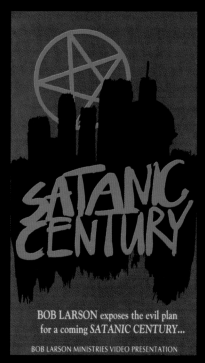

BOB LARSON exposes the evil plan for a coming SATANIC CENTURY...

BOB LARSON MINISTRIES VIDEO PRESENTATION

·976·
CHIAMATA PER IL DIAVOLO

una produzione HORRORSCOPE INC. per la CINETEL FILMS INC. un film di ROBERT ENGLUND "976: CHIAMATA PER IL DIAVOLO" (976 EVIL)
con STEPHEN GEOFFREYS · JIM METZLER · MARIA RUBELL · LEZLIE DEANE · J.J. COHEN
e per la prima volta sullo schermo PAT O' BRYAN e SANDY DENNIS nel ruolo di "ZIA LUCY" e con DARREN BURROWS · GUNTHER JENSEN · JIM THIEBAUD · MINDY SEEGER
direttore della fotografia PAUL ELLIOT cast di BARBARA CLAMAN, C.S.A. e MARGARET McSHARRY montaggio di STEPHEN MYERS
musica di THOMAS CHASE e STEVE RUCKER scenografia di DAVID BRIAN MILLER trucchi speciali della KEVIN YAGHER PRODUCTION
scritto da RHET TOPHAM & BRIAN HELGELAND
produttore esecutivo PAUL HERTZBERG prodotto da LISA M. HANSEN diretto da ROBERT ENGLUND

LIFE
INTERNATIONAL

Left and Right: Italian locandina artwork for *976-EVIL* (1988) and *Trick or Treat* (1986).

VIETATO AI MINORI DI 14 ANNI

MORTE A 33 GIRI

DE LAURENTIIS ENTERTAINMENT GROUP PRESENTA "MORTE A 33 GIRI" CON MARC PRICE - TONY FIELDS
E GENE SIMMONS nel ruolo di "NUKE" Con la partecipazione straordinaria di OZZY OSBOURNE
Musica originale scritta e interpretata dai FASTWAY Colonna sonora di CHRISTOPHER YOUNG
Direttore della fotografia ROBERT ELSWIT
Soggetto di RHET TOPHAM Sceneggiatura di MICHAEL S. MURPHEY - JOEL SOISSON e RHET TOPHAM
Prodotto da MICHAEL S. MURPHEY e JOEL SOISSON
Diretto da CHARLES MARTIN SMITH

DEG
DE LAURENTIIS ENTERTAINMENT GROUP

ULTRA★STEREO®

DISTRIBUZIONE
FILM**A**URO

Top: Lianne Dietz and the Devil from *Rock 'n' Roll Nightmare* (1987).
Bottom: The cast and crew of *Rock 'n' Roll Nightmare* watching the dailies.
Photos courtesy of Frank Dietz.

TOM HANKS
**MEINE TEUFLISCHEN
NACHBARN**
"THE 'BURBS'"

Ein Universalfilm im Verleih der UP

TOM HANKS
**MEINE TEUFLISCHEN
NACHBARN**
"THE 'BURBS'"

Ein Universalfilm im Verleih der UP

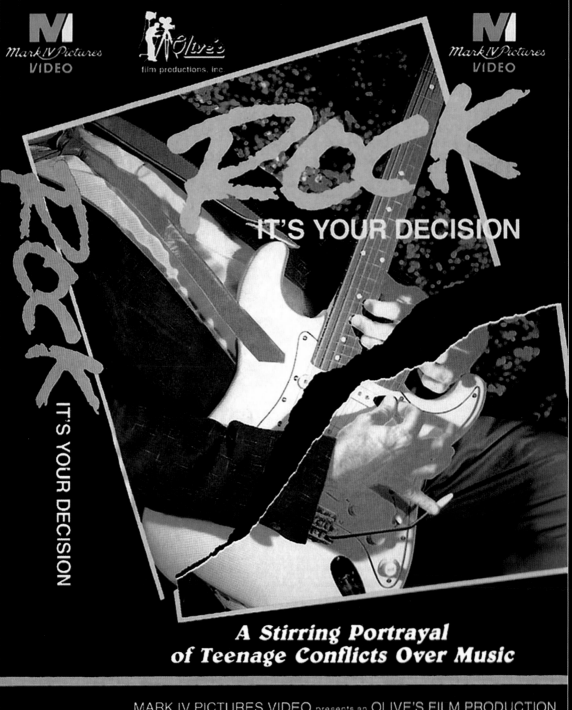

MARK IV PICTURES VIDEO presents an OLIVE'S FILM PRODUCTION
ROCK; ITS YOUR DECISION
starring TY TAYLOR • LAURA BRANSCUM • GLEN WILLIAMS • STEVE
WEDAN • PEGGY GRINER
Produced by DAVID OLIVE III   Directed by JOHN TAYLOR
Written by KAREN RICHARDSON
AN OLIVE'S FILM AND FAITH PRODUCTION

Consensus regarding the dangers of MTV spread farther than the private sphere of parents looking over their teens' shoulders. When MTV hit the cable network, many critics were standing by to declare their opposition. Dr. Richard M. Bridgberg banned the network at his mental health facility in Hartford, Connecticut, citing patient complaints and "ill effects" that he claimed to have witnessed in several patients. U.S. Surgeon General C. Everett Koop also declared MTV a liability. According to Koop, music videos were full of violence and pornography that would foster troubling relationships with people of the opposite sex. "Born again" rock lecturer Rob Lamb further condemned MTV's visual imagery, noting that children would no longer have to interpret the salacious messages of their favorite song, since they were explicitly pictured on screen.

MTV knew that an individual viewer's complaint could quickly garner greater support from an entire community, and its network carriage was threatened in several instances. In 1983, a Calvary Baptist Church youth supervisor in Emporia, Virginia was largely successful in petitioning city council to ban MTV. Though the channel was still offered for a $10 premium, MTV lost access to 1,500 homes. A year later, Mormon bishop and landlord Leo Weidner tried to ban MTV from his Provo, Utah apartment complex, which was inhabited primarily by university students. In the same year, two women in Meymouth, Massachusetts circulated a petition and had the network removed from the cable system, rejecting the cable company's offer of a channel-blocker.

Having succeeded in convincing the RIAA to label albums with potentially offensive content, the PMRC was at the forefront of tackling the music video industry. Backed by Dr. Thomas Radecki and the National Coalition on Television Violence (NCTV), the PMRC lobbied for warnings to appear on-screen before any "offensive" video was broadcast. Although more lenient Federal Communications Commission (FCC) guidelines for cable meant the PMRC and NCTV were fairly powerless on this point, MTV decided to cooperate to avoid controversy. MTV even invited members of the PMRC to visit their offices to discuss standards and practices to monitor a video's material.

MTV's Standards Department, created in 1984, reviewed video submissions for potentially "subversive" material, including song lyrics. Videos that showed drug use, excessive consumption of alcohol, graphic sex, gratuitous violence and negative representations of ethnic or religious groups, were either re-edited or rejected. There was, however, little consistency in applying the standards, and some potentially offensive videos still aired, especially those by extremely popular musicians, such as Michael Jackson's video for "Thriller." Even though the NCTV found the video offensive and rallied to have it banned from circulation, it received saturation play on MTV. The NCTV highlighted the video's violence and sexuality as deviant and sadistic. Nevertheless, the video marked a watershed moment for MTV as a new cultural force, breaking down the racial barriers and opening the door for other African-American musicians, who had previously been excluded from the network.

Clocking in at thirteen minutes long, "Thriller" revolutionized video production, supplementing the performance format with a more creative approach that brought filmmaking to the music industry. Although Jackson's video uses horror imagery like many of the heavy metal videos, the film format makes it easier to dismiss the imagery as pure fantasy. Moreover, Jackson requested that director John Landis include a "warning label" at the beginning that stated, "Due to my strong personal convictions, I wish to stress that this film in no way endorses a belief in the occult."

As late as 1987, parents were still advocating against MTV. *The New York Times* reported that Clinton, Connecticut's Gery Alexander came home one day to find his five-year-old daughter imitating a video that he considered offensive. When he called the cable company to have MTV removed, Alexander was offered a "lock out" box for $15, or a "tamper proof box" for $35. Eventually, after the town held a meeting to respond to complaints, the company provided lock boxes free of charge.

In a telephone interview, MTV's Vice President for Press and Public affairs, Barry Kluger, stated that MTV had set standards and that videos were edited, if necessary, before being aired. He also defended the network's broadcasting of anti-drug service spots by musicians and reminded the public that the network did not cater to little children.

In effect, MTV's "standards" were more like a philosophy of taste. When asked about

Above: Michael Jackson and friends in a publicity shot for his "Thriller" video, famously directed by John Landis in 1983.

her role in identifying which videos were deemed "suitable" for circulation, founding Standards Department employee, Michelle Vonfeld, stated, "We felt we were being consistent with a product that was inconsistent. No two videos were the same." There was no checklist of unacceptable content, only a case-by-case evaluation of each video.

Despite its inconsistencies, MTV's Standards Department did relegate certain videos to late-night hours. MTV cut back considerably on heavy metal videos because of the mounting pressure by conservative watchdog groups, but fans were unhappy with the disappearance of their favorite videos, and called the network to request more metal. In response, MTV launched its popular late-night heavy metal program, "Headbanger's Ball" in 1988. Heavy metal videos had finally been placed on the margins, where parents were less likely to see them.

THE SCAPEGOATING OF MTV

In a strange twist of fate, Ronald Reagan was elected President of the United States in the same year that MTV was launched. One of the first tasks of the Reagan administration was to cultivate a new image of "American-ness" for the 1980s. The country was still reeling from the backlash of Vietnam, and there was a sense that the U.S. had grown soft and weak under the previous Carter administration. Multiple discourses sprang up on American life and the "American Dream," which spilled out into the public sphere, dragging in issues such as pornography, abortion, sexuality and reproduction, marriage, personal morality and family values. Lauren Berlant, in her book, *The Queen of America Goes to Washington City*, suggests that "in the process of collapsing the political and the personal into a world of public intimacy, a nation made for adult citizens has been replaced by one imagined for fetuses and children." The Reaganite right capitalized on the image of the child as a means of securing its familial politics by proposing an agenda that focused on the preservation of the nation for "tomorrow's" children. An opposing progressive left challenged the administration by demanding change "now."

Instead of simplifying this multifaceted struggle as a political battle between left and right, it is perhaps more suitable to define America's culture war of the 1980s as contending worldviews, wherein an orthodox version of authority located in tradition, religion, and concepts of natural law clashed with a progressive, postmodern vision that favored more radical notions of subjectivity and relativism. The discord between the older orthodoxy of Christian values and the new radical cultural forces constituted the core of the culture war.

Media in the 1980s played a pivotal role in disseminating the conservative cultural politics and promoting this cultural war. The American dream came to be defined through the "good old values" system, which excluded others through racism, sexism, and classicism. If you worked hard, investing your energies in the family and in your job, then the nation would secure the social and economic conditions wherein your hard work would pay off, and you could live a dignified life. This philosophy tied the strength of the nation to private fortune which, by nature, was already exclusionary because the American dream is a fantasy inaccessible by the economically disadvantaged. The media reinforced this exclusion through images of impoverished, drug-addicted African-Americans, making drug use and poverty seem like something that did not affect white, middle-class families. Similarly, the rise of the AIDS epidemic was seen as either a scourge cast down by God to punish gay men or a product of drug use in the low-income areas. The media also helped to circulate a "mother-blaming" campaign that envisioned a child's physical or psychological abnormality as a failure by single mothers. The media portrayed these mothers as unfit and unable to raise productive members of society.

All of these issues were of debate in the public sphere during the rise of MTV. Many of the heavy metal music videos challenged the conservative's traditionalist values of work and family. For instance, in Ozzy Osbourne's video for "The Ultimate Sin," Ozzy pokes fun at the American dream and mocks the idea that hard work gets you ahead. Dressed as a caricature of J.R. Ewing from 1980s hit TV series *Dallas*, Ozzy sits in a corporate office, his feet on a desk. After a quick "business" call, where he seems to just yell at the caller, he rests his face in his hands, apparently bored. He perks up when he turns on the TV and finds a concert performance of his band. The video cuts back to Ozzy in a business meeting, where he continuously checks his watch and yawns. Finally, he offends all of the members in the meeting by taking his shoe off and smelling his sock. Through the caricature of Ewing, who inherited his fortune, Ozzy undermines the conservative value of hard work as the key to unlocking the American dream.

The body itself is a site of cultural tension in music videos. By their nature, the male members of heavy metal bands, strutting across the screen with long hair, make up, tight clothes and high-heeled boots threaten the image of the nuclear family; androgynous figures that blur the line between masculinity and femininity. In her essay, "Hard Bodies: The Reagan Heroes," Susan Jeffords discusses how the Reagan ideology controlled the idea of the body during the 1980s, categorizing the approaches as either the "soft body" or the "hard body." The "soft body" is an "errant body containing sexually transmitted disease, immortality, illegal chemicals, 'laziness,' and endangered fetuses." The "hard body" is a "normative body that enveloped strength, labor, determination, loyalty, and courage... the body that was to come to stand as the emblem of the Reagan philosophies, politics, and economies." The "soft body," identified as a female

Above: Ozzy Osbourne in his video for "The Ultimate Sin" (1986).

or person of color, was considered threatening because it could contaminate and was uncontrollable. Through assimilating feminine markers, the mostly white heavy metal bands became associated with the "soft body," disrupting the social fantasy of the "hard body" as a symbol of the national character, which was thought of as "heroic, aggressive, and determined."

Motley Crüe's video for "Smokin' in the Boys Room" demonstrates the threat of the "soft body." The video begins with a male student, dressed in denim, heading into school late. He encounters two authority figures, his teacher and his principal, and he tries to tell them that he was late because a dog ran off with his homework (an excuse that proves to be true). The principal humiliates the boy, who then sulks off to the "boy's room." Motley Crüe's band members appear and pull the boy through the mirror in the bathroom. Vince Neil looks directly into the camera with frosted hair and a pink polka dotted headband, pink lipstick, and silvery eye shadow. The band members then guide the boy through a fantasy tour of the "other side," where students sit in a classroom like drones while a teacher in a Nazi-esque coat zaps the students with a mechanism to make them conform. The video ends with the principal apologizing to the

boy after finding his homework, and the boy ripping up the homework and throwing it in the principal's face. In a blatant challenge to authority, the boy asserts his own subjectivity, which encourages an acceptance of the left's progressive, postmodern ideology, thereby subverting the traditional values of the conservative right.

CONCLUSION

In *Hollywood From Vietnam to Reagan...And Beyond*, film critic Robin Wood discusses how the 1980s met with a profound desire to reassure the public that everything would work out just fine. In the interest of the political/economic system, it was important for the country to experience a sense of helplessness. The *20/20* special and other TV programs at the time attributed the rising rate of teen suicide, drug abuse and murders (including the cases of Ricky Kasso, Sean Sellers and John McCollum) in "good," white middle-class neighborhoods to Satanic networks and their affiliates. These programs insinuated that heavy metal videos provided children with access to these networks through Satanic imagery, sexually explicit material, and depictions of substance abuse. By displacing the blame on MTV and the music videos, parents did not have to take the blame for their children's actions, as though MTV was more accountable for America's children than the parents.

Above: Motley Crüe's Vince Neil in their video for "Smokin' in the Boys' Room" (1985).

Skid Row's 1989 video, "18 and Life," incorporates the image of the "imperfect" white American middle-class family. The setting is a modest home, where domestic bliss is shattered as a young boy, Ricky, argues with his father and gets thrown through a glass door. A montage of Ricky on the streets shows him drinking, smoking and vandalizing property. At one point, Ricky breaks back into his parent's home. A photo on a bedside table projects a happy Ricky with his father. The image becomes obstructed when Ricky reaches across it, holding his father's gun. Ricky later shoots his friend and goes to prison. The emphasis on the fight and the close up of the photo suggest a return to questions about parental responsibility. Within the conservative fantasy of the child as image of a strong national future, Ricky's "fall from grace" throws apart the Reaganite right's familial politics.

By the end of the 1980s, the "good old values" only served to reinforce the internal fragmentation of the United States. Frustration, dissatisfaction, anxiety, greed and neuroticism over the national image still prevailed. With fast-paced images and postmodern pastiche, MTV proved to be too overwhelming for some parents. The network sold a way of life to teenagers, which subverted the traditional narratives held dear by the conservative right. But because of the Satanic imagery and themes that emerged explicitly in heavy metal videos, it was easy to blame MTV for corrupting the minds of America's youth. Similar to the 1970s religious cult scare, the 1980s Satanism scare became a rallying point for parents, a moral panic that they could use to adhere to Reagan's redefinition of the American dream for the 1980s, avoiding the very real issues their children were facing.

BIBLIOGRAPHY + REFERENCES:

Berlant, Lauren. *The Queen of America Goes to Washington City: Essays on Sex and Citizenship.* Durham: Duke University Press, 1997.

Binder, Amy. "Constructing Racial Rhetoric: Media Depictions of Harm in Heavy Metal and Rap Music." *American Sociological Review* 58.6 (1993).

Burr, Ty. *Gods Like Us: On Movie Stardom and Modern Fame.* New York: Pantheon Books, 2012.

Christe, Ian. *Sound of the Beast: The Complete Headbanging History of Heavy Metal.* New York: HarperCollins, 2003.

Coleman, Loren. *The Copycat Effect: How the Media and Popular Culture Trigger the Mayhem in Tomorrow's Headlines.* New York: Paraview Pocket Books, 2004.

Collins, Robert M. *Transforming America: Politics and Culture During the Reagan Years.* New York: Columbia University Press, 2007.

"Court Throws Out Suit Against Ozzy Osbourne." *The New York Times*, August 8, 1986

Def Leppard "Rock of Ages." *Pyromania*. Mercury, 1983. Music Video.

Def Leppard. "Foolin'." *Pyromania*. Mercury, 1983. Music Video.

Denisoff, R. Serge. *Inside MTV*. New Brunswick: Transaction Books, 1988.

Devil Worship: Exposing Satan's Underground. NBC/Universal Television Distribution, October 22, 1988.

Dio. "Rainbow in the Dark." *Holy Diver.* Warner Brothers, 1983. Music Video.

Dyrendal, Asbjørn. "Devilish Consumption: Popular Culture in Satanic Socialization." *Numen* 55.1 (2008).

Gruson, Lindsey. "In Northport, A Meeting on a Murder." *The New York Times,* July 17, 1984.

Gruson, Lindsey. "L.I. Murder Trial Opens; Confession is Described." *The New York Times,* April 5, 1985.

Hebdige, Dick. *Subcultue: The Meaning of Style.* New York: Routledge, 2002.

Iron Maiden. "2 Minutes to Midnight." *Powerslave.* EMI. 1984. Music Video.

Iron Maiden. "Number of the Beast." *Number of the Beast.* EMI, 1982. Music Video.

Jeffords, Susan. "Hard Bodies: The Reagan Heroes." *Hard Bodies: Hollywood Masculinity in the Reagan Era.* New Brunswick: Rutgers University Press, 1994.

Judas Priest. "Turbo Lover." *Turbo.* Columbia, 1986. Music Video.

Judas Priest. "You've Got Another Thing Comin'." *Screaming for Vengeance.* Columbia, 1982. Music Video.

Luhr, Eileen. *Witnessing Suburbia: Conservatives and Christian Youth Culture.* Los Angeles: University of California Press, 2009.

Marks, Craig, and Rob Tannenbaum. *I Want my MTV: The Uncensored Story of the Music Video Revolution.* New York: Dutton, 2011.

Megadeth "Wake Up Dead" *Peace Sells... But Who's Buying?.* Capitol, 1986. Music Video.

Megadeth. "Peace Sells." *Peace Sells... But Who's Buying?.* Capitol, 1986. Music Video.

Motley Crüe. "Looks that Kill." *Shout at the Devil.* Beyond, 1983. Music Video.

Motley Crüe. "Smokin' in the Boys Room." *Theatre of Pain.* Beyond, 1985. Music Video.

Nagler, Eve. "Company Meets Concern on MTV." *The New York Times,* August 30, 1987

Nuzum, Eric. *Parental Advisory: Music Censorship in America.* New York: Harper Collins Publishers Inc., 2001.

Ozzy Osbourne. "Ultimate Sin." *The Ultimate Sin.* Epic, 1986. Music Video.

Ozzy Osbourne. "Mr. Crowley." *Blizzard of Ozz.* Epic, 1980. Music Video.

Patters, N'Jai-An. "A Culture in Panic: Day Care Abuse Scandals and the Vulnerability of Children." *The 1980s: A Critical and Transitional Decade.* Eds. Kimberly R. Moffitt and Duncan A. Campbell. Lanham: Lexington Books, 2011.

Powers, Ron. *The Beast, the Eunuch, and the Glass-Eyed Child: Television in the '80s.* San Diego: Harcourt Brace Jovanovich, 1990.

Rather, John. "Trial Recalls Night of Death That Rocked Northport." *The New York Times,* April 7, 1985.

Ravo, Nick. "Corrupt Minds, Rebel Voices: It's Rock 'N' Roll." *The New York Times,* August 25, 1987.

Richardson, James T., Joel Best, and David G. Bromley. *The Satanism Scare.* New York: A. de Gruyter, 1991.

Rohter, Larry. "2 Families Sue Heavy-Metal Band as Having Driven Sons to Suicide." *The New York Times,* July 17, 1990.

Smith, Sally Bedell. "There's No Avoiding Music Videos." *The New York Times,* March 10, 1985.

"Stunned by Suicides, A Town Asks, 'Why?'" *The New York Times,* May 5, 1990.

"Teen-Ager Indicted on L.I. In Ritual Slaying of Youth." *The New York Times,* July 14, 1984.

"The Devil Worshipers." *20/20.* Disney-ABC Domestic Television. May 16, 1985.

W.A.S.P. "I Wanna be Somebody." *WASP.* Capitol, 1984. Music Video.

W.A.S.P. "Wild Child." *The Last Command.* Capitol, 1985. Music Video.

Williams, Lena. "For More Youths, It's Always Halloween: For More Youths, It's Always October 31." *The New York Times,* October 25, 1989.

Wood, Robin. *Hollywood From Vietnam to Reagan...And Beyond.* New York: Columbia University Press, 2003.

"Youth Arraigned in Ritual Slaying." *The New York Times,* July 14, 1984.

TRICK OR TREAT:
HEAVY METAL AND DEVIL WORSHIP IN '80S CULT CINEMA

BY SAMM DEIGHAN

There's something about teenagers behind closed bedroom doors that gets a suburban parent's imagination working overtime. Even when their mostly dutiful sons and daughters are simply competing in role-playing games, listening to loud music or popping the odd slasher movie into a VCR, adults still harbour fears that their teenagers may be overwhelmed and seduced by the things they consume. While heavy metal and horror have always been attractive to misunderstood teens and young adults who connect with inherent themes of escapism and fantasy, the Satanic Panic that gripped America throughout the 1980s aggressively targeted these teen counterculture obsessions as conduits for social rebellion, drug and alcohol abuse, illicit sex and occultism. Both reflecting and fuelling that fear was a loose collection of horror films that suggested that teens involved in these activities may be more susceptible to Satan's powers.

These Satanic Panic-inspired horror films of the 1980s included movies like *Rocktober Blood* (1984), *Hard Rock Zombies* (1985), *Trick or Treat* (1986), *The Gate* (1987), *Rock 'n' Roll Nightmare* (1987) and *Black Roses* (1988), films that infused the tradition of 1970s Satanic cinema with portrayals of heavy metal music as the locus of evil, violence and

Left: Tony Fields and Marc Price in Charles Martin Smith's *Trick or Treat* (1986).

moral corruption. Though these films didn't quite develop into a fully-formed Satanic subgenre, they featured a blend of cult movie influences and pop culture themes that made them a hybrid reflection of contemporary anxieties. However, most of these films were not directed by horror genre aficionados, but directors of low-budget exploitation films or Hollywood hopefuls, suggesting that the filmmakers, though they preyed on Satanic fears, only made use of these themes to boost ticket sales.

Throughout the decade, these horror films evolved from slasher riffs that used degenerate rock musicians rather than teens as serial killer bait to include an exploration of the occult and, finally, to incorporate popular themes of rebellion and escapism that dominated teen films at the time. As they changed, these films came to reflect the real-life climate of hysterical, out-of-touch parents and school authorities obsessed with the idea that music would introduce their children to sex, drugs, and Satan—or worse, turn them into sacrificial victims. Central characters were often lonely and misunderstood teens or young adults at odds with their families and society at large. Through it all, these films imply that their love of heavy metal—whether as fans or musicians—made them particularly vulnerable to evil.

Satanic heavy metal horror films may be the ultimate collision of rock music and occult themes, a connection that has existed in contemporary popular culture since bluesman Robert Johnson's alleged pact with the Devil in the 1930s. Following Anton LaVey's founding of the Church of Satan in 1966, the popularity of the occult exploded with an emerging counterculture and, by the 1970s, there were numerous heavy metal bands making use of Satanic themes. Following in the footsteps of Black Sabbath and Led Zeppelin, bands like Uriah Heap, Coven, Black Widow, Angel Witch, Pagan Altar, Cloven Hoof, Lucifer's Friend and Witchfinder General used lyrics and album imagery to pay homage to the dark lord (even if the band members didn't actually worship the Devil himself).

At the same time, Satan had made headway as a favourite topic of 1970s cult cinema. Aside from more mainstream Satanic movies like *The Exorcist* (1973) and *The Omen* (1976), there was a steady stream of films in which kids and teens were subjected to Satanic forces, such as *Satan's School for Girls* (1973) and *Satan's Cheerleaders* (1977), as well as films that linked the counterculture with devil worship, such as *I Drink Your Blood* (1970), *Lucifer Rising* (1972) and *Werewolves on Wheels* (1971).

This occult obsession continued into the 1980s, as Satanic motifs continued to prove popular amongst British heavy metal acts like Judas Priest, Iron Maiden, Motörhead, Diamond Head and Saxon, as well as their U.S. counterparts—the glam-influenced hair metal of W.A.S.P., Quiet Riot, Twisted Sister, Mötley Crüe and Poison. The glam-metal bands in particular skyrocketed into pop culture infamy, largely due to their use of makeup and conspicuous, gender-bending fashions. These musicians and their fans were perhaps more visible than their predecessors thanks to MTV and other music video channels that emerged during the decade.

Heavy metal and rock rebellion were also popular subjects for films in the 1980s.

Not only were there spoofs like *This Is Spinal Tap* (1984), which satirized a band's lifestyle and their enormous egos, but also comedies such as *Like Father, Like Son* (1987), in which a young metal fan and his dad accidentally switch bodies, and mainstream musicals like *Footloose* (1984), where a Chicago teen brings rock music and dancing to a conservative small town. Metal bands and their fans were also immortalized in documentaries like Jeff Krulik's short cult film *Heavy Metal Parking Lot* (1986) and the Penelope Spheeris documentary *The Decline of Western Civilization Part II: The Metal Years* (1988). Both films depict musicians, hopefuls and fans as somewhat unintelligent, obsessed with fame and sex, and in denial about their self-destructive lifestyles.

Drawing from this cultural stew, heavy metal—hair metal in particular—became a popular theme of horror movies throughout the decade, perhaps because of the musicians' unusual appearances, outsider lifestyles, and supposed interest in the occult. Two of the earliest films of the '80s heavy metal horror subgenre, *Terror on Tour* (1980) and *Rocktober Blood* (1984) referenced these widespread pre-conceptions about metal as they moulded tales of musicians targeted from within by a psychotic killer to the popular slasher film formula.

Terror on Tour revolves around a band known as The Clowns (a riff on KISS, who had appeared in one of the original horror-metal hybrids, the TV movie *KISS Meets the Phantom of the Park* (1978)). The Clowns are on the road touring when a number of hangers-on, including prostitutes and drug dealers, are killed by a mysterious figure wearing the same Satanic-themed makeup as the band members. Director Don Edmonds established his reputation as an exploitation pioneer with softcore films like *Wild Honey* (1972) and Nazisploitation classic *Ilsa: She Wolf of the SS* (1975), before turning to *Terror on Tour*, his only foray into the horror genre. This low-budget, largely ignored effort was filmed in just seven days and, according to IMDB, didn't receive an official release until 1988, when the band's music had become very dated.

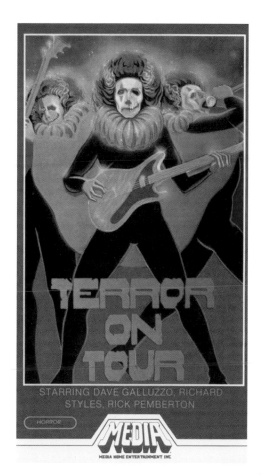

In the similarly-themed *Rocktober Blood*, a band is preparing for a blow-out reunion show years after the singer's murder spree, imprisonment, and execution. His girlfriend, also their new singer, claims he has returned from the dead and is stalking her, but no one will believe her, even as the bodies

Billy's back from the dead...
with a message from Hell!

Rocktober Blood

Starring
**TRAY LOREN DONNA SCOGGINS NIGEL BENJAMIN
RENE HUBBARD CANA COCKRELL**
Produced, Written and Directed by
FERD & BEVERLY SEBASTIAN

pile up. Much like *Terror on Tour*, *Rocktober Blood*'s director, Beverly Sebastian, was known for making low budget exploitation and action films—such as *The Hitchhikers* (1972), *The Single Girls* (1974), and *Delta Fox* (1979)—not horror movies. While neither *Terror on Tour* or *Rocktober Blood* tread new ground in the horror genre, these early examples show metal bands creating an environment ripe for violence due to their unconventional lifestyles and the atmosphere of drugs, partying and anonymous sex.

Another interesting early entry that falls somewhere between monster movie and heavy metal horror film is *Monster Dog* (1984), a low-budget Spanish-U.S.-Puerto Rican coproduction from director Claudio Fragasso (*Troll II*). By 1984, controversial rocker Alice Cooper had already starred in *Alice Cooper: The Nightmare* (1975), a horror-themed TV special co-starring Vincent Price, where he played variations of his stage persona. This approach continued with his starring role in *Monster Dog*—his character Vincent (Cooper's birth

name) is a disturbed, yet sympathetic rock star who returns to his possibly cursed ancestral home isolated in the countryside to record a new album with his band. Ultimately, Vincent is doomed—his father was a werewolf and he has inherited this demonic evil. Despite his best intentions, he is responsible for the slaughter of his bandmates.

In John Fasano's similar *Rock 'n' Roll Nightmare* (1987), Canadian rocker Jon Mikl Thor plays the singer of a heavy metal band, once again stalked and murdered by a mysterious,

The Fear...The Terror...The Nightmare...
They Will Never Forget It!!!

ALICE COOPER · VICTORIA VERA in
MONSTER DOG

supernatural evil. In a twist, it is revealed that Thor is actually an angelic hero disguised as a metal frontman, sent to battle the forces of darkness. Fasano has the distinction of directing the most heavy metal horror movies; after the relative success of *Rock 'n' Roll Nightmare*, he was able to get funding for *Black Roses* (1988), about a demonic rock band that invades a small town.

By the midpoint of the decade, heavy metal horror movies began to develop away from the slasher format to explore more overt occult themes, as well as issues of teen angst and high-school bullying. At the same time, news broadcasts, daytime talk show episodes (most notably Geraldo Rivera's 1988 special, *Devil Worship: Exposing Satan's Underground*), and Christian-produced documentaries like *Hell's Bells: The Dangers of Rock 'n' Roll* (1989), propagated stories that seem to be taken right from the

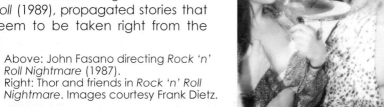

Above: John Fasano directing *Rock 'n' Roll Nightmare* (1987).
Right: Thor and friends in *Rock 'n' Roll Nightmare*. Images courtesy Frank Dietz.

plots of heavy metal horror. The *20/20* special, "The Devil Worshippers" (1985), alleged that widespread, underground Satanic activities were occurring throughout small-town America. Despite a lack of evidence, the special claimed that kidnapping, sexual abuse, and the murders of young children and pregnant women were commonplace Satanic practices. In the absence of actual perpetrators (often the only interview subjects were former cult members turned-right-wing Christians or young children whose accounts may have resulted from coercion), these news segments villainized metal musicians and pointed out a connection between the supposed Satanic cult violence and heavy metal.

One of the more well-known occult-themed heavy metal horror films—and one that directly references the hysteria-inducing daytime talk show phenomena—is *American Graffiti* alumnus Charles Martin Smith's *Trick or Treat* (1986). Many heavy metal stars appear in the film, which follows Eddie (Marc Price from *Family Ties*), a dejected metal fan who is constantly bullied at school. He worships rocker Sammi Curr (Tony Fields), who once attended the same school and is planning to play a Halloween show there. When Sammi's request to perform is rejected by the school board, he angrily burns himself alive in a Satanic ritual. The distraught Eddie believes Sammi is dead, but gets ahold of the only existing copy of Sammi's newest record, thanks to a friendly local DJ (played by KISS singer Gene Simmons). When Eddie plays the record backwards, Sammi arises from the dead—or perhaps from an infernal realm—to get revenge against his former high school. Though Eddie tries to stop him, Sammi is able to possess media technology: speakers, radios, record and tape players, and even a television, through which he kills an evangelist (played by Ozzy Osbourne) denouncing heavy metal on a talk show.

TRICK OR TREAT: A NEW HALLOWEEN HORROR FLICK FOR ROCK FANS!

Eddie Weinbauer (played by Marc Price, who is better known as "Skippy" on *Family Ties*!) is a typical teenage boy. He gets picked on by the high school bullies, like Tim (Doug Savant) and his goons, and then at home retreats into a fantasy world listening to his musical idol, heavy metalist Sammi Curr (Tony Fields). But soon his life will become atypical and dangerous.

Eddie learns of his rock idol's mysterious death in a hotel room fire. He visits the local rock d.j., Norman "The Nuke" Taurog (Gene Simmons) to find out more. He discovers that the town wouldn't allow Curr to perform at the Halloween

Gene Simmons of KISS (left) plays D. J. Norman "The Nuke" Taurog; Marc Price (bottom right) is nerd Eddie Weinbauer; and Tony Fields (upper right) plays heavy metalist Sammi Curr in October's Trick Or Treat.

Dance at his old high school. The Nuke also loans Eddie the only copy of Curr's last LP, which the d.j. plans to broadcast exclusively on Halloween night at the stroke of midnight! Eddie takes the album home knowing that Sammi Curr utilized the studio technique of back-masking (which is dubbing messages onto a record in reverse so that they can be understood only by playing the record backwards). The message Eddie discovers gives him an idea of how to get revenge on Tim and his

Marc Price ("Skippy" on Family Ties) stars with pretty Lisa Orgolini in Trick Or Treat.

Relaxing between the intense scenes of Trick Or Treat, Marc Price plays air guitar on the set.

friends. He also slips a cassette tape of the album into Tim's locker and a bad deed befalls Tim's girlfriend.

But soon, Eddie also discovers the danger that

One day Eddie notices that his sound system has been taken over by the spirit of heavy metalist Sammi Curr!

lurks within Sammi Curr's music. One day he notices that his sound system has been taken over by the spirit of Sammi Curr! Eddie becomes frightened and tries to destroy the stereo and speaker system, but a

blue bolt of lightning streaks out and knocks him down. After an explosive display of music, noise and electricity, an apparition of Sammi Curr emerges from one of the speakers. In a show of power, Sammi turns on the TV on which he sees Reverend Gillstrom, played by Ozzy Osbourne, on a talk show discussing the evils of heavy metal music. Sammi puts his

This was Charles Martin Smith's first and only horror genre work (with the exception of the pilot episode of *Buffy the Vampire Slayer*), one that he admitted was "not a particularly scary horror film" in a recent interview with *Collider*. It was essentially an assignment given to the first-time director by Dino De Laurentiis for his production company De Laurentiis Entertainment Group. With an opening weekend of nearly $3 million dollars, *Trick or Treat*'s success speaks more to the popularity of its themes than its effectiveness as a horror film. Unlike the earlier efforts in the heavy metal horror subgenre, this is less like a slasher film and more a riff on *Carrie* with a male protagonist. Eddie is tortured in a locker room by his peers early in the film, is raised by a struggling single mother, and unwittingly invokes a supernatural power to get revenge against his enemies, which ends with a fire at a high school dance.

While *Trick or Treat* villainizes metal to a degree, it also presents a more complex view of heavy metal music and fandom than its predecessors. Eddie wears band shirts, posters are plastered over his walls, and he has an extensive record collection that includes both popular and more obscure metal bands: Megadeth and Twisted Sister next to Impaler and Exciter. Hair metal band Fastway wrote and perform the film's metal

Left: German VHS cover for *Trick or Treat* (retitled *Ragman*).
Above and previous (Pg. 191): Images from a *Teen Beat* magazine spread on *Trick or Treat*, December 1986.

songs, and W.A.S.P. singer Blackie Lawless was initially approached to play Sammi Curr. Eddie is presented as an inherently good-hearted kid who is bullied and misunderstood, rather than being depicted as immoral or degenerate like the metalhead characters in earlier films such as *Terror on Tour* or *Rocktober Blood*.

Eddie's interest in metal is also portrayed as a viable option for his future and the movie ends on a positive note, with Eddie having defeated Sammi and Eddie planning to pursue a career as a radio DJ. But through Sammi and Eddie's devil worship, metal is still portrayed as a conduit for Satanic evil. Through a shared desire to get revenge, Eddie helps bring about Sammi's resurrection, but is horrified by the results. Some of his classmates are badly injured, people are murdered, and the climactic showdown involves Sammi trapping the high school students and teachers in the gym during a Halloween dance where he indiscriminately fries people to death with bolts of electricity from his guitar.

Trick or Treat's mainstream success allowed for a somewhat similarly-themed follow-up film, cult favorite *The Gate* (1987). Though no musicians are depicted, the two main characters Terry (Louis Tripp) and Glen (a young Stephen Dorff) are lonely and misunderstood pre-teens who listen to heavy metal records. Terry is like a younger version of *Trick or Treat*'s Eddie; he wears metal T-shirts, his room is adorned with posters, and he has an impressive record collection. Like Eddie, he is being raised by a single parent and spends much of his time fending for himself. The titular gate refers to a hole in Glen's backyard which turns out to be a gateway to Hell. Terry accidentally opens the gate by playing a record backwards and reading out a Satanic ritual written in the record's liner notes.

Director Tibor Takacs—whose career is made up of a combination of cult and mainstream films—describes *The Gate* as being a horror movie meant for children. In an interview with *Badass Digest*, he called it a creature feature and "an enchanting movie and not a hard-edged slasher film." This low-budget effort broke $13 million in the box office, becoming one of the highest grossing films of 1987— another indication that Satanic and heavy metal themes were increasingly in the public eye.

Above: Al (Christa Denton), Glen (Stephen Dorff) and Terry (Louis Tripp) in Tibor Takacs' The Gate (1987).

Like *Trick or Treat*, *The Gate* is another sympathetic look at heavy metal fans.

The atmosphere of *The Gate* summarizes the experience of young teens in a hostile world. While Terry struggles for the love and affection of an absent father who ignores him, Glen suffers his own form of domestic torment when his parents go out of town and he's left with his increasingly distant sister and her older, bullying friends. His childhood is decimated as the film unfolds: his beloved tree house is cut down and his dog dies during the course of the film, both of which lead towards the creation of the hell mouth in Glen's backyard. In *Heavy Metal Movies*, author Mike McPadden states:

> 66 *With perfect timing, The Gate arrived between Tipper Gore's anti-metal PMRC circus in summer 1985 and Geraldo Rivera's 1988 Halloween special on devil worship, the latter of which offered King Diamond a shot at NBC prime time. The 'satanic panic' of this era may never have been as widespread or taken as seriously as metal commentators pro and con will insist it was, but for '80s kids, hard rock demonology loomed everywhere: on T-shirts and blaring from the stereos of their older siblings, keeping congregants wide-eyed and worried during Sunday church sermons, and delivering socko TV news ratings one Ricky Kasso-style fuck-up at a time.*

Psychologists, such as Carl Pickhart in his article "Rebel with a Cause: Rebellion in Adolescence" for *Psychology Today*, generally consider rebellion to be a "poster characteristic of the teenage years, [marked by] behavior that deliberately opposes the ruling norms." Teen alienation— which ranges from asserting independence to the flouting of rules and self-destructive behavior— reached a head in 1980s cinema with everything from *Over the Edge* (1979) and *River's Edge* (1986) to mainstream films like *The Breakfast Club* (1985) and *Weird Science* (1985). Like Eddie, Terry and Glen, many of the characters in these films are outcasts, a theme nearly inseparable from heavy metal horror.

Above: Demonic creatures in *The Gate*.

Black Roses (1988), another post-*Trick or Treat* entry, takes the theme of teen rebellion a little further and satirizes it. The film depicts the quiet town of Mill Basin, where the local teenagers are anxious to hear metal band Black Roses play their first live show (though they are depicted as average teens and not specifically metal fans). Although their parents are initially against this proposed string of concerts, the high school principal and edgy English teacher remind everyone that teenage rebellion is perfectly normal and each generation has had their music targeted by shocked parents. Except that Black Roses—who appear to be tame pop-rock musicians with combed hair and clean blazers when the parents are around—are actually heavy metal-playing Satanists preparing to turn the town's kids into devil-worshipping zombies.

In an interview for this book, Frank Dietz, who collaborated with director John Fasano on production and acted in his films *Zombie Nightmare*, *Rock 'n' Roll Nightmare* and *Black Roses*, mentioned that *Black Roses* was meant to build on Fasano's earlier work. "It was intended to be another vehicle for Thor, who we enjoyed working with on the first two films," he says. "But somewhere between, there was a falling out between John and Thor, and the role eventually went to Broadway actor Sal Viviano. And even though our budget was much better on *Black Roses*, to appease the distributors we still had to use the same formula: monsters, nudity and rock music. So one film literally dove-tailed into the next."

Above: Frank Dietz in costume as the demon guitarist in John Fasano's *Black Roses* (1988). Photo courtesy Frank Dietz.

Dietz believes that, as with Fasano's films, so many Satanic horror films were made during the period in response to media events: "I think movies that mashed up heavy metal music and the Devil were popular to make in the '80s because they were topical at the time. It was a hot button topic, and filmmakers are always looking to the headlines for high concept script ideas. This was a no-brainer for horror filmmakers."

Director John Fasano stated in an interview with *Brain Hammer* that *Black Roses* was a morality play directly inspired by Tipper Gore's anti-metal censorship crusade. The genesis of the project began with him imagining, "what if Tipper Gore was right and some heavy metal band was not only playing music of the Devil, but was fronted by the Evil Dude himself. I figured the band would blow into some *Leave It To Beaver* town and corrupt the morals of the kids — they'd start drinking and smoking dope and having sex." Whether or not *Black Roses* was an intentional satire, both the conservative parents and wild high schoolers of *Black Roses* are shown as merely following the crowd, with amusing

parallels between the two. The film's only true misfit — and coincidentally its hero — is perhaps ironically the English teacher, a man trying to teach the values of independence and rational thought to a group of kids who just want to belong.

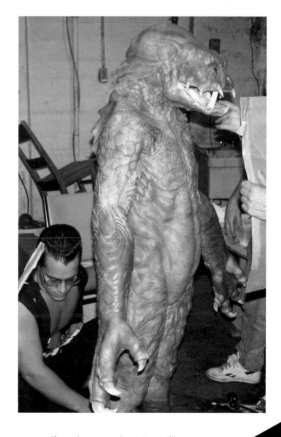

Following *Trick or Treat* and *The Gate* came slightly different riffs on a similar theme: *Halloween Night* (aka *Hack-O-Lantern*, 1988), *Hard Rock Nightmare* (1988)—not to be confused with the earlier *Hard Rock Zombies* (1985), where the members of a band are the rare good guys in the midst of a creepy small town—*Slaughter House Rock* (1988) and *Heavy Metal Massacre* (1989). The trend stretched into the early 1990s with *Dead Girls* (1990) and *Shock 'Em Dead* (1990). These films suggest that, even if metal is not directly responsible for evil, the type of person who would like heavy metal music or be involved with the counterculture is automatically susceptible to the influences of Satan and the occult.

Top: *Creature From the Black Lagoon*'s Julie Adams as anti-rock crusader Mrs. Miller in *Black Roses*.
Bottom: Behind-the-scenes monster makeup in *Black Roses*. Photo courtesy Frank Dietz.

One of the unifying themes throughout all of these heavy metal horror films is that the music itself is shown to be a corrupting influence, a conduit for evil through backwards–masked LPs, radios, stereos and headphones. Religious figures like Pastor Gary Greenwold and Lynn Bryson grabbed onto these ideas and spoke out about the moral evils of heavy metal, in particular the dangers of hidden messages in the music. This theme, a key plot point in *Trick or Treat* and *The Gate*, also appears in *Black Roses*, where the evil comes out of a radio and manifests as a murderous hell-monster. This can be seen even in non-metal-themed horror films like *Amityville II: The Possession* (1982), where a teen boy is demonically possessed by a force that spreads from music played in his Walkman.

Heavy-metal horror is perhaps unique as a cinematic subgenre in that, for nearly a decade, it paralleled real-life violence, moral panic, and a media firestorm, and was essentially the product of mass hysteria. As these movies were being released to VHS shelves across North America and beyond, stories of teens killing their friends in Satanic rituals flooded the news, and heavy metal bands enjoyed platinum and gold records and sold-out tours. In alignment with the news segments, Christian commentators and parental groups of the time, the 1980s heavy metal horror films played upon the fear that teenage rebellion leads directly to devil worship. And even though the directors behind these films probably laughed off the panic itself, they still suggested that even if your children started out as inherently moral, Satan was readily waiting in record players and VCRs to corrupt unsuspecting teens and transform them into violent Satanists.

REFERENCES + BIBLIOGRAPHY:

Christe, Ian. *Sound of the Beast: The Complete Headbanging History of Heavy Metal*. New York: HarperCollins, 2003.

Cohen, Stanley. *Folk Devils and Moral Panics the Creation of the Mods and Rockers*. Abingdon, Oxon: Routledge, 2011.

"Dolphin Tale 2 Interview: Director Charles Martin Smith." *Collider*. September 12, 2014.

"John Fasano Interview!!!" *Brain Hammer's Picks From The Crypt*. October 18, 2011.

McPadden, Mike. *Heavy Metal Movies: Guitar Barbarians, Mutant Bimbos & Cult Zombies Amok in the 666 Most Ear- and Eye-ripping Big Scream Films Ever!* New York: Bazillion Points, 2014.

Pickhardt, Carl. "Rebel with a Cause: Rebellion in Adolescence," *Psychology Today*, December 2009.

Showalter, Elaine. *Hystories: Hysterical Epidemics and Modern Media*. New York: Columbia University Press, 1997.

Victor, Jeffrey S. *Satanic Panic: The Creation of a Contemporary Legend*. Chicago: Open Court, 1993.

Walser, Robert. *Running with the Devil Power, Gender, and Madness in Heavy Metal Music*. Hanover, NH: University Press of New England, 1993.

Weinstein, Deena. *Heavy Metal: The Music and Its Culture*. Rev. Ed., 1st Da Capo Press ed. New York: Da Capo Press, 2000.

Right: Argentinean poster for heavy metal horror film prototype *KISS Meets the Phantom of the Park* (1978)

KISS téricos!
KISS tóricos!
KISS candalosos!

KISS
CONTRA LOS FANTASMAS

Una producción HANNA-BARBERA
con GENE SIMMONS · PAUL STANLEY · PETER CRISS · ACE FREHLEY
y con ANTHONY ZERBE · DEBORAH RYAN · CARMINE CARIDI
Escrita por JAN-MICHAEL SHERMAN y DON BUDAY · Producida por TERRY MORSE, JR.
Dirigida por GORDON HESSLER · Productor Ejecutivo LOUIS M. (DEKE) HEYWARD
Fotografía A. ROBERT CARAMICO · Efectos Especiales DON COURTNEY   COLOR

STEALING THE DEVIL'S MUSIC:
THE RISE OF WHITE METAL AND CHRISTIAN PUNK

BY DAVID BERTRAND

In the spring of 1984, the battle for the hearts and wallets of teenage metalheads was fought with fast licks, slick music vids and a moral war between God Most High and the River Styx. Metal titans Venom, infamous for their Satanic imagery and coining the term "black metal," released their third album *At War With Satan*—complete with a 20-minute title track hailing the Devil and his minions waging war against the heavens—just as Christian hard rock/metal act Stryper were hard at work preparing their debut EP, *The Yellow and Black Attack*.

By summertime, *At War With Satan* was pulled from the stores of music chain HMV over a possible breach of U.K. blasphemy laws, in one of the decade's first blows against objectionable lyrical content by conservative alarmist groups. Stryper, meanwhile, was on its way to becoming the first Christian hard rock/metal band to break out of the evangelical niche and achieve mainstream chart-topping success, eventually going platinum with 1986's *To Hell With the Devil*.

Left: Stryper in a 1980s publicity photo.

In the '80s, the music got louder and so did its critics, and the tug-of-war between God, church and righteousness against the audacious, hedonistic lure of hard rock was tauter than ever. Copping the Devil's music seemed a fine crusade, and what played out in record store bins that year was echoed in music collections across North America. As a heavy music fan growing up in the early '90s in Abbotsford, British Columbia—the epicenter of west coast Canada's Bible Belt—I watched as numerous friends underwent a born-again conversion and discarded their offending albums (which I promptly swooped up at a steal). The Christian stamp on heavy music was a big deal, edging some lesser bands into a bigger market share while slighting others from mass appeal. This is the story of how Christian metal and punk music snuck its way into the mainstream in the era of moral panic.

$7.95

WHY SHOULD THE DEVIL HAVE ALL THE GOOD MUSIC?
PAUL BAKER

JESUS MUSIC—
WHERE IT BEGAN,
WHERE IT IS, AND
WHERE IT IS GOING.

Early rock 'n' roll, R&B, country, blues, and other forms of popular music have always had a basis in spirituals, church hymns, and gospel choirs. But by the 1980s, popular music had been secularized for decades, and had shape-shifted through enough musical variants to thoroughly weed out any religious roots. It could be frustrating to be both a Christian and a serious fan of contemporary music. Larry Norman's 1972 boogie-woogie call-to-arms "Why Should the Devil Have All the Good Music?" from his album *Only Visiting This Planet*—the first Christian rock album admitted to the American Library of Congress registry, in April 2014—also became the title of a popular book by Christian DJ and journalist Paul Baker. Released in 1979, *Why Should the Devil Have All the Good Music?* was the first comprehensive text on the contemporary Christian music scene.

In his 1987 book *Religious Rock 'n' Roll: A Wolf in Sheep's Clothing*, defrocked (and refrocked) televangelist and gospel musician Jimmy Swaggart pins the beginnings of the contemporary Christian music industry to the rising Jesus Movement in Southern California in the 1960s and '70s, where:

> **❝** *Most of the new converts in the movement were young people burned out by drugs, shifting sexual morality, and hedonistic life-styles. Soon hundreds were flocking to Costa Mesa's Calvary Chapel, pastored by Chuck Smith, and other similar churches where the long-haired, blue-jean-dressed youths were welcomed.*

These lost kids loved folk music and rock 'n' roll before they ever loved Jesus. And part of the attraction of the Calvary Chapel and other ministries was the Saturday night jams. Musicians were plentiful at these gatherings, and looking for an outlet. Swaggart notes, disparagingly, that the resulting musical output—a blend of folk, rock, country and psychedelia mingled with overt Christian lyrics—was "an attempt to come as close as possible to secular rock 'n' roll without actually using the name."

Eric Strother's thesis *Unlocking the Paradox of Christian Metal Music* provides an excellent summary of the early developments in Christian rock, beginning with the seduction of acoustic hippiefied "Jesus Freaks" toward amplified heavy

blues rock like Cream and Led Zeppelin. One of the earliest Christian hard rock acts to follow this model was California's Agape, with their 1971 album *Gospel Hard Rock*. But it wasn't until near the end of the decade that the first true Christian metal band was born: Sweden's Jerusalem. Prog-tinged, ballad heavy and not to be confused with the

Above: The 1980 English release of Jerusalem's 1978 self-titled debut album.

British proto-metal band of the same name, Jerusalem's earliest albums were released in Swedish only, with later releases picked up and dubbed in English for Pat Boone's Lion & Lamb label. Leviticus—also Swedish—followed on their heels with a biting tone more in tune with the New Wave Of British Heavy Metal sound (Diamond Head, Iron Maiden, Saxon).

When Stryper signed to Enigma Records, they were still a secular act called Roxx Regime. But they soon adopted an explicit Christian lyrical approach, changed their name, and donned two-tone bumblebee spandex (drummer Robert Sweet's obsessive predilection for yellow and black stripes was, in a stroke of faith-marketing genius, attributed to Isaiah 53:5: "With his stripes we are healed"). Enigma then signed a distribution agreement with Benson Records, a Christian imprint. Stryper had the advantage of a double-whammy marketing arm in both mainstream rock promotion and Christian-specific publications and businesses.

The approach worked. In their wake, many acts (and many musical styles) followed, including Saint, Messiah Prophet, Barren Cross, Bloodgood, Sacred Warrior, and metal/punk crossovers like The Crucified. Most of these releases were distributed by new specialty labels—Pure Metal Records, Intense Records, R.E.X. Records. Many also had crossover record distribution agreements, such as Myrrh Records teaming with major player A&M. Sampler cassette tapes also proliferated at this time, such as *California Metal I* and *II* and *Heavy Righteous Metal I* and *II*, spreading the word on hot and unsigned Christian metal acts on the rise. These tapes played as big a role in the Christian scene as they did for secular metal and hardcore (Metal Blade Records' *Metal Massacre* series introduced the world to Metallica, Armored Saint and Slayer, for example).

Despite their success, bands like Saint (*Time's End*, 1986), Leviticus (*The Strongest Power*, 1985), and Stryper (*Soldiers Under Command*, 1985) faced an uphill battle fighting for legitimacy. Depending on who you asked, punk, rock and metal with an overt Christian agenda was either the answer to incessant moral decay—the kind identified by Tipper Gore's Parents Music Resource Center

Top: Roxx Regime, before they changed their band name to Stryper.

(PMRC)—or twice as alarming and objectionable as any lewd sexual allusions or cartoon Satanism. If the Church viewed religious rock as a perverse subversion of righteous gospel, secular rock fans saw it as a perverse subversion of rock music's lusting, exhilarating energy.

Likewise, the entire Contemporary Christian Music industry was recognized by friends and foes as an attempt to marry two disparate loves—the love of Christ, and the love of rock 'n' roll. In Marcus Moberg's thesis, *The Double Controversy of Christian Metal*, the author discusses Christian metal's demonization by conservative Christianity on one side and secular metal culture on the other, a persistent career headache for all involved in this increasingly lucrative extreme sidebar to the growing Christian music industry.

The most profound and enduring response to the Christian metal dilemma began in 1985, when Pastor Bob Beeman founded the "Sanctuary movement" in California. Updating the '60s/'70s Cavalry Chapel experience, this rock refuge was intended for Christian kids who felt alienated from traditional evangelical ministries due to their unorthodox musical tastes, dress, and social habits. Heavy music became the dominant genre of the rapidly spreading "metal

churches" that, according to Eric Strother, "not only encouraged their congregants to fully adopt the metal style and look; they also used metal music during church services and, to some extent, even embraced metal concert practices such as headbanging and moshing." These alternative parishes spread through North America, Europe and South America, offering metalheads a more appealing method of religious expression.

Sanctuary's success was such that, even today, Sanctuary International remains a relevant and adapting movement, having expanded, splintered and inspired numerous imitators (Pastor Dave Hart's Sanctuary in San Diego focuses on goth/industrial culture, for example). However, by no means did the Sanctuary movement smooth tensions inside or outside the Christian rock scene. As musical forms became more abrasive and intense—thrash metal, speed metal, hardcore, death metal, black metal, goregrind—the Christian mainstream's urgency to halt the defection of America's youth to a supposed worldwide Satanic element fueled by this new noise became more pronounced.

At the PMRC hearings of 1985, a hot topic was backmasking—intentionally adding messages recorded backward onto an audio track meant to be played forward. Bands like Slayer, Judas Priest and Led Zeppelin were all accused of using this technique for subversive or Satanic ends. At the same time, videos and TV specials made waves, from Geraldo Rivera's *Devil Worship: Exposing Satan's Underground* to Eric Holmberg's *Hell's Bells: The Dangers of Rock 'n' Roll* (1989). Though these rock exposés usually avoided

Above: A promotional card from Pastor Bob Beeman, founder of the metal-friendly Sanctuary movement.

the issue of Christian metal and punk—perhaps granting them a pass by omittance?—Christian metalheads were busy enough defending themselves to the church to jump to the defense of secular acts under fire, even those from who they copped their influences. And sometimes, religious rockers were the most critical.

In the March 30, 2012, episode of his podcast *Pastor Bob Daily*, Bob Beeman is asked to discuss televangelist Jimmy Swaggart's highly publicized attacks on rock music and the contemporary Christian music industry. In the episode, Beeman confesses regret at his role in the Satanic Panic paranoia during the late '70s to mid '80s, when he toured the USA with his presentation, "The Rock That Steals Your Soul." He claims, "Even though I'd love to forget it, I am one of the people—if not the person—who started [the panic over] backward masking. It's something I deeply regret. You know there are some things in your life, if you could go back and redo them, you'd do them a lot differently." Speaking to crowds of thousands, his early efforts to promote Christian rock/punk/heavy metal bands were defined by demonizing the alternative. Beeman bemoans, "I really created a monster."

Regardless, this sharp divide encouraged a self-proliferating industry. At the online forum *Christian Metal Realm* there is a substantial thread under the question: "Do you have anti-Christians/controversial bands in your discography?" The response varies, from those who claim to listen to 98% secular music with a couple of choice Christian acts in the mix, to those who steadfastly refuse to listen to any music of any variety that is not in overt praise of God. In between, there are those that will accept metal bands in the PG-13 range like Iron Maiden, or object only to cuss words and sexual content, and others who admit to enjoying much harsher music like Slayer, but skip the songs with overtly Satanic lyrics (interestingly, Slayer's Chilean-born frontman Tom Araya is a practicing Catholic).

A common refrain at the Christian Metal Realm forum is the symbolic ditching of one's record collection when the inner turmoil gets too much. Others found their own workaround. One forum member states about her black metal music collection, "I just can't respect the intelligence of blatantly Satanic bands, so that disarms some of the lyrical power. Nowadays I just skip blatantly Satanic bands, and if a band is too anti-Christian I might torrent instead of buying, or buy but not rip any songs that are particularly bad. The anti-Christian element is certainly in a different category from violence, sex or even nationalism/racism. Those themes don't really factor for me in the same way."

Teetering the line between criticism/acceptance of mainstream Church opinion and the communal support of the metal underground is a daily life struggle for Christian extreme music fans, and musicians especially. Hence the need for worthy fanzines to connect fellow soldiers (under God's command). *Heaven's Metal* was the first of the bunch, founded in 1985. It currently lives on as *HM Magazine*, a digital zine published monthly, bearing similarities to most other slick, contemporary heavy music sites, such as *MetalSucks.net*, *Brave Words & Bloody Knuckles*, *Metal Hammer*, or its fellow Christian publication, *Untombed.com*.

Top right: An early edition of *Heaven's Metal* magazine.
Bottom right: The impaled hand of Pastor Bob Beeman on Vengeance Rising's (then still called Vengeance)1988 album *Human Sacrifice*.

In the '80s, the interplay between the Sanctuary movement, *Heaven's Metal*, Christian music festivals, and new bands on the rise was very tight indeed. Vengeance Rising's 1988 album *Human Sacrifice* was the first prominent Christian thrash/death metal release, and voted by *HM Magazine* as #1 on their list of the top 100 Christian metal albums of all time. Roger Martinez, a pastor of a Sanctuary congregation, fronted the band, delivering harsh indecipherable guttural vocals, another first for Christian metal. Not only that, but for the album's controversial cover art, an iron spike is nailed to a cross through the bloodied hand of none other than Sanctuary founder Bob Beeman.

As the decade reached its climax and moved on, further subgenres were born and the Christian music community followed suit. Scandalous Scandinavian black metal inspired Horde's *Hellig Usvart*, the first Christian black metal (or "unblack metal") album, whose sole instrumentalist/vocalist Jayson Sherlock was also drummer for the first Christian pure death metal album, the eponymous release by Mortification (1991). Not unlike Stryper's mainstream label crossover years prior, both albums were released by popular main market metal label Nuclear Blast. The barrier to the secular market had thinned considerably by this time, even more so across the genre threshold at the world's most popular Christian punk label, Tooth & Nail Records (home to MxPx, P.O.D., Thousand Foot Krutch), whose releases sold at regular record stores as well as my local Christian book emporium, House of James.

But regardless of mainstream crossover, heavy music and Jesus were most often odd, embattled bedfellows. In his autobiography *Honestly: My Life and Stryper Revealed*, Stryper's lead singer Michael Sweet recounts being unwittingly booked to a death/thrash metal festival bill in Holland, where the band was greeted by chants of "Fuck Stryper! Fuck Stryper!" as they took the stage. An effigy of Robert Sweet's face—Stryper's drummer and Michael's brother—with a woman's body attached, was affixed to an inverted cross and burnt and torn to shreds as bottles were thrown, and a steel chain with a padlock nearly took off Michael Sweet's head. They were unwelcome invaders, treated accordingly. (The happy ending, according to Sweet, is that God anointed Stryper after the third song, and the crowd turned in their favour.)

Pre-conceptions hurt, too. The doom metal band Trouble—one of the finest riff metal acts to follow Black Sabbath's example through the '80s and '90s—was branded "white metal" by the marketing team at Metal Blade Records after hearing the positive Christian twist to singer Eric Wagner's grim lyrics of turmoil against the Devil's forces. This gimmicky tag was a play on the then-developing genre of first wave "black metal" used to describe Sodom, Venom and their stylistic adherents. It was a label—much to the chagrin of the band—that they still can't shake three decades later, alienating a potential fanbase before they even hear a note.

If it isn't hard enough to get metal fans on God's side, Christian metal's other burden is to convince believers and

Above: Reluctant "white metal" band Trouble's 1987 album *Run to the Light*.

the rest of the contemporary Christian music industry that heavy music isn't inherently Satanic. Many evangelicals feel that Christian rock is not just a "wolf" in sheep's clothing, but the deliberate work of Ol' Scratch himself. Jimmy Swaggart, for example, states that his biggest bone to pick with the genre is that Christian rockers are profiteering from their music and living like rock stars, whereas true disciples of Christ would never seek to profit from art in His name (never mind that Jimmy Swaggart Ministries profited handsomely from sales of his book). Coupling a quest for material gain with rock star idolatry and hedonism opens up accusations of outright Satanism—carnality, egoism, the worship of the flesh and the self, God's name used merely as the hook to bait and confuse believers.

A *Newsweek* report quoted in Swaggart's *Religious Rock 'n' Roll: A Wolf in Sheep's Clothing* claims that contemporary Christian artists sold more than 20 million albums in 1984, the year Christian metal made major waves. According to the Gospel Music Association, over 56 million units of Christian/gospel albums and tracks (both physical and digital sales) were reported in 2008. Only 17% of those sales fall into the "rock" category, which is further subdivided into metal and punk. And, of course, the Christian subsection has suffered with the rest of the music industry in the download/streaming age. But still, the contemporary Christian music industry is built on the same foundation as any industry: money.

Even Pastor Bob Beeman, who's spent a lifetime promoting and nurturing Christian metal, speaks frankly about the business, urging his listeners to enjoy music on its own terms because a Christian stamp is no sure guide. On the November 28, 2012 podcast of *Pastor Bob Daily*, he states: "There's just as much corruption, I think, in the Christian music industry as in the secular. A lot of the bands that are out there are singing for the Lord one minute and doing things they shouldn't be doing behind the scenes." In an earlier episode of his podcast from May 12, 2012, he also brings up this point: "There are those who look at Christian music as a profession. Something to break into. Something that catches people's interest. Something that they really do feel like, at some point in their lives, is a great idea. But it doesn't mean that everybody that's doing music is following the Lord and has a tight relationship with him. That is not the case. For the most part the Christian music industry really doesn't foster a lot of intense time with Jesus."

A more extreme criticism of the contemporary Christian music industry is best exemplified by one of Jack Chick's Christian mini-comic book Chick tracts, *Angels?* (1989), in which struggling religious rock band Green Angels are stuck in a rut playing the church circuit for poor financial returns. But the band soon hires a new manager, Lewis Siffer, who has promised them not only fame and fortune, but all the booze, drugs and groupies they can handle as well—as long as they sign a contract in blood. Lewis oversees the entire music industry via his worldwide organization "Killer Rock" (revealed via a hysterical wall chart that subdivides music into "Soft Rock (1950-60s)," "Hard Rock (1961-71)" and "Heavy Rock (1972-?)"). From Elvis and the Beatles to Black Sabbath, Kiss and Motley Crue, Mr. Siffer proudly boasts that his music, "pushes murder, drugs, free sex, suicide, to destroy country, home and education... And man... is it doing it!"

As the Green Angels become an enormous success (singing: "We're gonna rock, rock, rock, rock with the rock!"), one of the band members outs himself as gay and wants to marry his boyfriend. Lew, now revealed to be Lucifer, gives them AIDS as a wedding present. Another Angel ODs on stage, while a third gets "into vampirism." Luckily, a concerned fan slips the last remaining member a Chick tract, which he reads and immediately rediscovers God's grace. He confesses that Christian rock is a powerful demonic force and advises everyone to burn their rock records.

Like all the Chick tracts, this story has abrupt left turns, hammer-smashed messages, and is often outright ridiculous. But Swaggart and Chick's blanket cynical dismissal of the Christian rock scene may not be totally off the mark—recently, Tim Lambesis, lapsed Christian and ex-frontman of popular Christian metalcore band As I Lay Dying (and

Above and Right: Panels from Jack Chick's *Angels?* tract.
© 1986 Jack T. Chick.

currently serving a six-year prison sentence for soliciting an undercover cop to kill his wife), claimed in an interview with *Alternative Press* that "in 12 years of touring with As I Lay Dying, I would say maybe one in 10 Christian bands we toured with were actually Christian bands." He describes how even as he and other band members knew their faith was lapsing, they "talked about whether to keep taking money from the 'Christian market,'" but ultimately decided to continue, resulting in awkward encounters with fans and Christian press who wished to pray with them or hear the band members share testimony. Maintaining the myth out of a fear of loss of income, Lambesis assesses the real market value of the Christian brand, especially among teens: "A lot of Christian parents said, 'Yes, you can buy this As I Lay Dying CD because they're a Christian band.' They don't even think to actually check the lyrics."

This last statement is particularly intriguing when pitted alongside the central argument of Bruce Moore's e-book *Metal Missionaries: The Assimilation of Extreme Christian Metal into Mainstream Consciousness* (2010). As a promo piece on the book for *Blabbermouth* nicely explains, "For the first time, extreme Christian music has moved from the dusty back bins of the Christian bookstores to the front racks at super retailers like Best Buy, Wal-Mart, Target and Hot Topic." In the 2000s, the rare mold that Stryper broke in the '80s with its mainstream market success seems now the rule more than the exception, with metal/metalcore/hardcore bands sharing bills, record store bins and metal blog digi-ink with their secular ilk, and less and less objectors are batting an eye.

But, accepted or outcasts, Christian metal fans have long taken to justifying their love of the genre and take it seriously indeed. The *Christian Rock Apologetics* website features an extensive series of essays arranged by category to defend all possible criticisms of Christian rock. They believe Jesus would indeed approve of loud, abrasive music, and there are scriptures to prove it. From the King James Bible: *"Sing unto him a new song; play skilfully with a loud noise."* (Psalms 33:3)

And from Luke 19:37-40:

> **❝** *The whole crowd of disciples began joyfully to praise God in loud voices for all the miracles they had seen: "Blessed is the king who comes in the name of the Lord! Peace in heaven and glory in the highest!" Some of the Pharisees in the crowd said to Jesus, "Teacher, rebuke your disciples!" "I tell you," he replied, "if they keep quiet, the stones will cry out.*

The rock fans behind the *Christian Rock Apologetics* site take offense at portrayals of Jesus as a "loving wimp" (detailed under the questionable chapter heading, "The Feminization of the Gospel"). Early Christians were dirty, rough and tumble characters, outcasts who had sinned hard, and learned to repent just as hard, and to celebrate this conversion with volume, spirit and revelry. The Soulful, impassioned call and response chorus of Southern black Baptist churches is often thought of as the pinnacle of praise music with a power and beauty that transcends religious affiliation. But Christian Rock Apologetics argues that it's logically in line with Jesus' teachings that you should worship and revel in whatever way most stirs your soul. Any music is valid.

And many would agree: in 2007, *Revolver Magazine* proclaimed Christian metalcore's unprecedented swell of popularity as the "Phenomenon of the Year." Many of today's mainline Christian church denominations accept Christian rock, metal, punk, or rap in their services, to the point where younger generations may not realize there was ever a controversy. It is a tolerable middle ground where parents can give their children the music they want, even if they themselves do not enjoy or understand it, confident that at least the message will be positive even if the delivery is suspicious. If the battles fought by Jimmy Swaggart, Eric Holmberg, Tipper Gore and others to extricate this music from kids' lives was a decisive failure, then for Christian musicians to infiltrate, mimic and excel at these musical forms and become accepted by mainstream metal and punk fans must be a success.

Tough, heavy bands of the Satanic Panic era—in the eyes of Swaggart and the PMRC at least—tended to be lumped into the same bin of offensive, aggressive, indecipherable and subversive swill, with a few touchstones. To which Pastor Bob responds: "Some people need a platform, and you can find a demon behind any bush that you want to. If you're trying to find something, you'll probably find it whether it's there or not. And it's true that music isn't innocent. Music reflects our lifestyles, reflects our thoughts, our spirits, our aspirations. It reflects life. And because of that you have the good and the bad. That doesn't disqualify it. Instead of trying to find a hole to climb underneath, or talking about how horrible it is and how it offends us as Christians, we ought to listen to what they're saying, and respond."

But ultimately, by creating a separate, self-sustained (and lucrative) industry, Christians found a way to indulge in heavy riffs and rock 'n' roll pageantry while mentally and spiritually disassociating from the moral panic engulfing the music community at large.

At its worst, extreme Christian music can be a cynical knock-off with a heart in the heavens, supposedly, but a hand in your pocket. At its best, it can sway even the sternest crust punk or true metal headbanger to shout these immortal words:

"We are here to rock you and to say, TO HELL WITH THE DEVIL."

REFERENCES + BIBLIOGRAPHY:

Baker, Paul. *Why Should the Devil Have All the Good Music?* Waco, TX: Word Books, 1979.

Beeman, Bob. "Satanic Forces in Music," *Pastor Bob DAILY!* Podcast. Sanctuary International Matrix, March 30, 2012.

Beeman, Bob. "X-Christian Bands," *Pastor Bob DAILY!* Podcast. Sanctuary International Matrix, May 12, 2012.

Beeman, Bob. "Christian VS Secular Music," *Pastor Bob DAILY!* Podcast. Sanctuary International Matrix, November 28, 2012.

Chick, Jack T. *Angels?* Ontario, CA: Chick Publications, 1989.

Counelis, Paul. "Metal Missionaries: Christian Metal To The Extreme," *The Gate Music Magazine*, May/June, 2010.

The Christian Metal Realm: http://thecmr.forumotion.com/

Christian Rock Apologetics: http://www.mindspring.com/~brucec/craindex.htm

Downey, Ryan J. "Tim Lambesis World Exclusive Interview: The As I Lay Dying Singer Breaks His Year-Long Silence," *Alternative Press*, May 16, 2014.

"'Metal Missionaries': The Assimilation of Extreme Christian Metal Into Mainstream Consciousness," *Blabbermouth*, March 26, 2010.

Moberg, Marcus. *The "Double Controversy" of Christian Metal*. Sheffield, UK: Equinox Publishing Ltd., 2012.

Strother, Eric S. *Unlocking the Paradox of Christian Metal Music*. Kentucky: University of Kentucky, 2013

Swaggert, Jimmy with Robert Paul Lamb. *Religious Rock N' Roll – A Wolf in Sheep's Clothing*. Baton Rouge, LA: Swagger Ministries, 1987

Swank, Jonathan, et al. "The Top 100 Christian Metal Albums of All Time," *Heaven's Metal Magazine*. Taylor, TX, 2010.

Sweet, Michael with Dave Rose & Doug Van Pelt. *Honestly: My Life and Stryper Revealed*. St. Petersburg, FL: Big3 Records, 2014.

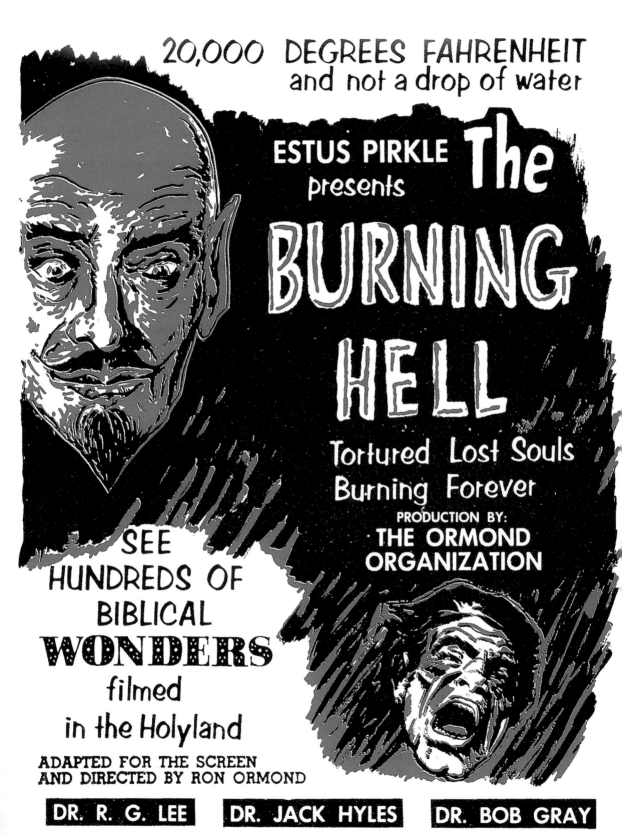

THE TRACKING OF EVIL:
HOME VIDEO AND THE PROLIFERATION OF THE SATANIC PANIC

BY WM. CONLEY

At some point in the late 1970s, the imagined death rattle of the cinema echoed throughout every frantic Hollywood boardroom and production house. While outlandishly expensive by current standards, home video players emerged as a viable technology for consumers. No longer dependent on the schedule of the cinema, moviegoers experienced film in the sanctuary of their living rooms on plastic-wrapped couches, accompanied by TV dinner trays and a great sigh of relief at the convenience of modern living. At the onset of this technology, most North Americans were watching *M.A.S.H.* on their home players, sprinkled with a pornographic film here or there. But as with all media consumption, there are always a few outliers whose viewing choices do not fit with the zeitgeist of their age. On the fringes of culture, a small and select flock of Christian evangelicals were watching VHS films that claimed that hundreds of thousands of youth were being influenced by Satanic forces, and participating in ritualistic sacrifices involving the slaughter of infants and children, often making "baby soup." Others were privy to the fact that He-Man was a tool of occult-Hinduistic-symbolism and ritualistic brainwashing.

Left: An original handbill for Ron Ormond's *The Burning Hell* (1974).

231

And, in case you've never heard, Satanic high priests in law enforcement were so powerful, they were able to kill with magical words and stares.

If such a dire and horrifying age of Satanic infiltration had emerged, then why were these films relegated to horribly produced endeavors on VHS? To be blunt, their claims are readily refutable and inconsistent. But in the insular glow of the home theater, removed from the outside world, madness becomes the word of God. In addition, home video served as an ideological apparatus for moralizing interest groups, most notably, a smattering of Christian Evangelicals in positions of localized political influence. The television screen was a 20th century burning bush, leading the chosen few on a path of supposed righteousness. In reality, these films laid a much more treacherous path, laying the groundwork for the Satanic scares of the 1980s and early 1990s. If it were not for the blatantly false claims and sensationalized imagery in these "films," the collective paranoia of a Satanic threat might never have reached the dizzying heights it did.

> **"** Your eye is the lamp of your body. If your eye is healthy, your whole body is full of light; but if it is not healthy, your body is full of darkness. Therefore consider whether the light in you is not darkness.
> –Luke 11:34-36

In the most basic sense, an Evangelical is a Christian who spreads the word of God. Due to the varied nature of Evangelical groups, a basic definition is as follows:

> **"** There are the four qualities that have been the special marks of Evangelical religion: conversionism, the belief that lives need to be changed; activism, the expression of the gospel in effort; biblicism, a particular regard for the Bible; and what may be called crucicentrism, a stress on the sacrifice of Christ on the cross. Together they form a quadrilateral of priorities that is the basis of Evangelicalism.
> (Bebbington 6-7)

The early successes of media evangelizing were not through film, but rather radio broadcasting. Groups like the 700 Club and Focus on the Family attribute their successes to radio broadcasting, not television or print. The Evangelical movement's flirtation with the film industry was not consistently observable until the 1950s, with Billy Graham's World Wide Pictures, a Christian filmhouse that released a variety of now oft-cited Christian cinematic endeavors. In some sense, location and access to media was the formula for Evangelicals spreading the gospel through the film industry. California boasted an extraordinary Evangelical population who migrated from the aptly named "Bible Belt" during World War II. This exodus to the sun-soaked 20th century Canaan was not a singular event for Evangelicals, but more so a shift in politics and populist ideology that propelled families and communities west. Ingrained in the migrants was not only a desire to spread the word of God, but for some to change the ways in which Evangelical worldviews were disseminated. A stroke of luck perhaps, that the home of television and film surrounded these communities.

In the past, Evangelicals had often capitalized upon broadcast media and drawn considerable audiences, however they saw the Hollywood film industry as producing media that went against the grain of certain Evangelical moral sensibilities. While religion speaks of truth to those with faith, these truths are subjective, dependent on communities and congregations. If anything, the notion of Evangelical factions and their acceptance of mass media cannot be characterized as a singular entity but a splintered population whose attitude varied from congregation and household.

Professor Nancy T. Ammerman, a notable sociologist and theorist on religious communities, commented on this point in an interview conducted in her office at Boston University:

66 *The notion in the Evangelical community has always been that there was something sort of dangerous about this whole [film and entertainment] industry. Because so much of it had to do with glamour and sex and violence and drinking, and all sort of things they don't want people to do. It's always had this sort of strange double-role in the community, where it can be a tool, but in this "we are very aware we're using the devil's tool when we do this" way.*

Regardless of the communities, varied perceptions on the profane notions of mass communication were easily pushed aside due to the scope of evangelizing that could occur. If Evangelicals could reach thousands, if not hundreds of thousands with films, media was seen as a minor transgression to save the souls of unbelievers and false prophets alike; the flicker of the screen, a small light to combat the darkness in a world torn asunder by evil.

Home video (particularly the formats of VHS and Betamax) began development in the early 1970s. VHS players did not arrive to the commercial market in the United States until 1977. The average cost of a trip to the movies was $2.23 USD in 1977, minuscule compared to the cost of one VHS film for $50 to $70 USD. The newly prevalent rental stores did not truly integrate with the Evangelical media market, however, preferring to

Above: *The Restless Ones* (1965) from Billy Graham's World Wide Pictures, wedded religion with the popular juvenile delinquent subgenre.

peddle horror films, adult films and a plethora of morally questionable material. While more palatable Christian films were certainly distributed in both national and local rental stores, video stores did not cater to a religious community that was at times distrustful of mainstream media, especially those communities which had historically shunned major media outlets on religious grounds.

The religious communities that paved the road for the Satanic Panic were very aware of their precarious position in the video market, and dodged this conundrum of faith by creating alternative means of dissemination. Evangelical film companies ultimately bypassed the economic system of mass media and popular culture by presenting and accumulating media through their own churches, companies and businesses. By creating a network of communication and distribution, Evangelical home media was able to garner ideological legitimacy through isolating itself to other like-minded Christians, while serving a product to a niche market that was eager for analog evangelizing.

Additionally, Evangelical home media allowed a fringe group to legitimize their beliefs for relatively low cost, avoiding the video store and going straight to pastors and religious leaders. The process of choice inherent in selection and viewing were in turn circumvented and the pastor was placed as a curator. Interestingly, this model of niche marketing has always been a tool of many organizations that are antithetical to Evangelical doctrine: punk and metal record labels, far-left publishing houses and even the Church of Satan itself relied on catalogs and mailing lists to distribute media in a pre-internet market. The difference for Evangelicals, of course, was that the selection of media was not individualistic but often based on the recommendations of a pastor or informed by other members of their religious community.

Ammerman elaborated on this as a trend, particularly the role of the pastor in selecting media:

> **❝** So you take the pastor's view of the world, his own view of their mission and ministry and congregation and what lands on his desk, and he's gonna do some sorting. He's gonna pick out what fits his view of the world and his ministry... You're not going to find that at Trinity Copley [an Episcopalian church in Boston's Back Bay]. It would be unlikely to land on that rector's desk because the producers are smart enough to know who their audience is. So there's a pretty elaborate filtering system that is in place before you ever get, "Here Mr. Jones, you should take this VHS home because you need to watch out for your teenage kid so they stick on the straight and narrow."

These films were more than simply vehicles to spread the Good Word. From the simple perspective of profit, Satanic-themed religious films on VHS were priced with the pockets of the producers in mind. As the Satanic Panic was a crisis of supposed massive infiltration on all levels, it would logically follow that many consumers would pay the price for a precautionary video rather than find their family pet chopped to pieces in the backyard on Halloween. Coupled with the fact that many church groups bought media through church funds rather than out of pocket, the model for production was one of quantity rather than quality work. Evangelical video groups not only knew their market, they also knew how to sell a product and sensationalized narrative to make a quick dollar.

Produced and distributed by a variety of Evangelical media companies, notable films such as *Exposing the Satanic Web*, *Not Just Fun and Games*, and *Doorways to Danger* are almost canonical in their contribution to the milieu of disinformation and reactive paranoia that marks the 1980s and early 1990s.

Exposing the Satanic Web is a ramshackle "documentary" of disinformation and shocking images set to poorly composed Christian rock that is arguably so weak and painful that it makes Stryper sound like the most evil music ever written. Viewers are greeted with an introduction by the inimitable Dave Roever, stern and concerned about the horrors he will impart upon his audience. The camera always faces directly at Roever whenever he speaks to the viewer; an apostle of mail-order analog truth that is assured of his duty to enlighten the world on Satanic forces that threaten the youth.

The film sets a tone of factuality by beginning with a heartfelt disclaimer. Roever, adjusting his glasses, warns that parents should not allow children in the room for the tape's length. The film quickly cuts to short vignettes of a cast of supposed experts and witnesses, who make claims as implausible as, "85% of the teenagers in Western Europe have been exposed to hardcore Satanism in school." This claim is shocking—so shocking, that it seems the producers forgot to include any reference to where that statistic was derived from. Roever addresses their research at the conclusion of the film, if any doubt was left in your mind. He states: "We've done our best in researching these people to qualify both their characters and claims. We believe in them, that they've been honest with you and with us." What a relief!

Above: Dave Roever's *Exposing the Satanic Web* (1989), not to be confused wth the Sean Sellers interview film *Escaping Satan's Web* (1987).

Exposing the Satanic Web is awash with disinformation and logical fallacies. A flier for a death metal gig is shown as a supposed invite to a Satanic mass. A school notebook drawing of the cover of Metallica's seminal album *Kill 'Em All* is used as an example of "Satanic threats" in school. In the conclusion of the tape, an expert on family therapy outlines two ways to prevent children from joining Satanic cults, presented in a well outlined freeze frame: "1. Strong family relationships" and "2. A belief in God." The producers bring it back to the nuclear family and religion, imposing the status quo of God and family on the viewer. As the credits roll, about half of the cast are revealed to share the same last name. A family that prays against Satanic infiltration together, stays together...

Jumping from hard rock to the toybox, the Canadian production *Not Just Fun and Games* (from Peter Lalonde, future producer of the *Left Behind* series) illuminates the occult tendencies of mass-produced toys and entertainment media. Released in 1991, when the Satanic Panic had begun to decline in intensity, *Not Just Fun and Games* is notable for its deeply unsettling footage of grown men in their Sunday best stalking the toy aisles for Christmas gifts that supposedly promote "Hinduism and humanism." The narrators proclaim that the Teenage Mutant Ninja Turtles toy line comes from the tradition of ninjutsu which, they say, is the practice of evil assassins murdering for the worship of occult forces. Aside from the fact that somebody let the cast into a toy store to film their delusions, there's something even more puzzling about where the director of this film first landed these ideas. There's nothing in biblical scripture that specifically cites children's toys as being evil, but the producers have many biblical references up their sleeves intended to legitimize their opinion. *Not Just Fun and*

Games highlights just how far removed from modern-day Evangelism the producers of many of these films were, incorporating a fringe belief system that was only presentable in the format of specialized home media.

Ouija boards, fortune telling and demonic possession are targeted by *Doorways to Danger*, a U.K.-produced Satanic scare film on VHS. The film unravels more like of a retelling of childhood ghost stories than a documentary. All but the last three minutes focus on people who have witnessed demons or malevolent forces when participating in "New Age" practices. One respondent claims that they saw a young girl thrown across the room after playing with a Ouija board, while another respondent claims that demons emerged in their room after using Ouija boards.

Doorways to Danger ends with a completely unprompted interview with an expert on Satanic Ritual Abuse, who posits that Ouija boards and astrology are major factors in the prevalence of Satanic cults in Britain. When compared to earlier VHS films on the subject, this video is very slick and well produced. However, the logic is clumsy and there's nothing more than stories of the supernatural, with a supposed expert begging to put away the tarot cards for the sake of the children. The film's supernatural nature is important to note, as VHS was the only viable format for such far-fetched tales. For many individuals who believed in the reality of Satanic forces, *Doorways to Danger* serves as a reminder to the metaphysical powers that Satan may unleash, tapping into more than just anxiety on supposed occultists.

Top: Toy store scrutiny in Peter Lalonde's *Not Just Fun and Games* (1991).
Above: Illustrated sequences from *Doorways to Danger* (1990).

> **❝** *Satan's sitting there, he's smiling / Watches those flames get higher and higher / Oh no, no, please God help me!*
> –Black Sabbath

Music, particularly that linked to youth culture, was one of the most targeted and scapegoated cultural forms of the 20th century. Lambasting and shrieking about the moral culpability of musicians and their messages has a long history that exceeds criticisms by Evangelical communities during the Satanic Panic. While moralizing interest groups have always targeted the impact of music and, in particular, its effect on youth, the Evangelical communities brought a particular brand of theatrics to their videotapes on the Satanic undercurrents of the music industry. Although the various incarnations of heavy metal at times seemed to embrace "evil" imagery as a metaphorical and symbolic position, to the Evangelical community these Satanic gimmicks were literal acts of wickedness not to be taken lightly. Most of the films already discussed touch on the dangers of music, but several films focused on music as the great catalyst towards Satanic domination.

Hell's Bells: The Dangers of Rock 'n' Roll is, foremost, a technical masterpiece compared to the other films discussed. The editing is well timed and synchronous with the narration. The film begins with a series of comical vignettes on rock's obsession with Hell and evil. As if that's not enough to suck in any confused teenager looking for a source of music their parents won't like, the first line uttered by the narrator is "What is wrong with this man?" accompanied by live footage of Fleetwood Mac. For a brief moment, the narrator seems like he could be vaguely relatable to any socially alienated teenager of the 1980s. Maybe he could own a Black Sabbath record or two. Or at least have a few Judas Priest singles?

The narrator in question is Eric Holmberg of Reel to Real Ministries. His casting as the narrator is deliberate, his presence exuding a relaxed and non-judgmental demeanor. Aside from sounding like a desperate high school guidance counselor, he is presented as an objective and informed source. "Well, don't get uptight... from the outset, try to keep an open mind," he pleads to viewers. "Don't anybody worry, we are not trying to control what people listen to," Holmberg smoothly assures.

Above: *Hell's Bells: The Dangers of Rock 'n' Roll* (1989) from left: title card, stoners in the park and Mick Fleetwood ("What is wrong with this man?").

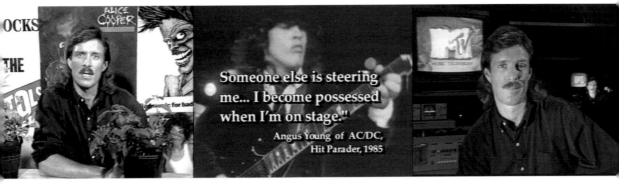

"Someone else is steering me... I become possessed when I'm on stage."

Angus Young of AC/DC,
Hit Parader, 1985

Holmberg's scripted narrative is a sort of soft-evangelizing in the beginning of the film. In an insidious form of moral normalization, he focuses more on the ideas of the "spiritual world" and various maladies of the soul, not simply the fire and brimstone of the other films. He avoids Satanic conspiracy, talking about the philosophy and history of music. There's something very logical and reigned in about the beginning of film. In part two of the film, the narration shifts as if the scriptwriter was replaced. The façade crumbles; Satanic conspiracy abounds, and the forces of darkness are everywhere. Listed as tools of Satanic deceit are hundreds of albums by the likes of Poison Idea, Mercyful Fate, Sonic Youth and… Creedence Clearwater Revival? Most puzzling is the amount of live footage of bands and great music that is played. One can easily imagine youth group members taking notes on what records to check out as soon as they were no longer under the watchful eye of adults.

A far less glamorous approach is taken by *Youth Suicide Fantasy: Does Their Music Make Them Do It?*, a video that burdens the viewer with fact after fact about the correlation between Satanism, suicide rates and rock music. The film must have been shot in one take, as narrators Dan and Steve Peters give each other smug grins as they obsessively talk about the "homosexual lifestyle" and "raw sexuality" that drives the spirit of rock music. The narrators stumble over each other and at times make statements that are absolutely nonsensical. On the creation of the term "rock 'n' roll," Steve Peters explains: "It was a sexual term called rocking and rolling with your girlfriend in the backseat of your car. It's a term, called sex." After delivering this line, Steve Peters blinks and stutters, the camera cutting quickly to his brother. Despite its

The Peters Brothers

Top: AC/DC's Angus Young flanked by Eric Holmberg of Reel to Real Ministries in *Hell's Bells*.
Above: Dan and Steve Peters in *Youth Suicide Fantasy: Does Their Music Make Them Do it?* (1984).

faults, the brothers hammer away at one point very smoothly throughout the frantic script: "We want you to go from the rock that breaks you, to the rock that makes you."

A documentary approach is often favoured over fictional narratives for these Evangelical scare videos, since shoddy acting and robotic dialogue from non-professionals often detracts from moral messages about the nature of sin. Watching

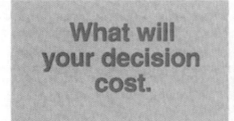

What will your decision cost.

In this thought provoking film, Jeff wrestles with his values. "What will this decision cost? My best friends? My relationship with my parents? My own identity?" At every turn is a challenge from family and friends, as they watch Jeff go through an agonizing struggle with facts and feelings. "Am I becoming a fanatic," he asks himself, "or am I finding my freedom?"

The decision is his. Discover the facts, as Jeff found them — **ROCK, it's your decision.**

55 minutes — in color

Above: VHS back cover of *Rock: It's Your Decision* (1982).

Rock: It's Your Decision, it's easy to see why—the story centers on a young man named Jeff in constant conflict with his parents over rock music. As Jeff becomes increasingly defiant to the limits set by his mother, his pastor has an interesting proposition: Jeff will research rock music and abstain from non-Christian music for two weeks. As Jeff alienates himself from his peer group and even his likeminded Evangelical friends, he comes to the realization that, "While we're trying to reach people for Christ, the record industry is trying to pump sex and Satanism into the minds of kids." At the film's conclusion, Jeff redeems himself in the eyes of his peers and church group, presenting a scathing critique of rock music. Rattling off a list of Satanic themed songs and sinful ideas inherent in rock lyrics, Jeff takes on the mannerisms of a tent revival preacher (or perhaps the actor is a preacher off the screen). In the greatest symbolic act in Evangelical media ever recorded, Jeff smashes a record in half and proclaims, "I've made my decision... what's yours?" *Rock: It's Your Decision* is different from the evangelizing in most of the more provocative informational Satanic Panic films, simply because there is no great appeal to a Satanic conspiracy. Originally released in 1982, the content of the film is not much of a classical "scare film," instead developing Jeff's faith-based reasoning as ample proof of rock's malevolent nature.

But not all Evangelical narrative films appeal to religious reasoning. *The Burning Hell* is a widely distributed shock film, originally shared via 16mm prints and shown in religious communities as early as 1974. Various Christian media groups reproduced the film throughout the 1980s, presumably duplicating the 16mm film reels that were once the primary format for viewing. The movie contains graphic depictions of hell and eternal damnation as if plucked from the films of the "Godfather of Gore" himself, 1960s horror director Herschell Gordon Lewis. Sinners burn, blood splatters and demons parade on the screen. While viewers could easily dismiss the film as shock footage, the piece is a fantastic and surreal ode to the foundation of Satanic hysteria. *The Burning Hell* is not simply a shock film, but a testament to the steadfast belief in the reality of Satan on this earth for evangelical communities.

These films, as well as countless others, were viable as mass produced products only in the context of home media. Productions on the VHS format allowed content to dribble out that would otherwise be relegated to small Evangelical communities' sermons, written works and the occasional radio broadcast. There is no fact-checking, only the same claim is repeated over and over again. However, this factual ambiguity accounts for precisely why home media was so successful for these scare films; they were viewed in small groupings, by people already prone to believing there was a massive cultural upheaval in the world around them. Due to the personalized nature of home media, individual pastors, religious communities and even those with probable clinical diagnoses centred on the distortion of reality were given a source of hyper-obsession for their "ontological insecurity." A term coined by Anthony Giddens, ontological insecurity presents a pervasive sense of dread at the social world one inhabits, where individuals feel as if their very being is threatened due to a disruption in routine and social events. Religious communities practiced a type of collective transference, where the anxieties of life in the 1980s were channeled into a singular threat that would rip apart their families and selves: in this case, Satanism, validated by home media.

This great rupture of stability spilled over as if shouted back and forth, amplified as it was repeated, twisted and internalized from video tape to parishioner to neighbour. In an attempt to liberate oneself from the slavery of Satan, Evangelical media companies did not simply spread factual deceit. They painted a reality where the world was a place of absolute evil, setting a precedent for prejudice and discrimination against those who fit into the broad category of "Satanic influence."

Eventually, the Satanic Panic became an issue not just for evangelical Christians, but a perceived threat to those in the fields of public education, childcare and therapy, with media that was produced for each of these industries on VHS format. *CultWatch Response*, a publication by Wiccans and occultists who hoped to bring awareness to the inaccuracies of this moral panic, lists the following selection of titles offered from Cavalcade Productions, a group that professes to produce media and resources for professionals working with children with trauma histories:

- *"Identification of the Ritually Abused Child"* (40 min, $225, rental $60, Cavalcade Productions)

- *"Treatment of the Ritually Abused Child"* (25 min., $195, rental $50, Cavalcade Productions)

- *"Ritual Child Abuse, A Professional Overview"* (30 min, $195, rental $50, Cavalcade Productions)

Any mention of these tapes is oddly missing from Cavalcade Productions' 2014 catalog; instead, all of their films focus on the current bio-neurological model of post-traumatic stress disorder and therapeutic processes, still for a hefty fee. The erasure of these films being part of a group's history is intriguing: were these films a cash-in? Or did the producers and owners of the company really believe that Satanic cults were systematically abusing children? Similarly, even Dave Roever, once so adamant in his renunciation of the Satanic forces in the world, has struck all references to Satanism from his current offerings. Attempts to contact Cavalcade Productions and Roever were unsuccessful. One can only hope that these films ended where they belong: filed in a dumpster somewhere, never to be seen again by an impressionable audience who blames those who stray from the flock for the suffering of the world.

Moral panics wax and wane, changing topics from crisis to crisis. While the Satanic Panic reached a respite in the 1990s, the disinformation propagated through home media towards groups labeled as prone to the Devil's influences is still observable as a residual belief. David V., a man I interviewed, spent several years, from 1995 to 1999, as a teenager in an Evangelical community in Massachusetts. While this was some time after the Panic had ended, David's experience was highlighted by feelings of isolation and extreme interpretations of the roots of his adolescent development:

> **"** *It's almost hard to believe it happened to me. It feels sort of dreamlike. It seemed like something that must have been a nightmare, I still have nightmares about the church. It's fucked. The place was fucked. I was getting into The Ramones, The Misfits, this harmless punk rock. This was considered a serious event at this time. I was not living with my parents anymore, through the school year I was living with other families. So one day I was in my room, I was staying with this family and they heard that I was listening to music on my CD player. They informed my father, and they informed the pastor and his wife. The next day I was summoned up to the pastor's office, and he informed me that one of the elders of the church was going to cast a demon out of me. It was clear that Satan had penetrated me with a demon, and had got into my life. They prayed over me. I didn't know what to do, you know? I felt more scared of them than I did of Satan. I was almost scared that a demon wouldn't come out of me, so I had to put on a show with them.*

When I showed David the aforementioned VHS films, he began to laugh. While he never saw these films directly, he remarked: "This sounds just like what they used to say. All this stuff about Satan... I mean they are right. It did corrupt me [laughs]."

David also recalls a community that shared their home media, where the group traded and bought films from other church groups across the country. David's church group would send a few select parishioners to regional and national meetings of like-minded Evangelicals, who would return with VHS tapes and literature. Finally, these films would be handpicked by the pastor and added to the congregation's library, which would be the primary source of religious information and at-home entertainment for parishioners. The second moralizing apparatus of the church was through the group's day school, which logically showed media that fit into the pastor's fears of Satanic domination of his parishioners. When media is curated and selected by an individual such as a pastor, the formation of an agenda occurs that may become an insidious part of that community's ideology for years to come and outlive the actual "reality" of the perceived threat. Perhaps these Satanic scare films still sit in a church's library somewhere, waiting to be dusted off and their clamshells snapped open, a Pandora's box of disinformation and fear to fuel the next Satanic Panic. Hopefully, the nearest VCR is broken, and these films are long forgotten.

VHS films are not the only cultural product to blame for the Satanic Panic—literature, political groups, television and law enforcement are all culpable, as well as a network of social and political forces. VHS films are a piece of the puzzle, and indicative of a shift in consumption of media from a pseudo-public space (a movie theater, library, etc.) to a private sphere, of individual homes or religious institutions. Media does not occur in a vacuum— it is an experience, and in the case of cinema, has always had an observable participatory element ingrained in the experience. According to Miriam Hansen, the experience of nickelodeons and early cinema can be paralleled to home media in its innovation, but fundamentally varied with its "enhanced powers of seduction, manipulation and destruction" producing a variety of experiences—but a radically altered perception of the information viewed.

Critical to the experience of the cinema as opposed to home viewing is the experience of the group. Specifically, the individual's reaction to a set of behaviors that are seen as minor acts of deviance in "open territories" and shared spaces, but are begrudgingly accepted as minor deviations. The crying baby, the drunken teenager and the jovial idiot who jokes over the movie: all these elements create a network of meaning that changes the reading of a film. Watching *The Last Temptation of Christ* at a late night showing in the late 1980s would be radically different if the venues of choice were a late night showing in Times Square or a North American suburban living room. Like a dose of "mother's little helper" or an "All-American cold one" after mowing the lawn, home video made people feel safe and undisturbed, able to tyrannize the screen with their own subjective truth on the essence of the flickering image.

In essence, the public spectacle, the reaction of the crowd and pleading whispers for quiet inherent in a trip to the cinema was reduced to no more than a package received by the mailman, or a few words spoken to a video store clerk. In the case of the Evangelical movement, the ability to watch films in isolation or within religious institutions was more than just a preference for convenience and normalcy, but an intricate process of the formation of a moral agenda. Home viewing produced a sort of warped worldview that could be likened to any devolved family grouping à la *The Hills Have Eyes* (1977) or *The Texas Chain Saw Massacre* (1974). With no audience to laugh at the claims of Satanic scare films and proclamations of factual legitimacy from supposed experts, the role of home media can be characterized as undemocratic and reactive when placed within small religious communities. This is not an indictment of the religious identities of Evangelical Christians, but a condemnation of the consumption of media as both objective truth and an unchallenged source of ideology.

We have progressed far from the days of The Salem Witch Trials and the Spanish Inquisition, which stand as tragedies that once eclipsed humanity in terror and monomania. These monuments of terror are slivers of human history, but repeated ad infinitum in both insidious and blatant forms. VHS Satanic scare films are documents of a civilization turned upside-down by fear in its most primitive source, as a source to rationalize the marginalization of others. In the final analysis, Satanic scare films were not targeting evil, but those who pushed back against the currents of cultural homogeneity and moral singularity. Cultural forms such as subversive music, drug culture and esoteric practices are all viable forms of meaningful experience, particularly in the context for youth of the 1980s. These have the characteristics of "Lucifer," of a mentality where "non-serviam" is the adage of living, where interrogating the social world is both life-affirming and liberating.

And what are the ideals of Satan, in a Biblical sense?

Satan is the great deceiver, "who uses all power, signs, lying and wonders" (Thessalonians 2:9). Satan is more than simply the pain and horror of this world. If this Satan is real, he dwells in the hearts of liars and false prophets, the wicked who accuse their neighbors and practice evil of all sorts. Is the mania of a modern day witch hunt—furthered by a simple VHS film—evil? Perhaps, if one believes in such things.

REFERENCES + BIBLIOGRAPHY:

Ammerman, Nancy T. Interview by author. September 23, 2014.

Bebbington, D.W. *Evangelicalism in Modern Britain: A History from the 1730s to the 1980s.* London: Routledge, 1989.

Black Sabbath. *Black Sabbath.* Warner Bros. Records/Rhino, 1970.

Copeland, Vicki. "Occult Crime: A Growth Industry." *CultWatch Response* Vol. II, Issue 1 (1989).

Dochuk, Darren. *From Bible Belt to Sunbelt: Plain-folk Religion, Grassroots Politics, and the Rise of Evangelical Conservatism.* New York: W.W. Norton, 2011.

Doorways to Danger. Dir. Tom Poulson. Sunrise Video Productions, 1990.

Durkheim, Emile. *Suicide, A Study in Sociology.* Glencoe, Ill.: Free Press, 1951.

Exposing the Satanic Web. Dir. Pat Titsworth. Roever Communications, 1989.

Giddens, Anthony. *The Consequences of Modernity.* Stanford, Calif.: Stanford University Press, 1990.

Hansen, Miriam. "Early Cinema, Late Cinema: Permutations of the Public Sphere." *Screen* 34.3 (1993).

Hell's Bells: The Dangers of Rock 'N' Roll. Dir. Erik Holmberg. American Portrait Film, 1989.

LaVey, Anton. "Welcome to the Official Website of the Church of Satan." Official Church of Satan Website.

Not Just Fun and Games. Dir. Peter Lalonde. Omega Letter Video Productions, 1991.

Rock: It's Your Decision. Dir. John Taylor. Olive's Film Productions Inc, 1982.

Tannenbaum, Frank. *Crime and the Community.* Boston: Ginn and Company, 1938.

The Burning Hell. Dir. Ron Ormond. The Ormond Organization, 1974.

The Holy Bible: Containing the Old and New Testaments with the Apocryphal/Deuterocanonical Books: New Revised Standard Version. New York: Oxford University Press, 1989.

V. (requested omission of last name), David. Interview by author. September 1, 2014.

Wasser, Frederick. *Veni, Vidi, Video: The Hollywood Empire and the VCR.* Austin, TX: University of Texas Press, 2001.

Youth Suicide Fantasy: Does Their Music Make Them Do It? Dir. Dan Peters. 1984.

BEDEVILING BOB:
PRANKING 'TALK-BACK WITH BOB LARSON'

BY FORREST JACKSON

Wayne the Happy-go-Lucky Satanist may have despised humanity, but he loved a lot of people and radio evangelist Bob Larson was one of his favorites. Wayne was friendly and well-meaning. He never sacrificed a black cat or a newborn brat and he didn't even like heavy metal music. If you heard him on the radio, you might have imagined him with stringy hair and a stinky black leather jacket, but in reality he was a preppy kid straight out of college. It's true he loved the goat more than the lamb. He certainly didn't fit the demographics of a Christian radio listener, yet every weekday he faithfully finished his office work as early as possible so he could tune in to *Talk-Back with Bob Larson* in the afternoons.

Yea, verily, Wayne admired this pipsqueak preacher for being a fighting man, a rude one who harangued half of his callers even as he begged listeners to keep his ministry afloat. The relentless fundraising was tiresome, but the topics were fascinating. Where else on the radio could you hear a widow relating the true crime of her pastor husband being slain in his church by a devil worshiper, a caller purporting to be a 15-year-old who had been beaten and impregnated by her father, and a heckler accusing "Beelze-Bob" of scripting all of these weird and wonderful phone calls? All of this and more happened during the same hour on

Left: Bob Larson in the 1970s.

January 18, 1995 and Wayne loved it. The only hitch was that Wayne the Happy-go-Lucky Satanist was not a real person. He was merely a character I created to prank my hero and adversary Bob Larson. At the time, it was just a goof. Little did I know that one day my prank calls would lead to meeting Larson, marveling at his typhonic combover hairdo in person, and having a room full of his faithful listeners pray for me.

In early adulthood Larson became a born-again Christian with a passion for fighting the Devil. Starting in 1967 he published books with titles like *Rock & Roll: The Devil's Diversion* and *Hippies, Hindus and Rock and Roll* in which he aimed his polemical barbs at the evils of rock music and Eastern religions. He also traveled the globe to push his faith. In places like Haiti, India, and Singapore, he witnessed ceremonies that convinced him of the reality of Satan and demonic possession.

By the time he started *Talk-Back* in Dallas in 1982, Larson was an autodidactic expert on cults and the occult. Invariably touting himself as a "best-selling author and commentator," Bob Larson was indeed a force to be reckoned with, especially when debating his listeners. As the popularity of his radio show grew, he became more outrageous, aggressive, and confrontational. The term "shock jock" accurately described him. He was quick of wit, 99% uncompromising, and relished bullying his callers. Always alarmist and an ally of alliteration, Larson knew how to pander to his

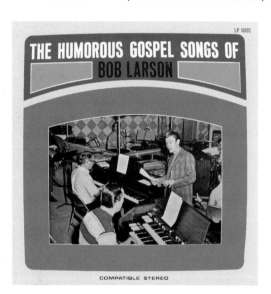

THE HUMOROUS GOSPEL SONGS OF BOB LARSON

LP 10105

COMPATIBLE STEREO

donors by calling them "heroes for the hurting." He begged for mystical-sounding sums like $111.56 and $223.12. Repeating these figures like numerological mantras, he insisted that donors of these amounts would "save" a station for a day or two. He made it sound like the ministry was perpetually on the brink of disaster.

Larson first gained mainstream attention in 1989 after touring with Slayer. He wrote about his experiences for *Spin* magazine and debunked the heavy metal band's Satanic image. He also produced videos like *The First Family of Satanism* in which he interviewed Anton LaVey's beautiful, bewitching, and intelligent daughter Zeena and her husband Nikolas Schreck. They told him that, if the miracles of the Gospels were true, Jesus was obviously a black magician. Bob prayed for their souls, but to no avail. Fascinating interviews with industrial music pioneer Boyd Rice, neo-Nazi James Mason, and demoniac Glen Benton from the death metal band Deicide were additional audio treats. And best of all, Larson occasionally performed exorcisms over the radio waves—between money-begging breaks, of course. In soliciting funds for his spiritual war against Satan, he always went for the scare and sometimes promoted conspiracy theories about generational Satanism and infernal crime syndicates. He cast a wide net of suspicions and considered demonic anything outside the Judeo-Christian belief system.

Starting in 1989, I called *Talk-Back* on occasion, hoping to get on the air to correct him on some point or other. Sadly, the soulless stammering of a busy signal always greeted me. One day the call rang through and I was surprised to hear a voice say, "Welcome to *Talk-Back*. What do you want to tell Bob?" My pulse raced. Larson claimed he frequently received death threats from devil worshipers, so I cleared my voice and explained how much I loved Larson, even though I spiritually opposed him. For whatever reason, I gave "Wayne" as my name. The call screener told me to turn off my radio to prevent confusing feedback when Larson took my call. I turned the volume knob counterclockwise, pressed the record button, and crossed my fingers the call would be worth saving. On hold I listened to the show on the phone. While I waited, I reminded myself that the goal was to be outrageous and confounding enough to keep Larson's interest as long as possible. Being from Texas, I hope you'll forgive me for comparing this task to a rodeo ride. Even though I don't own a pair of cowboy boots, the analogy rings true. Larson was a tough old bull and he bucked off most prank callers upon detection.

Each time he ended a phone call, I giddily anticipated that I might be next. When he finally picked up the line, I was nervous. At that time in my life I loved attention, so I found my jitters confusing. The adrenal thrill of finally getting on the air wasn't as fun as the pagan lust people like Larson will never know, but it was exciting in its own way. I psyched myself for the ride to come.

Left: Rare Bob Larson T-Shirt. Courtesy of the Robert Tilton Fanclub Archives.

"I'm going to talk to Wayne in Dallas."

In a peppy voice, I proclaimed Wayne to be a Satanist of sorts who loved listening to Larson. Wayne commended him for performing the interesting and valuable service of being Satan's best advertiser.

"So you don't want me dead?" Larson asked.

Hoping to drive him nuts, Wayne said, "No, I wouldn't know half of what I know now about Satanism if I didn't listen to *Talk-Back* every day."

Larson sarcastically thanked his devilish foil and said, "That's right, that's what I'm in the business of doing. Me and Moses, that was our calling. That's why Moses brought down the Ten Commandments. That's why he gave the people the Levitical Law, because they didn't know how to sin."

In vain, Wayne tried to interject, but Larson barreled onward.

"When Moses came along, he told them about incest, homosexuality, and bestiality and those poor people didn't know what to do until Moses explained it to them. I see, I have the Moses syndrome."

To which Wayne gleefully responded, "You've got the Moses demon."

"I've got Moses demons?"

With an all but audible grin, Wayne followed up, "Yes, the demon of Moses is inhabiting your body as we speak."

Knowing he'd been had, Larson exhaled in exasperation and kicked Wayne off the line. It hadn't been a funny phony phone call and it hadn't lasted very long. But, hearing that frustrated sigh was a delight, so I leaned back in my chair with a sense of satisfaction. My day was done.

I count myself among the simultaneously adversarial, skeptical, and amused demographics of Larson's audience. I'm not an atheist and I'm not angry with Christianity. The way I see it, since the universe seems infinite, anything is possible. So however unlikely the Bible's miraculous claims, Christianity deserves respect for helping people live in ways they feel are right. The same goes for all of the world's major religions when viewed objectively. And that means the same goes for cults and even joke religions like the Church of the SubGenius. Viewing established religions as valid primarily for the people who started them, I consider most of them ossified, if not dead. The solution, my brothers and sisters? Start your own love and terror cult! So, that's what my friends and I did, creating from scratch two small-time sects, the Diabolicrats of Disturbathon and a new religious movement henceforth referred to as Jacuzzism, which Larson eventually became familiar with.

If listening to *Talk-Back* was entertaining, then getting on the air felt like being part of the entertainment. I'm neither God's nor the Devil's gift to the world of prank phone callers, but I like to think that thousands of people were amused by my efforts. Often, he dispatched me within a minute. This became more problematic after Larson learned to recognize Wayne's voice. One time Larson expressed dismay that Wayne made it past the call screeners. Quickly, he asked what was planned for the summer solstice. The call didn't last long after Wayne replied, "nakedness, Jell-O pits, and goat loving." In another brief exchange in which Wayne praised Dr. Kevorkian, Larson resorted to name-calling. He called Wayne an "inexperienced 23-year-old jerk."

Wayne wanted to know, "Why am I a jerk? I've always been perfectly nice to you."

Flustered for a few seconds, Larson then resolved, "You're worse than a jerk. You're an abomination."

Wayne agreed, "OK, I'd believe that."

If the goal was to hang on to the airwaves as long as possible to confound Larson with outrageous claims and specious arguments, the nearly impossible task of leaving him speechless was like riding the bull for the full eight seconds. Flummoxing a professional broadcaster put joy in my heart. Hallelujah! I especially enjoyed hearing him repeat my words in disbelief while he marshaled his next thought. Sometimes, I had him on the run. Other times the hoaxes were too obvious, but succeeded in being so ridiculous that even Larson had to laugh. When the topic was the Avon Books edition of the *Necronomicon*, Wayne asked if he could use it to summon the spirit of H.P. Lovecraft. Larson said no, but a malevolent entity might manifest and claim the author's identity. The way I see it, Larson offered this non-committal answer to keep the Devil alive and well in the minds of his credulous donors. Then Wayne claimed that Larson, Lovecraft, and the pop star Prince were three of his favorite people and he had a tattoo on his back of them playing in a jazz trio. This got Larson laughing, sputtering, and laughing some more. Wayne elaborated that Bob was on banjo while Lovecraft was on drums looking askance at Prince, because Lovecraft was a racist. Larson urged Wayne to snap a Polaroid to confirm it.

Larson then changed tack. "You know you're not supposed to say Prince's name. He doesn't have a name anymore."

"I know and I'm also wondering if I could use a Ouija board to summon the old Prince. I don't like his new music now that he's changed his name."

"It's entirely possible, but if it happens, you'll have to take a bath afterwards. Do you want to know why?"

Knowing Larson was wise to the shenanigans, it was Wayne's turn to sigh. "Um, no. You can give me a quick one on this."

"Because if you do, you'll be totally drenched in purple rain."

Right: A 1994 issue of *Snake Oil Magazine* (formerly *The Robert Tilton Fanclub Newsletter*).

$NAKE OIL

YOUR GUIDE TO KOOKY KONTEMPORARY KRISTIAN KULTURE

$2.00

2

"MY DINNER WITH BOB LARSON"
exclusive interview with Boyd Rice!

plus........

THE BAD MOJO OF DAVID KORESH: BLACK MAGICIAN

REV. BOB MEETS THE STARS!
An Astrological Profile of Robert Tilton

Amused with himself, he told his audience to "mark one up for Bob." He went on to congratulate Vanity for ditching her nasty girl ways and becoming a born-again Christian. He even proclaimed, "There's hope for Prince, too." Yet, Larson would still deny hope for the multi-talented, re-renamed Prince who is now a Jehovah's Witness. For whatever reason, most Protestant Christians have no respect for their *Watchtower*-distributing spiritual brethren.

Eventually, I mustered the courage to call *Talk-Back* using my own name and this is what led to meeting Bob in person at one of his money-sponging rallies. Knowing his rigid, traditional values, one day I sought to subvert them by speaking in favor of the superiority of women. The topic was "Hillary for President," but I immediately started ranting about goddess worship. When I mentioned that I had called his show before, he exclaimed, "Oh! You are the idiot I remember." He may have recognized my voice, but hadn't identified me as Wayne.

"I don't think 'idiot' would be the word to describe me, Bob."

With haywire, circular non-logic, Bob told me, "You are an idiot, an absolute complete, total jerk. You're even more of a jerk than the guy who called a moment ago claiming that he needed spiritual help, which we discovered was a prank."

I knifed in, "This is no prank, Bob."

"I know you're not a prank; he was a jerk, you're an idiot. There is a difference."

When I said I wanted to "talk science," Larson asked how I could do that while worshipping the ancient Triple Goddess? I explained I was a materialist agnostic who worshiped her in a metaphorical sense and returned to the hypothesis of having Hillary Clinton for president.

"We should have a woman for president, but I don't necessarily agree with her politics. I agree with her anti-life stance and I disagree with her politics of economy."

"Whoa, whoa, whoa. Wait a minute. Did I hear you say you disagree with her anti-life stance?"

Speaking slowly with a pause after each word, I reiterated, "No. I agree with her anti-life stance."

This really set him off, as I knew it would. Praise Jesus, this call would last a while longer.

"You agree with her pro-abortion stance? Why would I be surprised that someone like you is pro-abortion?"

"I'm for the extermination of most men in the world. That doesn't include you, because you're very amusing. I think we could have a lot of fun with you and all the ladies of the coming future."

"The ladies of the coming future could have fun with me? And what would that be, putting me in a pillory and throwing rotten tomatoes at me? Where did you get this kooky idea? Did your mother not change your diapers or something?"

"Bob, I'm surprised you didn't talk more about underwear yesterday when the topic was Mormonism."

"I could have yesterday, but we'll talk about Bill Clinton's briefs later today if you'd like."

Larson next accused me of witchcraft. I objected and turned the topic to genetics. I told him that scientists had successfully completed an ova-fusing operation that would produce only women. The idea of making men obsolete really got under Larson's skin and the call lasted longer than I could have expected. My canard garnered me a rare, if back-handed compliment. "You know what's dangerous about you? You've got a brain."

"Yes, I do. I have a degree in organic chemistry."

I don't, but it sounded good at the time.

"You're half smart and that's what's dangerous about you. When I said you were an idiot, by the way, I meant spiritually."

"That will be for you and all of your gods to judge."

"Forrest, you're just mad and you're trying to take it out on Christianity."

I disagreed and referred to a rape victim who had recently called to ask for help from Bob Larson Ministries. Working in a Larson-laudable alliteration, I said, "You heard what those men did to Laura the Lucky Lesbian. If that's the kind of thing men do to women and men cause all of the problems in the world, then they should be exterminated."

"And when do they start with you?"

"That will be up to them. I don't place any great value on my life."

Again—and keep in mind this was music to my ears—Larson repeated my silly words, "Whoa, whoa, whoa. You don't place any great value on your life?"

"I value women and women's lives and their edification and superiority."

Confused, but still in control like a boxer holding his ground in the last round, Larson hit me again. "I just want to ask you another question, so play straight with me, Forrest.

You really mean this?"

"Yes. And we have a whole group of Jacuzzists here. We're not idiots and we're not goofing around. We're seriously promoting these ideas and we've written books about them." This last point was an extreme exaggeration, but I had extolled the virtues of the fair sex in a photocopied zine.

"Maybe you should send me copies of those books. I'm going to put you on hold in a moment so you can talk to the operator. Maybe we could do a whole show on this. I'm not interested in giving you publicity, but I am interested in finding out where you're coming from. And I'm very interested in this audience praying for you. I know that sometimes when you're sitting there listening to these people, you say, 'Larson, you're talking to a nut-case.' I think that anyone who is terribly discerning can listen to this kid and know that he's not just a nut-case. Yeah, he's nuts. Spiritually, he's crazy. But he's also a very bright and articulate young man. There are more kinds of dangerous, kooky cults out there than you could possibly fathom and none more so than the Church of Jesus Christ of Latter-day Saints." And of course, he went back to begging.

True to his word, Larson transferred me to his producer who jotted down my information, asked more questions, and implied they would get back to me. In anticipation of an invitation to Larson's Denver studio, I sent a videotape of the Disturbathon, a wild Halloween party my friends and I turned into a local legend that remains rife with rumors of bestiality, necrophilia, and devil worship. Larson watched

it and fixated on one outrageous aspect which he used to his advantage both on his show and when confronting us in person.

But now, a word about Jacuzzism. What was this dripping wet excuse for a religion? It was an affiliation of Dallas/Fort Worth area artists, zinesters, musicians, absurdists, and wannabe gnostics who sought a shared earthly paradise through sensory overstimulation. Owing to our reliance on sacraments of psychedelic chemicals, nitrous oxide, and coffee, our slogan should have been, "come for the drugs, stay for the disappointments." It bubbled up from philosophical and spiritual discussions my friends and I had while sitting in an apartment complex hot tub. It eventually deteriorated into communal bouts of weird video viewing and brain-numbing narcomania, the lame cousin of full-on hedonism. The jabberwockied tenets are not important. The point is, we were cultists in the eyes of people like Larson.

If Jacuzzism was kooky, Disturbathon was downright demonic. Now in its 25th year, Disturbathon remains a threat to all of Larson's values, so it's no surprise he views it as Satanic. If you search the internet for "disturbathon" you will likely find the website for the Texas Cult Awareness Network which describes it as "the most dangerous cult operating in Texas since the Branch Davidians." It says we use CIA-inspired mind control techniques and characterizes the pornographic Halloween party as a means of recruitment. The latter part is true and the Diabolicrats are kind of cultish, but the funny thing is that the Texas Cult Awareness Network is actually our own invention. Most people don't get the joke when they visit that site, but I assure you this disinformation is just another prank.

The upshot is, regardless of our intentions, we bolstered Larson's claim that cults remain a danger to God-fearing people everywhere. We were certainly good for business when Larson came to town on a "Save Our Kids from Satanism" tour in the mid-1990s. Keep in mind that even if his ostensible objective was to give "hope to the hopeless," cash for the coffers was really his number one goal.

My friends and I arrived early and found front row seating in the Metroplex Chapel, an ugly edifice that looked more like a convention hall than a church. I estimate there were almost a thousand souls in attendance. I was glad I'd decided to wear a tie. With my fresh haircut and shave, I looked as conservative as any devout Christian. I drew no strange looks from the flock. Not yet.

While waiting for the show to begin, I asked an usher to let Larson know the dreaded Jacuzzists were in the house. I had no expectation that he would deliver the message, but he must have done it because Larson soon singled us out. Immediately after emerging to applause and introducing a local pastor, he pointed our direction. Shaking his head, he told the audience, "These guys would be disappointed if they thought I didn't know they were here. You guys are strange. They call my show every once in a while and they are weird. They've got this thing called Jacuzzism. Remember them?"

Gasps and groans proved a few attendees had heard the prank calls.

He stepped down from the stage and jabbed the microphone in my face, so I heartily welcomed him to the home of Jacuzzism. Then, he addressed the guy sitting to my left. Clark said he had recently given his life to Jesus, which elicited much applause. Although it made him look like a shill, it was actually true. A few weeks earlier he'd had the "born-again" experience at a Power Team rally, where weight lifters showed their strength in Christ by wearing Spandex, picking up heavy objects, breaking boards with their bare hands, and the like.

With the fervor of the newly converted, Clark confessed, "I used to be associated with Jacuzzism, but since then I prayed to Jesus Christ and was delivered from drug and alcohol addiction."

Voice rising in pitch, Larson asked, "So you're with them?"

Clark truthfully answered, "No, but we're still friends. We're not so tight anymore since I gave my life to Christ."

Speaking to the audience more than to Clark, Larson said, "These guys are my friends, too. I just don't want to get into any hot tubs with them."

Next, Larson pointed the microphone to the person on my right. This was Percy who had made his own wacky calls about Jacuzzism and Disturbathon. In a nasal voice, Percy wheedled, "It's excellent to see you and we hope to have you come to the hot tub some time. We'd like to have you as our guest for dinner or the Jacuzzi to discuss religion."

Larson seized this opportunity to demonize us. It was then he used the ammo I had given him. "Now, you've got to understand something. These guys sent me a video of a naked man having sex with a goat's head in a vat of Jell-O." This strange but true accusation elicited more groans from the audience.

Addressing me, Larson asked, "Does your mother know about this?"

"Not specifically, but she knows about Disturbathon."

"Why don't you tell her about the goat-head sex in the Jell-O?"

"It never came up over dinner." This got a few laughs and set Bob up for a big punch line.

"If she ever saw the video, she wouldn't be able to keep down her dinner." A slow build of laughter ended up in hoots and hollers.

"Why do you guys do that kind of stuff? Don't you see that's demonic?"

Percy pitched in, "It's no more demonic than the Brethren of the Free Spirit, a Christian

sect from the 13th Century that said God is inside us and directs us."

"Wait a minute, you're comparing someone who says God is in my life and gives me direction to some guy having sex with a goat's head in a vat of Jell-O? Have you totally lost it or what? Why do you guys follow me?"

"We really enjoy your antics," I said.

Predictably, he took offense and then parlayed the exchange to his advantage. "These are not antics. Have you written a check to help out?"

"Not today, but I've given before," I said. Tempted by his premiums of books and videotapes, I had indeed donated to Bob Larson Ministries.

Turning to the audience, Larson admitted, "Actually, he has. He has probably given more than some of you. Even my enemies want to keep me on the air."

I clarified, "We're not your enemies, Bob. We love you."

Above: Bob Larson meets Forrest Jackson during his "Save Our Kids from Satanism" tour in the mid-1990s.

Some gasped, some groaned, and others laughed. Larson stepped back and smirked. Someone in the audience shouted, "They need some prayer!"

"I think that's a pretty good idea. But we're not going to have just anybody pray for you. We're going to have..." Larson paused dramatically and continued in an ominous tone, "the Intercessors pray for you. Where are those ladies?"

I stood straight up and grinned as the prayer warriors surrounded Percy and me. At the urging of the preacher, seven or eight Jesus-freaky women who called themselves "the Intercessors" supplicated our deliverance from evil. Eyes closed, they muttered curse-breaking prayers I could barely hear, much less understand. Were they speaking in tongues? Indeed, I heard some among the throng bless us with a little glossolalia. I continued to smile pleasantly inside the circle of good Christian ladies. They were mostly older, poofy-haired women wearing solid color dresses of conservative cut. I could have hoped for more pulchritude, but they didn't have to be sexy to make me happy. These women were praying for me and I loved it.

Larson led the prayer from the stage. The microphone gave him super powers as he intoned, "We pray for these young men and others like them. Lord, forgive them; they know not what they do. Lord, touch their hearts at the core of who they are and let them know your power and might and let them know you alone are God. And all those who blaspheme shall account for it on the Day of Judgment. Let them know this is not the Day of Judgment. This is the day of grace. The hour in which your mercy is extended to them and everyone who does not know you. In Jesus' name we break the bondage of evil by the authority of Jesus Christ, Amen."

To carry the hoax further, we should have played along and pretended conversion on the spot, but we didn't. I don't know if Jesus was listening, but the audience was enthralled. They, too, held up their hands and prayed aloud to break the curse that was not, in fact, upon us.

Having shown that the power of Christ could conquer kooky cultists, Larson went on with his show. He paced and harangued and cajoled and pleaded. Then he prayed and begged some more. At one point a springtime storm caused the electricity to go out. It was a spooky moment and Larson took the opportunity to say that it proved the Devil was mad at him. When the power resumed, he cried, "Let there be light!" And, unsurprisingly, he passed the plate again. When it was all over, a few people came forward to say they hoped we might find Jesus someday. We thanked them as sincerely as we could and sniggered on our way out.

Getting this much of Larson's attention was gratifying, but I'm sorry to say I never made it to his Denver studio. His radio show's popularity fizzled when he tried to break into televangelism with little success. Today, he focuses solely on casting out demons and he operates the online International School of Exorcism. For a fee, you can learn about exorcism through the ages and how to spot the demonically possessed. If you pay enough, you will receive a certificate that allows you to perform exorcisms on your own.

Right: Forrest Jackson with Bob Larson, 2014.
Photo by Brother Randall of the Robert Tilton Fan Club.

Cash, checks, money orders, credit cards, and even Paypal are all accepted. On two occasions I've seen Larson perform exorcisms, but it's hard for me to see his hypnotic actions as anything other than preying on the weak-minded. However, I don't think Bob Larson is a bad person. He's greedy, but not evil. Despite his devotion to Mammon, I think he is sincere on some level. Maybe he really does care about people.

In the months following the prayer circle fun, my interest in calling Talk-Back waned. I felt like I'd pestered Larson enough and I knew he was wise to me. Alas, the once effervescent waters of Jacuzzism grew tepid and dried up. Whether viewed as a valid religion or an outright hoax, it never amounted to anything. By contrast, Disturbathon continues to haunt the Dallas/Fort Worth Metroplex every Halloween. The fact remains that people like Bob Larson view it as a Satanic sex cult and with good reason. It really is a wild and licentious party. I remain supportive of the Diabolicrats and their devilish efforts to unbuckle the bible belt. Yet, like so many of my cohorts, I have mellowed with age. I'm no longer the attention-hungry kid whose pulse quickened whenever his call made it on the air. But, I can't complain. Life is good, and I try to keep it fun. And I still love the goat.

REFERENCES + BIBLIOGRAPHY

THE
SATAN
SELLER

CONFESSIONS OF A CREATURE FEATURE PREACHER:
OR, HOW I LEARNED TO STOP WORRYING ABOUT SATANISM AND LOVE MIKE WARNKE

BY DAVID CANFIELD

What I have to say about Satanic Panic, one of its leading architects Mike Warnke and my own relatively minor role in his rise and fall, comes back to me as a series of moments that, like theology itself, fails to paint a whole picture. I could probably spend the rest of my life trying to bring that picture into focus, but what does seem clear is that the story starts way before I ever heard of Satanic Panic. Like Hieronymous Bosch's famous triptych *The Garden of Earthly Delights*, it's a story crowded with all the detail one associates with Earth and Hell and Heaven, even as its momentum opens upward into a quiet blue sky where all is well even if everything below cannot be understood, much less taken in. But, if I look hard, I can still see the figure of a small boy in the corner clutching his first copy of *Famous Monsters of Filmland* magazine. Evangelist/comedian/occult "expert" Warnke is in there too. Be patient with me and I'll show you why the devil is in the details, the place where we lose the whole picture.

Left: The cover image for Mike Warnke's 1973 book *The Satan Seller*.

The place where Warnke and I both got lost. I found my way out. I hope he does too.

Warnke first came to mass media prominence with his 1973 autobiographical book, *The Satan Seller*. Released in the burgeoning days of what came to be known as the Jesus Movement, a Christian religious revival deeply tied to a sharp rise in societal interest in all kinds of spirituality in the early 1970s, Warnke's book detailed his conversion to Christianity vis-à-vis a tumultuous journey that included a stint in Satanism.

A would-be Christian personality could not have asked for a better calling card than *The Satan Seller*. After being orphaned at an early age and shuttled around between relatives, the book tells how Warnke met a mysterious friend who began inviting him to drug and sex parties, eventually revealing his deeper intention to draw the author into the Satanic underground. What follows is a graphic account of a life nearly destroyed by alcohol and drug abuse, all while Warnke runs a 1,500 member coven of Satanists in California. Demons are called forth and people are kidnapped, raped and sacrificed to the Devil. Warnke becomes so obsessed with power that his own coven turns on him, making him overdose on heroin and leaving him to die. Embittered, he joins the military and meets two soldiers who witness to him relentlessly until he accepts Christ as his personal savior. Requesting an early discharge, Warnke goes into full-time ministry work.

Warnke at Melodyland Christian Center.

Appendix II

How to Fight Occultism

What can you do to fight the spreading occultism in our country? You can do many things.

First you can realize that God is the answer to the lures of Satanism. By talking to Him and asking His guidance you will be far more effective than if you go out on your own without Him to help you.

A. Write Letters—Write to your Congressman and Senators. Also write to your state legislators for they read every letter and frequently take action. Tell them what is going on and ask them to help.

Write to your newspaper. Tell them what is happening and why you object to it. Keep your letters around two hundred to three hundred words. Remember the Letters to the Editor section of daily newspapers is one of the best-read sections of the paper. Also write to radio and TV stations about the problem.

B. Use Your Telephone—Call your newspaper editor and ask him to investigate the occult activities in your city. Also call your radio and television station and ask them to investigate too. Check to see if your Congressman or your state legislator has an office in your city and call him or his secretary to ask for a similar investigation. Call your city and county officials and ask them to take action on local problems with the occult.

C. Work with Your Church—Help the members of your church and other churches in the community to learn of the errors of the occult. Help them plan action programs to stem occult growth.

D. Investigate Your Schools—See what your schools are teaching. Check courses called "Mysticism" and "Literature of the Supernatural." See if teachers are pushing occult practices on students. Then take your case to the school board. Tell the newspapers, radio and television what you have found. Do not let the school administrators tell you to keep the information confidential. If it is wrong—tell the world.

218

Top: Warnke at the former Melodyland Christian Center in Anaheim, Califfornia, as captioned in *Cornerstone* Magazine #98.
Above: Appendix II from *The Satan Seller*.

The only problem with *The Satan Seller* was that almost none of Warnke's stories were true, a trail of deception outlined in "Selling Satan," a lengthy investigative report published in respected counterculture Christian magazine *Cornerstone* in 1992, where I worked at the time. That story, written by Mike Hertenstein and Jon Trott and researched by others including myself, outlined the life of a child who was orphaned at an early age, a man known for telling whoppers and who loved to be the centre of attention. Someone who discovered, in the Jesus Movement, a way to build a legend.

They say the truth will set you free, but Warnke seemed more interested in what his newfound notoriety allowed him to do in secret. By the article's publication in 1992, Warnke had gone through many adulterous relationships and four marriages, and his financial dealings were attracting much scrutiny. Even more devastating was the article's relentless historical timeline in which eyewitnesses to Warnke's day-to-day activities showed that, at the time he was supposed to be involved in a cult, Warnke was actually a typical nerdy college kid, who had accepted Christ at college and was engaged to a nice demure Christian girl. A photo, taken at the time when Warnke claimed to have long bleached hair and six-inch fingernails (as well as chronic addictions to every illicit drug on the planet and a number of shooting and stab wounds), showed a thick-spectacled, almost stereotypically nerdy young man in a suit who would have a hard time scaring an old lady, much less conducting an occult ritual that involved human sacrifices.

It appears Warnke and co-author David Balsiger cooked up the idea for *The Satan Seller* in the early 1970s for San Diego evangelist Morris Cerullo. Cerullo, impressed with Warnke's wild stories, suggested Warnke write a book that could be used in conjunction with a traveling exhibit of occult paraphernalia he had previously assembled for "educational" use. At this point, Warnke was given early discharge from the Navy to go into ministry work, and subsequently left Cerullo's ministry after demanding all of the book material back. Thus, *The Satan Seller* was born.

On the book's success, Warnke was invited to speaking engagements, one of which was recorded and released as his first album, *Mike Warnke Alive!* (Myrrh Records) in 1975. The recording was a weird mix of standup comedy and his supposed real-life history, delivered in an irreverent, but folksy style. It struck a chord with religious audiences and he soon found himself releasing record after record, each including stories of his days as a Satanist and all-round heathen bad guy and Vietnam vet

Above: One of Warnke's many albums on audio cassette.

MIKE WARNKE
Former Satanic Priest

hippie goofball. Warnke videos soon came, and he was constantly touring with comedy and preaching appearances. As his reputation as a former occultist grew, he was often asked to appear on news networks as an expert on the occult, culminating in an appearance on ABC's highly popular *20/20* news show on May 16, 1985 for a story entitled "The Devil Worshippers."

When the *Cornerstone* story came out, a team of staffers passed out copies at the yearly Christian Booksellers Association meeting while the rest stayed at the office to answer phones—and boy, did those phones ring. Warnke lost a lucrative recording contract with the largest Christian music label in the world. Publishing contracts and speaking engagements were cancelled. More importantly, people started asking how someone could become such a prominent figure in the church while basing their entire ministry on lies. Hertenstein and Trott later published a book (also called *Selling Satan*) that expanded on the article to tackle that very question.

By the time the *Cornerstone* article hit shelves in 1992, the Satanic Panic narrative Warnke helped launch and spread had done most of its damage. Warnke's appearance on *20/20* was part of a story on the McMartin pre-school child abuse case, a legal quagmire that was so clouded by erroneous accusations of Satanic Ritual Abuse that the real story will probably never be known. A lot of others got accused of Satanic Ritual Abuse too, all linking back to weird claims of a vast underground network of Satanists disguised as law-abiding citizens, spread by Warnke and like-minded Evangelicals. Parents, grandparents, babysitters and respected community members were all suspect. Many believed that kids were being kidnapped, sacrificed and converted by the thousands, while women and girls were abducted and forced to become baby breeders for Satanic rituals.

By the time the FBI debunked the Satanic underground in a special investigation on Satanic Ritual Abuse, so many authors and speakers had jumped on the gravy train that there was no way all their claims could be debunked. (1) Guests appeared on Christian talk shows, books sold—it was all business as usual and there was money to be made. It wasn't until the public got tired of this particular boogeyman that the carpetbaggers moved on to mine the next exploitable fear.

I suppose that, to Warnke, *Cornerstone* will always be the real devil. In an interview with leading Christian magazine, *Christianity Today*, Warnke accused authors Hertenstein and Trott of being Satanists. (2) Those involved in Warnke's exposure were certainly considered the devil for many Christians, as guests on programs like long-running Christian talk show *Praise the Lord* reasserted Warnke's accusations and did everything they could to support claims of Satanic Ritual Abuse.

Even though it was covered well in the *Cornerstone* article, other media that covered the exposé didn't give nearly enough attention to Warnke's roots. They overlooked

Right: The cover of the career-derailing 1992 *Cornerstone* magazine exposé on Warnke.

VOL. 21 ISSUE 98

Cornerstone

THE
MIKE
WARNKE
STORY

the story of a young orphan trying to make a name for himself, the little boy who lied for attention long before it became a way to make money and seduce women. In *The Satan Seller*, Warnke talked about his youthful fascination with high church (then Catholic courtesy of his adoptive parents) ritual and liturgy; how he would sit and listen with awe and wonder watching the priests, observing the lighting of the incense and glory and majesty of the architecture. This fascination grew as he aged and, after a period of self-study of the Syro-Chaldean tradition of Christian spirituality, Warnke was eventually ordained a Bishop in 1983 under the authority of independent Bishop Richard Merrill. (3)

As Warnke's career took off, so did other claims about his past and pedigree. He told stories about his exploits in Vietnam, including claiming he was wounded five times, including being shot with a bow and arrow and an encounter with a tiger (stories later found to be lifted from fellow soldiers' lives). He claimed he possessed a number of degrees, including two Bachelors, two Masters and a Doctorate of Philosophy. (4) In short, he wanted to be somebody—he wanted secret knowledge, he wanted the validation of the robe, the collar, and the degree, he wanted to give others that "I could tell you shit" glance the old guy does at the bar. He wanted his listeners, viewers and readers to believe in anything. But the thing he couldn't believe in was himself.

Where was I in the middle of this? Born in 1965, the occult and Satanism were a big part of the mainstream zeitgeist while I was growing up and, before I became a conscious Christian in the mid-1980s, I was well on my way to becoming a monster kid—a die-hard horror and science-fiction fanatic. I could tell you how I conned my parents into taking me to see *The Return of Count Yorga* (1971) or show you a note I wrote that reads: "Mom, if you let me stay up tonight to watch *Creature Feature* I'll write the name of the world's longest chemical name 1,000 times." But my story really begins April 1974 when I first found *Famous Monsters of Filmland* (issue #106) in the magazine aisle of Ernie's Thrifty Mart, mere months before Warnke's first album was released.

Famous Monsters was just part of a monster movie obsession taking root across North America in the 1950s and '60s, a flood of monster-based toys, books, comics and magazines accompanied by a stream of creepy hosts presenting classic horror films on TV. My friends and I pored over these magazines, and we weren't alone—future filmmakers and monster makers like George Lucas, Steven Spielberg, John Landis, and Rick Baker were avid *Famous Monsters* readers too. We collected back issues. We ordered 8mm films and Don Post masks out of the back of it from an outfit called "Captain Company." And, if we were really lucky, we made "Creep of the Week" and got our home-made monster faces in the actual pages of the mag. This cultural diet meant there was no way I was getting out of this zeitgeist alive, dead or undead without a little fake vampire blood on my lips.

And if I'm going to be honest my life as a monster kid wasn't just a matter of the "spooky gene," there were other genes at work too. Diagnosed at a very young age with severe hyperactivity—a diagnosis today that would probably have put me somewhere on the autism spectrum—I had a lot of difficulty controlling emotions and was awkward as hell in social situations. Then there were the night terrors. Horrific waking nightmares where I would wander the house screaming at the top of my lungs or wake up stuck to the bed sheets with my own sweat and urine. Anything could trigger them, monster-related or not.

Except for family baptisms and bible camp, I didn't have much direct contact with the church and, at the time, my beliefs about God and the universe were rooted more in popular culture. My encounters with ole scratchfoot were mainly on screen—I'd seen Ernest Borgnine change into a demonic goat in *The Devil's Rain* (1975), snuck in a viewing of *The Exorcist* (1973) and stared into the eyes of the son of Satan himself in *The Omen* (1976). I also watched TV shows like *In Search Of...*, in which host Leonard Nimoy offered glimpses into a shadow realm that seriously considered claims about the supernatural and cryptozoology.

Christian films like *The Late Great Planet Earth* (1979) and *A Thief in the Night* (1972) weren't much different, and at the time some Christian bookstores had special sections on the occult. There was a fear-mongering quality to all it—end times prophecy, delivering people from demons and a cultural commentary on ways the Devil held modern society captive. In my late teens, my friend Ken Cyr even played me Warnke's first record. It's easy to see in hindsight that these narratives, including the urban myth of the Satanic underground, were effectively a covert horror culture—a way for Christian folk to get those campfire story heebie-jeebies outside the verboten cultural arenas of secular entertainment. And it wasn't any less entertaining.

My own entrance into Christian faith itself was relatively mundane. My parents, like most people around the U.S. at that time, received a constant flow of unsolicited religious periodicals and tracts in the mail, and it was a copy of "Power For Living" (1983) a tract by American Vision, that got me saying the Sinner's Prayer when I was 19. As a young religious convert, I suddenly found myself in constant conversation with other Christians about religion and the search for a religious culture that I could use to express myself. As a self-styled entertainer, I was singing for pay at the time, including occasional stints as an opening stand-up act for bands, and my ultimate goal was to be a well-known Christian personality. It's more than fair to say I wanted to be like Mike Warnke. I also helped others with their ministry by promoting concerts. Distributing handbills, cold calling churches and helping backstage not only got me into concerts for free, but also taught me about the business and gave me the chance to meet my heroes.

I went to my first Warnke show when I was about 19 or 20. Ken and I joined a few other kids for the show and we were completely blown away. We laughed and, when Warnke talked about the Satanic Ritual Abuse survivors he and his wife Rose were sheltering, we cried. Warnke told us that Satanists were doing anything they could to find and kill them, and armed guards often accompanied him. Especially heart-breaking was Warnke's story of Jeffy, a young boy found crucified upside-down. I don't how much money was donated at the end of the spiel and I don't remember how many Warnke records I ended up buying for friends, but I do remember that I had to let everybody in the world know how great I thought Warnke was. (5)

When Warnke came back to town a few years later, the promoter offered me the chance to head up the behind-the-scenes preparations at the Morris Civic Auditorium in South Bend, Indiana. I jumped at the chance—it was fun getting the hall ready but more than anything I wanted to be the one to drive Warnke to the venue, even though I hadn't been behind a wheel long. The night of the show, it was dark and misty as I drove my dark metallic green Lincoln to Gippers Hotel and Lounge. The wait at Gipper's itself seemed long, but then again I was pretty nervous. When Warnke appeared it was almost a relief—*almost*. I think I hit that poor man with every geek move in the book. I sweated like crazy, stammered and stuttered, starting talking about my own standup, recited his own jokes back at him and basically worked myself up into a nice perfect lather. Warnke for his part said little. Then we got into the car. At least I think it was the car. It could have been a dimensional portal to my own personal hell based on the next series of events.

Before we started moving, I briefly panicked about a preacher saying something weird on the radio, worried that Warnke would think I listen to this kind of stuff all the time (which I did). But Warnke just looked at the radio the way you stare at a yappy little dog and said "Hmph." I switched the radio off and he turned to me to ask, "Whadja do that for?" Wide-eyed, I said something like "harglegarrrrr." He started looking at me the way he had looked at the radio and switched it back on.

Because of the misty weather, what should have been a short 10-minute ride to the gig turned into half-an-hour of me weaving all over the road. Warnke kept shooting me increasingly nervous glances until we arrived, and even then there was a problem—I couldn't remember where the backstage door was. First, I turned into an alley behind the auditorium where a slew of fans literally mobbed my car. Then, I got to the front where my way was blocked by a large stone flower pot, which I accidentally ran into hard enough to knock it over and lodge it under my front bumper. We were now five minutes late and Warnke said to me, "C'mon man. Get us outta here!" I threw the car into reverse and stomped on the accelerator just long enough to dislodge the flower pot, sending us lurching violently upwards. I remember Warnke asking me if I was okay at one point, but he also looked like he wouldn't have minded a sharp stick just in case the Satanists had sent me to assassinate their number one enemy. I drove backwards seventy feet or so to the other end of the alley, where I pulled a sharp turn and backed into a parked vehicle. Finally fed up, Warnke yelled, "Son, I used to be a Satanist high priest and you are scaring me to death!" At that moment, Warnke's travelling companion opened the stage door—I can still remember the sound of him laughing when he saw the state Warnke was in. I was heartbroken and never saw Warnke again, but at least I got to talk to him once.

This disastrous story illustrates exactly how my life was going at that moment, as I bounced from flipping burgers at dumpy dives to maddeningly mundane factory work and into high stress care giving for the mentally handicapped. Soon, still living in my parents' basement and unsure of how to make a living, I decided to visit Jesus People USA (JPUSA), a sort of art-centric mecca for Christian counterculture types in Chicago, Illinois which had about 400 fulltime communal group members. JPUSA not only worked with the homeless, they also had their own record label and two pastors were members of Rez, the first hard rock Christian band ever signed to a major Christian music label. I stayed after I experienced a profound sense of calling.

After short stints doing dishes, kitchen work and joining their house painting company (all of which I sucked at), someone got the idea that I should write for *Cornerstone* magazine. This meant late-night deadlines, sleeping behind my desk and the beginning of a lifelong coffee addiction, but I also got to share my Warnke stories in meetings when everyone pitched article ideas. Turns out the staff had their own stories, and they weren't warm and fuzzy ones. Many in the Christian publishing and recording world knew bad things were going on in Warnke's camp for a long time, and the general consensus at *Cornerstone* was that Warnke had been confronted privately enough times that it was probably time to do a well-researched exposé.

"Selling Satan" wasn't *Cornerstone*'s first exposé. The magazine was instrumental in exposing religious scammers like Lauren Stratford, a supposed victim of Satanic Ritual Abuse, as well as Jack Chick collaborators John Todd and Alberto Rivera, the latter of whom claimed special knowledge of a Catholic conspiracy to take over the world. The atmosphere was different than any I ever encountered. This was a crack team doing hard journalistic work and, as I read back issues, I was amazed at how my own understanding of faith was changing. They tackled racism in the church, greed and hypocrisy. Their question was always what the balanced world view was for the Christian in the 20th century. Naturally, everybody on both sides gave *Cornerstone* a lot of grief for failing to embrace extremes of hot button issues.

When the Warnke exposé got underway, it became a full time project for almost everyone at the magazine. I lived at the office and I wasn't even one of the writers. Instead, I helped manage a huge whiteboard that tracked all the major players in Warnke's life that we were trying to contact. Imagine, in the days before the internet, trying to find "Chuck" from a certain high school based on someone's vague memory. Sometimes I would search for weeks only to track them down to the local morgue. I actually had a contest running with a staffer over who would find the most dead people by the time all was said and done. (6)

Then came the day when all the hard work led to the inevitable. The article was all but done, and I was asked to help find Warnke himself. We knew he was aware of the exposé at this point, but it was unclear whether he'd agree to be interviewed before we went to press. But Warnke was just as hard to find as some of those faceless folks I'd spent so much time on, and I spent days hunched over my notes, calling people who didn't want to talk to me. In the end, it occurred to me that maybe he was married again, and I located wife number four in the phone book as I recall. A few finger taps later, I heard that familiar voice on the other end of the phone and quickly passed it off to our leading investigators. For a moment, I found myself staring off into space wondering what must be going through Warnke's mind and heart.

Despite *Cornerstone*'s article, Warnke still tours, telling modified stories about his days in the occult to whatever church is willing to pay him, only now he has a new narrative in the mix that involves the way Christians shoot their own wounded. Personally, I just shake my head—it's hard to believe people still hire the guy. But I did notice he and his fourth wife are still married and I can't help feeling glad. Does Warnke believe his own stories at this point? What keeps him out there? Is it just a living?

As for myself, more than two decades later, I'm no longer with the JPUSA (for about eight months as of this writing) and separated from my wife. I'm still a Christian, but I consider myself sexually fluid and sex positive. I still love horror movies and am a founding member of *Twitch Film*, the largest blog in the world devoted to genre film from across the globe. I don't believe there are any bad guys in this story, but I hope I have a little more humility than my wiseass young self that used to see music, comedy, writing and just about everything else as a way to become important. That's a lousy motive to do anything—sort of Satanic if you think about it. Maybe Warnke will someday realize that too.

NOTES:

1. An FBI investigation was inevitable due to the widespread nature of the Satanic Ritual Abuse claims, but a lack of evidence, except a few isolated cases of self-styled occult crime, helped deflate the concerns. Of course, local law enforcement all over the U.S. continued to investigate claims of Satanic Ritual Abuse and occult activity, drawing on self-appointed experts on occultism, including the infamous West Memphis Three case.
2. Jay Grelen. "Christian comedian says he lied about coven", *Lexington Herald-Leader*, November 3, 1992, page B1.
3. "Selling Satan", *Cornerstone* (98). 1992
4. Mike made so many claims about himself that it's impossible to track them all, however these claims were made on his album *Higher Education*, Myrrh Records, July 1982.
5. Many of the performers I volunteered for were absolutely sincere in their intentions and were great to work with, including Steve Taylor, Degarmo & Key, Sacred Warrior and Whiteheart.
6. I won. My tally was over a dozen.

Right: The cover of *Mike Warne Alive!*, 1975.

BOUC ÉMISSAIRE:
MANIFESTATIONS OF SATANIC ANXIETY IN QUEBEC

BY RALPH ELAWANI
(WITH THE KIND COLLABORATION OF GIL NAULT AND L'ABBATIALE DE LA LITURGIE APOCRYPHE)

While modern Satanism, as envisaged by Anton LaVey, never stood a chance of taking hold in Quebec, sordid crimes have been and are still committed there either in the name of Satan or as a means to keep him away. Home to a once highly religious population, Quebec's distinctive culture was largely dominated by Roman Catholicism until at least the 1970s. Although the Satanic Panic that rippled across North America and other parts of the world in the 1980s didn't make quite as many inroads into the cloistered Francophone media, it manifested in different ways, such as in the anxiety about the proliferation of cults and religious sects that bolstered the Dark Lord's supposed presence in what locals call "La Belle Province." While figures like Father Jean-Paul Régimbald (1931-1988) and Father John O'Connor (1929-2006) exorcised demons from local culture, tabloids jumped on stories that smacked of demonic doings as a number of cults and religious sects took advantage of Catholicism's waning influence.

Left: The cover for Father Jean-Paul Régimbald's book *Rock n' Roll: Rape of Consciousness Through Subliminal Messages* (1983).

In a culture where the aspergillum kept wagging ferociously, the stage for Quebec's own unique take on the Satanic Panic was set early on. From *La chasse-galerie* to *Rose Latulippe*, *Le sorcier du Saguenay* and *La griffe du diable*, trickster stories, morality tales and legends are at the heart of French-Canadian culture, which has largely been an oral tradition. Folktales have helped epitomize a notion that has not died off since the days of hunters and fur trappers: the idea that a shape-shifting form of evil somewhere is lurking.

This mentality was certainly dominant in Quebec. Until the Quiet Revolution of the late 1960s loosened the papal grip on the province, most Quebeckers grew up in a society where the clergy had power over most of the institutions—from the bedrooms or hospital beds you were born or died in, to the schools you received your education in. Only after this period of political and cultural upheaval—which coincidentally occurred around the time the Vatican was also evolving to keep up with more modern sensibilities—was control over certain institutions returned to the politicians, and the local arts flourished under a new sense of freedom.

At the same time that Quebec was re-emerging from its stiff and proper past, Anton LaVey was hard at work crafting misanthropic comments on modern complacency, and blasting those he saw as Bible-backed hypocrites. Charismatic and con man-charming enough to attract a motley cast of adepts into his organization, the Church of Satan, LaVey consecrated his world views with the publication of *The Satanic Bible* in 1969.

By publishing a "Bible"—not a manifesto, not a tract, not a grimoire, not a modern day version of the *Codex Gigas*—he accomplished a few things. First, he technically made his ideas available to anyone who would bother to explore them. (1) Second, he defined Satanism in an authoritative text; finally, he created a precedent by establishing that actions taken "in the name of Satan," such as child molesting and animal sacrifice, could not be called Satanic rituals.

In 1968, a book arguably as culturally incendiary as *The Satanic Bible* was published in Montreal by les Éditions Parti pris: Pierre Vallières' *White Niggers of America*. Vallières was a political prisoner to some, a terrorist to others, and his book, originally written in prison in 1966, became the Bible of the Front de Libération du Québec (FLQ). Founded in 1963 and influenced by post-colonial literature, Marxism, the Black Panthers and decolonization theories (as posited by those including Aimé Césaire, Albert Memmi and Franz Fanon), the FLQ made news all around the world in 1970 when they kidnapped two government officials (later killing one) during what is now known as the October Crisis. These events stand today as some of the province's darkest episodes.

Just as the Manson family murders in 1969 prompted questions about whether there were actually active networks of devil worshippers corrupting the youth, the events of October 1970 showed Quebeckers that evil had a name. Here was direct proof of an underground network of terrorists; a horizontal organization, a local "jihad," a band of anti-British monarchy and anti-capitalist guerilas. The Canadian government declared

Above: The original Quebec pressing (1968)
and the first English translation (1971)
of Pierre Vallières' *White Niggers of America*.

war measures during the October Crisis, so that arguably anybody could be arrested, which lasted until 1971. The resulting widespread panic and intellectual shortcuts, which led to the arrest of over 500 individuals (including *Montreal Star/Gazette* journalist Nick Auf der Mauer and future Parti Québécois minister Gérald Godin), cannot help but be compared to the patented stories and false accusations made against numerous groups and individuals during the Satanic Panic era.

> ❝ *It could be said that, with almost the best will in the world,*
> *we have created a hell and called it The American Way of Life.*
> –Gore Vidal

After the October Crisis, with the FLQ technically out of the picture, the Catholic Church in freefall and a film industry that started boiling, some major changes were taking place in Quebec.

In 1974, Montreal-based production company Cinepix (later responsible for producing films by David Cronenberg, George Mihalka and Ivan Reitman) drew on the population's anxieties and released one of the first horror films shot in Quebec: Jean Beaudin's *Le Diable est parmi nous*.

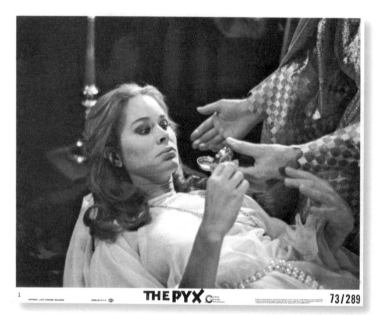

THE PYX   73/289

Featuring Daniel Pilon (*Red, Après Ski*) and Danielle Ouimet (*Valérie, Daughters of Darkness*), *Le Diable est parmi nous* was a landmark. For the first time, a fiction film dealt with the threat of Satanism in Quebec. Although documentaries such as La Cinémathèque Québécoise's founder Guy L. Côté's 1965 NFB-produced *Regard sur l'occultisme* had explored the world of card readers, astrologers, shamans and other occult aficionados, Beaudin's *Rosemary's Baby*-influenced thriller was one of a kind. Strangely enough, a year later, Cinepix would produce another horror film with a similar plot, but this time featuring Pilon's brother Donald: *The Pyx* (1975).

After Quebec's failed bid at sovereignty in 1980, a cold shower was thrown on the notion of provincial solidarity. (2) Following the tax-shelter film stabs at Satanism, major changes were happening in the music industry, and countercultures that shared some common ideas with the separatist Parti Québécois were thrown out with the bathwater. Although Quebec-based musicians such as garage rockers Les Sinners and macabre chansonnier/performer Serge Mondor had made use of devilish imagery on their album covers and in their songs during the 1960s, the 1980s saw an unparalleled level

Right: An orgiastic frenzy in Jean Beaudin's *Le Diable est parmi nous* (1974). Image © Cinepix.

of panic directed at rock 'n' rollers. While punk rock melted into new wave as a more marketable form of "youth culture," heavy metal played the role of a scapegoat, even in Quebec. Although the Catholic Church was no longer the powerful local institution it once was, heavy metal found plenty of French-Canadian opponents, as members of religious congregations maintained that the youth were being perverted by a type of music that served the interests of the Prince of Darkness, mirroring the criticisms from south of the border.

Aside from Ozzy Osbourne and Judas Priest, KISS was one of the most publicized groups accused of corrupting the youth. On January 12, 1983, KISS was scheduled to kickstart its Canadian tour at the Quebec City Coliseum, As Radio-Canada's coverage of the band's performance confirms, KISS met with opposition from members of the Pentecostal Church—a group that, until then, was arguably low on the cultural radar. Members of the church made a point of analyzing the group's name (which, depending on the rumours, stood for Kill in Satan's Service, Killers in Satan's Service, Knights in Satan's Service, Kings in Service of Satan or Kinder SS) and lyrics, and deemed them Satanically dangerous for teenagers. In the wake of the event, Dan Bouchard, goalkeeper for Quebec pro hockey franchise the Nordiques, even went as far as to recruit some of his teammates and place six open Bibles under the stage where KISS was set to perform.

Nevertheless, in terms of lyrical content and aesthetics, KISS paled in comparison to groups that would storm through town in the following years. British black metal originators Venom caused a remarkable commotion when they came to Quebec City towards the mid-1980s. Evangelical church Carrefour Chrétien de la Capitale received media attention when they announced they would hand out anti-Satanic tracts at the concert. They went as far as to plan on sending a group of preachers to infiltrate the crowd after the show to invite the audience to pray and save their souls. Unluckily for Carrefour Chrétien de la Capitale, Quebec City then hosted concerts by metal bands Krokus and Accept—groups that journalist Guy Tremblay said openly advertised their members' homosexuality in his TV news story on the Venom concert.

However, despite the repeated efforts of these religious groups, one man established himself as rock 'n' roll's main opponent in Quebec and made it his mission to denounce the "rape of consciousness" perpetrated by the Devil's music (among other things). Father Jean-Paul Régimbald (1931-1988) was among the few "charismatic" Quebecois priests to organize rallies and conferences to speak out against the evils that threatened to take over the world. (3) Afraid that the Illuminati and the Freemasons were on the cusp of establishing a new world order under the reign of Satan, Father Régimbald embraced conspiracy theories and was quick to speak out against subliminal messages contained in rock 'n' roll songs. In 1983, he published *Rock'n Roll: Viol de la conscience par les messages subliminaux* (4), in which he states that the 1980s would see the rise of punk rock groups whose music would drive their audience to violence, murder and suicide:

> **"** *Vous pensez peut-être que c'est la fin? Non, pas encore, car la perversion n'a pas encore touché le fond de l'abîme. En effet, les années 80 verront la naissance des groupes punk rock dont le but et la philosophie sont de pousser les auditeurs directement au suicide, à la violence collective et aux meurtres systématiques. Parmi les groupes les plus notoires, mentionnons KISS, Ted Nugent, Les Mutants et Aphrodite's Child (666).* (5)

Father Régimbald would not live long enough to witness the rise of the second wave of black metal, the terrorist acts of September 11, 2001, or even the publication of the Lanning Report in 1992 investigating claims of Satanic Ritual Abuse, which ultimately helped to defuse the Satanic Panic.

In the U.S., representatives of the Church of Satan such as Boyd Rice, King Diamond and Peter H. Gilmore were prompt to confront their detractors. Ironically, Quebec did not witness notable public debates on the topic of Satanism. As a result, the teenage basement brouhaha and the publication of books such as *Michelle Remembers* (1980), combined with the golden age of public access TV, helped provide the need for a theatre where Régimbald and other esoterists (such as UFOlogist

Above: Anti-rock crusader Father Jean-Paul Régimbald.

Richard Glenn) could perform their burlesque spectacle and reinforce, mostly for themselves, their ideas of morality and conspiracies.

THE JOY OF SECTS

> **❝** There is little or no evidence for the portion of their allegations that deals with large-scale baby breeding, human sacrifice, and organized satanic conspiracies. Now it is up to mental health professionals, not law enforcement, to explain why victims are alleging things that don't seem to have happened.
> –Excerpt from the Lanning Report

While Satanic influence seemed to be circling the film and music industry, a certain fringe of society had become disenchanted with city life and was retreating to the countryside to experience communal living. (6) With the void engendered by the crisis of faith among a population that, until recently, had been living under the authoritarian control of the Catholic Church, many commune dwellers became not only disconnected from the urban world, but also started experimenting with Eastern religions, macrobiotics and even the occult. But, as the "void" was slowly being filled, communal living was sowing the seeds for a future threat that would permeate the 1980s and run parallel to the Satanic Panic: the fear of religious sects.

It is no hyperbole to say that Quebec has had its share of controversial spiritual communities in the past 40 years. However, far from Claude Vorilhon's UFO-loving Raelians and André Moreau's Jovialists, the late 1980s and early '90s saw some gruesome acts perpetrated by groups that had very little to do with polygamous and new age-y swinger gatherings. Sects that had nothing to do with Satanism actually committed crimes far worse than what Satanists had been accused of in mainstream media. (7)

Montréal interdit, a Mondo-inspired pseudo-documentary directed by Vincent Ciambrone in 1990 tried to capture the sordid underbelly of city life. Also known as *Mondo Montreal*, the film covered everything from voodoo ceremonies to would-be Satanic cults that supposedly took place amidst members of the Ordo Templi Orientis. Nowadays regarded as a piece of kitsch cinema, *Montréal interdit's*

MONTREAL INTERDIT

directeurs de la photo
ROGER MORIDE
YVES DELACROIX
musique de
BAT TAYLOR

productrice déléguée
MONIQUE PRAVIE
réalisateur
VINCENT
CIAMBRONE

look at the Ordo Templi Orientis (OTO) can perhaps only rival *Le Diable est parmi nous'* orgiastic depiction of Satanic cults. (8)

However, Canada was once considered to be a rapidly growing OTO Caliphate. According to researcher Peter-Robert Koenig, Montreal's first Caliphate body was founded in 1981 with some 50 members and was called the Phoenix Lodge. In Koenig's words, the Phoenix's first Treasurer, Robert Deumié (who also owned the Café Thélème) was later expelled from the Caliphate for revealing some of their secret signs and rituals in a documentary broadcast on French television in Québec.

In addition, during the second half of the 1980s, an unparalleled number of articles dealing with sects began appearing in tabloids like *Allô Police*. For example, around 1985, Raymond Steele—self-appointed pastor of l'Église universelle de la raison éclairée—sequestrated, tortured and fed to his dogs a 22-year-old pregnant woman he suspected of being a witch. This story and others started filling up the pages of this publication that, until recently, mostly dabbled in the usual drug busts, sex worker arrests, astrology and other gang-related nonsense.

POLICE STORY

Detective M.P. is a retired agent of the Sûreté du Québec. (9) During her career, she investigated and infiltrated numerous street gangs and criminal organizations. When asked about ritualistic crimes and sects, her answer is straightforward: ritualistic crimes are real and a lot more frequent than one would think.

> Was there a considerable number of Satanic crimes perpetrated in Quebec during the 1980s and '90s?
>
> *From my experience, "rituals" are often performed by groups of teenagers. Small groups. Nothing very organized per se. I remember a case where a group of teenagers had broken into a church and stolen a chalice and other ceremonial items. They later mixed their blood in the chalice and performed a ritual. I personally knew a priest in Lévis [South Shore of Québec City], Father Gabriel Arsenault, who is what we refer to as a responsable des délivrances /accompagnateur spirituel. He has had to deal with many teenagers who were visibly "under the influence" of some kind of force. As a matter of fact, he told me years ago that he himself had been "affected" at some point. He recalled having had all of his energy pretty much sucked out of him. He had to seek the help of another priest who in turn taught him certain rites had to be performed on oneself before attempting to perform an exorcism on someone else. These are things that we do not hear about in the media, but apparently they do happen.*

What about more organized crime and sects?

Sects are always difficult to infiltrate. It's not like we have a crystal ball that tells us a group will commit suicide next month. Informants provide us with particular information about a group and we dispatch them to the right squads and keep an eye open. But many of these groups are very hermetic; one only needs to think of Moïse Thériault or of the Order of the Solar Temple, which culminated in a mass suicide in the early 1990s. Furthermore, when children are involved, like more recently with the ultra-Orthodox Jewish group Lev Tahor, we do our best to act quickly, especially when there is evidence that children are mistreated.

That being said, rituals are very common among street gangs. I think especially here of voodoo rituals performed by some members of the Haitian community involved in street gangs. I've seen searches where we stumbled upon candles and drawings on the floor. I also remember a case where a prostitute would keep mailing certain passages from the Bible to her pimp. Unbeknownst to us, she was performing a ritual to try to get him out of jail. (10)

We are forever lost
in the desert of eternal darkness
–Robert Desnos

The publication of books such as Yves Lavigne's *Hell's Angels: Le clan de la terreur* (1988) and Betty Mahmoody and William Hoffer's 1987 bestseller *Not Without my Daughter* reinforced a sense of unease among the population. (11) Kidnapping and sordid stories—often the result of what has been dismissed as "False Memory Syndrome"—made parents worried about their children's safety.

However, despite the surreal number of cases reported in the United States, very few publicized cases of Satanic Ritual Abuse made headlines in Quebec during the Satanic Panic era. One of the few widely-known cases surfaced in 1995, when Manon, a 28-year-old Eastern Townships resident, claimed she had endured physical and sexual abuse by members of a Satanic sect her mother had been part of for so long that it predated her birth (note that this assertion alone would make the sect predate the foundation of the Church of Satan).

Although Quebec Detective Luc Grégoire admitted to newspaper *La Presse* that Manon's tale of rape, black masses and physical abuse resembled at least half a dozen other cases he was aware of—all of which he insisted the police were taking seriously—nothing apparently came of Manon's case.

As these events unfolded, some of Canada's largest sexual and physical abuse scandals were disclosed between 1989 and 1995. Along with media coverage of horrific abuse in Residential Schools—government-sponsored institutions meant to "assimilate" Aboriginal children—allegations of physical and sexual abuse inflicted on residents of Mount Cashel orphanage in St. John's, Newfoundland surfaced in 1989, followed by criminal investigations that led to a Royal Commission. As card-carrying member of The Church of Satan (Magister) Robert Lang mentions:

> 66 *The notorious Mount Cashel Orphanage case, as well as other controversies within the Roman Catholic Church, fueled the public's view of organized religion towards a very low esteem. Certainly these things alone cried out for a new social pariah to be created and supported, something else for people's attention to latch onto.* (12)

Around the same time, the Roch "Moïse" Thériault case shed light on crimes committed by a sadistic ego-driven sex-crazed guru. Thériault, a self-proclaimed prophet of the Seventh-day Adventist Church was arrested in 1989 for a series of acts that had all the characteristics of Satanic Ritual Abuse cases.

Around 1977, Thériault persuaded a group of people to leave their jobs and homes and move with him to a commune in Gaspésie (they later relocated near Burnt River, Ontario). Over approximately 12 years, Thériault commonly inflicted beatings, rapes, torture and other forms of extreme punishments on members, including acts of scatophila, castration and unanesthetized circumcisions and other surgeries. During his reign over the commune, Thériault fathered near thirty children with multiple "wives."

In September 1988, while inebriated, the guru caused the death of Solange Boilard by surgically operating on her with a knife after she complained of an upset stomach. Thériault later asked

Above: Cult leader Roch "Moïse" Thériault.

his "wife" Gabrielle Lavallée to stitch up her fellow-devotee with a needle and thread. Lavallée escaped but ultimately returned to the commune. On returning, Thériault punished her by pinning her hand to a wooden table and later amputating part of her arm. When she finally escaped a second time, Lavallée contacted the authorities. Convicted of murder in 1993, Thériault was killed in prison by his cellmate in 2011.

In an effort to warn teenagers of the dangers of sects during the nineties, Lavallée would often visit high schools throughout Quebec to share her story. Teenagers from all over the province would not easily forget "the lady with a hook" whose presentation was an obligatory part of the curriculum.

Even within Canada, Quebec has always had and nurtured its own thriving culture that remains completely distinct from anywhere else in the world. The language difference has, to some extent, enabled the province to avoid saturation by American pop cultural exportation, but it's not completely immune to it, as evidenced by the way the Satanic Panic manifested in specific ways within the province's own films and musical output, and especially local reactions to them. However, even today, it is worth asking whether—had the Catholic Church maintained its control over state apparatus—Quebec would have witnessed the explosion of a wider variety of would-be Satanic cults in the 1980s.

NOTES:

1. Also known as the "Devil's Bible" because of a gigantic illustration of the devil on the inside and the legend surrounding its creation, the *Codex Gigas* is the largest extant medieval manuscript in the world. It is thought to have been created in the 13th century in a Benedictine monastery of what is now the Czech Republic.
2. In 1979, the Quebec government made public its constitutional proposal in a white paper entitled *Québec-Canada: A New Deal. The Québec Government Proposal for a New Partnership Between Equals: Sovereignty-Association.* The province-wide referendum took place on Tuesday, May 20, 1980, and the proposal to pursue secession was defeated by a 59.56 % to 40.44 % margin. [Fitzmaurice, John (1985). Québec and Canada; Past, Present, and Future. C. Hurst & Co. Ltd. p. 47.]
3. Other priests who jumped on the televangelist/charismatic take on priesthood in the style of Marjoe, Jerry Falwell and Pat Robertson, include Father Gagnon, whose church on Rue Papineau still bears to this day a gigantic neon sign that reads "Le salaire de ton péché c'est l'enfer" [literally: "the wage of your sin is hell"].
4. "Rape of Consciousness Through Subliminal Messages."
5. "You may think this is the end, but no. Perversion has not yet reached the bottom of the abyss. The 1980s will see the birth of punk rock groups whose purpose and philosophy are to push listeners directly to suicide, collective violence and systematic murders. Among the most notorious current groups, we should note KISS, Ted Nugent, Les Mutants and Aphrodite's Child (666)."
6. An exploration of communal living can be found in Pierre Maheu's NFB-produced

documentaries *Le Bonhomme* (1972), an entry into the life of a bus driver who turns to communal living, and *L'interdit* (1976) in which he explores the questionable practices and day-to-day life of an ex-psychiatrist who lives in a commune with many of his former patients.
7. Theologian Richard Bergeron (1933-2014), co-founder of the Centre d'information sur les nouvelles religions, was one of the first scholars in Quebec, alongside Bertrand Ouellet, to study Satanism and "new religions," as a means to foster a spirit of openness, critical intelligence and Christian discernment towards new spiritual and religious groups. In his book *Damné Satan*, he insists on the idea that groups that possibly dabbled in Satanism during the late 1960s rapidly moved on to become swinger groups (something that films like *Le Diable est parmi nous* would exploit).
8. *The Ordo Templi Orientis Phenomenon: A Research Project* by Peter-Robert Koenig. http://www.parareligion.ch
9. Her name has been changed to protect her privacy.
10. Personal phone interview with the authors, (October 2014).
11. *Hell's Angels: Taking Care of Business* [Ballantine Books, Eng Transl. 1989]
12. E-mail interview with the authors, fall 2014.

REFERENCES + BIBLIOGRAPHY:

Bergeron, Richard. *Damné Satan!: Quand Le Diable Refait Surface*. Montréal: Fides, 1988.
Bergeron, Richard. *La panique satanique*. Montréal: Centre d'information sur les nouvelles religions, 1996. Audiocassette.
Bergeron, Richard. *Le satanisme, ses forces, son contenu et les sources duphénomène*. Montréal: Centre d'information sur les nouvelles religions, 1992. Audiocassette.
"Le culte de Satan semble bien vivant au Canada". *La Presse* (Montréal), December 15, 1991.
Detective M.P., Phone interview by author. October 2014.
Dossiers Mystère. Canal D, 2006. TV series.
Du Berger, Jean. *La figure du diable dans l'imaginaire collectif québécois*. Montréal: Centre d'information sur les nouvelles religions, 1993. Audiocassette.
Fitzmaurice, John. *Québec and Canada: Past, Present, and Future*. New York: St. Martin's Press, 1985.
Introvigne, Massimo. *La peur de Satan*. Montréal: Centre d'information sur les nouvelles religions, 1996. Audiocassette.
"Kiss, un groupe satanique?" *Radio-Canada*. January 13, 1983. TV news report.
Koenig, Peter-Robert. "The Ordo Templi Orientis Phenomenon." *Ordo Templi Orientis Phenomenon: A research project done by Peter-Robert Koenig*. Accessed May 27, 2015. http://www.parareligion.ch/.
Lavigne, Yves. *Hell's Angels: Taking Care of Business*. Toronto: Ballantine Books, 1989.
Lepage, Yvon. *Satan aime-t-il le rock?* Montréal: Centre d'information sur les nouvelles religions, 1991. Audiocassette.
Montréal Interdit. Dir. Vincent Ciambrone. 1990.
Pichette, Jean. "La nouvelle inquisition." *Le Devoir*, July 23, 1996.
"Satan in music" *Caméra 80-90*. TV series.
"Témoignages terrifiants sur les rites sataniques". *La Presse* (Montréal), December 15, 1991.

Right: English cover art for Governor General's Award-winnning Quebecois author Anne Hébert's 1975 novel, *Les enfants du sabbat*.

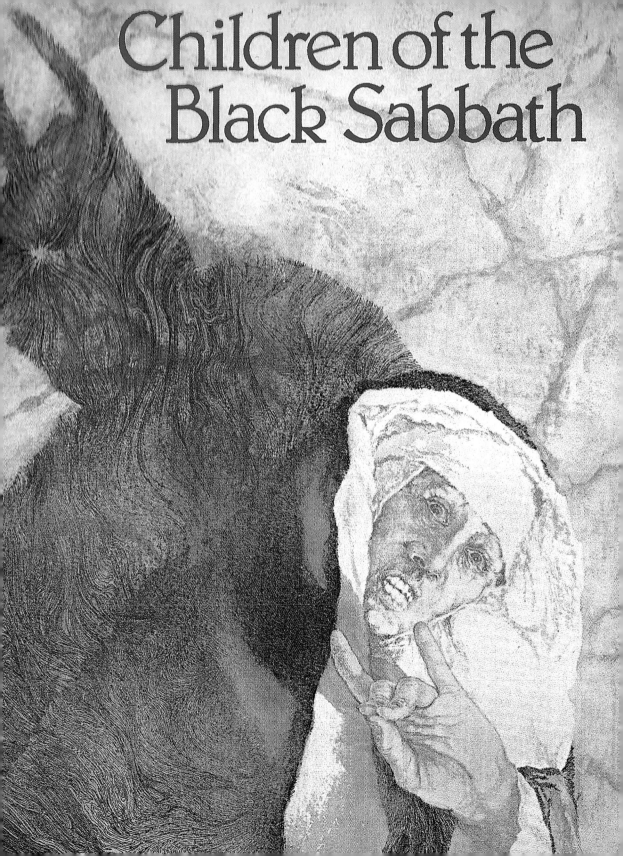

Children of the
Black Sabbath

THE DEVIL DOWN UNDER:
THE SATANIC PANIC IN AUSTRALIA, FROM ROSALEEN NORTON TO 'ALISON'S BIRTHDAY'

BY ALEXANDRA HELLER-NICHOLAS

When the McMartin pre-school trial collapsed in the United States, Satan decided to try his luck elsewhere. In a pre-internet world, Australia suffered from a kind of scandal lag: the Satanic Ritual Abuse controversy that had appeared on both sides of the Atlantic during the 1980s took a little longer to arrive but, when it did, it was just as spectacular and scandalous. Satanic Ritual Abuse burst into the Australian popular consciousness in October 1990 in a TV special hosted by *60 Minutes* journalist Ian Leslie called "The Devil Made Me Do It," heavily influenced by Geraldo Rivera's *Devil Worship: Exposing Satan's Underground* (1988). Featuring almost word-for-word repetition in many places, this program also mirrored the impact of the U.S. TV special: soon after its broadcast, police phone lines were swamped with reports of Satanic Ritual Abuse in Australia.

Like Europe and North America in the 1980s, an entire professional network rapidly appeared around Satanic Ritual Abuse in Australia during the 1990s. Even the prestigious Royal North Shore Hospital in Sydney was not immune, hosting a seminar on the subject in 1991 with the nation's most reputable medical and mental healthcare professionals in attendance. It was not until the Royal Commission into the New South Wales Police Service's final report in 1997 that

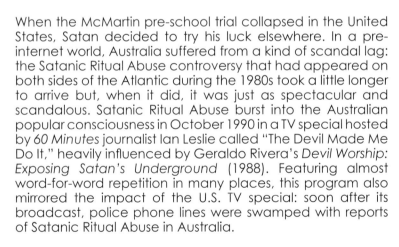

Left: Poster art for Ian Coughlan's *Alison's Birthday* (1981).
Image from the collection of Mark Hartley.

a lengthy official rejection of Satanic Ritual Abuse appeared in Australia. After an unambiguous dismissal of the claims that an organised Satanic criminal conspiracy existed in Australia, the report's unnamed author listed a number of reasons why both the public and many professionals (including police officers) believed in the existence of Satanic Ritual Abuse so readily. One of these included that a "large amount of fictional but sexually explicit, violence-oriented and occult material has been available in the form of films, videotapes, and video games, along with heavy metal and other music with an emphasis on similar themes."

The foundations for Australia's moral panic linked to Satanic Ritual Abuse were laid decades earlier. It begins with the media circus surrounding artist and self-identifying white witch Rosaleen Norton, and how this scandal manifested in the Australian popular imagination. Before *The Devil Made Me Do It,* Satanic cult practices notably featured in two popular television serials, *Homicide* (1964-77) and *Number 96* (1972-77), and were fetishized further in Ozploitation classics such *Australia After Dark* (1975), *Night of Fear* (1972), *Alison's Birthday* (1981) and the documentary *The Occult Experience* (1985). All these examples illustrate how the groundwork was set for the 1990s Satanic Ritual Abuse phenomenon in Australia, providing context for how the controversy itself unfolded.

While the *60 Minutes* television special can fairly be considered ground zero for Satanic Ritual Abuse in Australia, the same long international history of fear and suspicion that has accompanied occult practices such as witchcraft had—perhaps predictably—a strong lineage in Australia too. In the context of Australian cultural history, however, these anxieties were predominantly framed as a distinctly urban threat, bucking the trend that tended to manifest colonial fears as linked explicitly to the Great Outback Unknown. Famous examples of Australian horror stretching from *Wake in Fright* to *Picnic at Hanging Rock* to *Razorback* to *Wolf Creek* all share a vision of the bush as wild, untamed and dangerous, constructing a powerful yet implicit vision of urban Australia as its Other: safe, controlled, and distinctly Eurocentric.

The iconic Rosaleen Norton typified this urban aspect of the threat of occultism in Australia. As the infamous "Witch of Kings Cross"—Kings Cross being an inner suburb of Sydney—Norton became something of a tourist attraction at the peak of her notoriety, where crowds of tourists would gather at the inner-city suburb's cafes—particularly The Apollyon or The Kashmir—hoping to catch a glimpse of Norton and her fellow devil worshippers. Born in New Zealand, legend holds that when Norton was born she had an extra strip of skin that began at her armpit and ran down to her waist, identified by many as a third breast that housed the all-important third nipple, marking her as a "true" witch. Moving to Sydney with her family when she was eight years old, the young Norton had begun drawing supernatural figures at the age of three, and was a self-identifying witch by seven. She was later expelled from her school at 14 because teachers were concerned her interest in the supernatural would be a negative force on other students.

An openly bisexual bohemian with a taste for sadomasochism and a life-long interest in the occult, Norton modelled for iconic Australian painter Norman Lindsay but was also an artist in her own right. She was renowned for her occult and pagan-themed paintings, noted for their intense and often perverse sexuality. During the highly conservative 1950s in Australia she was a significant bohemian force. Wild clothes,

Right: Rosaleen Norton's controversial drawing *Fohat.* Image © Walter Glover.
Inset: Rosaleen Norton.

blood red lipstick and—perhaps most of all—her naturally pointy, pixie-like ears marked Norton as something altogether outside the norm. She had no interest in the surrealist art movement that was so in vogue at the time in Sydney (although she adopted the practice of automatic writing), and looked to earlier inspiration from pagan and medieval art.

Norton's first public exhibition in 1947 was described by one newspaper as "artistic maladjustment," and an exhibition at the University of Melbourne in 1949 was raided by police and had four works removed. Even at this stage, Australia was a relatively secular society and while Christianity was present and certainly a cultural force of some note, there was no established central church as such: that Norton's work caused such a strong reaction was therefore as much to do with its explicit and supposedly "deviant" sexuality as it was its occult content. A natural exhibitionist, Norton relished the attention: she and her lover Gavin Greenless even had a sign on their flat door in Kings Cross that said "Welcome to the house of ghosts, goblins, werewolves, vampires, witches and poltergeists."

Released in 1952, *The Art of Rosaleen Norton with Poems by Gavin Greenless* was a book of her work that solidified her reputation as "The Witch of Kings Cross." Deemed almost immediately an "offensive publication," it was also was banned from entry into the United States. As her notoriety grew, Norton courted both fame and controversy, even sending copies of the 1952 book to everyone from C.S. Lewis to Albert Einstein. The publication resulted in obscenity charges being laid against her publisher.

Certainly Norton was interested in the occult, and conducted rituals with figures including the conductor of the Sydney Symphony Orchestra at the time, Sir Eugene Goossens. In 1956, customs seized occult objects and a large number of pornographic photos in his luggage, leading to a police investigation, his being fired from his job and divorced by his wife. The Goossens scandal was one of the most scandalous and public downfalls of the decade, and Norton played a central role in his shift from honour to notoriety. Norton would continue to be linked to these kinds of scandals and, on September 14, 1955, a mentally ill New Zealand immigrant named Anna Karina Hoffman told police that she had been to a black mass at Norton's apartment on Brougham Street in Kings Cross, insisting that she was not a vagrant but a victim of Norton's rumoured occult practices. Hoffmann told police that the masses were in fact just orgies where people dressed in black, and ultimately confessed that she had not actually attended any ceremonies, but had heard rumours about them.

But it was too late: the press ran with the Norton beat-up, and wrote stories including Norton's participation in animal sacrifice (a personally abhorrent idea to the animal-loving Norton). With the attention reaching fever pitch, the Vice Squad raided her apartment on October 3 that year and she was arrested on the basis of supposed photographic evidence supplied to the *Sun* newspaper by two men who stole photographs of Norton and her lover making fun of precisely these kinds of rituals after a recent birthday party. The press went wild during the court hearings as Norton was forced to defend her pagan beliefs while articulating their difference from Satanic worship and black masses. A number of her paintings were confiscated from The Kashmir and she was charged with obscenity. After a lengthy two-year trial, Norton and her lover Greenless were fined £25 each. Exhausted from the after effects of her long-term zealous affection for both Methedrine and Dexedrine, the hearings exhausted

Norton but were to have a more serious influence on Greenless, who was diagnosed with schizophrenia soon after, and spent the rest of his life institutionalized.

Although the punishment was both token and mild, by the following year, it was clear that the damage to Norton's reputation had been done. The *Australian Post* ran a number of stories about her Satanic connections, including one called "I Am A Witch!—The Chilling Admission of Rosaleen Norton, Sydney's Worshipper of Elder, Darker Powers." The similar look between the Devil and Norton's true source of worship—Pan— was apparently too much for the Australian press to let slide. But she was no victim, and certainly played up associations: in one article, she said "If Pan is the Devil…then I am indeed a Devil worshipper." Norton continued to play up this image throughout the 1960s, and even made money selling potions and charms. By the end of that decade, however, the rise of the civil rights movement and its involvement with burgeoning youth subcultures saw the wildness that Norton represented distinctly out of date. She died in relative poverty in 1979, and it was not until the mid 1980s that interest in her was revived, particularly through a 1984 reissue of *The Art of Rosaleen Norton* and Barry Lowe's play "Rosaleen: Wicked Witch of the Cross." Though her name is rarely heard today in Australia, she is a crucial figure not only in the history of the Devil's antipodean adventures, but also in the nation's sadly underwritten history of strong, creative and difficult women.

Due in large part to Norton's notoriety, Kings Cross became widely linked in the public's mind to the occult and the bizarre. According to Australian pulp fiction expert Andrew Nette, Attila Zohar's (a.k.a. James Holledge) gloriously sensational pulp investigation into the subject, *Kings Cross Black Magic* (Horwitz, 1965), lived up to his previous works, all with equally salacious titles like *Australia's Wicked Women* (1963), *Crimes Which Shocked Australia* (1963), *Teenage Jungle* (1964), *Women Who Sell Sex* (1964) and *What Makes a Call Girl* (1964). *Kings Cross Black Magic* emphasised this connection with the city and occult practices, its blurb reading:

> **66** *Behind the glittering panorama of strip joints and all male shows the Cross has another facade… mysterious sinister, that ensnares the unwary into Satanic séances and the depraved orgies of black magic. Frenzied sex rites take place which stun and horrify.*

Even before Norton's legal scandals hit the press, however, Australian newspapers were littered with controversy-baiting titbits seeking to reveal the ubiquity of occultism both within Australia and around the world. Reports of Australian links to "witch cults" spanned back to at least 1931 and, in April 1950, Perth's *Sunday Times* newspaper declared that "People still practise sorcery—or pretend to practise it—even in this Atomic Age!" As elsewhere, interest in the occult in Australia was on the rise by the early 1970s: the use of Ouija boards and tarot cards were widespread, and the Church of England even launched an internal investigation into the influence of the occult, handed down in 1975, which found that orthodox religion had failed contemporary Australians and they were turning to glitzier, darker sources for spiritual fulfilment. Again, newspapers provoked these anxieties, with one 1974 report claiming "half of Sydney's high school students have had dealings with the occult and Satanism." That same year, news stories linked black magic from the isolated outback town of Kalgoorlie to disused churches in the prestigious Adelaide Hills.

PB 232 4/9 48c

KINGS CROSS BLACK MAGIC

Attila
Zohar

This growing interest in the occult during the 1970s was in large part triggered by the international success of films such as *Rosemary's Baby* (1968), *The Exorcist* (1973) and *The Omen* (1976), which were popular enough to rate mention in even the most genteel of Australian media outlets: for example, nestled between recipes and knitting tips, the October 1976 issue of *The Australian Women's Weekly* bubbled excitedly in its review of *The Omen* that "Satanism can be as big a box office draw as *Jaws*." The commercial allure of occultism and the supernatural had already been firmly established on Australia's small screen, however. *The Evil Touch* was a 26-episode anthology series produced by the Nine Network that ran from 1973-74, with host Anthony Quayle emphasising the viewer's own susceptibility to dark forces as he announced at the introduction to each episode of the "touch of evil in all of us."

Earlier still, two popular Australian television series both opted for "devil worshipper" storylines. *Homicide* was a police procedural that ran for an impressive 13 years, and its tendency to base its storylines on real-life cases gave it a degree of urgency and gravitas that proved extremely successful with local audiences. Episode #218, "The Devil May Care," debuted in late August 1969 and addressed the murder of a young woman found dressed as a wolf and the involvement of two local witches in the crime. In 1972, the beloved Australian soap opera *Number 96*—another series with a long shelf life, running from 1972-1977—also included a devil worship episode called "The Black Mass," where a hypnotist employed to help one of the series regulars quit smoking is revealed to be a devil worshipper, leading to a climactic ritual complete with velvet altars and sacrificial virgins. The focus on Satanism in *Number 96* was prime evidence of just how much a fascination with black magic had infiltrated mainstream Australian culture, even by the early 1970s.

A similar image is privileged in what is arguably the first "real" post-New Wave Australian horror film, *Night of Fear* (1972). (1) One of the greatest achievements of underrated Australian genre auteur Terry Bourke, *Night of Fear*'s gimmick is that it is completely free of dialogue, effectively functioning as a kind of Australian horror version of Eric Sykes' *Rhubarb Rhubarb* (1969). Influenced heavily by *Willard* (1971) and predating both *The Hills Have Eyes* (1977) and *The Texas Chain Saw Massacre* (1974), *Night*

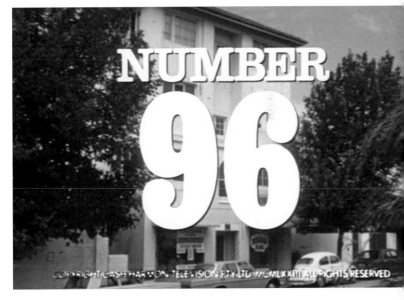

of Fear culminates—somewhat randomly, admittedly—in a bizarre Satanic ritual by its creepy protagonist (played by Australian actor Norman Yemm). While *Night of Fear* locates the demonic and perverse in the rural, in John D. Lamond's exploitation "documentary" *Australia After Dark* (1975) it is nestled within suburban Melbourne: in

Left: One of Attila Zohar's many occult-themed pulp paperbacks.
Image from the collection of Andrew Nette at Pulpcurry.com.
Above: The title card of Australian soap opera *Number 96*.

the book tie-in to Mark Hartley's extraordinary Ozploitation documentary *Not Quite Hollywood* (2008), Lamond confesses that the sequence was filmed in his mother-in-law's backyard with the assistance of a smoke machine and "some bird paid to writhe on the altar."

With the U.S. publication of Lawrence Pazder and Michelle Smith's *Michelle Remembers* in 1980 and the McMartin pre-school case beginning in 1983, the anxieties and fears that underscored the explosion of the Satanic Ritual Abuse phenomenon in the United States already had their groundwork laid in the Australian pop cultural consciousness. Still unavailable on DVD, Australian horror film *Alison's Birthday* (1981) is a lost classic, and one of the notable gaps in Hartley's documentary (although to his credit, it does make an appearance in the accompanying book). The film begins with 16-year-old Alison (Joanne Samuel, who had previously starred as Mel Gibson's wife in 1979's classic *Mad Max*) and two friends from high school indulging in a séance. The sequence is marked by some gloriously excessive, decade-specific cinematography as a camera shoots the girls through a glass-topped coffee table upon which they undertake their occult ritual. Nervous about the séance, her friend reassures her "it can't hurt you, everyone does it." An aggressive spirit appears, shattering the glass and telling Alison that her family is cursed by evil and that she must conquer it before she turns 19.

Above and Right: John D. Lamond's *Australia After Dark* (1975).
Images from the collection of Mark Hartley.

The voice, which explains he's Alison's deceased father, also cautions her to beware of "Mirne." But his frightened voice then announces that Mirne has found him, and the room explodes into violence as debris flies and a bookshelf falls and crushes Alison's friend to death.

Leaping forward three years, Alison—who lives in a small town on the New South Wales south coast—is unable to excuse herself from birthday celebrations with her Aunt Jenny (Bunney Brooke) and Uncle Dean (John Bluthal, who would later appear in 1998's *Dark City* and 1997's *The Fifth Element*) in Sydney, and visits them with her boyfriend Pete (Lou Browne). Uncomfortable with her family's over protectiveness, Pete becomes increasingly suspicious but Alison reassures him there is nothing more malign going on. As the family's hostility towards Alison's boyfriend becomes more overt, he turns these suspicions into investigative action.

It is in the middle-class suburban domain that Alison finds herself under dramatic threat by her family, and the demon-worshiping cult to which they belong. The cult wants to transfer the spirit of goddess Mirne from the dying body of Alison's grandmother to the younger woman herself.

Discovering a miniature Stonehenge in their back garden (curiously predating *This Is Spinal Tap* (1984) by three years), exposition provided by Pete's witchy ex-girlfriend Helen (Robin Gibbes) reveals that Mirne is a Celtic demoness who has manifested as a British woman named Isabel Thorne for centuries, whose followers must find a new young body for her to live in when the previous one grows too old. Kidnapping Alison as a baby, Thorne's followers murder Alison's real parents and Jenny and Dean raise her with the sole intention of sacrificing her on her 19th birthday.

Alison's Birthday was not a commercial or critical success, and its occasional slow-pacing is dragged down by what are often laborious or even frankly silly moments of supposedly supernatural spectacle. But there are moments—such

Left and Right:
Ian Coughlan's
Alison's Birthday (1981).

as the scenes of the mysterious, elderly Grandmother Thorne in her bedroom—that are beautiful and haunting, emphasizing powerful yet monstrous women that link it as much to Dario Argento's *Suspiria* (1977) as to specifically Australian instances of hagsploitation, such as *Night Nurse* (1978). Quality aside, however, *Alison's Birthday* is a significant film for a number of reasons. Most immediately, it continues Rosaleen Norton's legacy of demonic threat in Australia being linked explicitly to the city. Again, this is notable in this particular national context, because it is predominantly the outback or other rural environments—wild, untamed, and unknowable to the colonial imagination—that are traditionally coded as the site of horror.

More significant, however, is the wholesale importation in *Alison's Birthday* of its central mythology. The film even says outright at one point that the Mirne cult moved from Somerset in the United Kingdom when the witch hunts became too difficult for them, and hurriedly suggested that the coven simply "moved somewhere else": apparently (and randomly), this was Sydney, Australia. This reveals a trend that again can be linked back at least to the scandal surrounding Rosaleen Norton, and certainly through to the Satanic Ritual Abuse phenomenon as it played out in Australia: that this particular representation and construction of "evil" is coded as distinctly Western and imported. The appeal of the evil that all these examples share is one that locks in directly to colonial anxieties: North America! Europe! We share your demons! We are, therefore, one of you.

Left and Above: Devilish dealings in *Alison's Birthday*.
Images from the collection of Mark Hartley.

A notable exception to this was the documentary *The Occult Experience* that screened on Australian television in 1985, partially funded by the Australian Film Commission. Directed by noted Australian oral historian Frank Heimans and co-produced and narrated by Rosaleen Norton's biographer Nevill Drury, *The Occult Experience* is effectively a Mondo-styled exploration into various manifestations of occult-related practice across cultures, looking at Shamanism, Egyptian mysticism and the increasing popularity of the occult in Western cultures at the time, particularly in relation to the growth of Wicca and the Temple of Set (a spin-off of Anton LaVey's Church of Satan). Although not perhaps consciously exploitative, as one online review eloquently puts it, *The Occult Experience* is "a one way ticket to lolzington via blisstopia." Including interviews with a range of intriguing figures—everyone from the Temple of Set's Lilith Sinclair to Wiccan priestess and occult author Margot Adler to Swiss surrealist H.R. Giger—what the documentary lacks in credible tone it makes up for in titillating perversity.

Regardless, from a purely Australian perspective, *The Occult Experience* is an intriguing historical document that explicitly places local occult ritual practice in a global context that is neither purely Euro- nor North America-centric. It speaks of a history of ritual practice beyond a colonial paradigm, implying that these beliefs have their own long, natural history. In effect, *The Occult Experience* seeks to defamiliarize—or "de-demonize"—occult practice. Ironically, however, by placing these practices under the spotlight, the documentary was one of the many cultural elements that played a role in the increasing public fascination with the occult, paving the way for the Satanic Ritual Abuse moral panic to unfold in Australia during the early 1990s.

Whether positive or negative, the cultural trickle-down effect from the North American Satanic Ritual Abuse scandal of the 1980s was making its presence in Australia felt. By the late 1980s, self-styled anti-occult missionary and ex-policeman David Lentin was appearing with increasing regularity in national newspapers with his stories of a rise in devil worship in Australia. While it took time for his stories to contain the element of sexual abuse, one report from 1987 included his claim that he "carried out a raid several years ago in an old house with the police and when I went up to the second story... they were all in a room with children eating a live chicken and the blood was pouring down their mouths." Even at this stage, he linked Satanic cult activity to missing persons cases, grave desecrations, suicides and animal sacrifice, insisting that there were up to 1,000 occult groups currently active within Australia.

In retrospect, it is intriguing just how closely the Australian Satanic Ritual Abuse scandal cut-and-pasted the major elements of the United States version onto this specific cultural context. The Australian iteration of the controversy was directly linked to many key experts from the United States who had brought the phenomenon to the media's (and thus the public's) attention. In August 1986, Sydney hosted the largest child abuse conference in Australia's history, the Sixth International Conference on Child Abuse and Neglect. Special guests included key investigators in the McMartin pre-school case such as Kee MacFarlane, Dr. Astrid Heger and conservative sociologist David Finkelhor.

As the Australia Satanic Ritual Abuse phenomenon unfolded, many industry professionals were convinced by arguments such as those presented at the conference. For most, the claims of an organised international Satanic child abuse network was proven simply because they so closely replicated allegations made internationally. It is curious that the seeds for these beliefs were planted by Satanic Ritual Abuse evangelists so convincingly into a national consciousness that is otherwise relatively secular (especially in comparison to the United States) but, as noted, in Australia these fears already had a long history in Australian pop culture.

Australia didn't have the McMartin pre-school trial, but it did have its own version in the notorious "Mr. Bubbles" case. This case focused on alleged abuse committed by Anthony and Dawn Deren, who ran a private kindergarten in the Sydney suburb of Mona Vale. A mother of one of the children in their care had suspicions her daughter had been sexually abused, and reported it to police. Launching Operation Bubbles—named so after the clown Mr. Bubbles that Anthony dressed as to allegedly assault the children—the couple were charged in 1989 with over fifty counts of sexual assault and abduction of 17 children. The trial was significantly weakened by claims of interference in the questioning of the children, and Judge David Hyde declared in late 1989 that the witnesses had been contaminated—again, not wholly unlike the McMartin pre-school trial.

The Mr. Bubbles case was a media circus, and public opinion—swayed in large part by the moral panic drumbeat emitted from the nation's major television news programmes and newspapers—was predominantly of the opinion that the Derens had got away with their shocking crimes. After the case collapsed, a television interview with Anthony was interpreted by many as suggesting that he had been previously charged with past sexual offences against children. More significantly, the fundamentalist Anthony himself claimed that Satan influenced investigators: this latter statement neatly paved the way for Satanic Ritual Abuse to unfold in Australia.

In this context, the *60 Minutes* special "The Devil Made Me Do It" was a metaphorical match in the tinderbox. Channel 10 shrewdly broadcast it in the 9:30pm timeslot on Tuesday night in mid-September, directly after the 1990 Dally M. Awards (the highlight of the Rugby League calendar). Police call centres were immediately jammed with claims of similar stories to those documented in the lurid program: a Sydney Crimestoppers spokesperson said that "the phones here have been ringing constantly since we opened them this evening," and that the reports of rape, child abuse and cannibalism were, "rather consistent in what they told us and in the things they said." Not everyone was swept away with the TV special's sensationalist claims, of course. In one newspaper review, Mark Wallace dismissed it for what it was: a cynical

Thursday, July 20, 1989

Satanism linked to kindergarten sex cases

By JACQUELYN HOLE

Allegations of satanism and involvement in the occult sometimes accompany charges of child sexual assault in "kindergarten" cases, an expert on child sexual abuse told Glebe Local Court yesterday.

Dr Ralph Under Wager said: "Some people investigating child sexual assault cases have alleged there is a world network of satanists who seize children for rituals. As a theologian and as a historian I must say there has never been any charge of organised satanic worship that has been sustained."

Dr Under Wager had been flown in from the United States to give evidence in the case of Dawn Deren, the director of a northern beaches kindergarten, her husband, Anthony Deren, and two assistants, Rima Muir and Louise Bugg, who have been charged with sexually assaulting a group of pre-school children.

The Crown is alleging that Anthony Deren dressed up as a clown, Mr Bubbles, to entice the children at parties. It is also alleged that the defendants involved the children in occult ceremonies.

Dr Under Wager, a member of the American Psychological Association, told the court that he had investigated 36 alleged "kindergarten" sexual assault cases in the US.

"Generally they begin with an innocuous statement, as in this case, that Mr Bubbles is a nice man," Dr Under Wager said.

"But then it moves from innocent actions to fondling and then to acts of penetration with an object, frequently toys, and then to the suggestion of drugs and hypnosis.

"Then to adults doing strange things in bizarre costumes and finally to a form of satanic, ritualistic behaviour."

With continued pressure from their parents "the children are driven deeper into their own fantasy life".

Dr Under Wager criticised the way the Mona Vale police station had investigated the case.

The hearing continues today.

attempt to boost ratings, because "Satanists put bums on pews." Wallace dismissed Satanic Ritual Abuse as an "imaginative jamboree," calling the special "frivolous," its guests (many of whom were lifted wholesale from the 1988 Geraldo special) "absurd," and commenting, "no expense was spared to make this froth seem sustainable." It took some years, but the hysteria surrounding Satanic Ritual Abuse in Australia eventually died down. The 1997 Royal Commission into the New South Wales Police Service's final report explicitly identified the negative influence of international hysteria, asking how otherwise seemingly rational professionals in Australia could be sucked into believing in an international conspiracy of such a huge scale with so little evidence to support it.

In retrospect, the real damage done by the Satanic Ritual Abuse controversy—both in Australia and elsewhere—is that it diverted both public attention and essential funds away from the very real and tragically ubiquitous horrors of child sexual abuse of an altogether more earthly nature. For these survivors, that their trauma was not linked to an international Satanic conspiracy seemed to imply that their suffering and abuse was not as important or serious, adding gross insult to very literal injury. Like elsewhere, this is the true tragedy—and the real crime—linked to widespread Satanic Ritual Abuse paranoia.

The Satanic Ritual Abuse brouhaha diverted real money and real attention from where it was most desperately needed, and in Australia—like elsewhere—media representations of cult activity and the fetishization of figures like Rosaleen Norton fed archaic fears that were literally centuries old. As films like *Starry Eyes* (2014), *The House of the Devil* (2009), *Drive Angry* (2011) and *Kill List* (2011) suggest, however, demonic cult activity is still a source of fascination that shows little indication of losing its appeal. The longevity of this interest suggests it is deeply ingrained in the cultural imagination, making it likely that a future moral panic surrounding ritual and cult practice is inevitable.

NOTES:

1. *Wake in Fright* (1971) was released the year before *Night of Fear*, but it was made by a Canadian director, Ted Kotcheff.

REFERENCES + BIBLIOGRAPHY:

Alison's Birthday. Dir. Ian Coughlan. David Hannay Productions, 1981.

Coughlan, Ian. *Alison's Birthday*. Cammeray N.S.W.: Horwitz, 1981.

Creswell, Toby. *Notorious Australians: The Mad, The Bad and the Dangerous*. Ultimo: ABC Books, 2008.

"Cult calls jam police lines", *The Canberra Times*, October 30. 1991.

Drury, Nevill. *Pan's Daughter: The Strange World of Rosaleen Norton*. Sydney: Collins 1988.

Eisenhuth, Susie. "The Omen: Sortie into Satanism." *The Australian Women's Weekly*, October 20, 1976.

Guilliatt, Richard. *Talk of the Devil: Repressed Memory and the Ritual Abuse Witch-Hunt*. Melbourne: Text Publishing, 1996.

Hammond, John. "There are Still Witches About." *Sunday Times* (Perth), April 23, 1950.

Harbutt, Karen. "Investigator Shines Torch on Occult." *The Canberra Times*, August 4, 1987.

Harris, Paul. *Not Quite Hollywood: The Wild Untold Story of Ozploitation*. Melbourne: Madman, 2008.

Hill, Michael. "Satan's Excellent Adventure in the Antipodes." *The Institute for Psychological Therapies Journal*, Volume 10, 1998.

Homicide. Seven Network, 1964-1977. TV series.

Lynch, Timothy. *Satan's Empire: The Panic over Ritual Abuse in Australia*. Saarbrücken: VDM Verlag Dr. Müller 2011.

Nette, Andrew. "Pulp Friday: Kings Cross Black Magic." *Pulp Curry*. May 24, 2013.

Night of Fear. Dir. Terry Bourke. Terryrod Productions, 1972.

Nowra, Louis. *Kings Cross: A Biography*. New South: Sydney, 2013.

Number 96. Cash Harmon Television, 1972-1977. TV series.

"Royal Commission into the New South Wales Police Service", *Volume 4: The Paedophile Inquiry*. August 1997. Sydney: Royal Commission into the New South Wales Police Service, 1997.

Saunders, Kay. *Notorious Australian Women*. Pymble: HarperCollins, 2011.

"Student Interest", *The Canberra Times*, August 14, 1975.

The Devil Made Me Do It. Network 10, 1990. TV special.

The Evil Touch. Nine Network, 1973-1974. TV series.

The Occult Experience. Dir. Frank Heimans. Cinetel Films, 1985.

"The Occult Experience." *The Documentarian*. Accessed September 12, 2014. http://thedocumentarian.tumblr.com/post/8424961761/the-occult-experience-by-frankheimans-1985.

Wallace, Mark. "The Devil Made Me Watch It." *The Canberra Times*, September 17, 1990.

GUILTLESS:
BRITAIN'S MORAL PANICS,
SATANIC HYSTERIA AND THE STRANGE CASE
OF GENESIS P-ORRIDGE

BY DAVID FLINT

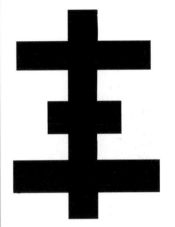

In 1992, as Britain's own uniquely hysterical version of the Satanic Ritual Abuse panic reached its peak, musician and artist Genesis P-Orridge became the local movement's highest-profile victim, accused of being complicit in Satanic rituals that involved rape, forced abortions and murder. Though not exactly a household name, the former Throbbing Gristle and Psychic TV frontman was forced to temporarily flee the country to escape the collective madness that had gripped social workers, police officers, journalists and other people of power and influence. Not long after Psychic TV's video release, *First Transmission*, P-Orridge became an unfortunate casualty for a growing moral panic that continues full swing across the U.K. in the wake of revelations about British TV personality Jimmy Savile.

As an island nation, Britain is especially suited to moral panics that essentially boil down to a fear of the "other"— the malign foreign influence, outsiders who fail to toe the line of polite middle class society and young people, whose activities are viewed with deep suspicion and fear

Left: The cover image from Psychic TV's *Live in Tokyo* album, 1986. From the archives of Genesis Breyer P-Orridge.

by previous generations (all of whom seem to forget what it was like to be a teenager by the time they turn 30).

The British often like to see themselves as superior to the rest of the world—especially the "uncultured" Americans. But, sure as night follows day, every American social and cultural trend (short of widespread gun ownership) eventually makes its way across the Atlantic, to be absorbed and reinterpreted in various ways. This is particularly the case with the writings and actions of U.S. sociologists, activists and self-styled experts. These "Big Ideas," often consisting of nothing more than the musings of a professor with a book deal, frequently have an extraordinary influence as they are absorbed, reinterpreted and recreated by their British equivalents. It's especially true where the ideas in question fit in with existing agendas of otherwise disparate movements.

As such, it was inevitable that the 1980s panic about Satanic Ritual Abuse would make its way across the pond and mutate into a full blown public panic. Fears of Satanic Ritual Abuse first emerged in North America with the publication of Michelle Smith and Lawrence Pazder's *Michelle Remembers* (1980) and continued almost unchallenged throughout the 1980s. It was a panic particularly suited to the British psyche, and was further fuelled by concerns over the influence of VHS tape "Video Nasties," the increased profile of religious cults and the emergence of active pedophile groups.

British video distributors and high street shops that sold and rented horror and exploitation movies on VHS were accused of conspiring to corrupt public morals in the early 1980s during what became known as the Video Nasties era. Although the story of the Video Nasties is beyond the scope of this essay (I would recommend the documentaries on the subject directed by Jake West and produced by Marc Morris), the press, politicians and decency campaigners like Mary Whitehouse used the corruption of children (rather than harm to adults) to increase censorship on these films. Not only did they rely on dubious research and apocryphal tales of traumatized ("damaged") young people, they also supported the idea that these films contained images so horrific that they could possibly "possess" a child and warp them forever. The connections to the Satanic Panic are interesting, as the more hysterical descriptions of Satanic murder in these cases often mirror atrocities supposedly depicted in Video Nasties.

On top of this fear was increased suspicion of religious cults operating in the U.K. From the Rajneeshees to the Children of God, it seemed that strange and unfamiliar (and therefore probably sinister) religions were springing up constantly, many of which were accused of "brainwashing" followers and having an unsavoury emphasis on sexuality.

Above: Mary Whitehouse (second from right) in one of her many public protests.

In addition, parents saw children joining these cults and often cutting off all contact with their families. It was no surprise that the very idea of non-established religions bred all sorts of fears, rumours and misinformation.

Finally, there was an overdue shift in attitude towards child abuse and exploitation, which were previously treated with a certain legal and social casualness. This was fuelled by a few events, including the U.K. government's outlawing of the production, sale and possession of child abuse pornography in 1978 (under the *Protection of Children Act*, which singled out material involving children even though all hardcore porn was illegal at the time) and the consternation caused by U.K. pedophile advocacy group The Paedophile Information Exchange (PIE), who further outraged the press and the public by demanding the government legalize adult-child sex. But what perhaps concretized this new vigilance was the rape and murder of 14-year-old Jason Swift in 1985 by a pedophile gang led by Sidney Cooke. The facts of this genuinely horrific crime were further sensationalized by the press through unfounded rumours that Swift's

death was captured in a "snuff movie." The tabloids (falsely) claimed that the mythical movie was recovered in police raids on horror video traders in the early 1990s as part of the Video Nasties investigations.

However, as Britain was poised to be swept away by Satanic hysteria at the end of the1980s, it was controversial artist and musician Genesis P-Orridge who was placed at the centre of this perfect storm. As far back as the 1970s, P-Orridge had been able to push buttons. He was the founder of performance art collective Coum Transmissions, who in 1976 mounted a show called "Prostitution" at the Institute of Contemporary Arts (ICA) in London—a venue unfortunately positioned across the road from Buckingham Palace and so an easy target for tabloid hysteria whenever they mounted a controversial show.

Jason sex ring face quiz over child murders

By JOHN TWOMEY
Crime Reporter

FOUR child-sex attackers found guilty yesterday of killing a 14-year-old schoolboy hold the key to the fate of up to 20 other youngsters, police believe.

The catalogue of unsolved abductions, sex assaults and deaths include the murders of Susan Maxwell, 11, and Caroline Hogg, five, who was snatched on her way to a fairground.

Choirgirl Sarah Harper, 10, is another. She went to a corner shop and was never seen alive again.

Detectives are convinced the four men found guilty of suffocating schoolboy Jason Swift can provide them with the breakthrough they are looking for.

They are said to be members of a massive underground paedophile network which stretches across Britain and into Europe.

A senior police officer said: "Paedophile groups operate very secretly and very closely with each other.

"Each unit is linked with others forming a chain stretching across the country and on to the continent.

"It is possible that the people convicted of killing young Jason may have information about attacks on other children over a fairly long period of time."

Activities

The four men found guilty at the Old Bailey were last night facing long jail sentences for killing shy Jason in a homosexual orgy.

They were tracked down after a multi-million pound investigation. More than 5,000 men were interviewed including doctors, former police officers and bank managers.

Detectives even heard allegations that a former Cabinet Minister and other MPs were involved in child-sex activities. None was questioned.

The four found guilty were Sidney Cooke, 61, of Kingsmead Estate, Hackney, East London; Leslie Bailey, 35, Robert Oliver, 34, both of Frampton Park Estate, Hackney, and Steven Barrell, 27, of Dagenham, Essex.

All were convicted of manslaughter and conspiracy to commit an indecent offence.

Bailey was found guilty

of attempting to choke Jason. He and Cooke were also convicted of perverting the course of justice. All four will be sentenced on Monday.

Police are to question fairground worker Cooke about a chilling list of crimes against children associated with funfairs.

They believe Cooke, who has a string of convictions for attacks on children, could give them vital information. The cases are:

● The murder of Susan Maxwell, who vanished after playing in Coldstream, Scotland, in 1982. A girl was operating in the area at the time. Her body was discovered 200 miles away.

● The murder of Caroline Hogg, five, who was snatched on her way to a

fairground in Edinburgh in 1983. Her body was found at Leicester.

● The murder of Sean McGann, 15, found strangled in April 1979, after going to a fair in Northampton.

● The murder of Vishal Mehrotra, eight, in July 1981. His body was found in a wood at Rogate, Sussex, close to the winter quarters of a funfair.

● The disappearance of Mark Tildesley, seven, who vanished after visiting a fair in Wokingham, Berkshire, in July 1984. His body has never been found.

Detectives also hope to question Cooke and the others about the murders of Chris Laverack, nine, six-year-old Barry Lewis and Sarah Harper.

Sarah went to a corner

Gang boss 'is traced'

Detectives who tracked down Jason's killers believe they have identified the homosexual who organised the orgy which led to his death.

The man, a former West End "rent boy", is suspected of running a network of young male prostitutes in London.

The four found guilty had been accused of murder, but this was reduced to manslaughter.

Three of the men have previous convictions for sex offences.

Sidney Cooke was once jailed for indecency, Leslie Bailey was jailed for attacking a woman, and Robert Oliver has been jailed for procuring young boys and assault.

shop near Leeds three years ago. Weeks later, her body was spotted in the River Trent at Nottingham.

Details of tragic Jason's death in November, 1985, at a flat in Hackney shocked the jury.

The men each paid £5 to take part in the orgy.

The slightly-built boy was subjected to horrific abuse before he was suffocated. He took between 15 and 20 minutes to die.

Then his naked body was dumped behind brambles on a copse near Ongar, Essex.

Jason's mother, Joan, said: "His killer deserves to be hanged."

The killers face a rough time in jail, hated by other prisoners. Bailey has already been beaten up in police cells.

Suffocated: Tragic teenager Jason

Guilty: Oliver   Guilty: Bailey   Guilty: Cooke   Guilty: Barrell

---

Above: The investigation into the organized pedophile gang behind Jason Swift's 1985 murder continues in *The Daily Express*, May 13, 1989.

October 19th-26th 1976

SEXUAL TRANSGRESSIONS NO. 5

PROSTITUTION

COUM Transmissions:- Founded 1969. Members (active) Oct 76 - P. Christopherson,
Cosey Fanni Tutti,Genesis P-Orridge.Studio in London.Had a
kind of manifesto in July/August Studio International 1976. Performed their works
in Palais des Beaux Arts,Brussels; Musee d'Art Moderne, Paris; Galleria Borgogna,
Milan; A.I.R. Gallery, London; and took part in Arte Inglese Oggi, Milan survey of
British Art in 1976. November/December 1976 they perform in Los Angeles Institute
of Contemporary Art;Deson Gallery,Chicago;N.A.M.E. Gallery,Chicago and in Canada.
This exhibition was prompted as a comment on survival in Britain,and themselves.

2 years have passed since the above photo of Cosey in a magazine inspired this
exhibition.Cosey has appeared in 40 magazines now as a deliberate policy.All of
these framed form the core of this exhibition.Different ways of seeing and using
Cosey with her consent,produced by people unaware of her reasons,as a woman and an
artist, for participating.In that sense,pure views.In line with this all the photo
documentation shown was taken,unbidden by COUM by people who decided on their own
to photograph our actions.How other people saw and recorded us as information.Then
there are xeroxes of our press cuttings,media write ups.COUM as raw material.All of
them,who are they about and for? The only things here made by COUM are our objects.
Things used in actions,intimate (previously private) assemblages made just for us.
Everything in the show is or sale at a price,even the people. For us the party
on the opening night is the key to our stance,the most important performance.We
shall also do a few actions as counterpoint later in the week.

PERFORMANCES: Wed 20th 1pm - Fri 22nd 7pm

Sat 23rd 1pm - Sun 24th 7pm

INSTITUTE OF CONTEMPORARY ARTS LIMITED
NASH HOUSE THE MALL LONDON S.W.I.   **BOX OFFICE** Telephone 01-930-6393

And "Prostitution", which traded on P-Orridge's then-partner Cosey Fanni Tutti's side career as a stripper and porn star (P-Orridge himself had joined her in some photo shoots for magazines like *Whitehouse*), was certainly controversial, featuring explicit imagery, blood and other bodily fluids and an in-your-face look at sexuality. The show was enough to cause Conservative MP Nicholas Fairburn to famously label the group "wreckers of Western civilisation" for producing the publicly funded show.

After COUM disintegrated, P-Orridge and Cosey (along with Chris Carter and Peter "Sleazy" Christopherson) founded Throbbing Gristle, effectively launching the industrial music scene as they continually stoked the fires of controversy. Linked to (but forever a step removed from) the punk scene, TG traded on dark imagery and pushing the envelope. Not only did many punks feel the group's music was too "out there," TG also used words and images that flirted with underground sexuality, serial killers and child murder. P-Orridge was not, by any stretch of the imagination, your average rock star.

Left: Original poster for the *Prostitution* show, 1976.
Above: Throbbing Gristle, from left: Peter "Sleazy" Christopherson, Genesis P-Orridge, Cosey Fanni Tutti and Chris Carter. From the archives of Genesis Breyer P-Orridge.

Following the demise of Throbbing Gristle in 1981 (the band would reunite in 2004), P-Orridge launched Psychic TV, a video art and music group that underwent several incarnations over the years, ranging from TG-like industrial sounds to semi-commercial pop (such as "Godstar," which almost saw the band achieve mainstream popularity) and into the U.K.'s burgeoning dance music scene. Featuring songs made under assumed names, the band's fake acid house collection, 1988's *Jack the Tab*, was hugely influential on the Ecstacy-fuelled warehouse scene, the most high-profile youth movement in the U.K. since punk. The combination of drugs and unlicensed gatherings resulted in another moral panic that saw the police granted new powers to act against events that played music "characterized by the emission of a succession of repetitive beats" — a description straight

out of the 1950s. While P-Orridge's involvement in the popularization (and arguably the invention) of rave culture wasn't widely known, it seems likely that the powers that be were aware of the connection.

P-Orridge was already an artist of dubious status for the mainstream media when he founded PTV off-shoot Thee Temple ov Psychick Youth (TOPY). Some cult watchers and suspicious newspaper journalists saw this collective of artists, chaos magick practitioners and PTV followers as a sinister religious organization preying on young "pop fans" (any teen listening to music was a "pop fan" to the tabloids, though Psychic TV were never going to sell to the Spice Girls audience). After all, TOPY's very name conjured up (deliberate) connections to Jim Jones' People's Temple (PTV even used the infamous tape recording of the mass suicide/murder at Jonestown in Guyana) *and* young people. That TOPY was a dangerous cult was a hysterical and

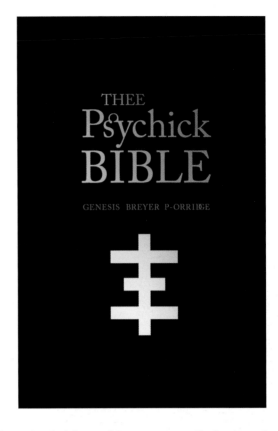

fatuous belief, though it's unlikely that TOPY's actual philosophies, as currently featured on their website, would be any more comforting to Middle England:

> **❝** *Thee Temple ov Psychick Youth (TOPYNA 1985-2008) existed to promote a system ov functional, demystified magick, utilising both pagan and modern techniques. It is a process ov individual and collective experimentation and research with no finite answers, dogmas or unchallengeable truths. It is for each to discover his or her own understanding ov thee questions that suggest themselves, and through that voyage ov discovery to find their personal and true identity, thee True Will.*

In a TOPY exposé, sensationalist U.K. tabloid *The Sunday People* dubbed P-Orridge "the most evil man in Britain"—quite a claim, given that Britain was home to serial killers like Ian Brady and Peter Sutcliffe, as well as the aforementioned Sidney Cooke. P-Orridge's unconventional lifestyle, which at the time included very public interests in magick, body art and other subversive forms of creative expression, ensured that he was a ready-made bogeyman for the more reactionary elements of the media

Left: Peter "Sleazy" Christopherson and Genesis P-Orridge in a Psychic TV pictorial in *Sounds*, November 6, 1982. Photo by Sheila Rock.

(which, at that time, was pretty much all of them). It's hard to imagine how he could have avoided being caught up in the growing hysteria about Satanic abuse, given that it was rapidly involving everyone from occult bookshops to pagan organizations.

One of the reasons for the scrutiny was TOPY's videotape release *First Transmission*, produced circa 1982/3. Available via mail order through TOPY's philosophical volume *Thee Grey Book*, *First Transmission* is a mix of endurance-testing minimalism, performance art, video nasty pastiche and experimental filmmaking, and was almost certainly illegal under the U.K.'s strict video censorship laws. At almost three-hours long (there are rumours of longer versions, and shorter edits are available online) it features two particularly controversial sections—a graphic castration scene and a crudely shot sex magick initiation ritual.

In the first sequence, titled "Polarvision," a doctor in an undisclosed location experiments with electrical implants on street kids. The worryingly convincing penis removal scene remains one of the most unsettlingly disturbing things I've ever seen, as it seems too authentic to be faked. It is, though, entirely staged. Christopherson, who, aside from his musical endeavors was also a partner in noted album sleeve design agency Hipgnosis, shot the film in Islington during studio downtime on a music video shoot, and used realistic blood effects that he had apparently learned as a member of the Casualties Union. According to P-Orridge, the original edit was even more explicit and disturbing than the final version. "The film was meant to be an exploitation satire on video nasties," said P-Orridge in an e-mail to the publisher. "When he showed me the original edit we said, 'Look Sleazy, that is too realistic! People will not be able to tell it's fake.' We then suggested he re-edit the castration to make the edits more clumsy and make the fakery more obvious. We warned him it would bring down heavy establishment attention otherwise! My prediction was correct."

The ritual sequence is more of a conscious piece of performance art, involving blood, urine, ritual scarification and generally decadent sexuality. It's slow, it's vague and it's probably very unsettling if you have no knowledge of the outer limits of BDSM (on the other hand, if you've been a regular at the harder edged fetish clubs, this will seem very tame to you). It would be this latter sequence, surprisingly, that would cause all the trouble.

It's unclear how many copies of *First Transmission* were sold—the tapes seem to have been duplicated to order, so it likely wasn't exactly flying out the door. But thanks to the U.K. VHS tape trading scene that began in the wake of the Video Nasties ban, many more "unofficial" copies were in circulation. And given the widespread rumours about snuff movies, Satanic abuse rituals and weird sex cults that abounded at the time, it's perhaps unsurprising that some people, possibly watching nth generation copies of the already murky footage, were all too prepared to believe that the content was evidence of whatever urban myth they most wanted to subscribe to.

In 1991, the British Satanic hysteria was at its height, with children being snatched in the middle of the night from families across Orkney, Rochdale, Nottingham and London.

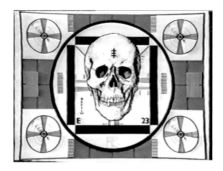

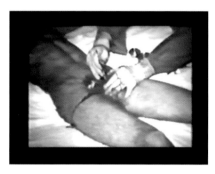

That same year saw the release of *Blasphemous Rumours*, a book by fundamentalist Christian writer Andrew Boyd. Readers enticed by the cover blurb, "Is Satanic Ritual Abuse Fact or Fantasy? An Investigation" and hoping for an independent, even-handed study were severely disappointed, however. In the book, Boyd accepts that all claims are true, and happily repeats every outlandish claim and apocryphal story without question.

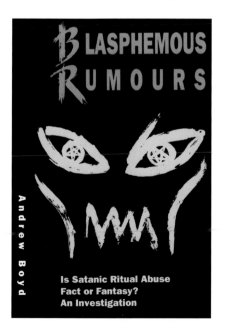

Boyd briefly mentions TOPY in a chapter of *Blasphemous Rumours* dealing with various Satanic and occult groups around the world. The reference mostly draws from the hysterical and error-laden *Sunday People* report, which claimed that *First Transmission* "shows scenes of a pregnant woman being tied to a dentist's chair and raped and a naked man being urinated on by Orridge [sic]." Boyd also compares TOPY to Nicholas Schreck's Werewolf Order and disapprovingly suggests that P-Orridge is "an admirer of Charles Manson." In a book that posits the idea of entire communities engaged in child abuse, forced abortions, human sacrifice, cannibalism, snuff movie production and every other atrocity that you can imagine, liking Manson and producing kinky movies seem fairly insignificant crimes.

Top: Various scenes from *First Transmission*, 1982/83.
From the archives of Genesis Breyer P-Orridge.

Still, it appears that the *Sunday People* story piqued Boyd's interest in obtaining a copy of *First Transmission*.

Dispatches is a U.K. current affairs TV show that has gained a reputation, over the years, for occasionally playing somewhat fast and loose with the truth. Their most notorious documentary, "Beyond Belief," was produced and presented by Boyd on February 19, 1992, the day before *Blasphemous Rumours* was published. The episode features much the same sort of material as Boyd's book, but also featured a trump card—an interview with an actual Satanic Ritual Abuse survivor that included video footage of a ritual that she took part in. The survivor, "Jennifer," is filmed in silhouette and talks about how she was forced to sacrifice one of her own children (and several other kids) during her time in the Satanic ring. This is followed by murky ritualistic video footage that Jennifer reveals was shot by the same ring. She's unequivocal about the origin of the film—she recognizes the location and the ritual, telling Boyd that the footage features a fetus being aborted.

This is shocking and sensational stuff, but it's also a complete lie. The clip is actually the same ritual from *First Transmission*, which was obvious to anyone familiar with the tape. It was not made by a shadowy group of Satanic abusers and it does not show an abortion taking place. Although the use of the clip provides a fascinating insight into how believers could misrepresent and twist facts to further their own agenda, with few channels to disseminate this information, many of those who saw Boyd's presentation of this "ritual" may still believe it to be the truth. British newspaper *The Observer* also published a hysterical piece supporting the validity of the evidence that, as it turns out, was written by a *Dispatches* researcher.

Interviewed on another program, *Right to Reply*, a week later, Boyd admitted that he knew of the clip's connection to TOPY, but decided to use it anyway. Jennifer was later identified by *The Mail on Sunday* as Louise Errington, a mother of two who, it turns out, only "remembered" her involvement with the Satanic ring during "recovered memory therapy" at a fundamentalist Christian healing centre.

By the time Boyd's claims in *Dispatches* were demolished, it was already too late for P-Orridge. In what seems like a suspiciously co-ordinated effort between the police, a TV broadcaster and a commercial publisher, officers of the Obscene Publications Squad had raided P-Orridge's Brighton home on February 15, 1992, four days prior to the broadcast—the evidence supporting the raid being the video clip and the testimony of "Jennifer." The police seized huge amounts of material, including the irreplaceable PTV archives, and began an investigation into P-Orridge and TOPY that continued even after the programme and its claims were quickly discredited.

Regardless of whether they were true, the *Dispatches* claims gave the British establishment an excuse to carry out a legally sanctioned raid and bring down a controversial artist. According to P-Orridge, the police told his lawyers that they knew the suggestions of sexual abuse were without foundation even before they carried out the raid—it was more about intimidation. Indeed, as P-Orridge explained in an e-mail:

"At one point my lawyers told me that if we told them who made [the segments] "Polarvision" and "Psychoporn" (both Sleazy solo) they'd return my two tons of property and leave me alone. They said it was those two videos they were trying to prosecute as they featured teenage boys. Sleazy was amused that psychedelia could be sexually subversive. Obviously we ain't no snitch, but when we told Sleazy we were protecting him from a shit storm *and* prison time, unbelievably he literally said, "So what," throwing myself and my family under the bus, as they say. We lost everything overnight, and we could have got it all back but we believe you protect your own. It's still my creed, but that betrayal by Sleazy really hurt."

By a stroke of luck, P-Orridge and his family were in Nepal at the time of the raid. "Through my friendship with Lama Yeshe at Samye Ling Tibetan Buddhist monastery in Scotland we chose to go there on his advice and help with their soup kitchen project," recalls P-Orridge. "We collected a large amount of good warm baby and young children's clothes from the TOPY network. Then at our own expense we travelled to Kathmandu, staying at the Vajra Hotel run by the Institute of Ecotechnics. Every morning we'd get up at dawn and go to Boudhanath Stupa. There we'd help monks from a sister monastery to Samye Ling prepare rice and dhal over an open fire and then feed all the beggars, lepers and myriad Tibetan refugees. We also gave each person fresh pure water. Caresse, Genesse, Paula and myself did this twice a day to help keep up to 300 people fed and warm. Of course the British rags never once told the truth that we were using our savings to help refugees, lepers and beggar children survive."

Fearing that the courts would issue a protection order and his children would be taken from him, P-Orridge decided not to return to the U.K., laying a false trail of information as to his whereabouts (it was claimed he was anywhere from Thailand to Amsterdam at the time) and eventually making his way to California, where the family settled and started again, having literally lost everything – their homes, their possessions and their entire history. In the liner notes of the 1993 album *Kondole*, Orridge writes of "having been forced into exile, victims ov thee psychological warfare that is sweeping through Poor Britain as it degenerates inconclusively into a withered mirror ov 1930s Germany"—his bitterness and fear plain to see. Of course, had the police genuinely wanted to charge him with a major crime, they could have attempted to extradite him—San Francisco is hardly a safe haven for international fugitives from justice. That they didn't speaks volumes about the real motivation behind the raids.

As it turns out, P-Orridge's exile was fairly short. While he remained in the U.S. as resident, his marriage collapsed soon after, and the artist was back performing in London before the end of the decade. P-Orridge never faced criminal charges and many recognized the idea of Satanic cults carrying out human sacrifices as mass hysteria by 1994. The Satanic Panic appears to have been led by religious groups and its claims were often the result of False Memory Syndrome, in which therapists with an agenda made vulnerable people believe that terrible things had happened to them in their past. There was no evidence linking actual Satanists, let alone organizations like TOPY, to any crimes.

Despite this, Satanic paranoia never really went away in the U.K. There are still therapists who whole-heartedly believe in its existence, and still people who, through recovered memories, remain convinced to this day that they were victims. I used to know one, and have no doubt that she genuinely believed her recovered memories to be true, even though any observer was quickly aware that her stories were inconsistent and that her wider grasp on reality was tenuous at best. It's worth noting that there are two claims of Satanic activity against allegedly prolific abuser (and former DJ, TV presenter, charity worker and National Treasure) Jimmy Savile, both from patients of the same therapist, Valerie Sinason, who in 2012 claimed that "Satanists are breeding babies for ritual murder." If there were anything to these claims, it seems that there would be more people amongst the hundreds of Savile's accusers who would have brought up these Satanic rituals.

For the unrepentant witch hunters, revelations recently emerging in the U.K. about Savile and child abuse rings (usually and conveniently involving now-dead politicians), are a vindication of the stories circulated decades ago. The voices of reason that brought the Satanic Panic's house of cards crashing down in the early 1990s are either silenced or ignored, and the internet's echo chamber allows delusional and unproven claims to be accepted as fact. Innocent people are spending months, if not years, under very public investigation, their careers often ruined as they wait to see if the police will ever press charges. And meanwhile, actual cases of child abuse—sometimes involving large rings of men—flourish because they have to do more with child protection than with celebrity culture or horror movie-inspired ideas of Satanism.

To question any of this is to commit a secular blasphemy. Yet, if the case of Genesis P-Orridge tells us anything, it's that people will lie, high profile individuals are easy targets and moral panics lead to the destruction of lives and families much more certainly than any mythical Satanic cult ever could.

REFERENCES + BIBLIOGRAPHY:

Breyer P-Orridge, Genesis. E-mail to publisher. May 27, 2015.
Boyd, Andrew. *Blasphemous Rumours: Is Satanic Ritual Abuse Fact or Fantasy? : An Investigation*. London: Fount, 1991.
Doward, Jamie. "How Paedophiles Infiltrated the Left and Hijacked the Fight for Civil Rights." *The Guardian*. March 2, 2014. http://www.theguardian.com/politics/2014/mar/02/how-paedophiles-infiltrated-the-left-harriet-harman-patricia-hewitt.
Jones, Barbara, and Ian Walker. "The Truth about Jennifer's Story." *Mail on Sunday*, March 1, 1992.
McClellan, Jim. "Genesis P-Orridge: Sexual Exile." *I-D*, November 1, 1992.
Morris, Nigel. "Rotherham Child Abuse: Commissioners Take over as Council Is Judged 'not Fit for Purpose'." *The Independent*, February 4, 2015.
Thompson, Damien. "The People Who Believe That Satanists Might Eat Your Baby." *The Telegraph*, March 22, 2002.

Right: From the opening spread of Jim McClellan's article "Genesis P-Orridge: Sexual Exile"

INTERVIEW BY **JIM McCLELLAN**
PHOTOGRAPHY BY **STEFAN RUIZ**

From confrontational art with COUM and The Temple Of Psychick Youth to avant-garde music with Throbbing Gristle and Psychic TV to his involvement with SM, tattoos and piercing, Genesis P-Orridge has shocked his way from the '60s to the '90s. But this year, after a film of alleged satanic abuse allegedly made by him was shown on TV, he was forced into hiding in America. Here he speaks to a British magazine for the first time about his ordeal.

FALSE HISTORY SYNDROME:
HBO'S 'INDICTMENT: THE MCMARTIN TRIAL'

BY ADRIAN MACK

Satanic Panic or not, ritual abuse and organized child abuse are real. From the occult-based horrors that happened in the Hosanna Church case in Ponchatoula, Louisiana—a story ultimately woven into the HBO series *True Detective*—to the details of a U.K. VIP pedophile ring that are still emerging in the wake of BBC personality Jimmy Savile's death, the evidence for both is depressingly abundant. When North America succumbed to the Satanic Panic of the '80s and '90s, these two realities merged, plunging them into the realm of tabloid sensationalism and fomenting, understandably, a strong collective psychological resistance to the complex realities of either.

At the very least, a cartoonish model of so-called "Satanic Ritual Abuse," as defined in such venues as Geraldo Rivera's infamous 1988 TV special, left us with a kind of reflexive skepticism about any and all eruptions of organized pedophilia, regardless of any cult, ritual or Satanic elements. As such, "Satanic Ritual Abuse" and organized child abuse have apparently become confused in the public imagination. The media, meanwhile, appears prejudiced

Left: James Woods as defense lawyer Danny Davis in Mick Jackson's *Indictment: The McMartin Trial* (1995).

by undue attention to the dangers of false accusations. In this environment, skepticism has arguably evolved into an all-consuming orthodoxy. Twenty-five years after it ended in an unprecedented glare of public attention, the McMartin pre-school trial remains one of the primary sources for this murky state of affairs.

Time has significantly eroded our already heavily mediated memories of the finer points of the McMartin trial, the most inflammatory of daycare abuse cases in which the operators of a pre-school in the affluent Californian community of Manhattan Beach (the stomping ground of arch-paranoiac Thomas Pynchon) were charged with abusing hundreds of children under their care. There were no convictions against Ray Buckey or the other defendants when the case finally ground to a halt in 1990 after five agonizing years. It seems to have been forgotten, however, that this grotesquely complicated trial, in the words of a 1990 *People* magazine cover story, would "leave everyone hurt—and no one satisfied."

In a press conference immediately after the trial, seven jurors admitted they believed that at least some of the McMartin pre-schoolers had been molested but that the prosecution had failed to prove where, when and by whom. "The Buckeys were not proven innocent," said juror John Breese, 51, a biomedical-equipment technician and father of eight. "We just found them not guilty, based on the evidence."

Today, the case feels indistinguishable from the myth of Satanic Panic. While some attempted to spin the anxiety around McMartin as an expression of society-wide sexual repression, others took the view that evangelical Christians had converged with Reagan-era conservatives to launch an all-out attack on reason itself. A third, more moderate line, blamed the scare on overzealous childcare workers, lawyers, and the media—an angle made concrete in the years since.

All seven jurors at a posttrial press conference raised their hands when asked if they believed the children were molested.

As the historical record was distorted, a kind of contagion took hold, and daycare abuse cases, often spiced with hints of occultism, began to pop up across the States. To this day, a tight complex of pundits reinforces the impression that McMartin sparked a wave of false accusations of child abuse.

Arriving in the context of the Satanic Panic, the 1995 HBO movie *Indictment: The McMartin Trial* satisfied the public's appetite for denial. It remains a key text in assessing

Above: McMartin jurors as depicted in the February 5, 1990 edition of *People* magazine.

The woman who trapped D.C.'s Mayor Barry

FEBRUARY 5, 1990 ■ $1.95

People
weekly

Barbara Stanwyck,
1907–1990

The
McMARTIN NIGHTMARE

America's most notorious
child sexual abuse trial gave no
one justice. The defendants are
acquitted, but ruined. The children
feel betrayed. Parents are outraged.
Here's what went wrong.

Kyle Daniels,
a witness in the
McMartin trial, with
his parents, Paula and
Larry, still claims he was
molested. Insets: acquitted
defendant Peggy McMartin
Buckey; the deserted schoolyard

how we automatically greet cases of organized abuse with pat objections to the reliability of witnesses; the integrity of parents, prosecutors and social workers; and the credibility of media. Finally, it helped to front-load subsequent eruptions of organized abuse with the discrediting whiff of Satanism, regardless of its relevance to individual cases.

An Emmy Award-winning docudrama directed by Mick Jackson and starring James Woods, *Indictment* presented itself as the last word on a grim, national nightmare, serving as the popular front in an effort to allay public fears about organized child abuse. In conferring a kind of sainthood on the defendants while simultaneously crucifying the press, the film works hard to reframe the McMartin trial as a story of political ambition, media irresponsibility, and the perversion of due process. But some had their suspicions about the motives of writer/executive producer Abby Mann, who made it his personal mission to get *Indictment* produced.

INDICTMENT OR INCITEMENT?

The McMartin pre-school case began in 1983 when Manhattan Beach mother Judy Johnson noticed blood in her two-year-old son's diaper. Johnson's pediatrician referred the case to child care specialists, igniting a police investigation that resulted in the arrest of seven of the daycare centre's employees. Among those charged were the daycare's owner, Virginia McMartin, her daughter Peggy McMartin Buckey, and grandchildren Peggy and Ray Buckey.

In the maelstrom that followed, the Children's Institute Inc. (CII, under the direction of social worker Kee McFarlane) claimed to have identified close to 400 victims. Skeptics complained that CII had massively overstated the scope of the crimes, biasing the claims of children with "leading questions." Meanwhile, the media focused on the most sensational details of the case, in particular the assertions that kids had been used in pornography and bizarre Satanic rituals.

But the McMartin case fell apart, ending seven years and $15 million later with no one behind bars. Charges against five of the seven defendants were dropped in 1986—justifiably, to be fair—by DA Ira Reiner (who inherited a wildly escalating situation from predecessor Robert Philibosian). Gradually, the remaining defendants, Peggy and Ray Buckey, were acquitted of 52 counts

Above: Social worker Kee McFarlane.

of molestation. Ray was retried on 13 counts, ending in a hung jury. Following the acquittal, the immediate community response was to march through the streets of downtown Manhattan Beach. *The Los Angeles Times* reported:

> 66 The crime that occurred inside the courtroom was almost equal to the crime that occurred outside the courtroom," Tim Wheeler, the father of two former McMartin pupils, told about 500 cheering supporters at a rally after the mile-long march. "I think the jury did what they thought was best," said protest spokeswoman Elizabeth Aleccia. "I think the judge did an excellent job too. I think the system itself is what failed. It made the children feel like they were to blame."

Summing up the situation years later, University of California child psychiatrist Roland Summit wrote:

> 66 After more than five years of glaring public exposure and 33 consecutive months of the longest and most expensive trial in history, the verdicts of January 8, 1990 left most parents angry and confused but at least reconciled to a return to private life. The willingness of a few to protest the failure of prosecution on television talk shows exposed them to a peculiar kind of vilification. They were the perfect scapegoats for a small band of investigative journalists out to save the world from superstitious nonsense. The backlash gospel is simple: Those who trumpet the hazards of ritual abuse are the ones responsible for creating it. And they should be punished.

Once the case ended, the spin began, persisting to this day. Debbie Nathan's 1995 book *Satan's Silence: Ritual Abuse and the Making of a Modern American Witch Hunt* (written with Michael Snedeker) is widely cited in *Wikipedia*'s entry on the McMartin case, even though its author's career has been dedicated to sowing doubt about child abuse cases, ritual abuse, and the effects of trauma.

Said one juror of Ray Buckey (after acquittal, above, with friend Barbara Ferrante): "He clearly had problems."

The Abuse of Innocence: The McMartin Preschool Trial, a gossipy account of the courtroom proceedings written by Paul and Shirley Eberle and published in 1993 also features prominently in this *Wikipedia* entry. Some 20 years earlier, however, the Eberles had been the publishers of notorious porno rag, *Finger*, which featured stories like "Sexpot at Five,"

"My son would never harm a child," said Peggy McMartin Buckey, leaving the courthouse after the verdicts.

Above: Defendants Ray Buckey and Peggy McMartin Buckey, as depicted in the February 5, 1990 edition of *People* Magazine.

"My First Rape, She Was Only Thirteen," and "What Happens When Niggers Adopt White Children." "There were a lot of photos of people who looked like they were under age but we could never prove it," said Donald Smith, of the LAPD's vice division in a 1988 *Ms. Magazine* article about *Finger* and the Eberles.

The dangers of favouring a skeptical view of McMartin and other such cases has been discussed by Brown University political science professor Ross Cheit, author of the 2014 book, *The Witch Hunt Narrative: Politics, Psychology, and the Sexual Abuse of Children*. In a 2014 *Huffington Post* article, Cheit notes that the problems "go beyond the distortion of the historical record about these cases. There's the larger truth that, as the witch-hunt narrative took root, prosecutors became increasingly reluctant to bring cases, the media sided with the defense, and children were less likely to be believed—all based on a narrative that is at its core inaccurate."

Asked about a witch-hunt narrative that "often includes a 'hero,' a journalist perhaps, who helps an innocent person escape a false conviction," Cheit told the *Providence Journal*: "We love this story... My concern is we love it so much even when it isn't true."

THE MAKING OF INDICTMENT

The HBO film *Indictment* came with an impressive pedigree, boasting Oliver Stone as its executive producer along with screenwriter Abby Mann. Mann, also the film's executive producer, had serious liberal bona fides, with an Oscar on his mantelpiece for *Judgment at Nuremberg* and further acclaim for writing and directing the Martin Luther King teleseries *King*. The legendary anti-fascist researcher Mae Brussell remained unimpressed, however, stating bluntly in a November 1987 radio broadcast: "I never trusted Abby Mann." Brussell was referring to the screenwriter's questionable involvement with the McMartin defense team—the details of which never made their way into his script.

For example, as a defense sympathizer, Mann offered his services as an investigator in the earliest days of the case. *The Los Angeles Times* reported that Mann and his wife, Myra, who helped research the film, believed "the McMartin trial was a modern-day witch hunt. They got involved in the case before the first trial, locking up the defendants' story rights and even sharing information with the defense lawyers."

Mann also appears to have played a role in the defection of assistant prosecutor Glenn Stevens, who left the case in January 1986 claiming that prosecutors had withheld evidence from the defense.

Above: *Indictment*'s writer/producer Abby Mann, with a spread of McMartin-related news clippings.

Although this drama has never been adequately explained, McMartin parent Jackie McGauley says Stevens was initially forced to resign because he was leaking information to the press. During an in depth (and apparently inebriated) tape-recorded interview with the Manns for *Indictment*, Stevens offered his misgivings about the case and accused his former colleagues of prosecutorial misconduct, statements which "became a major controversy during pretrial maneuvering in the case," according to *The Los Angeles Times*. *The New York Times* further confirmed that Stevens accepted a book and movie deal from the *Indictment* crew. It's conceivable that Stevens' discomfort with the case was authentic. But the airbrushing of Mann's influence and Stevens' less principled motives torpedoes *Indictment*'s credibility.

The Los Angeles Times anointed the Manns with "a crucial behind-the-scenes role" in the McMartin trial and observes that their influence on the defense team and in Stevens' apostasy was seemingly scrubbed from any reportage, as was the couple's role in bringing *60 Minutes* onboard to produce a sympathetic portrayal of the defendants in 1986 (videotaped, as it happens, right in the Manns' living room).

In a later article defending his paper's coverage of the trial, *Los Angeles Times* editor Noel Greenwood was more direct in his fulminations against the Manns, noting "a mean, malevolent campaign conducted by people... whose motives are highly suspect and who have behaved in a basically dishonest... and dishonorable way." It's of no little significance that the Manns so forcefully pushed the witch hunt narrative, an idea now routinely introduced into any dialogue about organized child abuse—and one that has subsequently encouraged "the complete negation of the evidence," as Cheit puts it. "We like to think we are different from Salem," was Mann's characteristically loaded comment as the McMartin trial collapsed.

SETTING THE WOODS ON FIRE

Mann wasn't the only true believer who worked on *Indictment*. In a fascinating *Los Angeles Times* piece published in 1995, director Mick Jackson offered a kind of inadvertent doublespeak when he said, "[People] don't know the defendants were actually not guilty." To state, as Jackson does, that Peggy and Ray Buckey "were acquitted on most of the charges and the jury actually said there is nothing we can commit to in the end" minimizes the continuing suspicion—even within the jury itself— that justice had been derailed by the defence team's delaying tactics; a strategy that terrorized and exhausted the parents and children. As one juror lamented, "I don't know how you could get 12 people to be unanimous in this case. There are too many unanswered questions. Too much time has passed."

In the same *Los Angeles Times* piece, *Indictment* star James Woods describes the issue of guilt or innocence—presumably the key point in any trial—as "irrelevant." "[It's] not as important as the deprivation of due process that happened in that case to an extent that's probably unparalleled in American history," thundered Woods. "These people were deprived of their life, their liberty and their pursuit of happiness to such an extraordinary extent that it's overwhelming. Nobody bothered to ask what their constitutional rights were. Nobody bothered to protect them except for their defense attorneys, who were fighting a tidal wave of press-induced hysteria."

Nobody or nothing, that is, besides the perception-shaping juggernaut of popular culture. If *Indictment* intends to redress the constitutional rights denied to the defendants, it pays scant attention to the victims, whose trauma, genital injuries and instances of sexually transmitted disease, as reported by political researcher Alex Constantine among others, could hardly be attributed to a tidal wave of press-induced or any other kind of hysteria. Even if *Indictment* is right about Buckey, its disregard for the kids and families speaks volumes.

As played by Woods, *Indictment* presents Ray Buckey's attorney Danny Davis as a sleazy "back alley lawyer" elevated by McMartin to his destined role as crusader for justice. Assistant prosecutor Glenn Stevens (Joe Urla) is shown to be the minority voice in the DA's office; the lone bulwark against a dishonest prosecution and frenzied media

Above: Henry Thomas and James Woods as *Indictment*'s Ray Buckey and Danny Davis, respectively.

all in collusion with inept child services worker Kee McFarlane (played with smug self-possession by Lolita Davidovich). Woods, at least, turns in a characteristically enthralling performance, but his onscreen chops don't make Indictment any less insulting to the viewer.

"We'll just conduct our own investigation," fumes one journo, early in the film, as the media mob clamors for the grand jury transcript and police reports. "Whoa, let's be careful here," chides the chief of police, "or some innocent people might be hurt!" The scene abruptly shifts to county jail, where we're treated to the admittedly snicker-worthy spectacle of Peggy Buckey (Shirley Knight) being knocked to the floor by a braying horde of women prisoners straight out of Chained Heat (1983). Peggy manages to pick herself up, wipe the blood from her mouth, and then tell her boyish attorney Dean Gits (Scott Waara)—with irrepressible maternal concern and decency still intact—"You're much too thin."

In case we didn't get it, Jackson and Mann put Peggy Buckey through another faceplant later in the film, not to mention a strip search cheesily overplayed as molestation. "Pull open your vagina," barks the conspicuously butch guard. Critics of the film magnanimously avoided mention of Knight's turbo-Shelley Winters Götterdämmerung as Peggy.

Indictment also tries to demonize the parents in a sequence which deliberately echoes the film's garish depiction of the press as cartoonish jackals. In the film's final scene, meant to echo the parents' protest after the acquittal, Peggy and Ray Buckey are violently heckled as they stroll along the pier at Manhattan Beach, ending on a note of high sanctimony as the wheelchair-bound Virginia McMartin stares at the Pacific Ocean and intones: "Don't blame God. What happened to us was all the work of people. God wasn't let into it. Who had the time to stop and listen to God? They were all too busy watching television."

Indictment offers over two hours of this kind of melodramatic manipulation. Glenn Stevens is the troubled man-of-conscience, while prosecuting attorney Lael Rubin is a cutthroat political bully, child abuse specialist Kee McFarlane is an incompetent narcissist, and the parents are no better than an unruly mob. But Indictment saves its nastiest prejudices for Judy Johnson, the mother whose suspicions aroused the community in the first place.

THE TRAGEDY OF JUDY JOHNSON

Judy Johnson, the Manhattan Beach mother who first alerted authorities about her son, tragically died of alcohol poisoning in 1986 before she could testify at the pretrial hearing. She's routinely dismissed to this day as a "psychotic alcoholic," a belief that has since become enshrined in popular memory. For example, Wikipedia asserts she was "diagnosed and hospitalized with acute paranoid schizophrenia" and "was found dead in her home from complications of chronic alcoholism." But debate lingers over the details of Johnson's heartbreaking demise.

Cheit notes that, "although Judy Johnson died of alcohol poisoning in 1986, making her an easy target for those promoting the witch-hunt narrative, there is no evidence that she was 'psychotic' three years earlier." Cheit's investigation into McMartin spanned 32 boxes of court documents along with medical records and video tapes. He continues that, "a profile in the now-defunct *Los Angeles Herald-Examiner*, published after Johnson died, made it clear that she was 'strong and healthy' in 1983... Yes, many strange things were said by parents in February and March 1984. But that does not mean they were all 'psychotic' then, let alone half a year earlier. The case was not started by the rantings of a mythical crazy woman."

Likewise, McMartin mom Jackie McGauley insisted that Johnson "was never, repeat never, diagnosed with any mental illness, much less schizophrenia. That is a great example of how a lie gets repeated over and over until people just take it for a fact without questioning."

"Sympathizers of the Buckeys in the press have gone to great lengths to portray Johnson as 'crazy'," echoes Alex Constantine. "She lived in fear, felt it necessary to keep a gun in the house. Her estranged husband appeared to have joined in the harassment campaign. She took to alcohol. She was allergic to alcohol. It poisoned her."

Above: Sada Thompson (of TV's *Family*) as Virginia McMartin.

Psychiatrist Roland Summit offers perhaps the saddest account of Johnson's predicament in the wake of the investigation:

> 66 *It is painful even to contemplate the stresses this young mother tried to endure during the succeeding years [...] She had always been an anomaly among McMartin parents, an outsider without access to the supportive social groups that had patronized the pre-school. She was alienated from her husband and increasingly reclusive in a small house with her two children, one a putative victim of a formless conspiracy and the other dying of a brain malignancy. She barricaded herself against the menacing strangers who patrolled her yard. Who knows if they were intimidating conspirators or toxic hallucinations? Her hyperprotective stance toward her children warranted protective service and mental health intervention and she was hospitalized briefly. I did not recognize Judy Johnson the last time I saw her alive, in the summer of 1986. She was bloated and somewhat incoherent, visibly damaged.*

In his own trial testimony, Glenn Stevens even allowed that, in his initial impression, Johnson was "pleasant and very lucid." Yet he apparently reassessed her "importance to the case" after speaking with Abby Mann. A subsequent attempt by the assistant prosecutor to organize a meeting between Johnson and the producer, busy shaping McMartin's behind-the-scenes narrative, was scuppered when Johnson died. As played by Roberta Bassin, *Indictment* appears to base its bug-eyed version of Johnson on a diagnosis that sadly, if probably by design, persists to this day. *Indictment* even brings a suspiciously ghoulish relish to her onscreen death. Livid, naked cadavers drooling corpse-goop from their mouths might be a common enough sight these days on *CSI* or *Bones*, but they were hardly cluttering up the screen back in 1995. More to the point, *Indictment*'s entire premise hinges on this merciless portrayal of a dead woman.

TUNNEL YOUR WAY OUT OF THIS ONE

You could throw a dart at any point in *Indictment* (no, really, you should throw a dart at it!) and find another distortion of the truth. A key sequence early in the film shows defense attorneys Danny Davis and Dean Gits paying what appears to be their first visit to the pre-school after it was attacked by arsonists in May, 1984. The bulk of the damage was to one particular room that, according to numerous children, led to tunnels allegedly used as a venue for abuse and trafficking.

Save for a brief mention in a montage showing the kids' testimony on video, *Indictment* ignores the controversial issue of the tunnels. We should hardly be surprised. Mann's precarious construct collapses in light of an independent survey in 1990 which—assuming we remain open to its veracity—found the tunnels precisely where the kids said they were. Led by archeologist E. Gary Stickel PhD, the dig was organized at their own expense by a group of parents after an earlier investigation by the DA's office neglected to use the necessary ground penetrating radar and was otherwise focused on the wrong part of the property. This left some observers to infer that it was a hollow effort to begin with.

In the words of the final summary of Stickel's report:

> 66 *The McMartin Tunnel Project confirms that a functional pattern of tunnels once existed under the McMartin Preschool, that the tunnels provided access outside the walls of the structure, that they must have been constructed after the structure was built in 1966, and that they were subsequently completely repacked with extraneous soil and implanted artifacts at some time prior to May, 1990... If the stories of the children were bogus fantasies, there is no excuse for the tunnels discovered under the school. If there really were tunnels, there is no excuse for the glib dismissal of any and all of the complaints of the children and their parents.*

Late as it came, with the trials winding to a close and an exhausted DA's office eager to move on, the results of the dig were never considered in court. Similarly fatigued, the media quietly looked the other way. It makes Mann's omission no less notable, particularly with *Indictment*'s eager, context-free focus on any number of contentious issues that undermined the prosecution's case. Between the dig and the

Above: The McMartin Pre-school.

production of *Indictment*, Mann had four years to conjure an explanation for Stickel's findings. And yet he conjured nothing.

Arguably, this is even more compelling considering the criticisms that have been directed at Stickel's findings in the intervening years, notably in a paper authored by Marshall University's W. Joseph Wyatt in 2002. Today, the consensus achieved by McMartin's debunkers is embodied in a flip dismissal of the archeological dig on *Wikipedia*. To paraphrase McMartin mom Jackie McGauley, skepticism has reified into conventional wisdom, any nuance is lost, and minds have been pre-emptively closed. "*People* magazine sent a reporter to interview Dr. Stickel," recalls Roland Summit. "She reported to headquarters the remarkable misunderstanding that the project found nothing. Hearing this I called Dr. Stickel, who was dumbfounded: 'I told her the children said there were tunnels and we found tunnels. It was as simple as that.' With some inside pressure, the magazine researched a more definitive appraisal of the project but it was bumped by more urgent priorities of space, perhaps by an unexpected celebrity marriage or divorce."

FALSE MEMORIES

In the binary world envisioned by the Satanic Panic, there's either a global Satanic conspiracy molesting and sacrificing our kids or there's an immense network of social workers and lawyers bent on persuading children that they were raped. This is the legacy of McMartin. While movies like *Indictment* cemented the latter idea in popular culture, the False Memory Syndrome Foundation (FMSF) took the other side of the campaign to the media, courts, and academia. It's outside the purview of this essay to explain the motives of this small but influential constituency, but by their fruit shall we know them.

Formed in 1992 out of the University of Pennsylvania in Philadelphia and the Johns Hopkins Medical Institution in Baltimore, the FMSF, per its own website, "saw a need for an organization that could document and study the problem of families that were being shattered when adult children suddenly claimed to have recovered repressed memories of childhood sexual abuse."

Since then, the FMSF has lobbied hard for the theory of False Memory, which it defines as a psychological condition in which a person "remembers" events that never occurred, or whose memories—echoing McMartin—were implanted in therapy. False Memory Syndrome isn't recognized in the Diagnostic and Statistical Manual of Mental Disorders (DSM IV), yet it has powerful sway in the public mind.

Less well-known is that the FMSF was formed under a dark cloud of abuse accusations levelled against its executive directors Pamela and Peter Freyd by their adult child, Jennifer, a decorated professor of psychology at the University of Oregon. Meanwhile, the FMSF's Scientific and Professional Advisory Board has boasted the involvement of people with a vested interest in seeding doubt about the reliability of victim testimony.

Among these were Martin Orne and Richard Ofshe, both key figures in the CIA's notorious mind control program MK ULTRA. Elizabeth Loftus is a high profile expert on memory, although her work has been met with widespread peer criticism. Arch-skeptic James "the Amazing" Randi is a stage magician who brings no scientific credentials at all to the Foundation's board, while Dr. Ralph Underwager was removed from the FMSF when he told the Dutch magazine *Paidika: The Journal of Paedophilia* that "paedophiles can boldly and courageously affirm what they choose." Subsequently, Underwager was no longer called upon for his "expert testimony" in child abuse cases.

On the other side of this battle over public perception is a stalwart community of therapists and survivors advocating for the victims of state and non-state torture. Lynn Schirmer is a 52-year-old Seattle-based artist who suffered cult abuse as a child and was then tendered to the U.S. government for human experimentation. Her art confronts the trauma she experienced.

"I was born into a family that was part of an organized crime group," Schirmer told the author by phone. "They made pornography. I was prostituted from a very young age, four-and-a-half, and my family had a connection with a general in Detroit who was involved in the CIA's mind control programs. They picked their victims through contact with families like mine, who were already involved in abuse and child trafficking. In my case, when the kids were accepted into programs to be experimental subjects, the status of the family rose in the minds of the rest of the network. It's a twisted, underground world, and I wouldn't be surprised at all if that was happening at McMartin."

Schirmer also concedes that McMartin, at this point, is unknowable. Discerning the truth or resisting the momentum of decades of disinformation is virtually impossible, in lieu of the time and resources available to people like Cheit. And even then, he occupies a marginal position. When *The New York Times* produced *Anatomy of a Panic* in 2014, a handsomely made documentary about the case detailing how America had fallen prey to hysteria and moral panic, journalists like Debbie Nathan were tapped to appear onscreen, not Cheit.

"Utterly defeated" is how Schirmer describes her reaction to this seemingly insurmountable cultural bias. Of the 29 user reviews on the *IMDb* page for *Indictment: The McMartin Trial*, 24 of them praise the film's importance in exposing the hysteria that fueled Satanic Panic. The *Project Gutenberg* website nails the wider impact of *Indictment* in a single elegant line: "The film is cited as a watershed in the shift of ideas about satanic ritual abuse in the United States, recasting Ray Buckey as a victim of a hysterical conspiracy *rather than a child abuser*." (My emphasis.)

It's a powerful delusion. While the film treats the ritual trappings of the case with the cinematic equivalent of an eye-roll, Jackie McGauley has been unequivocal about the long-term effect of bringing the Devil to McMartin. "I can't speak for all of the parents and families, but I can tell you that the trial was about child molestation, not Satanism," she told Jeff Wells. "Once the concept of Satanism entered the picture, the defense ran with it."

In the same interview, McGauley clarifies the role Ted Gunderson assigned for himself in the escalating McMartin investigation. Gunderson worked for the FBI for almost 30 years, rising to the position of senior SAC in Los Angeles in 1977. Gunderson was officially retired from the Bureau and working as a private investigator when he introduced himself to the Manhattan Beach community. Later he lived with McGauley.

"I want you to know that allowing him to be involved was the demise of any credibility we had," she said. "Who wouldn't trust the retired chief of the Los Angeles division of the FBI who introduced you to senators and former state attorney generals?"

Added McGauley: "His reputation was well known by law enforcement, but he is such a slick con man that we had no clue what we were getting ourselves into. I have to say that it was mostly my fault for letting him be involved. Later I found out he was COINTELPRO. Years later when I read the description of that program it all made perfect sense."

The implication is clear: former counterintelligence specialist Ted Gunderson thrived in the ensuing years as one of Satanic Panic's great carnival barkers, famously appearing on Geraldo's seminal 1988 special to trumpet, in the most lurid terms, a vast nationwide network of murderous devil worshippers. Until his death in 2008, Gunderson's constant evangelizing reduced his apparent obsessions with elite Satanists and CIA mind control programs to a tawdry "conspiritainment" spectacle tailor-made for David Icke's sensation-hungry audience. "I dunno—sounds like McMartin," is how Jeff Wells, in the introduction to his interview with McGauley, described "a typical reaction to virtually every allegation of the organized, ritual abuse of children in America."

A "SCARE"?

If Gunderson's antics kicked Satanic Panic into the trash TV and tabloid ghetto, *Indictment* debunked its origin story for the rationalists who occupy the middlebrow. This was handsomely mounted, expertly crafted, and ever-so-slightly smug entertainment for those who wanted McMartin to just go away. Returning to *IMDb*, we find a telling comment descended directly from the film's shrill propagandizing of the witch-hunt narrative. "At the time of writing," it reads, "we are witnessing yet another child abuse scare in the U.K. Plus ça change."

A *scare*? In mid-February of 2015, after more than 20 years of persistent rumour, Northern Ireland's High Court allowed victims of child sexual abuse to make their case for a full inquiry into the extent of State involvement at the notorious Kincora Boys School in Belfast—a case dubbed "one of the biggest scandals of our age" by Amnesty International.

It's only one of multiple fronts being fought in the UK. With the Haut de la Garenne orphanage in Jersey, the Elm Guest House in London, and the Dolphin Square complex in Westminster, organized pedophile rings with direct ties to the highest establishment figures have surfaced in the public sphere, finally legitimized by the same mainstream media that scorned those allegations for decades previously. In all cases, it's the Intelligence and security services that profited from the cover-up, either through their control of compromised public figures or the more mundane but lucrative business of human trafficking and child porn.

There's a tantalizing echo of McMartin in the failing official stories presented for so many years to the British public, right down to the easily dismissed and conveniently discrediting chatter about occult rituals at Haute de la Garenne. In the United States and Canada, however, these deep political realities are still too indecorous to confront and too wild to believe. Sadly, that might be the real indictment.

Above: Shirley Knight (Peggy McMartin Buckey), Henry Thomas (Ray Buckey) and Sada Thompson (Virginia McMartin) with the children of *Indictment*

REFERENCES+ BIBLIOGRAPHY:

Berry, Jason. "How the 'Witch Hunt' Myth Undermined American Justice." *The Daily Beast*. July 12, 2014. Accessed May 26, 2015. http://www.thedailybeast.com/articles/2014/07/12/how-the-witch-hunt-myth-undermined-americanjustice.html.

Bramson, Kate. "In new book, Brown University professor aims to discredit 'witch-hunt narrative' of child sexual-abuse cases." *Providence Journal*, March 23, 2014.

Cerone, Daniel Howard. "HBO Reopens the McMartin Pre-School Case" *LA Times*, January 13, 1995.

Chambers, Marcia "Prosecutor's Film Story Snags Molestation Case." *The New York Times*, November 30, 1986,

Cheit, Ross. "Mythical Numbers and Satanic Ritual Abuse." *Huffington Post*. July 11, 2014. Accessed May 26, 2015. http://www. huffingtonpost.com/ross-cheit/mythical-numbers-and-sata_b_5578078.html.

Cheit, Ross. "Unlearned Lessons of the McMartin Preschool Case." *The WitchHunt Narrative*. March 31, 2014. https://blogs.brown.edu/rcheit/2014/03/31/unlearned-lessons-of-the-mcmartin-preschool-case/.

Constantine, Alex. *Psychic Dictatorship in the U.S.A.* Portland, OR: Feral House, 1995.

Constantine, Alex. *Virtual Government: CIA Mind Control Operations in America*. Venice, CA: Feral House, 1997.

Harris, Michael D. "Some McMartin Data Withheld, Ex-D.A. Testifies." *LA Times*, January 21, 1987.

King, Susan. "HBO Movie Packs the Seven Years of LA's McMartin Preschool Case into Two Hours." *LA Times*, May 14, 1995.

Lacey, Marc "500 Marchers Protest Verdict in McMartin Case." *LA Times*, January 28, 1990.

Laurina, Maria. "Paul and Shirley Eberle: A Strange Pair of Experts." *Ms. Magazine*, December 1988.

Mann, Abby, and Myra Mann. "Indictment: The McMartin Trial." *Project Gutenberg*. http://self.gutenberg.org/articles/Indictment:_The_McMartin_Trial#cite_note-1.

McMartin Preschool: Anatomy of a Panic. The New York Times - Retro Report, 2014. Film.

"McMartin Preschool Case – What Really Happened and the Coverup." *S.M.A.R.T. Ritual Abuse Pages*. Accessed May 26, 2015. https://ritualabuse.us/ritualabuse/articles/mcmartinpreschool-case-what-really-happened-and-the-coverup/.

Schindehette, Susan. "The McMartin Nightmare." *People Magazine*, February 5, 1990.

Shaw, David. "Media Skepticism Grew as McMartin Case Lingered." *LA Times*, January 21, 1990.

Shaw, David. "Times McMartin Coverage Was Biased, Critics Charge." *LA Times*, January 22, 1990,

Stickel, E. Gary. "Archaeological Investigations of the McMartin Preschool Site, Manhattan Beach, California." *WHALE*. http://www.whale.to/b/stickel.html.

Summit, Dr. Roland C. "The Dark Tunnels of McMartin." *Journal of Psychohistory* 21 (Spring 1994).

Wells, Jeff. "Interview with Jackie McGauley, Part One." *Rigorous Intuition*. July 1, 2005. Accessed May 26, 2015. http:// rigorousintuition.blogspot.ca/2005/07/interview-with-jackie-mcgauley-part.html.

Wells, Jeff. "Interview with Jackie McGauley, Part Two." *Rigorous Intuition*. July 1, 2005. Accessed May 26, 2015. http:// rigorousintuition.blogspot.ca/2005/07/interview-with-jackie-mcgauley-part.html.

World Watchers International. KAZU-FM, November 16, 1987.

Wyatt, W. Joseph. "What Was Under the McMartin Preschool? A Review and Behavioral Analysis of the "Tunnels" Find." *Behavior and Social Issues*, 2002, 29.

END OF THE '80S:
PARANOIA AS COMIC CATHARSIS IN JOE DANTE'S 'THE 'BURBS'

BY KURT HALFYARD

> **❝** *There are over one million Satanists in this country...The majority of them are linked in a highly organized, very secretive network. From small towns to large cities, they have attracted police and FBI attention to their Satanic ritual child abuse, child pornography, and grisly Satanic murders. The odds are that this is happening in your town.*
> –Geraldo Rivera (1)

> **❝** *I want to kill everyone. Satan is good. Satan is our pal.*
> –Art Weingartner

In the late 1980s, following a decade of hysteria surrounding Satanic subversion into American society, filmmaker Joe Dante captured and skewered the Satanic Panic in his Universal Studios comedy *The 'Burbs*. Though many upsetting Satanic Ritual Abuse trials were still in the courts in early 1989 when the film opened in cinemas across the country, Dante deflated and satirized the rising moral panic with the story of several bored suburbanites

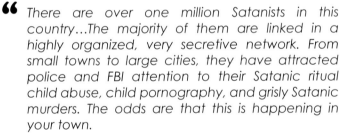

Left: Art Weingartner (Rick Ducommun) and Ray Peterson (Tom Hanks) discover what they believe to be the remains of their neighbour in Joe Dante's *The 'Burbs* (1989).

attempting to purge the neighbourhood of perceived threats, only to drag their idyllic cul-de-sac into Hell.

Featuring dense production design and a literate, referential script that serves as a comic exegesis of several decades of Satanic-cult cinema, The 'Burbs is more than just a riff on or redress of Hitchcock's Rear Window with a devil-worshipping twist—it's a comedy of manners, a slapstick cartoon, a self-deprecating social critique, a horror send-up and a buddy comedy all in one. Mainly, however, it mocks America's conformity and xenophobia during the Reagan years, when fears that your closest neighbours might be holding candle-lit black masses in their breakfast nooks barnacled itself to the national subconscious. Hysteria in popular television and best selling torture-memoirs (2) bubbled to the surface of North American pop culture, it seems only natural that a filmmaker would come along to poke fun of the collective rush toward fear. The 'Burbs deals largely (often playfully) with the tension between suburban America's quiescent façade and the destructive paranoia required to maintain it.

The 1980s-everyman Tom Hanks stars as Ray Peterson, a perfectly average husband and father who is, often reluctantly, self-appointed with the task of "dealing" with the eccentric new neighbours recently moved next door. After having decided to spend his week of summer vacation in his own backyard, he becomes increasingly obsessed by the reclusive Klopeks, who not only refuse to mow their lawn, they don't even have a lawn to mow. While fending off the pleas of his wife, Carol (a close-cropped Carrie Fisher) to take the family to their cottage on the lake, Ray can't help but notice Hans Kopek's (Children of the Corn's Courtney Gains) peculiar method of garbage disposal or Uncle Rueben (performance artist Brother Theodore) leaning out the window or especially the entire Klopek clan digging up their backyard during a violent rainstorm. When an elderly neighbour, Walter Seznick (sitcom stalwart Gale Gordon), goes missing, but leaves his tiny white poodle ownerless, dirty and shaking, civility goes out the window and vigilantism is on the menu.

Ray and his street-sharing pals—the boorish gossip Art Weingartner (Rick Ducommun) and uniformed and aviator shade sporting war vet Mark Rumsfield (Bruce Dern)—convince themselves that the Klopeks are full-blown Satanists and responsible for Walter's disappearance, and are agents of change, radically upsetting the status quo.

After establishing all the hale, white principals, the film takes the first stab at introducing the Klopeks by way of conflict through communication. After gossip, speculation and breakfast, Ray and Art hesitantly put their best foot forward—not really though, it is more of a childish dare. Hans peeks out onto his dilapidated porch to fetch the newspaper. Dante frames the sequence first as an elegant tracking shot from Hans' point of view out at the entire street, a marvel of both film geography, but also a perfect visual representation of the pressure of being stared at, accused. When the point of view returns to Ray and Art practically pushing each other up the sidewalk, Hans has retreated back into the house, either timid or sinister (take your pick), and the tone shifts to a mock-Sergio Leone Spaghetti Western, complete with all the hush,

Right: Ricky Butler (Corey Feldman), Ray Peterson (Tom Hanks), Art Weingartner (Rick Ducommun) and Bonnie and Mark Rumsfield (Wendy Schaal and Bruce Dern) in The 'Burbs.

anticipation and Ennio Morricone score. Rumfield's young wife Bonnie (Wendy Schaal) admonishes her husband, "We shouldn't stare like this." But really she is talking to us.

The neighbourhood is rounded out by teenager-at-large Ricky Butler (played by ubiquitous '80s brat, Corey Feldman) who is no stranger to staring ("Hey Mrs. Rumsfield! No tan lines this morning, looks nice!"). But along with his laid-back slacker peers, he is content to observe the neighbourhood antics as if they were a source of chuckle-worthy entertainment conducted just for them. And, for that matter, us. These shifts in points of view were noted and underscored in Jonathan Rosenbaum's astute 1989 review of the film:

> **❝** *The movie can be read as a satire about suburban conformists and snoops—xenophobic busybodies who can't tolerate the presence of any sort of eccentricity in their midst. Or the movie is a cautionary tale about the dangers of insulation and ignorance—minding one's own business and being unaware of the horrible things that are happening right next door. Or, finally, one can take the noncommittal stance assumed by the teenage characters in the movie, who are as undisturbed about the mysterious neighbors as they are amused by the xenophobic snoops trying to uncover them; the kids are simply around to enjoy the show. By building all three seemingly contradictory attitudes into this movie, Dante and screenwriter Dana Olsen aren't abdicating their moral responsibility. It might be more accurate to say that they're honoring the pluralistic and democratic possibilities of their story, and doing so in such a way that the viewer doesn't have to adopt any one of these three attitudes exclusively.*

In the film's only concession to feminine propriety, Carol and Bonnie (the only two women with any significant visibility in the film) suggest in firm motherly fashion that they all make a friendly visit to welcome the Klopeks to their suburb; albeit noteworthy that the ladies are similarly hoping to ferret out the secrets that are eluding the men. Once inside, the wives attempt polite conversation with Hans and Uncle Rueben in a

way that only highlights the vast cultural gulf between "them" and "us." An encounter with a sardine and a pretzel in all its awkward reaction-shot glory threatens a stalemate that is somewhat smoothed out by the arrival of the charming head of the household, Dr. Werner Klopek (character actor Henry Gibson). With a passive-aggressive veneer of politeness on both sides and a convoluted series of events involving a hot cup of tea, a Great Dane canine and Art doing his own reconnaissance in the garden, Ray stumbles upon Walter's toupee in the basement, whereupon he convinces Art and Rumsfield (who actually need no convincing) that further, more extreme, investigation is necessary.

With the Klopeks away the next day (and Carol at her sisters) Ray, Art and Rumsfield break into the house next door looking for evidence. While digging in the basement for buried bodies, Ray accidentally hits the gas-line, blowing up the house (and himself) in the process. The Klopeks arrive with the police, to witness the destruction of their house in a fiery inferno. Emergency crews and media invade the self-contained street as Ray rises from the ashes—a comic phoenix not only battered and broken, now aware that Walter wasn't murdered after all, but simply in the hospital for mild angina. The neighbourhood has collapsed under the weight of its fear and xenophobia, but as Ray is taken away in an ambulance, he learns that the Klopeks are Satanist killers after all, and is vindicated as the police discover a cache of their victims' bones; literal skeletons in their closet (or rather the trunk of Uncle Ruben's Oldsmobile).

Left: Carol (Carrie Fisher) and Bonnie make conversation with Hans Klopek (Courtney Gains).
Above: Rumsfield, Ray and Art spy on their strange new neighbors.

Mayfield Place, the cul-de-sac where the entirety of the film takes place, is turned upside down over the course of the film, as Ray's paranoia transforms it from a peaceful community to a garbage-strewn, passive-aggressive warzone, undermining the very security and sense of safety that the suburbs were originally designed to provide. As a civil design concept, the suburbs appeared shortly after World War II. The first planned neighbourhood of its type, Levittown, New York (along with identically named sister developments in New Jersey, Pennsylvania and Puerto Rico) was the template and engine for the post-war boom in America, the perfect place to raise an industrious family. But Levittown and other suburbs were equally criticized for their bland homogeneity as well as racial and class exclusivity, a general rejection of racial and social minorities (or the "Other") that sought to keep the neighbourhood "unspoiled" by those who didn't conform to a general suburban consumerist lifestyle.

Throughout the decades, the exact nature of this Other has evolved from Japanese-American citizens in World War II, Communists in the 1950s, counter-culture hippies in the 1960s along with urban African-Americans in the 1970s, all the way up to Muslims in the 21st century. Gross caricatures of the Other are enabled in part by media reports

Above: An aerial shot of one of the original Levittown communities.

and a popular culture that feeds on the collective anxieties all the while attempting to see them back to the unsuspecting consumer. In the me-decade 1980s, Christian evangelists and uncritical media latched on to the idea of an intruder from within, a cabal of lurking Satanists infiltrating suburban comfort with a measured, detailed plan to recruit unsuspecting citizens into a culture of sacrifice and ritual abuse.

Dante and Olsen make comic hay with the tension between the self-appointed guardians and the infiltrating cults by pushing the already dubious ideas of suburban bliss and the Other to extremes. *The 'Burbs* is set in an impossibly idealized suburb, shot entirely on Universal's "Mayfield Place" backlot using the very same TV-perfect houses embedded in the cultural unconsciousness via pastoral TV sitcoms like *Leave it To Beaver* and *The Munsters*. But where Ward and June always had out a welcome

mat, the many outsiders who visit *The 'Burbs'* Mayfield Place receive an unpleasant reception. In a throwaway scene early on, Ray tries to splash coffee on a paperboy who hits him with the morning paper. Dante regulars Dick Miller and Robert Picardo play garbage men (or "garbies" in the film's curious vernacular) who argue with Rumsfield

Above: The Klopek's house, previously home to *The Munsters*.

and Art about going through the Klopek's trash. Subtly, Picardo wears a rainbow patch on his work-coveralls whereas the more pragmatic Miller (who would rather blow off new-age crystal seminars in favour of league bowling) offers a pointed soliloquy to nobody (and everyone): "I hate cul-de-sacs: there's only one way out and the people are weird." Ray and company strongly imply that if you don't already belong, you're just not welcome.

But the neighbourhoods embedded Others are the Klopeks, who are not only of different racial background ("Is that Slavic?" asks just about everyone over the course the film), but are also aloof and strange. The 'Burbs' God's Eye pre-credits sequence zooms from the Universal studio logo's spinning globe all the way down through an aerial shot that echoes similar archival photography of Levittown, to the neighbourhood itself, past the suburban homes of indistinct architectural conformity before settling on the Klopek's spooky old manor, completely bereft of the grass and leafy greenery that characterizes the rest of the street. The title card pops onto the screen at the exact moment of tension between sleepy normality and a singular piece of eccentric decay. It's clear that the property line between Ray and the Klopek's houses is the threshold of the Other. The first real shot of the film is Ray, clad in his PJs and slippers, staring up at the monstrous house on the edge of his oh-so-straight property line as he lifts up his foot from his own verdant pitch towards the Other, the wind swirls and the lightning crashes.

Interestingly, an early draft of the film proposed that Ray was not in actuality on vacation, but fired from his job. Perhaps the stress of which may have not only disrupted his judgment, but also led to his "bullish" protection of his neighbourhood. As a subversive bit of casting, Kevin McCarthy, the iconic paranoid protagonist of the cold war sci-fi classic Invasion of the Body Snatchers (1956), was to play the role of his boss. The persecution of minority Others has been in many cases rooted in cultural and political factors such as a flagging economy, a failed war effort or evolving social trends. While these scenes of Ray losing his job never made it into the final film (a single scene of actor Kevin McCarthy playing Ray's boss exists as a deleted scene available on Arrow video's 2014 Blu-ray release), tendrils of backstory may have subtly coloured Ray's actions (and Hanks' performance) over the course of The 'Burbs.

Screenwriter Olsen explains: "What could be in your perfectly developed neighbourhood, it is that one house on the block where the people just behave unlike anyone else and it is everything we project onto the family that looks different." The film is primarily concerned with the suburban men spying on and plotting against the Klopeks. The film poses an unspoken question: Even if there are Satanists behind the white picket fences, do we have a right to bully them out to maintain a utopian veneer? Indeed, one of the repeated mantras in The 'Burbs is for Ray to "mind his own business," to stop peeking in the windows and vaulting over the fences of the admittedly eccentric Klopeks" (later, Ray admits to Werner that he figures "a man's furnace is his own business"). The film insinuates that, in monitoring the Klopeks, the average suburbanites run the risk, through insularity and hubris, of becoming their own cul-de-sac cult. This is mirrored in small acts of vandalism (from the owl in Ray's yard, to a plate of Walter's cookies) and the ever-present garbage that builds up in the street over the course of the film; visible detritus of the destructive paranoia that progressively sullies the neighbourhood right until explosive final act.

As in many of his films, Dante continually delights observant viewers of The 'Burbs with esoteric cinema lore, but in this case he uses the film to reference a whole history of Satanic movies, not the least of which is Jack Starrett's Race with the Devil (1975). In exploring the way Satan's worshippers have become a film culture icon, Dante offers a kind of cinematic history of purging the Other, starting with popular works like Roman Polanski's superb Rosemary's Baby (1968) and William Friedkin's pop-culture phenomenon The Exorcist (1973). Dante also tips his hat to a whole slew of Satanic movies, both Hollywood hits as well as indie and drive-in classics.

For example, a colony of bees lurks behind the Klopek's house number sign (669), let loose when Ray knocks on the door and the aging 9 swings upside down to a 6, resulting in a swarm that recalls the flies in The Amityville Horror (1979). At another early point in The 'Burbs, Ray is out for an evening stroll with the dog, smoking a cigar and chatting with Art and Ricky. After Art shares his tale of Skip, the average guy who ran soda fountain and one day for no apparent reason snapped and murdered his family, hiding the bodies in his home, Ricky brings up Michael Winner's trashy The Sentinel (1977). In that film, a young actress (Christina Rains) rents a Brooklyn apartment in a building that doubles as the gateway to Hell. Ray, of course hasn't seen it, and takes the opportunity to retreat from the bombastic conversation by going to watch game shows with his wife. Later, Ray and Art consult a book, Theory and Practice of Demonology by Julian Karswell, featuring some impressive woodcut prints of the incubus, the succubus and sacrificial mutilations. Karswell was the name of the eccentric warlock in Jacques Tourneur's Night of the Demon (1957) who leads a cult of rural British farmers and summons demons via ancient runes.

Dante's brief tour of horror film history comes to a head in the film's dream sequence centerpiece, in which all of Ray's anxieties converge. Framed with Race with the Devil, the drive-in classic where Warren Oates and Peter Fonda play motorcycle enthusiasts on an RV vacation and accidentally witness a ritualistic human sacrifice by cloaked cultists. After they report what they saw to the authorities, everyone from sheriff on down to local housewives try to silence them, leading to realization that there is a massive conspiracy of stealthy disguised "normal Americans" who have pledged allegiance to Satan. Race with the Devil is an appropriate comparison for The 'Burbs, since it too involves a neighbourhood-wide conspiracy intended to purge the Other—only in that film, it is a community of Satanists out to stop the infiltrating normals instead of the other way around. Ray and his friends may not be robed cultists, but their methods of ousting the Klopeks are only marginally less sinister.

The dream sequence begins as Ray falls asleep while channel surfing past the Satanic sacrifice in Race With The Devil, the vomiting sequence in The Exorcist, and Leatherface making a grand and bloody entrance in The Texas Chainsaw Massacre 2 (1986). On waking up to the snowy glow of the TV, evoking Poltergeist (1982), Ray wanders alone in his house, and a chainsaw rips through the wall, cheekily sawing the family portrait in half. Smoke pours in and, in standard dream logic, Ray is then pulled onto an oversized barbecue by robed cultists. Art, Carol, Walter (with an axe in his head), and the garbageman played by Dick Miller are present, while Hans Klopek wields the chainsaw and Uncle Rueben brandishes a sacrificial dagger. In a perfect pantomime of *Race with the Devil*, Rueben angrily snarls, "Mind your own business!" before plunging the dagger down. Screaming, Ray is jolted awake to his suburban reality with Mister Rogers on the TV set, singing "Won't You Be My Neighbour?" This cut features a bit of Americana repurposed as the height of irony considering Ray's headspace at the moment. Mister Rogers' serene openness is how America wants to see itself, but paranoid and fearful of terrors domestic and foreign, particularly in the throes of one media panic or another, is often the situation in which the collective consciousness finds itself.

By the end of *The 'Burbs*, Dante has exposed the anxieties of mainstream America by equating the danger of cult infiltration into the well-manicured cul-de-sacs with the wholesale scorched-earth consequences of those same nosy busybodies. As Ray emerges from the smouldering remains of the Klopeks' exploded house, he delivers a Gregory Peck-style monologue that encapsulates all the themes of the film in a very tidy package:

> **❝** *Remember what you were saying about people in the 'burbs, Art, people like Skip, people who mow their lawn for the 800th time, and then SNAP? WELL, THAT'S US. IT'S NOT THEM, THAT'S US. WE'RE the ones who are vaulting over the fences, and peeking in through people's windows. We're the ones who are THROWING GARBAGE IN THE STREET, AND LIGHTING FIRES. WE'RE THE ONES WHO ARE ACTING SUSPICIOUS AND PARANOID, ART. WE'RE THE LUNATICS. US. IT'S NOT THEM. It's us.*

The 'Burbs posits that the destructive Other is us, and always has been such. Should we, unlike Ray, mind our own business? In the film's coup de grâce, depending on how you feel about studio executive interference, Dante subverts his own message by vindicating Ray and revealing the Klopeks to be the Satanic killers they were always suspected of being. In Dante's original, much darker ending, the Klopeks were to murder Ray, but the studio would not let them as he puts it, "kill Tom Hanks," due to the actor's star power. Making Ray "right," and allowing him to live to point the finger at the ensuing media circus so that the end justifies the means, obfuscates all the morally reprehensible behaviour that came before it. One wonders whether Dante (or the studio itself) was wary of concluding the film on a note that suggested that average suburban busybodies were ultimately more dangerous than the suspected Satanists that they targeted.

Following a decade of network news stories, criminal trials, and bestsellers that fuelled a national panic of Satanic Ritual Abuse, The 'Burbs ends as the media circus arrives, willing participants who help spread Ray's homespun paranoia beyond the cul-de-sac and into the annals of popular culture. Geraldo Rivera is coming to excavate the Klopek's basement, live on TV—it's obvious how that will turn out, and the whole cycle will begin again, only played out on a larger stage.

As a laceration of the conformity that is endemic to suburban America (and the resulting fear of the Other), The 'Burbs effectively diffuses the Satanic Panic by both irreverently mocking it, and weaving throughout the variety of film and television image-systems that may have been the germinating seed of the Satanic Panic in the first place. Comedy is often a way of indirectly addressing society's most sinister corners and speaking truths that nobody wishes to hear. In this way, The 'Burbs points a finger, and gives us all the finger, in regard to the damaging effects of moral panics. We laugh at what is on the surface, a harmless slapstick comedy, the last humourous hurrah from Tom Hanks as he evolved towards Oscar feted dramas in the 1990s. And yet watching Dante's critique-robed-in-farce unfold on screen is akin to swallowing anti-venom, seeded with the potent stuff that got us sick in the first place.

Left: Ray with Dr. Werner Klopek (Henry Gibson).

REFERENCES + BIBLIOGRAPHY:

Amityville Horror. Dir. Stuart Rosenberg. American International Pictures, 1979.

Baskar, Nil. *FilmmuseumSynemaPublikationen: Joe Dante*. 1. Aufl. ed. Wien: SYNEMA Gesellschaft Für Film Und Medien, 2013.

Burnett, Thom. *Conspiracy Encyclopedia: The Encyclopedia of Conspiracy Theories*. New York: Chamberlain Bros., 2005.

Children of the Corn, Dir. Fritz Kiersch, New World Pictures, 1984.

Dana Olsen and Calum Waddell commentary, *The 'Burbs*. Arrow Video Blu-ray, 1988.

Devil Worship: Exposing Satan's Underground. NBC/Universal Television Distribution, October 22, 1988.

Higgens, Chris. "Stop Saying 'Drink the Kool-Aid'." *The Atlantic*. November 1, 2012.

"Interview with Joe Dante." March 1, 2011. Online video. Interview with Joe Dante, March 2011/ https://www.youtube.com/watch?v=yK5QV1zWeml

Invasion of the Body Snatchers. Dir. Don Siegel. Allied Artists, 1956.

"Joe Dante Talks The Burbs at Lightbox - August 2013." August 22, 2013. Online video. https://vimeo.com/73217090.

Lanning, Kenneh V. "1992 FBI Report -- Satanic Ritual Abuse." *1992 FBI Report -- Satanic Ritual Abuse*. http://www.skeptictank.org/fbi1992.htm.

Leave It To Beaver. Universal Studios for CBS Television, 1957. TV series.

Mister Rogers Neighborhood. CBC Studios, 1963. TV series.

Night of the Demon. Dir. Jacques Tourneur. Columbia Pictures Corporation, 1957.

Race With The Devil. Dir. Jack Starrett. Twentieth Century Fox Film Corporation, 1975.

Rosemary's Baby. Dir. Roman Polanski. Paramount Pictures, 1968.

Rosenbaum, Jonathan. "Split-Level Comedy." *Chicago Reader*. February 23, 1989.

Smith, Michelle and Pazder, Lawrence. *Michelle Remembers*. New York: Pocket Books, 1987.

The Texas Chainsaw Massacre 2. Dir. Tobe Hooper. Cannon Film Group, 1986.

The 'Burbs, Dir. Joe Dante. Universal Pictures, 1989.

The Exorcist. Dir. William Friedkin. Warner Bros., 1973.

The Munsters. Universal Studios for CBS Television, 1964. TV series.

The Sentinel. Dir. Michael Winner. Universal Pictures, 1977.

AUSTIN CHRONICLE

THE AR...
FOOD D...
SX...
W...
FILM Rev...
MUSIC Liv...

imaginary FIENDS

The little kids at Fran's Day Care in Oak Hill played games, gardened, and rode horses. Then one troubled girl told her mom that "bad things" happened there. When the grown-ups were through "investigating," Fran and Danny Keller went to prison for life.

BY JORDAN SMITH P.22

AFTERWORD

BY JOHN SCHOOLEY

On May 20, 2015, just days before the first edition of this book went to press, the Texas Court of Criminal Appeals overturned the child sexual assault convictions of Dan and Fran Keller. The Kellers served 23 years in prison after being convicted of abusing several children as the owners of Oak Hill Pre-school, a suburban Austin, Texas daycare center. Though the charges against them were dropped, the state did not go so far as to declare the Kellers innocent, possibly to avoid payment for the decades they remained in prison while wrongfully convicted. The Oak Hill Pre-school case could well have served as the embodiment of the 1980s Satanic Panic era, save for one fact: Fran and Dan Keller were convicted in 1991. A full year into the 1990s, and a year after the close of the more widely covered McMartin trial, police and prosecutors around the country continued to repeat the same mistakes that plagued the McMartin case.

The Oak Hill case shared many similarities to the McMartin case, and while the McMartin trial was perhaps seen as the end of the Satanic Panic era, it did not mean the end of the hysteria. The prosecution's failure to convict any of the McMartin defendants, even after the longest and most expensive trial in American legal history, did not necessarily lead authorities to approach allegations of Satanic criminal activity with greater skepticism.

Left: The cover of the March 27, 2009 edition of *The Austin Chronicle*, featuring the Jordan Smith article that spearheaded the appeal process for Dan and Fran Keller.

As in other cases, the Kellers had been convicted of outrageous crimes, with little to no evidence supporting the allegations. The *Austin American-Statesman* outlined the charges:

> **"** The children [...] accused the Kellers of forcing them to watch or participate in the killing and dismemberment of cats, dogs and a crying baby. Bodies were unearthed in cemeteries and new holes dug to hide freshly killed animals and, once, an adult passer-by who was shot and dismembered with a chain saw. The children recalled several plane trips, including one to Mexico, where they were sexually abused by soldiers before returning to Austin in time to meet their parents at the day care.

The only physical evidence against the Kellers came from an emergency room doctor with little training in child sexual abuse, who later admitted that his diagnosis was incorrect. The rest of the case rested on accusations coaxed from children by therapists and police using faulty interview techniques.

Like Ronald Reagan's presidency in the United States, leg warmers, and "Where's The Beef?", the Satanic Panic is largely associated with the 1980s. Yet the moral panic and the hysteria it generated lingered well into the next decade. South Africa, for example, endured a similar moral panic throughout the 1990s, resulting in the creation of a special police task force, the Occult Related Crimes Unit, in 1992. In America, the Oak Hill Pre-school case and similar cases still cropped up from time to time but, as time went on, the furor died down and claims of Satanic involvement in crimes became less frequent. Police, prosecutors, and parents became less likely to accept Satanic explanations at face value. The press and public began to doubt the widespread influence of Satanic cults, once feared and accepted as fact by many.

In 1994, just two years after the Kellers' conviction, three teens in West Memphis, Arkansas were convicted of murder, and seemingly the only straw the prosecution could grasp at to attain their conviction was the accused's alleged Satanic activities (listening to Metallica, wearing rock band T-shirts and reading Stephen King novels, mostly). It was enough for the local jurors, but the wider public were able to judge on their own when a documentary film about the case, *Paradise Lost: The Child Murders at Robin Hood Hills*, was released in 1996. The defendants—Damien Echols, Jessie Misskelley Jr. and Jason Baldwin—were dubbed the West Memphis Three and became causes célèbres among many fans of heavy metal, punk rock and underground music.

It was galvanizing for many to see these three teens convicted of murder when their only crime was apparently listening to records and wearing clothes that their small-town neighbors didn't like. People who had grown up (or were currently living in) similar circumstances could see themselves in the West Memphis Three, and the case managed to stay in the public eye more than other, similar cases due to publicity for *Paradise Lost* and its two sequels as well as the interest taken in the case by well-known

Your friend or classmate develops:

a **new** or **odd** way of behaving;

becomes unusually **aggressive**,
very quiet or secretive;

loses concentration or suddenly does poorly at
school despite the fact that he or she was once a
brilliant learner;

insists on wearing **black** clothes, dyes her hair
black and/ or regularly wears black make-up;

talks about being in touch with the devil or about
black magic;

shows **addiction** to reading or watching black
magic books and movies;

boasts about having **spiritual powers** that could
cause harm to others;

forces you to join his/her religion and does not
listen when you refuse;

shows fascination with blood,
especially **human blood**;

speaks of killing or hurting animals or people;

speaks of attempts to **cut herself/himself**;

expresses deep hatred about **someone and
insists on getting rid of that person**;

shows you **strange signs** or symbols.

musicians. As the original fears that spawned the Satanic Panic faded into memory, the whole idea of widespread Satanic cult activity seemed increasingly absurd.

In his book *Satanic Panic: The Creation of a Contemporary Legend*, author Jeffrey S. Victor says that witch hunts and moral panics result when "societies construct imaginary scapegoat deviants as a way of dealing with rapid change and social stress." Now that Ozzy Osbourne is better known as a doddering old man on a reality show and a Slayer concert is probably considered a wholesome father-son outing, scapegoating music fans just doesn't seem as satisfying. Society still deals with rapid change and social stress, but thinking that, say, an Iron Maiden fan is in any way responsible for these discomforts is now laughable. The popular image of the metal fan is now more akin to the interview subjects in Jeff Krulik's documentary short *Heavy Metal Parking Lot*— loveable stoners that are maybe a little dumb, but hardly dangerous.

That doesn't mean that the Satanic Panic didn't have a grave effect on many people. Having personally lived through the era while growing up in a small town,

Above: A pamphlet circulated by South Africa's Occult Related Crimes Unit—renamed the "Harmful Religious Practices Unit"—as recently as 2014.

I find it hard to believe now just how seriously fears of Satanic influence were taken at the time. Lives were ruined over things that, in hindsight, seem patently ridiculous. It's also amazing how few repercussions the authority figures that fanned the flames ultimately suffered for their actions. Police and prosecutors who pushed for convictions on dubious evidence were rarely forced to so much as publicly apologize. Ministers who (profitably) fed the fears of believers suffered little loss of reputation when those fears were revealed to be unfounded. Even Geraldo Rivera went on to enjoy a successful and lucrative career in journalism after his much-maligned television special. It seems that everyone just wanted to forget that the whole thing ever happened.

Although we consider ourselves more sophisticated now, and less likely to fall victim to outlandish fear-mongering, it's more likely that new fears have merely supplanted old. For example, the undercurrent of homophobia that underscored Satanic Panic fears has given way to a more widespread acceptance of homosexuality, and concerns about computer and phone lines serving as conduits for Satan have been forgotten in our constant interactions with technology. People carry a combination phone and computer around everywhere they go; they probably listen to Judas Priest on it, too.

At the same time, gangster rap and violent video games have replaced heavy metal and VHS horror movies as the parental concern du jour, while Islamic terrorists are now feared in the same way that Satanists once were. The absurdity of many of the unfounded anxieties of the era is mirrored in equally absurd conspiracies today—delve into the world of Sandy Hook "truthers" who claim, among other wild accusations, that a school shooting was staged by President Obama to increase support for gun control.

But there's one outlandish notion of the Satanic Panic era that has become a confirmed reality—organized conspiracies of child abusers. The credulity given to often dubious claims in the 1980s made it hard for the public and the media to accept the reality of continuing revelations of pedophile rings in high levels of government in Great Britain or the cover-up in the Penn State football program in the United States. Society has grown both more worldly and more gullible, seemingly in equal measure. That we are destined to repeat recent history, rather than learn from it, seems inevitable.

While moral panics may appear in new forms to deal with evolving fears and anxieties, the enduring cultural legacy of the Satanic Panic era lies in the pop-culture artifacts it produced. The paperbacks, music, comics, movies, talk shows and religious tracts that argued for or against the Satanic Panic, or that sometimes lampooned it, are unique documents that give you a feel for what it was like to live through the period. Rather than being dry pieces of social-cultural history, these artifacts of the era are still engaging as entertainment when taken at face value, or as kitsch. Whether they illustrate the fears of parents and authority figures, or take a sympathetic view toward the typical long-haired teenage metalhead, it would be impossible to truly understand the era without them.

Right: Damien Echols in 1996.
Inset: The West Memphis Three: Jesse Misskelley Jr., Damien Echols and Jason Baldwin.

ee teens charged with murder
layings of West Memphis boys

By Steve Jones

Ark. youths
could face
the death
penalty

By Bartholomew Sullivan
The Commercial Appeal

pect
ary,'
of
iping
vil

Perrusquia
mercial Appeal

ayne Echols carried
around with him at
outinely dressed in

MISSKELLEY
JESSIE
LOYD JR

ECHOLS
DAMIEN
WAYNE

BALDWIN
CHARLES
JASON

POLICE DEPT.
W. MEMPHIS, AR

POLICE DEPT.
W. MEMPHIS, AR

POLICE DEPT.
W. MEMPHIS, AR

CONTRIBUTORS:

ADAM PARFREY founded or co-founded the publishing companies Amok Press, Feral House and Process Media. He also had his hand in writing or editing *Ritual America: Secret Brotherhoods and Their Influence on American Society, Cult Rapture, It's a Man's World: Men's Adventure Magazines, the Postwar Pulps, Apocalypse Culture, Apocalypse Culture II,* and *The Secret Source*.

KIER-LA JANISSE is the owner and Editor-in-Chief of Spectacular Optical, founder of The Miskatonic Institute of Horror Studies and author of the books *House of Psychotic Women: An Autobiographical Topography of Female Neurosis in Horror and Exploitation Films* and *A Violent Professional: The Films of Luciano Rossi,* as well as co-editor of Spectacular Optical's first book, *Kid Power!*

ALEXANDRA HELLER-NICHOLAS is a film critic and academic from Australia. She is a co-host on Triple R's film programme *Plato's Cave,* and author of *Rape-Revenge Films* (2011), *Found Footage Horror Films* (2014) and *Devil's Advocates: Suspiria* (2015). She is also on the editorial team of the online journal *Senses of Cinema.*

ALISON NASTASI is a writer and artist from New York City. She is the weekend editor of *Flavorwire.* Her work has appeared on *Fandango, Fearnet, Moviefone, MTV, Rue Morgue, Shock Till You Drop* and more. Alison inherited some incredible occult texts from her father and now has her own collection.

GAVIN BADDELEY is an English writer specialising in the devilish and decadent, with a special interest in the darker fringes of history. He's penned ten books and written for numerous periodicals. An honorary priest in the Church of Satan, Baddeley's in demand as a speaker in both academic and media circles.

PAUL CORUPE Since 1999 Paul Corupe has shared his passion for Canada's film history at Canuxploitation.com, a site recognized as the essential source for uncovering the forgotten films of Canada's past. He regularly writes about genre film and Canadian cinema in publications including *Rue Morgue* magazine and *Take One: Film and Television in Canada*, and has appeared in several documentaries about Canadian film.

JOSHUA BENJAMIN GRAHAM is a freelance writer and editor living in Mahone Bay, Nova Scotia. He received a Master of Arts in English from the University of Alberta. Currently, he's working on a novel that deals with the fallout of Satanic Panic in rural New Brunswick.

KEVIN L. FERGUSON is Assistant Professor in English at Queens College, City University of New York. He teaches undergraduate and graduate courses on college writing, contemporary literature, digital humanities, and film adaptation. His current book project, *Eighties People*, examines cultural strategies for fashioning self-knowledge in the American 1980s.

LESLIE HATTON created the pop culture website *Popshifter.com* in 2007 and also contributes to the Toronto International Film Festival's Vanguard and Midnight Madness blogs, *Rue Morgue Magazine* and, most recently, *Everything Is Scary. com*. Her favorite movie of all time is Todd Haynes' 1998 glam rock fantasy *Velvet Goldmine*. She refuses to have a Ouija board in her home.

ALISON LANG is a lapsed Satanist and current editor of *Broken Pencil* magazine. She lives in Toronto.

LISA LADOUCEUR writes about music and the dark side of culture, and is the author of two books, *Encyclopedia Gothica* (2011, ECW Press) and *How to Kill a Vampire: Fangs in Folklore, Film and Fiction* (2013, ECW Press). She lives in Toronto with a black cat.

STACY RUSNAK Dr. Rusnak, Assistant Professor of Film at Georgia Gwinnett College, holds a Ph.D. from Georgia State University in Moving Image Studies and a M.A. in Spanish. Her article, "When 'Nation' Stops Making Sense: Mexico and Giorgio Agamben's 'State of Exception' in *Children of Men*," appears in *The Postnational Fantasy*.

SAMM DEIGHAN is a Philadelphia-based writer and editor. She's has contributed to *Fangoria*, *Diabolique* and *Paracinema*, among others, and has an essay in *Screening the Dark Side of Love* (2012). She is the founder of film blog *Satanic Pandemonium* and is writing a really long book about WWII and cult cinema.

DAVID BERTRAND is a writer, filmmaker, drummer, DJ and dad living in Toronto, Canada. His film and music musings have been published in *The Nerve*, *Cashiers du Cinemart*, *Spectacular Optical* and *Fangoria Magazine*. He co-founded Montreal's Blue Sunshine Psychotronic Film Centre, and has worked with the Fantasia International Film Festival and the Toronto After Dark Film Festival, as well as the TV writing room, most notably with CBC's *The Border*.

WM. CONLEY writes and edits for the zine *Death Wound*. His topics of interest include conspiracy theory, religious cults and continental philosophy. He resides in Boston, Massachusetts.

FORREST JACKSON Happiest when surrounded by goth girls, goats, and grimoires, Forrest Jackson is a bookbinder and antiquarian bookseller who lives in Dallas, Texas. He and Rodney Perkins are the authors of *Cosmic Suicide: The Tragedy and Transcendence of Heaven's Gate* (Pentaradial Press, 1997).

DAVE CANFIELD is one of the founders of Twitch Film, the world's largest world cinema blog, a member of the Chicago Film Critics Association and has a sister who looks uncomfortably like Linda Blair—a fact he first realized after sneaking into his first screening of *The Exorcist* while babysitting her.

RALPH ELAWANI is the author of *C'est complet au royaume des morts* and *Les marges détachables*. He has contributed a chapter on David Duchovny in *Bleu nuit: Histoire d'une cinéphilie nocturne* and is currently working on a novel and a dictionary of Jim Wynorski's films.

GIL NAULT is a photographer, graphic designer and musician. He has worked for the National Film Board of Canada and the Montreal Museum of Fine Arts. Nault was also a member of bands Mi Amore and Cobra Noir. He still keeps the fire burning with his blog *Liturgie apocryphe*.

DAVID FLINT is a freelance writer, sometime filmmaker and full time angry misanthrope who has edited *Sheer Filth*, *Divinity* and *Headpress*, authored *Babylon Blue* and *Zombie Holocaust*, co-edited *Ten Years of Terror*, and has written for publications ranging from *Rapid Eye*, *Bizarre* and *Skin Two* to *Penthouse*, *Loaded* and *Mayfair*.

ADRIAN MACK writes about film, music and fascist death cults. Adrian lives in Vancouver with his wife and two kids, considers himself a militant bike rider, enjoys arguing with "new atheists," and once wrote a song that was covered by reggae legend Dennis Alcapone. He hopes to become a threat to national security.

KURT HALFYARD Research chemist by day (toiling in the building where 1988's *The Brain* was filmed), cinema enthusiast by night, Kurt was blessed with parents who took their children to every kind of film as a child. Currently contributing to Twitchfilm, editor at Rowthree, and taking his own kids to the movies often.

JOHN SCHOOLEY is a musician and writer whose first record as a one-man band was released in 1996. His latest album is *The Man Who Rode the Mule around the World*, on Switzerland's Voodoo Rhythm Records. Follow his blog and check out his recordings at: www.johnschooley.com

RICK TREMBLES has been published internationally in books, periodicals & anthologies such as Russ Kick's *The Graphic Canon*, Robert Crumb's *Weirdo* and Fantagraphics' *Pictopia*. FAB Press published two books of his *Motion Picture Purgatories*, & the strip appears monthly at canuxploitation.com. His film *Goopy Spasms* has toured globally. He plays music in American Devices & Sacral Nerves. Find him at snubdom.com.

THE EDITORS AND AUTHORS WISH TO THANK:

Adam Parfrey, Genesis Breyer P-Orridge, Zeena Schreck, Michael A. Aquino, Ryan Martin, Mark Hartley, Mike King, Jim VanBebber, Frank Dietz, Brother Randall of the Robert Tilton Fan Club, Todd Brown and Twitch Film, Movie-INK Amsterdam, Robert Dayton, Karim Hussain, Harvey Fenton, Spencer Parsons, Katie Hoffman, Rodney Perkins, Mitch Davis, Pierre Corbeil and the whole Fantasia team, Dean Brandum, Eleanor Colla, Lee Gambin, Andrew Nette, James Tierney, Laura-Jane Halfyard, Andrew James, Matt Gamble, Dan Gorman & The Time Bandits Podcast, Joe Dante, Universal Studios, Jordan Janisse, Karen Ray, Paul A. Ray, Michel P. Janisse, Virginia Offen, Patricia Morse, Tom Morse, Clint Enns, Will Erickson, Samuel Zimmerman, Chris Alexander, Rebekah McKendry, Dejan Ognjanovic, Daniela Konishi, Victor Teles, Stuart "Feedback" Andrews, Sean Hogan, Virginie Selavy, Josh Saco, Mark Pilkington, Greg Dunning, Colin Geddes, Katarina Gligorijevic, Anthony Timpson, Zack Carlson, Bret Berg, Kristen Bell, Don May Jr., Matthew Kiernan, John Rusnak, Russell Hill, JPUSA Covenant Church, Cornerstone Magazine, Tom Pappalardo, Shaun Hatton, Aaron Christensen, Cimminnee Holt, Dominic LaRochelle (CROIR), Éric Falardeau, Fabrice Montal, Félix B. Desfossés, Frédéric Maheu, Jean Décarie, Laura Beeston, Magister Robert Lang, Simon Lacroix, Simon Laperrière, Kezia Ofiesh, Andrew Osborne, Coco Roy, Jim Conley, Marie, Margot and Eve Ferguson, Andrea Subissati, Alexandra West, Hal Niedzviecki, Eric Duncan, Nattie and Beverage, Lali, Monte Hellman, Ewan Cant, Bob Beeman, Jennifer Idems, Ronin Idems-Bertrand and Spectacular Optical's many Indiegogo contributors, without whose support the first editon of this book would never have been published.

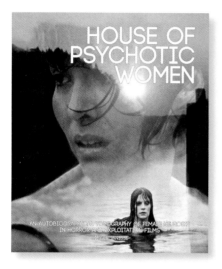

HOUSE OF PSYCHOTIC WOMEN
An Autobiographical Topography of Female Neurosis in Horror and Exploitation Films
By Kier-La Janisse

ISBN 978-1-903254-69-1
£19.99 (UK) / $29.95 (US)

Few things are more transfixing than a woman losing her mind onscreen. Horror provides the most welcoming platform for these histrionics: masochistic death-wishes, crippling paranoia, desperate loneliness, apocalyptic hysteria, dangerous obsessiveness. This book examines these characters through a daringly personal autobiographical lens. Anecdotes and memories interweave with film history and confrontational imagery to create a reflective personal history and examination of female madness, both onscreen and off.

"God, this woman can write, with a voice and intellect that's so new. The truth in the most deadly unique way I've ever read." ~ Ralph Bakshi, director of Fritz the Cat

"Fascinating, engaging and lucidly written: an extraordinary blend of deeply researched academic analysis and revealing memoir." ~ Iain Banks, author of The Wasp Factory

SHEER FILTH!
Bizarre Cinema Weird Literature Strange Music Extreme Art
Edited by David Flint

ISBN 978-1-903254-76-9
£14.99 (UK) / $24.95 (US)

Published between 1987 and 1990, SHEER FILTH! offered a heady mix of reviews, features and interviews with icons of cult cinema and adult entertainment. Mixing serious analysis with wild enthusiasm, SHEER FILTH! covered everything from XXX-rated cinema to true crime novels, from sleazy rock 'n' roll to experimental movies, and from pulp fiction to cutting-edge art. It was the first publication to cover the likes of Psychic TV's First Transmission and Nekromantik, and includes interviews with cult movie legends like David F. Friedman, Samuel Z. Arkoff and Annie Sprinkle, as well as articles covering the likes of SPK, Robert Bresson, Cicciolina, Archaos Circus and GG Allin.

"SHEER FILTH! is one of the rockingest zines... eruditely penned yet heartily low class."
~ SCREW magazine

"Draws the reader into a hermetically sealed world of sleaze."
~ Shock Xpress magazine

THE GOSPEL OF FILTH
A Bible of Decadence and Darkness
By Gavin Baddeley with Dani Filth

ISBN 978-1-903254-51-6
£24.99 (UK) / $39.95 (US)

The Gospel of Filth is the most comprehensive and authoritative guide to the realms of darkness and devilry ever published. Taking in every significant milestone and major landmark, this lavishly illustrated volume is the definitive guide to the dark side. From ancient formulae for conjuring the goddesses of hell, to the latest research on the psychopathology of serial murder, no tombstone remains unturned in this wide-ranging and witty dissection of the uncanny and unholy, of the esoteric and erotic. Music forms The Gospel's entry point, but every medium, from movies and literature, to comics and computer games is considered.

"The tome of all tomes! The amount of info is ridiculous, it'll probably take me the entire year to get through it, a marvellous piece of work!" ~ Ville Valo

"The most realized band in the Black Metal realm... Cradle of Filth always create with an intelligence and self-awareness that reveals a great art." ~ Rolling Stone magazine

RICK TREMBLES' MOTION PICTURE PURGATORY
An Incomparable Collection of Comic Strip Concoctions Configured to Critique Films
By Rick Trembles

ISBN 978-1-903254-30-1 & ISBN 978-1-903254-59-2
£11.99 (UK) / $19.95 (US)

FAB Press published two anthologies of internationally-published cartoonist Rick Trembles' best work. Legendary underground cartoonist Robert Crumb has called Rick Trembles' comix "even more twisted and weird than me" and renowned alternative cartoonist Chester Brown cited him as an early influence with "immediate impact." The choice of films covered in both volumes of Rick's amazing insightful reviews, all presented in his much lauded unique comic-strip style, demonstrate his deep knowledge of cult cinema, from the most obscure to the most mainstream.

"Rick combines his seemingly endless knowledge of all kinds of film with his signature artistic style. You've never seen anything like this before. This is a great book." ~ Creature Corner

"Clearly the work of a deranged genius – film reviews for psychos."
~ Bookmunch